❧ The Good Immig

The Good Immigrants

HOW THE YELLOW PERIL
BECAME THE MODEL MINORITY

Madeline Y. Hsu

PRINCETON UNIVERSITY PRESS

Princeton and Oxford

press.princeton.edu

Cover photograph: 1959 publicity still of refugees in Hong Kong boarding one of the last Pan Am planes chartered by the voluntary agency Aid Refugee Chinese Intellectuals, Inc. ARCI Collection, Box 1, "Chartered Flights." Courtesy of the Hoover Institution Library & Archives, Stanford University.

Cover design by Amanda Weiss

Second printing, and first paperback printing, 2017
Paperback ISBN 978-0-691-17621-5
Cloth ISBN 978-0-691-16402-1

British Library Cataloging-in-Publication Data is available

This book has been composed in Sabon Next LT Pro

Printed on acid-free paper. ∞

Printed in the United States of America

For Izzy

Contents

List of Illustrations
ix

List of Tables
xi

Abbreviations
xiii

Note on Transliterations
xv

CHAPTER 1
Gateways and Gates in American Immigration History
1

CHAPTER 2
"The Anglo-Saxons of the Orient"
Student Exceptions to the Racial Bar against Chinese, 1872–1925
23

CHAPTER 3
The China Institute in America
Advocating for China through Educational Exchange, 1926–1937
55

CHAPTER 4
"A Pressing Problem of Interracial Justice"
Repealing Chinese Exclusion, 1937–1943
81

CHAPTER 5
The Wartime Transformation of Student Visitors
into Refugee Citizens, 1943–1955
104

CHAPTER 6
"The Best Type of Chinese"
Aid Refugee Chinese Intellectuals and Symbolic Refugee Relief, 1952–1960
130

CHAPTER 7
"Economic and Humanitarian"
Propaganda and the Redemption of Chinese Immigrants
through Refugee Relief
166

CHAPTER 8
Symbiotic Brain Drains
Immigration Reform and the Knowledge
Worker Recruitment Act of 1965
198

CHAPTER 9
Conclusion
The American Marketplace of Brains
236

Acknowledgments
251

Appendix
257

Notes
259

Bibliography
313

Index
325

Illustrations

Figure 1.1.   Ronald Reagan awarding Medals of Liberty,
              July 3, 1986   2
Figure 2.1.   Yung Kuai and Mary Burnham, 1938   24
Figure 3.1.   Formal opening of China House, December 1, 1944   73
Figure 4.1.   *Terry and the Pirates*, 1937–1938   82
Figure 5.1.   Li Zhengdao and Yang Zhenning   106
Figure 5.2.   Zhao family portrait, 1946   121
Figure 6.1.   Ernest Moy with Chiang Kai-shek, 1957   138
Figure 6.2.   Chinese refugees waiting to board a plane in
              Hong Kong chartered by ARCI, December 1958   153
Figure 7.1.   Illegal immigrant heroine of *Flower Drum Song*, 1961   168
Figure 7.2.   John F. Kennedy with Anna C. Chennault,
              chairwoman of Chinese Refugee Relief, 1962   170
Figure 7.3.   "Red Past, Red Future," 1962   182
Figure 8.1.   Yi-fu Tuan conquers the American West, 1954   199
Figure 8.2.   I. M. Pei supervising construction of the
              John F. Kennedy Library during the 1970s   228
Figure A.1.   International students from six major
              sending countries, 1923–1975   257
Figure A.2.   Total international students in the
              United States, 1923–2000   257

Tables

Table 2.1. Chinese Students in the United States, 1903–1945   48

Table 2.2. Number of International Students, by Major Sending Countries
of Origin, 1923–1947   49

Table 2.3. Educational Background of Listees in *Who's Who*, by Country
of Study and Selected Years (in percent)   51

Table 8.1. Number of College Graduates from Taiwan Going Abroad
for Study and Returning from Abroad in Selected Years   212

Table 8.2. Temporary Nonimmigrants (H-1, H-3, J-1, and F-1) Who
Changed to Immigrant Status, by Country or
Region of Previous Residence, Fiscal Year 1967   219

Table 8.3. Number of Immigrants from Taiwan Entering the United States,
by Decade, 1950–2000   226

Table 9.1. Educational Attainment, Employment, and Income Data for
Adults in the United States, 2010   241

Abbreviations

ARCI	Aid Refugee Chinese Intellectuals, Inc.
CCBA	Chinese Consolidated Benevolent Association
CEM	Chinese Educational Mission
CFRFS	Committee on Friendly Relations among Foreign Students
CIA	Central Intelligence Agency
CRR	Chinese Refugee Relief
CSCA	Chinese Student Christian Association
FERP	Far East Refugee Program of the United States Escapee Program
ICA	International Cooperation Agency
IIE	Institute of International Education
IPR	Institute of Pacific Relations
IRC	International Rescue Committee
MSA	Mutual Security Agency
NRC	National Resources Commission
ORM	Office of Refugee and Migration Affairs, Department of State
PRC	People's Republic of China
RRA	Refugee Relief Act
RRP	Refugee Relief Program
STEM	Science, technology, engineering, and mathematics
UNHCR	United Nations High Commission for Refugees
USEP	United States Escapee Program
USIA	United States Information Agency, Department of State
USIS	United States Information Service, Department of State
YMCA	Young Men's Christian Association

Note on Transliterations

THE HOST OF CHINESE DIALECTS and competing systems for transliterations makes it difficult to attain consistency in rendering names and places
into English. In most instances, when the characters are available, I convert Chinese names into the *pinyin* Romanization system. Following Chinese practice, surnames are followed by given names, as with Li Zhengdao
and Yang Zhenning, who are also widely known as T. D. Lee and C. N.
Yang, respectively. H. H. Kung is thus rendered as Kong Xiangxi, Paul Chih
Meng as Meng Zhi, Yuen Ren Chao as Zhao Yuanren, T. V. Soong as Song
Ziwen, Chiang Mon-lin as Jiang Menglin, and Hu Shih as Hu Shi.

Some individuals and places are known pervasively by irregular romaniza-
tions, and I follow these common usages for Chiang Kai-shek (Jiang Jieshi),
Peking University (Beijing University), Tsinghua University (Qinghua University), I. M. Pei (Bei Yuming), Yung Wing (Rong Hong), V. K. Wellington
Koo (Gu Weijun), Yi-fu Tuan (Duan Yifu), and Hong Kong (Xianggang). I use
the Nationalists or Nationalist Party rather than the plethora of names referring to the Chinese Republican Party, the KMT or Kuomintang, or the
GMD or Guomindang.

Readers should note distinctions between unsanctioned entry, employment, and residency in the United States by Chinese. Many of the Chinese
discussed in this book entered through temporary visas as students, diplomats, and technical trainees, statuses that did not, however, confer legal
rights of employment, permanent residency, or citizenship. Legislative and
procedural measures that enabled them to remain had to address these various components of resettlement. They cannot therefore be described as un-
documented, although many remained and worked in the United States
without permission or legal permanent status.

CHAPTER 1

Gateways and Gates in American Immigration History

UNDER CLEAR SKIES on July 3, 1986, in a ceremony broadcast around the world from Governor's Island, President Ronald Reagan presided over the first of a four-day commemoration of the hundredth anniversary of the Statue of Liberty with a one-time presentation of Medals of Liberty to twelve outstanding immigrants.[1] These highly select acclaimed Americans included no less than *three* individuals of Chinese ancestry—the architect I. M. Pei (Bei Yuming, b. 1917), the computer scientist and entrepreneur Wang An (1920–1990), and the astronaut Franklin R. Chang-Díaz (b. 1950).[2] From the vantage point of the early twenty-first century, the celebration of Chinese Americans as exemplary immigrants seems unsurprising given the pervasive image of Asians as model minorities whose educational and professional attainments surpass that of any other racial group, including whites.[3] This is very recent history, however. Such an honor would have been inconceivable, and legally impossible, just a century before and as recently as World War II, when Asians categorized by race were barred from naturalized citizenship and subjected to highly limited rights of entry. The earliest American law concerning citizenship, the Nationality Act of 1790, had set aside Asians as racially ineligible, and the earliest enforced immigration laws (1875–1943) had targeted Chinese by race, who thereby became the first illegal immigrants against whom the legal and institutional foundations of American border controls were established. Under such circumstances, how did Pei, Wang, and Chang-Díaz, as Asians but particularly as Chinese, ascend so rapidly to become model American immigrants?

I. M. Pei's life story surfs astride the shifting ideological, political, and legal tides that advanced the integration and visible successes of Chinese. Individual brilliance aside, Pei had excellent timing, for his arrival in the United States in 1935 at age seventeen coincided with the onset of major changes in the relationships between immigration priorities and practices, the politics of foreign relations, and views of domestic racial inequalities that transformed the positioning and possibilities available to Chinese. The immigration histories of Pei and his generation of fellow students, heretofore

Figure 1.1. Ronald Reagan awarding Medals of Liberty, July 3, 1986. A dozen exemplary immigrant Americans were honored at this one-time ceremony to celebrate the centennial of the Statue of Liberty. I. M. Pei is third from the left, next to Franklin Chang-Díaz and Wang An. Courtesy of Ronald Reagan Library.

treated as exceptional to the mainstream of Asian American history, require our attention because they illuminate the many intersections between immigration history and international relations, underscoring that the evolution and institutionalization of American border controls emerged not just from domestic political agendas and racial ideologies but as manifestations of American ambitions and constraints abroad. The twentieth-century turn from restriction to selection gained momentum as the U.S. government—chiefly the executive branch and the Department of State but in conjunction with internationalists active in education, missionary work, and public policy—realized and co-opted the use of educational and cultural exchanges as means first to advance American foreign interests and eventually to develop national reserves of economically enhanced human resources. Immigration policies and practices shifted from a set of defensive measures protecting America from unwanted immigrants seen as posing dangers to the state to a set of selective processes recruiting immigrants seen as enhancing the national economy.

Pei entered the United States as a student, which, along with merchants, diplomats, and tourists, was one of the few exempt classes of Chinese permitted legal admission, although only for temporary residence. A banker's son, he came to study architecture first at the University of Pennsylvania but then transferred to MIT and continued to Harvard University for graduate study. As did other Chinese students, and even some American-born Chinese facing discrimination in the United States, Pei anticipated working in China, where professional careers were more readily available to ethnic Chinese. The Sino-Japanese War (1937–1945), the Chinese Civil War (1945–1949), the outbreak of the Cold War (1948), and the hardening of political divides with the Korean War (1950–1952) shattered these plans and transformed him from a relatively privileged professional-in-training with a secure future in his homeland to a stateless refugee with uncertain prospects for either residence or employment. Unlike most Chinese in America, stigmatized as working class, ghettoized, and inassimilable, however, Pei had abundant talents, bicultural adeptness, and top-notch educational credentials that brought opportunities knocking at his door. On graduating in 1940, he received the Alpha Rho Chi Medal, the MIT Traveling Fellowship, and the AIA Gold Medal and continued his studies at Harvard with leading architects such as Walter Gropius, garnering special attention and teaching assignments. Pei was not alone in receiving support and succor from Americans. In 1948, alerted to the plight of thousands of elite Chinese students and technical trainees rendered homeless in the United States by the tragic turn of events, Congress made legal and financial provisions to provide sanctuary that included payments for tuition and living costs, stays of deportation, and legal employment. In the mid-1950s the Department of State came to accept the permanence of China's communist government and sought ways for the "stranded students" to gain permanent residence and eventually citizenship in the United States, a strategic move in light of the intensifying Cold War competition in the arms and space race.[4] In 1954 China's assistant foreign minister, Wang Bingnan (1908–1988), had issued an open invitation for overseas Chinese scientists and technicians to return and help rebuild their homeland, a move that prompted the State Department to make U.S. citizenship available to selected resident Chinese refugees of good standing and demonstrated usefulness, such as Pei and Wang, who were otherwise unable to regularize their status because of restrictive immigration laws.

They and others in their cohort of student-refugees, such as the Nobel Prize–winning physicists Li Zhengdao (T. D. Lee, b. 1926) and Yang Zhenning (C. N. Yang, b. 1922), are also early examples of the phenomenon later criticized in the 1960s as "brain drain," the dynamic of educated elites departing their developing homelands to work in advanced economies, chiefly that of the United States, seeking better professional opportunities and working conditions, resources conducive to intellectual development, and political stability. In the face of Chinese with such outstanding capacities, and in the context of the mounting Cold War refugee crisis and intensifying competition for highly valued knowledge workers, changing the priorities and practice of U.S. immigration controls to privilege individual merit rather than race and national origin presented compelling imperatives.[5] The product of these shifting considerations, the Hart-Celler Act of 1965, facilitated the transformation of Asian Americans into model minority groups by prioritizing employment and educational criteria over race and national origin in potential immigrants. *The Good Immigrants* traces the longer history of such selective processes to the exemption for students articulated in the 1882 law restricting Chinese entry by race, a differentiation that laid the ideological and legal foundations for the role of Chinese students and refugees in enabling this dramatic turn in American immigration strategies, racial ideologies, and foreign relations, as immigration controls turned from emphasizing restriction to selection, with the aim of enhancing America's international political and economic agendas.[6]

Considering immigration as both a restrictive *and* a selective process makes several major interventions. At a basic level it integrates students and intellectuals into standardized narratives of excluded, largely working-class Asian immigrants, thereby providing the connections between the dominant, early twentieth-century trope of Asians as a yellow peril to the late twentieth-century positioning of them as model minorities.[7] Furthermore, it alleviates the scholarly neglect of the Cold War era by tracing how the international alliances and enmities of World War II and the Cold War improved acceptance for certain kinds of Asian immigrants and conditions for their permanent resettlement in ways that foreshadow the transformations more usually associated with the 1965 Hart-Celler Act. Although some monographs have addressed social and cultural history dimensions of race and foreign relations during the Cold War, none so far has addressed how international politics and fiscal considerations contributed to significant shifts in immigration laws, practices, and ideologies that in turn transformed the demographics, attributes, and trajectories of Asian American communities and U.S. immigration policies more broadly.[8]

The Good Immigrants contributes to discussions concerning the relationships among foreign policy, the naturalization of neoliberal principles, American immigration laws, and domestic ideologies of racial difference and inequality. Celebratory narratives emphasizing the successes of Asian "model minorities" have obscured how selection processes serve economic purposes by screening immigrants for educational attainment and economic potential, thereby eliding domestic limits on access to opportunities and systems enabling upward mobility and success for those without such advantages. Cold War politics laid the groundwork for transformations associated with the Civil Rights era in repositioning Asians, here particularly

Chinese, as capable of, and even ideally suited to, participating in American democracy and capitalism. Attributed with exemplary economic, social, and political traits, educated and readily employable Chinese, and other Asians, gained preferential access to "front-gate" immigration as permanent residents eligible for citizenship, in the framing of Aristide Zolberg. In contrast, "back-door" immigrants such as refugees and unsanctioned migrant laborers face greater, sometimes insurmountable, barriers to naturalization.[9] To these I would add the "side door" through which migrants such as students, paroled refugees, and now H-1B workers legally enter through less scrutinized temporary statuses yet routinely gain permanent status leading to citizenship. Between 1948 and 1965, such side doors enabled thousands of Chinese screened for educational and employment credentials to resettle in numbers far exceeding quota allocations as part of campaigns for general immigration reform. The H-1B visa side-door system, which primarily admits Asian workers in the high-tech sector, exemplifies twenty-first-century priorities in immigration selection that demonstrate how this metamorphosis has become naturalized, thereby rendering invisible how our systems of border controls continue to designate certain racial and ethnic groups for success while severely penalizing others.

Legacies of Exclusion

Asian Americans have featured most prominently in U.S. history in the Gold Rush period, as workers on the transcontinental railroad, and as the innocent victims of incarceration during World War II. After the shocking attack by Japan on Pearl Harbor, Japanese Americans were categorically treated as "enemy aliens" who were liable to engage in sabotage or espionage if allowed to remain within one hundred miles of the West Coast. "Military necessity" justified removing about 120,000 Japanese Americans, a majority of whom were American-born citizens, from their homes to isolated, hastily erected, "relocation camps" in the interior. Although no evidence of espionage or treason ever came to light, the U.S. Supreme Court affirmed the constitutionality of such mass civil rights violations in cases such as *Hirabayashi v. United States* (1943) and *Korematsu v. United States* (1944), decisions that were not vacated until the 1980s.[10] That the executive branch enacted such mass incarceration against targets defined by race as bound to enemy national origins, a move sanctioned by the highest reaches of the judicial branch, illustrates the pernicious prejudice with which ethnic Asians have been viewed as essentially foreign, inassimilable, and therefore probable threats to national security if allowed to enter and remain in the United States.

The impossibility of Asians becoming U.S. citizens was established early in America's history. As noted earlier, Asians had been excluded from citizenship when the Nationality Act of 1790 confined naturalization rights to "free white persons," a category that then referred to white, male property-owners. The groups eligible for citizenship expanded with the inclusion of Mexicans through the Treaty of Guadalupe Hidalgo (1848) and African Americans with the Civil War (1861–1865) but Asians not fully until 1952.[11] Asians thus existed for most of American history as "aliens ineligible for citizenship," a legal category underpinning discriminatory legislation such as the alien land laws that prevailed in many western states during the first half of the twentieth century and used to ban their entry altogether with the Johnson-Reed Immigration Act of 1924.[12] The move to restrict the admission and residence of racially incompatible Asians had begun much earlier with Chinese, who were the first to arrive in noticeable numbers during the Gold Rush. These numbers only grew as economic development in the western states enticed workers with abundant job opportunities in trade, agriculture, fishing, service industries, manufacturing, mining, and railroad construction. Although Chinese constituted but 0.2 percent of the national population during the 1870s, some 70 percent of this number lived and worked in California, which spearheaded efforts to impose limits on their entry as early as the 1850s. During the 1870s the most severe economic contractions yet experienced by the United States, anxieties regarding the economic and racial legacies of recently abolished slavery, the restoration of southern Democrats to Congress after the Civil War and Reconstruction, and California's influence as a swing state in razor-close presidential elections[13] propelled the anti-Chinese movement into a heated national campaign. Presidential candidates of both parties in 1876 and 1880 featured platforms that declared the racial incompatibility and inferiority of Chinese—as marked by their status as unfree, heathen, coolie laborers; the undermining of white, working-class family men through unfair economic competition; and the sheer numbers of Chinese poised to take over the West Coast if allowed to enter unchecked. Charles Darwin's *On the Origin of Species*, published in 1859, seemed to grant scientific authority to such beliefs in intrinsic racial inequalities and incompatibilities and the imperative to segregate different "species" of men otherwise bound to erupt into evolutionary competition and violence.[14] Such arguments justified the transformation of America from a nation founded by free immigrants to a "gatekeeping nation" that began shutting its doors by targeting Chinese.[15]

Congress first passed what came to be popularly known as the Chinese Exclusion Law in 1882 under the title "An Act to Execute Certain Treaty Stipulations Relating to Chinese" (47th Congress, Sess. I, Chap. 126; 22 Stat. 58). This law restricted Chinese entry by enacting the terms of the Angell Treaty of 1880 in which China had acknowledged America's sovereign powers "to regulate, limit, or suspend" the entry of laborers with the stipulation that certain exempt classes, including students, merchants, merchant family members, teachers, tourists, and diplomats were "permitted to come and go of their own free will and accord."[16] In practice the United States interpreted the law much more severely than the Chinese government had expected, a source of tension for decades to come, so that *all* Chinese not of the exempt classes were presumed to be laborers and therefore barred from entry. The 1882 law also affirmed the ineligibility of Chinese for naturalized citizenship and set the United States onto the path of securing its borders—evolving from a nation of free immigration to one preoccupied by excluding unwanted migrants as expressed through restrictive laws with an expanding array of targets and a growing bureaucracy for enforcement. This institutionalization of American nativism ran against the determined dexterity of Chinese in continuing to pursue the greater economic opportunities in the United States by defying the thickening jungle of laws and enforcement strategies of surveillance, interrogation, confinement, and deportation by challenging their constitutionality in court, sneaking across land borders, assuming fraudulent statuses and identities, and multitudinous other manipulations and evasions of American laws and bureaucratic practices. These contestations laid the foundations for the legal, ideological, judicial, and institutional implementation of America's border control regime in all its twenty-first-century contradictions, abuses, and ineffectiveness. From enforcement of Chinese exclusion developed legal and procedural strategies such as the sovereign and plenary powers of the U.S. government to enact immigration laws, the executive branch's sole authority over border controls, an explicitly funded and designated immigration bureaucracy, standardized profiling, practices of documentation and authorization, early versions of green cards, deportation of illegally resident aliens, the limited rights of such aliens to access American courts, and the caste-like inability of unsanctioned immigrants to gain legal status.[17]

From Chinese, immigration restrictions extended to paupers, those with diseases, and illiterate people in 1891; to Japanese in 1908 through the diplomatically negotiated Gentlemen's Agreement; to a legislated "barred zone" in 1917 reaching from Palestine to Southeast Asia; and capping overall numbers by imposing a quantitatively discriminatory quota system based on national origins and applied to most of the rest of the world in 1924, accompanied by an absolute bar against immigration by "aliens ineligible for citizenship." Historically and academically the legacies of Asian exclusion have framed the chief contributions of Asian Americans to the evolution of the United States as a nation-state through racial definitions of what peoples cannot participate fully in its republic as citizens, who should therefore be restricted from entry, and the rationales for marking and maintaining such differential statuses. The emergence of Asian exclusion illuminates America's continuing ambivalence about the meaning of constitutional assertions of equality, specifically the priorities and criteria we should apply in determining whom and how many others we should admit and welcome to become fellow citizens.

Much of immigration studies scholarship has usefully focused on the goal of *restriction*—the targeting of certain populations as unwanted in the United States. Such gatekeeping agendas were critical to American nation-state formations by positioning certain categories of people, and particularly Chinese and other Asians, as essential outsiders and threats against whom the United States ideologically, legally, and institutionally defined its boundaries.[18] Until 1965 race and national origin were the chief criteria framing immigration laws, revealing deeply held convictions concerning racial incompatibilities and differing potentials for national integration. By focusing on restriction, however, the scholarship has neglected the *selective* aspects of immigration laws, which not only erected *gates* barring entry to unwanted persons but also established *gateways* that permitted admission to peoples deemed assimilable but also strategic, as determined by a variety of revealing rationales. We should strive not only to understand who America has tried to keep out and why, but also who America has chosen to admit and the priorities guiding such choices. Rather than emphasize the "centrality of race in immigration restriction,"[19] *The Good Immigrants* explores why certain categories of Chinese, particularly students, were deemed exempt from such racialized restrictions and what support for their continued mobility can tell us of how considerations of class, political and economic pragmatism, and individual attainments mitigated Asian exclusion and immigration restrictions more generally.

From the earliest implementation of immigration restriction, distinctions based on class, cultural capital, and political and economic utility justified differential treatment for certain categories of immigrants. Earlier precursors to Chinese exclusion, such as the "Act to prohibit the 'coolie trade' by American citizens in American vessels" (1862) and the Page Act (1875), specified limits on the importation of prostitutes and coolie workers, permitting continued entry by other classes of Chinese.[20] By examining how processes of immigration *selection* had existed alongside restriction from its beginnings, *The Good Immigrants* underscores that debates regarding immigration involved many highly invested constituencies apart from labor organizations and segregationists. This broader and more nuanced view reveals the dynamic and inextricable relationships between immigration controls, foreign diplomacy and internationalist agendas, competing racial ideologies, and economic prerogatives. Restricting immigration demonstrated America's status as a sovereign nation while satisfying domestic pressures clamoring for more secure borders,[21] domestic priorities that often impeded efforts to strengthen international relationships by offending the governments of excluded peoples, thereby inhibiting trade and other forms of economic cooperation and the expansion of American influence abroad. For such reasons, a group that Michael Hunt has called "the Open Door constituency," which included missionaries, cultural internationalists,[22] educators, business leaders, and diplomats, worked alongside Chinese government representatives to ameliorate the drive toward Chinese exclusion by advocating for selected ranks of Chinese migrants seen to possess useful attributes such as education and skills, economic contributions, and the potential to enhance America's foreign influence while advancing China's modernization. In particular, for a variety of reasons and by a range of advocates, Chinese students were regarded not as inassimilable, barbaric coolies but as a malleable leadership class whose education in America and employment in China could foster stronger ties between the two countries while spearheading China's advance into a Christian, democratic republic. Such high hopes attracted a breadth of supporters and advocates for Chinese to study in the United States, so that even at the height of the Asian exclusion period, Chinese students were constantly among the most numerous of international student populations attending American universities and colleges.

Studies of Asian American and immigration history tend to leave out students, who, after all, are commonly seen as but temporary presences in America that do not participate in struggles for settlement and acceptance. However, students demand greater attention for several notable reasons. Despite their low numbers relative to the total population of Chinese in America—around 1,300 compared to 102,159 in 1930 for example—even in the thick of the exclusion period they were consistently among the most numerous international students from the 1910s through the 1940s. In 1931 they were second in numbers only to Canadians out of a total of 9,806 international students overall.[23] The contradiction between the relatively high percentage of Chinese among international students compared with the very low number allowed to immigrate speaks to important nuances and slippages in the standard narrative of racialized segregation and exclusion. For example, missionaries and educators emphasized cultural differences that were mutable, rather than the essential difference of biological race. Students such as I. M. Pei demonstrated the possibilities of cultural convergences between Chinese and Americans and presented living examples that Americans could welcome and economically benefit from the presence of the right kind of Chinese: educated, Westernized, well-mannered, and possessed of practical skills and talents. Although Pei presents an exceptional profile in terms of ability and success, he nonetheless reflects a critical minority strand in the history of Asian immigration, revealing what would become a prevailing discourse in U.S. immigration by the late twentieth century. Such students could benefit the United States not only by returning to become leaders in their home countries but also by resettling permanently and contributing their professional and technical skills to the

American economy. Highly educated and skilled Chinese students such as Pei, who gained U.S. citizenship after becoming a refugee, illustrated the possibilities of such alternative rationales for immigration control, in which individuals could be selected by inoffensive and highly strategic criteria such as political alignment, personal merit, and attainment rather than the often impractical group criteria of race and national origin.

Despite their apparent challenge both to foreign policy and to constitutional ideals, gatekeeping priorities have dominated both practice and scholarship in the United States. Nativism and fear of economic competition as the governing principles for immigration restriction gained ascendance in the 1870s, grew in intensity through the 1920s, and staved off immigration reforms until 1965. However, throughout the eras of Asian exclusion (1882–1952) and national origins quotas (1921–1965), internationally minded advocates of more measured and less offensive immigration controls remained active and gained standing, particularly with the rising importance of America's foreign relations during World War II and the Cold War. Throughout America's exclusionary era, missionaries, educators, and internationalists developed and funded an expanding set of institutions promoting cultural exchanges, with Chinese as particularly valued participants, while they and business leaders continued to press the Immigration Bureau to respect the rights of exempt Chinese to enter and receive fair treatment. During the 1930s such international education programs gained State Department backing as inexpensive, soft diplomatic measures to strengthen relations with America's neighbors in the Western Hemisphere. Through technical training programs, U.S. corporations gained access to international students as cheap but highly trained temporary workers. As technological innovation emerged as a key force in economic competitiveness, maintaining access to suitably educated knowledge workers became necessary to maintaining America's capitalist edge.[24] World War II broadened the array of nations that the United States needed as allies, as did the revolutionary wave of decolonizations in Africa and Asia during the Cold War. International exchange programs increased in scope even as America could no longer afford to shut out by race and national origins the citizens of the many new governments in the Third World confronting miniscule immigration quotas and the tracking of Asians by race rather than by citizenship or nativity. These global shifts compelled a bipartisan succession of presidents—Truman, Eisenhower, Kennedy, and Johnson—to press for immigration reforms so that America might present to the world a less discriminatory face.[25] For well over a decade, however, the only modifications that could get through Congress were stopgap, limited measures that acknowledged the compelling demands of America's wartime allies, family ties, and refugees. This long campaign finally culminated in the much delayed passage of the Hart-Celler Act in 1965, which displaced considerations of race and national origins by prioritizing family reunification, employability, and refugees with some consideration for investors.

As the earliest targets of race-based exclusion, Chinese as students, and then as refugees prioritized for educational and professional attainments during the 1950s, contributed to the working out of how the United States might displace race and national origins criteria for those of individual attainment and merit by providing reassurances that America's racial and cultural essence could be preserved even as it enhanced its political and economic interests through more strategic selection of its immigrants. Students such as Pei and others of his cohort presented highly persuasive examples of why the United States should make it more feasible for them, and others of high educational attainment and useful technical and scientific training, to remain and work permanently. With the growth of international education programs, and the likelihood that those trained in science, engineering, and technology fields could readily find employment and convert from student to permanent resident status in the United States, increasing numbers of ethnic Chinese, Indians, and South Koreans chose such specializations to position themselves to immigrate to America. The Hart-Celler Act of 1965 facilitated such resettlement by ending the offensive quota system and making employment preferences part of general law. These transitions in immigration law and racial ideologies drew on the pivotal role of Chinese students as a strategically malleable category in immigration policy and practices, racial theories, economic expansion, and diplomatic outreach, transformations that are inexplicable if we consider only the racial implications of Asian exclusion without due attention to the mitigating circumstances of selected admissions based on individual class and merit, but also the international implications of immigration controls.

International Imperatives in American Immigration Controls

Seen solely from a domestic perspective, border control is a matter primarily of defense, protecting the nation against those who might undermine or dilute the coherence and security of the state. International perspectives, however, emphasize the many necessary relationships entwining the United States with other nations and their peoples and how select and strategic types of migration enhance political and economic agendas both abroad and at home. For both America *and* its foreign allies, circulating people in the roles of, at a minimum, diplomats and businesspersons, but additionally technical, cultural, and economic experts, relatives and family members, military personnel, students, and tourists, is essential to projects acknowledging, promoting, and seeking advantage from our sharing of the world. This book highlights the international dimensions of American immigration control that are revealed through Chinese student and refugee migrations to provide necessary complication for narratives that have emphasized domestic motives and impacts.[26] We cannot conjoin the state of America's immigration controls at the beginning of the twentieth century to the situation at its end unless we track the systematic privileging of educated and other kinds of economically and politically useful migrations.

Emphasizing domestic rationales for exclusion obscures the range of American opinions regarding racial difference and the need to strengthen foreign relations rather than isolate the United States. For example, the extensive American Protestant missionary establishment, for which China had been a major field of activity starting in the 1830s, opposed Asian exclusion. Although with some variation and inconsistencies, missionaries did not believe that essential racial differences divided Chinese from Americans. As expressed through the eyes of Presbyterian missionary William Speer (1822–1904), who ministered to Chinese in both China and San Francisco, the key divide was that between heathen and Christian, which "encompassed superiority and inferiority in social and moral life, just as hierarchical theories of race did, but provided a changeable and individualistic base for this difference—Christianity." In response to the competing discourse of scientific racism, missionaries such as Speer's Methodist counterpart, Otis Gibson (1826–1889), pursued "antiracist" projects that "attempted to better the lot of racially oppressed groups and individuals," with the only meaningful differences between people stemming from their religions.[27] Both Speer and Gibson were outspoken opponents of the anti-Chinese movement during the 1870s, despite virulently hostile attacks from other Americans. With their belief in the "universal brotherhood of man and fatherhood of God" and their considerable investment in physical infrastructure in China, such as missions, schools, hospitals, and thousands of human agents, missionaries had powerful ideological and material reasons to advocate for Chinese immigration rights before restriction began and for the mitigation of exclusion after it was implemented.[28] Such ecumenism battled with Christian paternalism and continuing assumptions regarding the superiority of Western civilization, fundamental contradictions that limited the impact of missionary projects in China despite the tremendous efforts expended.

The missionary establishment was but one component of the overlooked minority but nonetheless influential coalition of interests emphasizing that exclusion damaged America's relationships with foreign nations. Even the commonly used term "Chinese Exclusion Act" misleads by obscuring its roots in diplomatic negotiations and overstating original intentions. As described earlier, the law passed in 1882 enacted terms negotiated diplomatically with the Chinese government in the Angell Treaty of 1880, including the emphasis on entry by laborers while preserving admission for the exempt classes. Reflecting the limited nature of its initial scope, the law was called the Chinese Restriction Act, with "exclusion" applied only in 1883 in a *San Francisco Chronicle* editorial criticizing lax enforcement of the law and conveying Californian pressures for a more extensive ban. The drive to exclusion quickly gained steamed, and in 1888 passage of the Scott Act eliminated the rights of returning laborers to regain entry, whereby restriction became known as exclusion, which was then applied retroactively to the earlier period.[29] The exempt classes retained their legal rights of entry even if at times—particularly between 1897 and 1908 when organized labor leaders gained control—an overzealous Immigration Bureau attempted to enact complete exclusion, only to be reined in eventually by presidential fiat in response to the 1905 anti-American boycott led by Chinese students and merchants and lobbying by their diplomatic representatives and the Open Door constituency.[30]

Hunt describes the "special relationship" between Americans and Chinese ironically in arguing that the efforts of the "Open Door constituency" to present the United States as friendly to China and supportive of Chinese were not entirely benevolent. This group consisted of "American businessmen, missionaries, and diplomats—with a common commitment to penetrating China and propagating at home a paternalistic vision . . . of defending and reforming China" with the aim of protecting access to markets and China's millions ripe for conversion.[31] Through the Open Door policy developed by Secretary of State John Hay (1838–1905) in 1899, the United States did present a less rapacious image by pressuring other foreign powers to respect China's national integrity and not claim separate territorial concessions in order to maintain commercial access for all on equal terms. Absolute exclusion undermined such efforts by limiting the mobility merchants needed to conduct trade and by offending Chinese who could choose not to convert, not to study in America, and to consume others' products.[32] These considerations, along with the rising challenge of Japan in the western Pacific and concerted lobbying by the Open Door constituency and Chinese diplomats, led President Theodore Roosevelt to modify course and allocate funds to sponsor scholarships for Chinese to study in the United States through the Boxer Indemnity Fellowships (1909–1937) and insist that the Bureau of Immigration respect the rights of the exempt classes to enter without undue harassment if properly documented. From the nadir of Chinese entry rights at the turn of the twentieth century, the pendulum would swing back so that educated and other economically useful Chinese would become among the most valued of immigrants to the United States.

Understanding this transformation requires that we acknowledge and track the activities of missionaries and business leaders such as those who formed the American Asiatic Association to facilitate trade with East Asia, neither of which exhibits the domestic and security perspectives that frame the exclusion interpretation of American immigration history. Akira Iriye's explorations of internationalism help to break through the silos of such nation-based histories. Iriye defines internationalism as manifested in "an idea, a movement, or an institution that seeks to reformulate the nature of relations among nations through cross-national cooperation and interchange." He is particularly interested in "cultural internationalism, the fostering of international cooperation through cultural activities across national boundaries," including exchanges of ideas and persons across borders and regions. Although before World War I proponents of this worldview confronted the problem of "allegedly immutable racial distinctions," in the aftermath of World War I's devastating display of the destructiveness of nationalism, internationalism became seen as "civilization's universalizing force [which], many even began to argue, could in time obliterate differences among people."[33]

Educational exchange programs became key vehicles through which internationalists sought to promote world peace that extensively involved the missionary establishment. Entities such as the Young Men's Christian Association (YMCA, founded 1844), its affiliated Committee on Friendly Relations among Foreign Students (CFRFS, founded 1911), and the Institute for International Education (IIE, founded 1919) devoted funds, personnel, and buildings to providing services that encouraged and facilitated students from around the world, and very prominently Chinese, to come to the United States with the idea that such personal encounters were critical to mutual understanding and world peace.[34] The Chinese and American governments readily collaborated on organizing and funding programs for Chinese to study in the United States, although in service of different agendas that superficially enhanced the image of a "special relationship." Their highly effective collaboration around international education masked the potential for conflict as China sought to strengthen its national economy through the acquisition of relevant knowledge and training while the United States aimed to extend its political influence and trading advantages. As China stabilized and sought to reclaim greater sovereignty during the Republican era (1912–1949), even friendly programs such as educational exchanges could not prevent clashes with an imperially minded United States.

The international historian Paul Kramer urges the concept of "imperial history" to highlight the relationship between how the global "pursuit of power and profit . . . transformed 'domestic' settings." By emphasizing "the way power is exercised through long-distance connections," we can understand advocacy for migration by exempt Chinese as forms of "imperial openings" maintained "because empire-builders in both China and the United States in different ways freighted these social groups with geopolitical significance, as the means to advance their respective states' power." Class-based exemptions drew lines between civilized and uncivilized Chinese, enabling their mobility as conveyors of "nonimperialist expansion" that eschewed expensive military ventures and territorial expansion in ways that allowed the United States to retain rights to trade, fish, proselytize, and conduct business. Through expanding expressions of soft power, missionaries and educators "began to make their presence conspicuous" in both China and America by the 1890s.[35]

Kramer has developed a typology of educational exchange to capture the variety of motives, expectations, and imperial ambitions that shaped such programs and convey the changing complexity of Sino-American political and economic relationships they reflect. China's primary focus was self-strengthening as a means to halt its precipitous nineteenth-century decline by acquiring technical, military, and economic expertise to reinvigorate national development. However, from its earliest organized efforts with the Chinese Educational Mission (CEM) (1872–1881), study abroad has provoked tremendous ambivalence in Chinese, who weigh the necessity of emulating more advanced, powerful societies against deeply rooted anxieties that the essence of Chinese values and culture will thereby be lost and that Chinese foreign students will become "denationalized."[36] Even so, Western-educated Chinese have attained positions of great visibility and influence in the shaping of modern China.[37] Kramer also points to "colonial and neocolonial migrations" organized by imperial states for "crafting a loyal, pliable, and legible elite in the hinterlands with ties to metropolitan society and structures of authority," a strategy most visible in the *pensionado* program that sought to mold elite Filipinos into an acculturated leadership class and was one justification for the Boxer Indemnity Fellowships for Chinese. Christian organizations such as the YMCA and the CFRFS facilitated "evangelical migrations," although with uncertain and limited outcomes. Perhaps most successful were "corporate internationalist" migrations, as implemented by the IIE and developed after World War I "among educators and business and philanthropic elites preoccupied with the causes of the war and possible ways to forestall future conflict." In practice, however, education leaders working with their corporate funders "fastened and often subordinated pacifist idioms to projects in the expansion of U.S. corporate power through the training and familiarization of foreign engineers, salespersons, and administrators in U.S. techniques and products for potential export."[38] This co-optation of international education by corporate interests accelerated with technical training programs during and after World War II. Although Kramer considers these categories inapplicable to Cold War dynamics,[39] after World War II state-facilitated corporate-internationalist migrations evolved to synchronize with economic agendas and facilitate development through student resettlement patterns that became known as "brain drain." Although this book will treat these migrations more as forms of knowledge circulation and transnational corporate collaboration, such international partnerships facilitated America's Cold War drive to integrate developing economies into global systems of capitalism that it dominated.

Growing acceptance that educated Chinese as valuable workers should have access to employment, residency, and permanent status in the United States accompanied shifts in conceptions of racial difference. During the 1930s and 1940s, culture, articulated as ethnicity, gained ground over race as an explanation for differences between peoples. As such Boasian conceptions of race and culture gained general recognition, bringing the mainstream more in line with views long held by missionaries, once immutable categories based on essential biological, racial incompatibilities and hierarchies became increasingly untenable.[40]

International conflicts and competition reinforced pressures for Americans to demonstrate their capacities to integrate all peoples, regardless of race. During World War II, "official and unofficial propagandists celebrated America as a racially, religiously, and culturally diverse nation," contributing to the process of "transform[ing] the ethnic immigrant from a marginal figure into the prototypical American."[41] According to Christina Klein, "Questions of racism thus served to link the domestic American sphere with the sphere of foreign relations, proving their inseparability: how Americans dealt with the problem of race relations at home had a direct impact on their success in dealing with the decolonizing world abroad."[42] And so the Chinese Exclusion Act had to be repealed in 1943 so that Chinese and later other Asian allies of the United States gained naturalization rights. Such transitions accelerated into the 1950s, for the established and emerging nations of Asia gained strategic importance during the Cold War, with the United States committing unprecedented levels of political, military, and economic resources in efforts to foster alliances to construct a defensive belt enclosing the People's Republic of China (PRC) that extended from South Korea through the islands of Japan and Taiwan, enfolding Southeast Asia and reaching to the Indian subcontinent. Cultural exchanges such as the Fulbright programs assumed a central role in this building of relationships and common values that brought unprecedented numbers of Asians to study in America even as "hundreds of thousands of Americans flowed into Asia during the 1940s and 1950s as soldiers, diplomats, foreign aid workers, missionaries, technicians, professors, students, businesspeople, and tourists."[43] The balance of such movements was decidedly uneven, with a large proportion of Asian international students finding means to remain and permanently resettle in the United States, unlike the usually temporary sojourns by their American counterparts. The direction of such flows would not recalibrate until conditions of political stability and economic opportunities in sending states more closely approximated those in the United States starting in the 1970s.

Refugee admissions were another increasingly accessible means of immigrating, as about thirty-two thousand Chinese under this status did between 1948 and 1966.[44] Although Chinese barely register as refugees if they are acknowledged at all in most accounts of refugee or Asian American history, the State Department's refugee programs advanced the image of Chinese as politically sympathetic, or anticommunist, and assimilable, ready-made immigrants. As argued by Carl Bon Tempo, these two traits constituted the main thrust of State Department but also liberalizers' efforts to gain support for refugee admissions and to press for general immigration reforms.[45]

Klein identifies the "global imaginary of integration" that operated on "the Cold War as an opportunity to forge intellectual and emotional bonds with the people of Asia and Africa. Only by creating such bonds . . . could the economic, political, and military integration of the 'free world' be achieved and sustained. When it did turn inward, the global imaginary of integration generated an inclusive rather than a policing energy." Despite the "global imaginary of containment" propelling the struggle against communism, this campaign was primarily "directed inward and aimed at ferreting out enemies and subversives within the nation itself." Klein points out that integration "originated in the nation's fundamental economic structures" and fed into the constant expansion needed for the American capitalist economy to remain healthy. This underlying agenda fueled "the double meaning of integration in the postwar period: the domestic project of integrating Asian and African Americans within the United States was intimately bound up with the international project of integrating the decolonizing nations into the capitalist 'free world' order."[46] The seeming idealism of racial and ethnic integration had at its core the pragmatic agendas of economic and political expansion that impelled immigration reform and the elevation of Chinese into model immigrants.

Outline of Chapters

The Good Immigrants explores the emergence of the Asian model minority through competing immigration agendas and reforms. Chapter 2 begins with the story of Yung Kuai (1861–1943), a CEM student who graduated from Yale but remained in America for the rest of his life where he married a Euro-American woman and raised a biracial family, which he supported by working as a diplomat at the Chinese embassy. Yung Kuai's story reveals the holes in Asian exclusion, from the welcomed presence of the CEM in New England even at the height of the anti-Chinese movement in California, and highlights the efforts of Americans such as missionaries, educators, and diplomats who treated Chinese as culturally distinct yet malleable in ways that could be turned to advantage. Fears that unilaterally imposed immigration restrictions might damage relations with China meant that initial forays into imposing controls came through diplomatic negotiations. Even as domestic constituencies such as organized labor, segregationists, and the politicians catering to them pressed for absolute exclusion, Open Door advocates and the Chinese themselves campaigned for the rights of exempt Chinese. Particularly after 1905, both Americans and Chinese agreed on the usefulness of educating Chinese in the United States, although for different agendas. The "imperial opening" of the Boxer Indemnity funding provided the foundations for the development of international education institutions and policies in the United States molded in large part by the experiences of Chinese students. The Theodore Roosevelt White House threw its support to this coalition, helping to set exempt Chinese migrations on a different path from that of excluded laborers.

Chapter 3 examines the ready institutionalization of this form of Sino-American collaboration through the China Institute in America. Meng Zhi (1901–1990) directed this organization for thirty-seven years (1930–1967) and helped the Chinese government gain greater influence over the selection and training of Chinese students in the United States. In so doing, he became a valued participant in the development of America's international education establishment as spearheaded by the Institute for International Education under the leadership of Stephen Duggan. Meng effectively advocated on behalf of Nationalist Chinese agendas and Chinese students to claim growing levels of support and accommodation from entities such as the IIE and later the Department of State. This shifting balance resulted in part from rising tides of Chinese nationalism, the growing conviction of liberal missionaries that their role was to abet but not convert Chinese in their modernization, and rising hostilities with Japan, which positioned China as a crucial ally in the western Pacific.

Chapter 4 describes how international war compelled repeal of the Chinese exclusion laws, which were seen as unacceptable insults to a wartime ally. As the first liberalization of immigration law since 1924, the campaign for repeal showcased long-simmering contradictions between foreign policy agendas, nativist racism, ethnic and religious groups, organized labor, and economic priorities that would channel and distort the long struggle for immigration reform and eventual passage of the Hart-Celler Act of 1965. With her Christian upbringing, American education, and proximity to power in China, Madame Chiang Kai-shek served as a potent symbol of the humanity and assimilability of Chinese as well as the possibility that long-cherished missionary dreams for the transformation of China into a Christian, democratic nation might be realized. Despite the international conflict, Chiang Kai-shek continued to send significant numbers of Chinese students and technical trainees. His preparations for China's postwar development coalesced with State Department agendas to promote foreign relations by assuming greater management and expansion of the once privately run field of international education, particularly through technical training programs that located highly skilled and talented Chinese, such as Wang An, in cutting-edge research facilities in the United States.

As explored in chapter 5, the best-laid plans often fall apart. As illustrated by C. Y. Lee, the author of *Flower Drum Song*, Chinese present in the United States on temporary visas as students, technical trainees, diplomats, sailors, and so forth suddenly found themselves "stranded" by the Communist victory in the Chinese Civil War. Lee was rescued from refugee status by changes in immigration laws and procedures that allowed resident Chinese in good standing to receive permanent status. On behalf of this group of elite, highly educated Chinese, the State Department and Congress made accommodations rather than force such usefully trained workers to return to a now hostile state. Lee's transformation from student to refugee and then to legal immigrant mirrors that of thousands of other Chinese intellectuals, some not as famous, many in scientific and technical fields, who received American assistance to remain, enter the U.S. workforce, and become citizens. The decade after World War II was a time of flux in which China's future remained uncertain; it also revealed the responsiveness of the U.S. government in providing the sequence of piecemeal legislation, including the Displaced Persons Act (1948), the China Area Aid Act (1950), and the McCarran-Walter Act (1952), which set many of the "stranded students," particularly those with strategic skills, on the road to becoming model immigrants.

Chapters 6 and 7 address the neglected topic of Chinese refugees and their roles in reframing American perceptions of Chinese as exemplary immigrants by entwining exigencies of the Cold War, economic competitiveness, and domestic race relations in ways that compelled immigration reform. Identified as a crucial population in East and Southeast Asia, overseas Chinese and their loyalties had to be channeled away from the PRC despite U.S. willingness to provide only limited aid and resettlement options. Vigorous media campaigns sought to magnify both American benevolence and the deserving traits of Chinese refugees that entwined foreign outreach with domestic immigration reforms.

Chapter 6 describes the enactment of political agendas under the guise of humanitarian outreach through the operations of the CIA-funded Aid Refugee Chinese Intellectuals, Inc. (ARCI). This ostensibly nongovernmental agency targeted intellectual Chinese for assistance and migration, first to aid the Nationalists on Taiwan and then to the United States in fulfillment of the Refugee Relief Act of 1953. Congress had allocated Asians only a few thousand refugee visas, a drop in the bucket compared to the estimated 1.5 million refugees in Hong Kong alone, and a token gesture of American concern insisted on by a former China missionary, Representative Walter Judd (R-MN) (1898–1994).[47] Despite the limits of U.S. assistance, the Department of State through the Office of Refugee and Migration Affairs (ORM) and the U.S. Information Agency (USIA), sought to maximize the impact of such symbolic relief programs. Cold War propaganda, the "battle for hearts and minds," proclaimed American friendship and concern for Chinese overseas while reassuring Americans domestically that applicants vetted not only for political views but also for prearranged employment and U.S. citizen sponsors guaranteed that even Chinese refugees were readily integrated into the United States. The political imperatives of admitting deserving Chinese refugees paralleled the dismantling of the "paper son" system of immigration fraud to apply growing pressures for the reform of American immigration laws to admit immigrants on the basis of individual merit rather than attributions of racial inferiority.

As described in chapter 7, the mandate for refugee relief and widespread publicity that magnified the merits of Chinese applied further pressures for U.S. immigration reform. Hong Kong's refugee crisis of 1962 provided opportunity to affirm the transformed image of Chinese with White House authorization of parole for over fifteen thousand with popular and congressional support. Committee hearings promoted the deserving traits of Chinese as refugees but also as immigrants, described culturally as highly employable and self-sufficient, politically conforming, and with family values that minimized social burdens on the public so that whether admitted on the basis of individual merit, family reunification, or refugee status, their likely success as Americans demanded more general immigration reform based on such criteria rather than race and national origin. This concerted push, spearheaded by Philip Hart in the Senate, failed yet again, although Congress passed a less sweeping measure, Public Law 87–885 in October 1962, titled "An Act: To facilitate the entry of alien skilled specialists and certain relatives of United States citizens," which made permanent the economic nationalism at the core of President John F. Kennedy's vision for replacing the discriminatory national origins system.

Chapter 8 explores immigration reform and the knowledge worker recruitment aspects of the Hart-Celler Act of 1965 to track the intensifying convergence of educational exchange programs, economic nationalism, and immigration reform. During the Cold War the State Department expanded cultural diplomacy programs so that the numbers of international students burgeoned, particularly in the fields of science and technology. Although the programs were initially conceived as a way of instilling influence over the future leaders of developing nations, international students, particularly from Taiwan, India, and South Korea, took advantage of minor changes in immigration laws and bureaucratic procedures that allowed students, skilled workers, and technical trainees to gain legal employment and eventually permanent residency and thereby remain in the United States. This so-called brain drain became an international crisis during the 1960s, with European and Third World "losers" of "brains" accusing the United States of stealing their investments in human resources. Considering this phenomenon over a longer term of decades reveals that "knowledge circulation" is a more apt description for relationships with countries that managed to develop manufacturing sectors that benefited from a symbiotic cycle of exchanges that both sending and receiving countries rationalized as driven by market forces. As described by the British economist Brinley Thomas, the employment preferences of Public Law 87–885 and the Hart-Celler Act of 1965 had turned immigration selection into an aspect of fiscal policy. The growing influence of such neoliberal principles has masked emerging forms of inequality in global migrations that privilege the mobility of educated elites, particularly for those concentrated in what are now labeled STEM, or science, technology, engineering, and mathematics, fields, and most prominently from Asia.

The conclusion, chapter 9, considers early twenty-first-century immigration controls as furthering national economic advantage. The exemplary immigrant I. M. Pei, with his imported talent and skills, illustrates the diminishing of racial inequality through his exceptional accomplishments and success even as he reflects the hollowness of such civil rights victories. The quantified overattainment by the Asian American model minority emanates in large measure from immigration preferences that privilege those most likely to succeed educationally, economically, and now entrepreneurially. America's anxieties about immigration invasion have shifted toward its problematic, unenforceable southern border, which has admitted millions of unsanctioned immigrants just as eager for gainful employment but unscreened for educational and employment credentials. In contrast, few criticisms attend the geometric growth in the ranks of international students, particularly in STEM fields, and the expanding H-1B visa program for skilled workers seen as advantaging the U.S. economy by admitting primarily Asians who immigrate through employment preferences to the benefit of corporate interests. Although largely dependent on the importation of foreign talent, model minority successes have served as rebukes to less well performing minority populations by implying that their failure to attain equal standing does not result from past and ongoing discrimination but is somehow attributable to a lack of the kind of cultural values that would produce upward mobility in the land of equal opportunity, which a race-blind America had already become. Since its earliest articulation in the mid-1960s, the model minority image has become a pervasive, pernicious trope that attached higher standards of academic and employment expectations to ethnic Asians, while blaming other communities of color for failing to attain equitable status, thereby masking ongoing forms of racial inequality in the United States.

The Good Immigrants demonstrates the close relationship between the emergence of Asians as model minorities and selective processes deliberately encased in immigration law that serve neoliberal ends. The Asian American population has exploded since 1965, with a significant component entering through the preference system that privileges those with educational credentials, work skills, and professional and entrepreneurial proclivities. This importation of a middle-class minority has transformed the face of race relations in the United States. Twenty-first-century battles over immigration restriction and concurrences over immigration selection reveal the uneven fashion in which Kennedy's push toward economically rational principles have become naturalized and reworked racially. General consensus supports the use of H-1B visas to attract more workers in STEM fields, who are presumed to be educated Asians, whereas entrenched resistance meets proposals to allow normalization of status for unsanctioned immigrants, even those brought as children and of long residence in the United States, who are coded as primarily Latino. Simultaneously, even as Asians are positioned as highly sought after technical workers and entrepreneurial talent, as mobile, transnational subjects they remain vulnerable to yellow peril anxieties that readily situate them as hostile foreign agents, as illustrated by the 1999 espionage campaign waged against Wen Ho Lee.

The importation of a model minority obscures the failure of domestic educational and employment structures to advance historically disadvantaged populations of color. Moreover, educational attainment and socioeconomic class tend to be replicated across generations. Some of the most visibly successful American-born Chinese, including Secretary of Energy Stephen Chu, author Amy Tan, architect Maya Lin, writer Iris Chang, journalist and activist Helen Zia, and presidential speechwriter Eric Liu, are products of refugee and brain-drain families. If many Chinese Americans, and other post-1965 immigrants, bear the markers of "model minority" achievement, such educational and professional attainments were prerequisites for both their entry and their settlement in the United States. If we are to comprehend the character of racial inequality in the twenty-first century, we must address the distortions and privileges naturalized and enacted through our systems of immigration controls.

CHAPTER 2

"The Anglo-Saxons of the Orient"

STUDENT EXCEPTIONS TO THE RACIAL BAR AGAINST CHINESE,
1872–1925

YUNG KUAI (1861–1943) PENNED "Recollections of the Chinese Educational Mission" within a few years after graduating from Yale University in 1884. He dedicated the project to Mary Burnham (1868–1952) "as a token of warmest, truest, and purest love."[1] It seems only natural that Yung Kuai married Mary in 1894 and raised seven children with her. However, theirs was an era of mounting anti-Chinese hostilities that had become so intense on the West Coast that Congress had taken the unprecedented step of restricting immigration in 1882, with Chinese designated by race as the first targets. The so-called Chinese exclusion laws, which remained in effect until 1943, gave rise to a host of other discriminations, primarily in western states, in the form of riots, employment and residential restrictions, antimiscegenation laws, and other everyday harassments. Thus the interracial romance of Mary and Yung Kuai and the latter's lifetime employment in the United States were exceptional for their time.

Yung claimed his future in America by completing a PhB degree with honors at Yale and then working in New York and Washington, DC, first as a journalist but then primarily in the Chinese embassy.[2] When he died in 1943, his New York Times obituary called him "the permanent Chinese diplomat" for his fifty years of service as a translator, counselor, interpreter, and cultural liaison. Yung spent all his adult life in America and was buried in Glenwood Cemetery in Washington, having seen at least two of his sons also graduate from Yale, with one, Dana Young (1904–1996, class of 1926) teaching at their alma mater and ascending to the rank of Sterling Professor of Engineering and dean of the Sheffield Scientific School (1955–1961).[3]

This otherwise classic narrative of immigrant striving and family attainment masks the unusual timing and difficult circumstances of Yung's success and integration into American life as a Chinese man. Yung had arrived in America in 1873 among the second cohort of students sent under the auspices of the Chinese Educational Mission, which had the goal of training future Chinese officials in Western military and technological skills to advance

Figure 2.1. Yung Kuai and Mary Burnham on September 4, 1938, after forty-four years of interracial marriage. Courtesy of Dana Young.

national development. The students, most of whom arrived as teenagers, by and large thrived academically *and* socially and lodged with receptive Euro-American families in their New England homes even in the thick of the anti-Chinese agitations on the West Coast. Some seemed to get along too well with their hosts, and in 1880 CEM supervisors dismissed Yung together with another student, Tan Yaoxun (1861–1883), for having converted to Christianity.[4] Rather than return with their classmates in 1881 when the mission disbanded under a fog of uncertainty about whether and how Western training would benefit China, both Yung and Tan managed to remain in the United States and attain their college degrees, Yung with financial help from his distant relative, CEM founder Yung Wing (Rong Hong, 1828–1912), and annual donations from American supporters including Mark Twain. Although Tan died of tuberculosis in 1883, Yung achieved a fulfilling personal and professional life on the East Coast even as other Chinese faced discrimination and expulsion elsewhere in the United States.[5]

Because he does not fit standard narratives of exclusion, Yung Kuai is scantly mentioned in most accounts of Asian American or immigration history, or even in the many excellent studies focusing on Chinese exclusion. Although his trajectory was highly unusual, it nonetheless provides important reminders that unlike their despised "coolie" compatriots, Chinese students experienced America through the privilege of their presumed usefulness to both China and the United States as vehicles conveying Western modernity to their ancestral homeland. For example, as a diplomat and translator, Yung functioned literally as a bridge between China and America while facilitating China's emergence into modern systems of international relations. Unlike the detested Chinese laborer, Chinese students along with other useful sorts such as merchants and diplomats retained legal rights to enter the United States, with their studies often facilitated by missionary, internationalist, and higher education organizations throughout the country.

Yung Kuai's diplomatic career reflects the exclusion-era reality that educated Chinese had scant possibilities for professional or white-collar employment by Americans. Not until the watershed of World War II would Chinese, and other peoples of color, break through such barriers in significant numbers. Until then both Chinese and Americans accepted that the place of even the best educated, most Westernized Chinese was at home advancing China's modernization, a process over which the Chinese government gained greater control during the 1930s. In contrast, American hopes that educational exchanges could extend the influence of the United States often clashed with Chinese intentions for its educated elite. Despite such competing nationalist agendas, both sides viewed American-educated Chinese students as strategic resources who required protection for their continued mobility and assistance to facilitate their studies.

Although they constituted but a small, and usually temporary, component of Chinese society in the United States, Chinese students demand our attention because they illustrate that China and the United States actively and systematically cooperated to facilitate certain kinds of migration with the goal of strengthening relations through diplomatic, cultural, educational, and economic exchanges.[6] Such visitors would become permanent resettlers in growing ranks during and after World War II, when America's aspirations for global leadership ran into the impediments of its discriminatory immigration laws. The economic usefulness and ready assimilability of educated Chinese provided persuasive examples of why and how the United States could reform its immigration laws by privileging such value-added types of individuals. Tracking the alternative trajectories of Chinese students and their mitigated experiences of exclusion highlights the ideological and institutional foundations for how quickly Chinese transitioned from being racialized as an unwanted yellow peril to become welcomed model minorities within the span of one generation.

American Missionaries and Educational Outreach to Chinese

Not all Americans agreed that Chinese were irredeemably different and inferior as a race. Most notably, missionaries were among the most committed and institutionalized constituency working concertedly toward the belief that Chinese could adapt to Western civilization and be converted. To this end, over the rough century of their activities in China, American mainline groups made tremendous investments in the form of the thousands of missionaries who dedicated their entire adult lives to the China field, sometimes across multiple generations of families, and built hundreds of schools, churches, and hospitals to win over Chinese. Missionaries were responsible for the earliest exposure of Chinese to Western learning, both in China and abroad. Even as they developed American ties to Chinese through protracted activities in China, this influential, highly networked, transnational coalition of organizations informed public opinion in the United States through a prolific and steady stream of articles, books, letters, and lecture tours by returned evangelicals soliciting funding for their overseas programs. Through such wide-ranging activities, missionaries not only laid the early foundations for Western learning in China but also advocated vocally and with increasing effectiveness for the exempt status of students and eventually equitable immigration and citizenship rights for Chinese more generally.

Missionaries emphasized the capability of Chinese to adopt Western beliefs and practices in stark contrast to the exclusion movement, which presumed their essential difference. From their perspective, China's long traditions of high culture and literacy, albeit in decay during the nineteenth century, imbued Chinese with great potential to adopt Christianity. Chinese were viewed as particularly amenable targets for conversion, for in addition to their sheer numbers, they were seen as a literate, hardworking, and disciplined people with greater capacity to embrace Christian beliefs and ways. Just after the turn of the twentieth century, John R. Mott, general secretary of the World Student Christian Federation and the YMCA International Committee, summarized such views. Chinese were "the Anglo-Saxons of the Orient," as demonstrated by "six major points why China fit especially well into this educational scheme for Christian evangelism . . . the long tradition of China where scholars ruled, China's uncertainty of its future at the moment, China's vast land and population, and the traits of the Chinese people that were thought compatible with Christian values—'industry, frugality, patience, tenacity, great physical and intellectual vigor, independence, and conservatism.'"[7] Not only were Chinese capable of realizing the superior values and spirituality proffered by Christianity, their conversion would provide their salvation, as individuals and as a civilization. Such beliefs in Chinese convertibility nonetheless existed in tension with views of them as "savages" and heathens, inspiring missionaries to pursue their heavenly rewards by risking their corporeal and spiritual selves to intermingle with lesser races.[8]

Western missionaries had visited China as early as the sixteenth century. Jesuits such as the polymath Matteo Ricci (1552–1610) visited the Ming dynasty court (1368–1644), whose emperors admired European astrological techniques, paintings, and mechanical trinkets such as clocks but remained otherwise indifferent to either trade goods or religious beliefs. Chinese disdain for Western ambitions led them to restrict Westerners to the Portuguese colony at Macao in 1557 and the tiny island of Shamian in Guangzhou during the 1750s. Undaunted, the first Protestant missionaries arrived in 1807, led by Robert Morrison of the London Missionary Society.[9] Decades of tensions and recriminations ensued as merchants and missionaries alike chafed against their severely limited scope of activities and lack of impact on Chinese. This state of affairs shifted irrevocably with China's ignominious defeat in the first Opium War (1839–1842), when a coalition of governments led by Britain, France, and the United States decided to go to war to insist on their right to sell drugs to Chinese. The resulting Treaty of Nanjing (1842) initiated China's era of semicolonial subjugation with the imposition of treaty ports, extraterritoriality, and greater rights for Westerners to travel and reside in China. China's very decline motivated missionaries who saw opportunity in the decay of this once magnificent civilization. Despite continued clashes and hostility from Chinese, the number of American missionaries increased from a dozen or so in 1840 to 1,296 in 1889.

At the turn of the twentieth century, China had become the largest field for American Protestant missionaries. As the fabled silks and spices of the Orient had lured Marco Polo eastward, so too did missionary dreams of their bountiful harvest of Chinese souls. In addition to the China-born offspring of multigenerational missionary families such as Henry Booth Luce (1898–1967), Pearl Buck (1892–1973), and John Leighton Stuart (1876–1962), members of the Student Volunteer Movement (SVM), founded in 1886, were among the most enthusiastic expatriates to arrive in China.[10] The inspirational leadership of Arthur Tappan Pierson (1837–1911) had attracted many of America's best and brightest college graduates to join the SVM, particularly in China. During its first decade, of nearly 3,800 Protestant missionaries sent overseas, 3,100 labored in the China field, reaching a peak of 8,325 in 1926. Even after the wartime upheavals of 1927 and growing ambivalence among nationalistically inspired student protests against their influence during the 1920s, U.S. missionaries still did not decline in number below 4,000 through the 1930s.[11]

Despite this considerable commitment, direct ministry in China met with almost complete failure, which left missionaries little choice but to provide incentives such as medical care and education with hopes of attracting Chinese eventually to the benefits of the Christian religion. Protestant missionaries had established schools and taught Chinese for almost as long as they had proselytized in China. Through education, Chinese could be converted and trained as assistants to help recruit the millions of other souls requiring salvation. Just a year after arriving in 1844, the first American Presbyterian missionary established the Ningbo Boys' Academy, which eventually expanded to become Hangzhou Christian University.[12] By 1863 there were about seventy mission schools scattered in a dozen cities, primarily treaty ports.[13]

Chinese had dismissed such forms of alternative learning since their first encounters with Western envoys, but successive military defeats at the hands of foreigners after the first Opium War forced them to realize the necessity of adapting Western knowledge for their own purposes. Under the rule of the Qing dynasty (1644–1911), China's seventeenth-century greatness had ebbed over the eighteenth century through the combined decay of demographic crisis, diminishing tax revenues, official corruption, and the increasingly debilitating trade in opium with foreign powers. Its failure to use military force to reject the trade forced the Qing to accept a once unthinkable reality: that China would have to adopt Western ways. The Qing initially sought to limit such acquisitions to practical skills such as languages, military strategy, and technology. To this day Chinese remain ambivalent about the loss of core spiritual and cultural values that surely must accompany the acquisition of foreign knowledge, ideas, and practices even in the name of national survival and competitiveness. In 1862 the Qing established language schools in several cities, and by 1866 it had added arsenals to two to further the study of Western technology. Under the urging of Yung Wing, the first Chinese to graduate from an American university (Yale, 1854), the Qing initiated the first formal study abroad program in 1872, the Chinese Educational Mission, with the goal of acquiring useful rather than cultural or philosophical knowledge about technology and military science. As discussed in the next section, the CEM's contested goals and implementation reflect late nineteenth-century Chinese ambivalence about whether and how to acquire Western learning without losing a core of Chinese values weighed against the necessity of learning from ascending powers. This conflicted mission had now forced Chinese officials to journey overseas.

Chinese Students in America:
Yung Wing and the CEM, 1871–1881

Most of the earliest Chinese travelers in Western countries were brought by missionaries, usually as students and converts. For example, Andreas Zheng (Zheng Andeluo, n.d.) was one of the first Chinese to visit Europe when he traveled to Rome in 1650 with the Polish Jesuit priest Michael Boym (1612–1659) to help with translation projects. Chinese visited the West only occasionally until the nineteenth century, when missionary schools more systematically provided language training so that more Chinese could study abroad, particularly in the United States.[14] Among the earliest were five boys who had attended the Foreign Mission School in Cornwall, Connecticut, run by the American Board of Commissioners for Foreign Missions during the 1820s. Upon return, such Western-educated Chinese were positioned to greatly influence Sino-American interactions because they were so few in number. For example, one of the Cornwall students, Alum, returned to China and translated for the leading Qing official Lin Zexu (1785–1850) on the cusp of the first Opium War. During the 1840s the first Chinese to attend an American college, Zeng Laishun (n.d.), came to America with returning missionaries and entered Hamilton College in New York in 1847.[15] The most famous nineteenth-century student, Yung Wing, had studied in the Morrison Education Society School in Macao and came to America in 1848 with the missionary Dr. Samuel Robins Brown. Yung Wing became the first Chinese to graduate from an American institution when he became a Yale alumnus in 1854. This experience positioned him to propose and then direct the CEM, the first Chinese government-sponsored program to educate Chinese in the United States.

Yung Wing saw no contradictions in pursuing with equal fervor both an American liberal arts education and patriotic projects supporting China. As argued by K. Scott Wong, he serves as an early example of the possibilities and problems of being both Chinese and American.[16] By studying in New England under the sponsorship of missionaries, Yung avoided anti-Chinese conditions on the West Coast and even escaped enforcement of the 1790 ban against Asian citizenship and naturalized upon his graduation. Despite his admiration and affection for America, Yung prioritized his Chinese patriotism in refusing a scholarship intending him for a missionary career and chose instead to pay his own way through college so that he might place his American education in the service of China. Yung articulated his vision in a letter to Yale's president written when he graduated. He aspired to bring other Chinese to study in the United States so that "the rising generation of China should enjoy the same educational advantages that I had enjoyed; that through Western education China might be regenerated, become enlightened and powerful."[17]

Yung Wing took seventeen years to win the backing of powerful, modernizing, government officials such as Zeng Guofan (1811–1872) and Li Hongzhang (1823–1901), who had led efforts to quell the Taiping Rebellion (1850–1864), for this unprecedented venture in Western learning. Rather than the traditional route of immersion in Confucian texts and taking examinations to enter the most prestigious career path of government service, the CEM would provide its participants with fifteen years of training consisting of English-language lessons in Shanghai, after which the teenage participants would be tested to select those continuing for study in America, with the ultimate aim of enrollment in West Point or the Naval Academy. Upon graduating, they would return to work for the Qing on self-strengthening projects. CEM officials, including Zeng Laishun, who taught English, struggled to find families willing to relinquish their sons to this unproven career path. Most of the students, such as Yung Kuai, were related to CEM officials or came from areas already familiar with Western influence, such as Guangdong, Fujian, and Zhejiang provinces.[18]

The Qing intended CEM students to study topics considered critical to China's self-strengthening efforts, such as "the sciences related to army, navy, mathematics, engineering," so that "all the technological specialities of the West may be adopted in China, and the nation may begin to grow strong by its own efforts."[19] From the outset, however, tensions beset the program concerning the attempted melding of Chinese and American knowledge and values and whether Chinese could learn from the West in ways that did not undermine the essence of Chinese civilization, moral ethics, and social systems. According to Y. C. Wang, Yung Wing believed that Chinese needed not only to learn "the progressive, technological culture of the West" but to acquire Western viewpoints as well. Having originated the idea for the CEM, and knowing more about America, "he became the moving force behind it. Under his direction, a marked change developed in the boys' attitude and conduct: they played baseball, dated American girls, refused to show respect to the head of the mission, and neglected their Chinese studies to such an extent that they forgot how to speak the language. Some became Christians."[20] These signs of unwanted acculturation fostered tensions between Yung Wing and his more traditionally Chinese colleagues.

The ready integration of CEM students into small New England communities contrasts markedly with the virulent anti-Chinese campaigns then convulsing the West Coast. More families than there were boys available offered to provide housing, tutoring in English, and socialization to prepare them for matriculation into college.[21] Under such hospitable conditions, the young men, many of whom were only thirteen or fourteen at the start of their American sojourns, quickly adapted to Western clothes and hid their queues in order to play baseball, row crew, engage in other sports, attend social events like dances, and win a range of academic awards while coming to despise their lessons in the Chinese language and Confucian texts at the "hellhouse" of the CEM headquarters in Hartford, Connecticut.[22] Their very successes in adapting to Western society set off alarm bells for the CEM's less Westernized administrators.

According to a report filed in 1878, the Qing supervisors doubted whether the students and even Yung Wing himself would prove useful to China because they had become "denationalized." Yung was Christian and had married a Euro-American woman, Mary Kellogg. As described earlier, converts to Christianity such as Yung Kuai and Tan Yaoxun were expelled. However, when the program ended, it did so because the U.S. government refused to abide by stipulations in the Burlingame Treaty (1868) and denied the CEM students their ultimate goal of admission to the U.S. Naval Academy or West Point. With these targets of American public education beyond the students' grasp, the Chinese government withdrew from the attempt altogether and recalled the students, most of whom never attained their undergraduate degrees. Only those who could muster private funds and connections, such as Yung Kuai, completed their studies in the United States.[23] The rest returned to a China still deeply suspicious of Westernized Chinese even as Congress voted to pass immigration restrictions banning the entry of most of their countrymen.

Despite uncertainties about how their American training could be usefully employed in China, many CEM students went on to assume leading roles in China's modernization through work on the railroads, mining, international trade and business, and the diplomatic service. In 1923 former CEM student Wen Bingzhong (1862–1938), superintendent of customs at Suzhou, delivered a speech to students at the Customs College in Beijing recalling the attainments of his fellow students: Zhong Wenyao (1861–1945) became the chief of customs at Hankou, a foreign minister in the Qing dynasty, and minister of communications in the Republican government;[24] Liang Dunyan (1858–1924) and Tang Shaoyi (1862–1938) helped found the Customs College; Cai Tinggan (1861–1935) became an admiral and director-general of the Water Bureau; and Zhan Tianyou (1861–1919) founded and led the building of the Beijing-Zhangjiakou Railroad.[25] Other graduates went on to serve in the diplomatic corps and were instrumental in building relationships and institutions that would make China one of the major senders of students to the United States by the 1920s. It took a couple of decades, but the CEM and its participants would prove their critical value in the emergence of modern China, not least in providing the foundations for the educational exchanges that are perhaps the most meaningful of Sino-American collaborations today.

Legislating Exclusion: Immigration and the Struggle between Foreign and Domestic Agendas

The breaches of treaty terms that led the Qing to end its support for the CEM illustrate American ambivalence regarding Chinese. Even as the CEM students joined New England society to warm welcome from local residents, labor organizations and other nativist and segregationist forces were propelling the anti-Chinese movement to its boiling point in California, culminating in America's earliest enforced immigration restrictions, which singled out Chinese as a race for virtual exclusion from the United States. During the 1870s, economic contractions combined with deeply rooted nativist pathologies to identify labor competition from Chinese laborers—in stark contrast to their educated, New England contemporaries—as racially inferior, inassimilable coolies who posed dire threats to America's working class and its young, Christian, and democratic republic. Widespread unemployment and violence associated with labor unrest set the backdrop for exaggerated fears that a tidal wave of Chinese might readily cross the continent and overwhelm all America, particularly after completion of the Transcontinental Railroad in 1869. As home to 70 percent of Chinese in the United States, California was both at the heart of anti-Chinese agitation and a critical swing state whose electoral votes would decide presidential elections.[26] This confluence ensured that the state's anti-Chinese platforms assumed national prominence, with both Democrats and Republicans vehemently agreeing that the Chinese "problem" required resolution, even though Chinese constituted only 0.2 percent of the national population and diplomats, missionaries, and business leaders' concerns that laws singling out Chinese for immigration restriction might insult China.

From the beginning, attempts to restrict Chinese entry focused on both race *and* class. Responding to efforts by Southern planters to replace slaves with pliant Chinese coolies during the Civil War, Congress passed "An Act to Prohibit the 'Coolie Trade' by American Citizens in American Vessels" on February 19, 1862, banning "the inhabitants or subjects of China, known as 'coolies;'" from being transported on American ships.[27] As explained by Moon-ho Jung, the law's definition of "coolies" was so vague that it could not be enforced. The law marked ideological linkages between African slavery and Chinese contract workers that conflated significant differences between the two labor systems and signaled the difficulties of distinguishing admissible individuals from those facing restrictions.[28]

Despite passage of the 1862 law, Americans remained divided about the benefits or harm of Chinese workers. Railroad construction and large-scale industrial and agricultural projects across the western and southern United States demanded large numbers of laborers, a reality reflected in the signing of the Burlingame-Seward Treaty in 1868, which contravened Chinese prohibitions against emigration to secure American access to Chinese workers. Both the U.S. and Chinese governments agreed to "the inherent and inalienable right of man to change his home and allegiance, and also the mutual advantage of the free migration and emigration of their citizens and subjects ... for the purposes of curiosity, of trade, or as permanent residents."[29] Despite the economic and diplomatic rationales for the treaty's terms, Congress made further attempts to restrict Chinese immigration. The Page Act, passed on March 3, 1875, singled out unfree Chinese workers and prostitutes by targeting the "immigration of any subject of China, Japan, or any Oriental country, to the United States" to ensure that it was "free and voluntary" and forbade bringing in any woman for "lewd and immoral purposes."[30] The law significantly reduced the number of Chinese women landing in West Coast ports.

At this juncture, the U.S. government had not sorted out authority over immigration restriction and whether it was a matter of foreign policy, subject to international negotiation, or of domestic policy to be decided by Congress. The balance seemed to be shifting toward Congress, which in

1879 attempted a more general restriction by passing the Fifteen Passenger Act limiting the number of Chinese who could arrive per ship. In the face of such an insult, China's first diplomatic delegation to the United States pressed for a presidential veto by requesting that Americans friendly to Chinese immigration, such as businesspeople and missionaries, protest to their congressional representatives and lobby Secretary of State William Evarts. S. Wells Williams, Yale University's first professor of Chinese language and literature and a former missionary and diplomat who had helped negotiate the Burlingame Treaty, mobilized his colleagues to sign a petition warning that the proposed laws violated America's treaty agreements, which could lead Chinese to abrogate American extraterritoriality rights. President Rutherford Hayes agreed with these concerns, reiterating some in explaining his veto: the need for "maintaining the national faith" and that the United States should "deal with all nations on the same principles—footing. We should deal with China precisely as we would expect—and wish other nations to deal with us."[31] Hayes feared that enacting immigration restriction without some consent from China would lead to an international crisis, leading Evarts to start working to induce Chinese to renegotiate the Burlingame Treaty's guarantees of "free migration."

Evarts selected a bipartisan team to handle this delicate mission, led by the moderate James B. Angell, then president of the University of Michigan, along with John F. Swift of California and William H. Trescot of South Carolina. Angell accepted this responsibility only after receiving reassurances from Hayes and friends in the Senate that the negotiations were intended not to prohibit Chinese immigration but to correct "the abuses now connected with the immigration . . . as a restraint." The U.S. group was split, with Swift demanding outright prohibition and Angell and Trescot preferring to request the right of the U.S. government to *regulate* the immigration of Chinese laborers.[32]

Their Chinese counterparts, who included prestigious grand councilors and foreign ministry officials, were prepared to allow American restriction of Chinese immigration although they disagreed about the trade-off between retaining U.S. friendship and opposing use of the term "prohibit" and limiting the scope of the term "laborer." In the end the U.S. mission gained the right to "regulate, limit, or suspend" the coming or residence of Chinese laborers. Only those coming as "teachers, students, merchants, or from curiosity, together with their body and household servants, and Chinese laborers who are now in the United States" retained the right "to go and come of their own free will and . . . be accorded all the rights, privileges, immunities, and exemptions which are accorded to the citizens and subjects of the most favored nation."[33] Although U.S. preferences dominated the proceedings, the Chinese government had some influence in staving off outright prohibition, a small conservation of entry rights that would be reiterated in the versions of U.S. immigration restriction that followed passage of the law in 1882. From this point onward, however, priorities for immigration restriction moved steadily away from concern for potential damage to foreign relations with China and toward implementing border controls intended to secure an ideologically driven conception of America's fundamentally white, Anglo-Saxon heritage.

The working out of how to implement immigration restriction continued after the signing of the treaty. Congress first passed what came to be popularly known as the Chinese Exclusion Law in 1882 under the title "An Act to Execute Certain Treaty Stipulations Relating to Chinese" (47th Congress, Sess. I, Chap. 126; 22 Stat. 58). In early 1882 Congress passed the first version of the Chinese restriction law, applicable for a twenty-year period. The Chinese minister to the United States, Zheng Caoru, protested to Secretary of State Frederick T. Frelinghuysen that this was too long. When President Chester A. Arthur vetoed the bill in April, he cited Zheng's reasons and the need to avoid offending China's honor and the inevitable harm to commerce. By May Congress had swiftly rewritten the bill by shortening its effective term to ten years. Arthur just as readily signed this version, and Chinese restriction became law on May 6, 1882.[34]

In practice, America's limits on Chinese immigration ultimately proved stricter than Chinese officials had expected in permitting entry *only* to those of the explicitly stated exempt classes. Despite early concerns for maintaining friendly ties to China, anti-immigration sentiments intensified through the final decades of the nineteenth century with the U.S. federal government assuming increasingly sovereign understandings of its authority to restrict immigration. The Scott and Geary Acts (1888 and 1892, respectively) imposed further restrictions on Chinese entry by abolishing the exempt status of returning laborers, requiring Chinese to bear Certificates of Residence to verify their legal entry, and authorizing deportation of those found to have landed illegally.[35] Chinese government complaints that the American immigration bureaucracy treated even admissible Chinese as "suspects and criminals" rather than "subjects of a friendly power"[36] only prompted Congress to enact exclusion permanently in 1904, reflecting the growing willingness of Congress and U.S. presidents to unilaterally impose immigration restrictions despite the risk of retaliation against American business and expatriate communities in China.

The United States could insult China in part because the latter's precipitous decline had continued, marked by the imposition of more onerous treaty conditions, exactions of payments, and, in 1894, its unprecedented naval loss to Japan culminating in the Treaty of Shimonoseki and the ceding of Taiwan. In contrast, when the United States sought to limit the entry of Japanese from the rising world power in 1907, it did so by treaty negotiations that produced the so-called Gentlemen's Agreement. Unable to protect itself in either battle or diplomatic negotiations, China saw its international stature wane with the waxing of Western, military-backed, economic and missionary activities and influence. Christian educational facilities increased in numbers and attendance, particularly after 1905 when the abolition of the imperial examination system that had emphasized Confucian learning opened up the most prestigious career path of government service to those with foreign training. Growing American investment by missionary groups in educating Chinese resulted in the establishment of over 6,380 Christian schools in China by 1918 and growing numbers of Chinese traveling to study in the United States.[37] Missionary efforts to civilize Chinese and shape China's destiny ran into serious interference from the intensification of exclusionary activities in America, which imposed hostile entry conditions on Chinese students and fostered highly alienating, discriminatory conditions of residence.

Although students were legally exempt from exclusion, the immigration bureaucracy that implemented the laws tended to treat all Chinese as racially ineligible for admission without consideration for distinctions of class, education, or legal status. This overenforcement subjected Chinese diplomats, merchants, students, and other elite Chinese to humiliating treatment, such as extended stays on board ships or in unsanitary detention facilities, invasive medical inspections, and even strip searches only to reject their documents and refuse them permission to land. Although the Qing did not dispute the U.S. right to limit immigration, it did object to harassment and efforts to turn away those Chinese whose rights to enter had been enshrined by treaty and by law.[38] According to Adam McKeown, by the turn of the twentieth century, states generally accepted the principle that nations could control their borders, although selective restrictions on mobility could convey dismissive and denigrating attitudes to those facing barred gates.[39] Americans such as missionaries, business groups, internationalists, and educators joined their voices to protest the injury inflicted on their aspirations abroad by such hostile treatment toward representatives of a friendly nation.

Enforcing Exemptions:
The Strategic Value of Educating Chinese

The turn of the twentieth century witnessed the nadir of Chinese entry rights into the United States. Presidents such as Grover Cleveland and Theodore Roosevelt had appointed organized labor leaders and activists in the anti-Chinese movement, such as Terence Powderly in 1897 and Frank P. Sargent in 1902, as commissioners of immigration. Powderly and Sargent directed the Immigration Bureau to complete exclusion by assuming that even Chinese of the exempt classes were attempting fraudulent entry. Any

Chinese seeking to enter America, including diplomatic representatives, faced humiliating medical exams and nitpicking evaluations of entry documents that turned many away in violation of the legal entry rights of exempt Chinese. Against such exclusionary forces, "Open Door" advocates for maintaining amicable relations mobilized to protect their educational and commercial aspirations for China in light of the considerable damage inflicted by their national inhospitality to Chinese visitors, who found that the reality of America fell far short of the model of advanced civilization and civility proclaimed by missionary educators. In 1905 a confluence of events enabled this coalition to persuade Roosevelt and his sympathetic secretary of state, Elihu Root, that benign treatment of Chinese students was strategic to the advancement of U.S. interests in the western Pacific.

The missionary establishment openly criticized such excessive enforcement of the laws and the concept of exclusion itself as violations of American ideals of democracy and justice that undervalued the character and potential of individual Chinese.[40] In perhaps the most famous case, in September 1901 a Presbyterian missionary, Luella Miner, returned to the United States accompanied by two Chinese students on their way to attend Oberlin College. Not only were the two Methodists from staunchly Christian families, Fei Chihao (Fay Chi-hao, n.d.) and Kong Xiangxi (H. H. Kong, 1881–1967) had also distinguished themselves during the Boxer uprisings by risking their lives to save Americans. They bore letters verifying their admission to Oberlin and guarantees of their student status from the leading Chinese official, Li Hongzhang. Nonetheless, immigration officials held them in San Francisco on the technical grounds that their documents were improperly written in Chinese rather than in English and did not include all the required information. The young men remained on the West Coast a full year, first in the infamously oppressive detention facility on the docks of San Francisco known as "the Shed" and then confined in a hospital while Miner rallied letters of support from the American Board of Foreign Missions, the "renowned missionary" Judson Smith, the Ministers Union of Oberlin, Representative Theodore Otjen of Wisconsin, and the widow of a missionary killed in the Boxer uprisings. Ambassador Wu Tingfang protested as well.

Miner herself was a particularly influential advocate who published widely and to broad acclaim through vehicles such as the *Advance, Independence,* and *Outlook.* She evoked constitutional and Christian ideals and reminded merchants and missionaries of how America's Open Door policy advanced their interests. Through this agenda the United States aimed to protect its commercial interests in China by urging other foreign powers to maintain equitable trade conditions for all with reduced interference in Qing government tariff policy. She stressed the foolishness of antagonizing well-connected students such as Fei and Kong and explicitly warned that at a time when the Chinese government was encouraging study abroad, competitors such as

Germany, Russia, and England were receptive to Chinese students in contrast to the United States. Miner bluntly predicted that trade opportunities would almost certainly channel elsewhere as well.[41]

Fei and Kong reached Oberlin after a delay of more than a year. Miner publicized their case to attack the exclusion movement through a double autobiography that depicted their travails. She underscored her personal commitment to their cause by dedicating all her royalties to fund their American educations, predicting great returns on this kind of investment for "if these young men succeed[ed] in their noble purpose of obtaining in America a mental and spiritual training," they would be positioned for "lifting China out of the darkness of her past into the light of the new century, and into the glorious possibilities which lie before her as a nation."[42] In Miner's eyes, Fei and Kong could accomplish this great destiny in a number of ways: "It remains to be seen whether the training received abroad ... will lead them into the high calling of the ministry, or into that of the teacher with its boundless opportunities for molding the intellectual and spiritual life of the new China, or into that of the editor and translator, with its ever-widening influence."[43] Proselytizing was not the only path by which American-educated Chinese could help their homeland.

Miner directly attacked the Chinese exclusion laws, pointing out that they not only undermined efforts to influence Western-educated Chinese but also violated America's Christian ideals. Evoking "the grievous wrong inflicted on these noble men by our Chinese exclusion laws," she appealed to ideals of Christian acceptance for all peoples regardless of race while reminding her readers that national origin was a poor measure of individual quality: "We have made the laws; if they are working injustice it is ours to change them. Is it not a sad anomaly—the doors of a Christian land bolted and barred against Chinese Christians who have shown such heroic loyalty and tender love to her citizens, while they are swung open wide to the off-scouring of every other nation under heaven?"[44] Miner pointed out the flaws of a system of immigration restriction based on race and urged that individual merit be the chief criterion instead. Although articulated in the twentieth century's first decade, this alternative principle of immigration selection would gain ground only when the Sino-American coalition of World War II ate away at the racialist imperatives of exclusion.

The Appeal of Americanized Chinese:
The Song Siblings

Westernized individual Chinese presented some of the most compelling examples of why the United States should rethink exclusion and admit Chinese for education, both as appealing examples of Chinese biculturalism and as effective spokespersons for Chinese rights and national agendas. The Song family offered perhaps the most prominent demonstrations of how persuasively Chinese who were educated and acculturated could convince Americans of their impact in shaping Chinese modernity. The Songs' ascent to power and wealth was the most visible example of the emergence of this influential class in Chinese cultural and political affairs.

Charlie Jones Song (Song Jiashu, 1866–1918) founded this powerful Christian dynasty. He came to America at the age of twelve in 1878 with an uncle. Frustrated by his relative's refusal to send him to school, he ran away and worked as a ship's mess boy. The ship's captain, a devout Methodist, decided to aid the promising boy, who was baptized as Charles Jones Soon in 1880. Recognizing his potential as a missionary, friends helped him enter Trinity College, later Duke University, where the owner of Bull Durham Tobacco, General Julian Shakespeare Carr, helped to pay his tuition. Through these useful connections, Charlie graduated and returned to China in 1886, intending to become a missionary. After a brief flirtation with this poorly paid and largely fruitless endeavor, and frustrated by the lower status of Chinese in missionary organizations, he turned to publishing Bibles and made his fortune in business, a success that enabled him to marry into a prestigious and wealthy Methodist family in Shanghai.[45] He fathered six children whose lives would shape the first half of the twentieth century of Chinese history. The three Song daughters all made highly strategic marriages to prominent Christian men: the eldest, Ailing [pronounced ī'-ling] (1890–1973), to the Boxer Uprising hero Kong Xiangxi, who became the wealthiest man in China; the second, Qingling (1893–1981), to the idealistic Nationalist Party founder Sun Yatsen (Sun Zhongshan, 1866–1925); and the third, Meiling (1898–2003), to the powerful generalissimo and future president of the Republic of China, Chiang Kai-shek (Jiang Jieshi, 1887–1975). The eldest son, Ziwen (T. V. Soong, 1891–1971), would become premier and finance minister under his brother-in-law's leadership. After immigrating to America in the late 1940s, he and Kong became influential members of the China Lobby.

Charlie Song and his wife settled in the International Settlement of Shanghai, where they attended the Moore Methodist Church and sent their daughters to the McTyeire School for girls. At the age of fourteen, Ailing determined to attend college in the United States, and in 1904 she set out for Wesleyan College in Georgia. In anticipation of the likely difficulties facing her in San Francisco, Charlie arranged for his daughter to have a Portuguese passport obtained at Macao and respectable escorts in the form of a homebound missionary couple. Nonetheless, immigration officials confined Ailing aboard the Pacific Mail steamer *Korea* for three weeks while deliberating her papers. San Francisco authorities leaned toward sending her away, but many influential people interceded, including Seth Ward of the Board of

Missions of the Methodist Episcopal Church together with the president of Wesleyan College. In the end, Ailing's case was appealed to the Washington, DC, immigration office, which verified her right to enter and allowed her to proceed to the East Coast.[46]

Through her prominent family connections, Ailing soon had the chance to convey her ill impressions of America to persons with the power to implement reforms. While visiting her uncle Wen Bingzhong, formerly of the CEM and posted on a diplomatic mission to Washington in 1905, she attended a reception also attended by Theodore Roosevelt. Ailing confronted the president about the contradiction between the United States' reputation as a democracy and its discrimination against Chinese. "America is very beautiful, and I am very happy here, but why do you call it a free country? Why should a Chinese girl be kept out of a country if it is free? We would never treat visitors to China like that. America is supposed to be the Land of Liberty." According to Song's biographer and contemporary, Emily Hahn, "The President said he was sorry."[47] Shortly thereafter Roosevelt had opportunity to act on his apology.

Respecting the Entry Rights of Exempt Chinese

In 1905 international circumstances aided Chinese and the "Open Door constituency"—a loose coalition of American businessmen, missionaries and diplomats—in gaining an amelioration of exclusion for the exempt classes by persuading Roosevelt, Root, and Congress that not only should the United States respect the rights of the Chinese students, merchants, and diplomats to enter under reasonably civil circumstances but funding outstanding Chinese students to study in the United States could bring significant benefits.[48] An accumulation of Chinese protests against the excesses of overzealous enforcement of exclusion and growing competition with Japan for influence in the western Pacific fueled the pressure for the United States to make gestures of friendship toward China.

The Immigration Bureau's intensified exclusionary campaign paralleled rising Chinese anger against foreign incursions in their homeland and ignited with the Boxer Uprisings (1899–1901), which had occasioned the heroics of Kong and Fei in saving white Christians from attack. Driven by desperate poverty and intense nativism, a primarily peasant army comprising members of the heterodox Righteous Harmony Society (Yihetuan) began attacking Westerners, Western objects, and Westernized Chinese with the goal of purging China of foreign contamination. A string of early Boxer victories led the Qing to see the attacks as an opportunity to rid China of pernicious outside dominance, and the Empress Dowager sent the Imperial

Army to aid the Boxers in laying siege to the Beijing Foreign Legations for fifty-five days in 1900. After inflicting sustained hardship on thousands of British, French, Germans, Italians, Russians, British, and Americans, many of whom went on to publicize their ordeal, the conflict ended badly for the Qing. An international military alliance vanquished the Chinese troops, and a coalition of eight governments imposed the Boxer Protocol, which exacted heavy financial punishment amounting to more than China's total annual income. America's share of the Boxer Indemnity was $25 million, more than double the damages it had actually incurred.[49]

Anti-American protests extended beyond uneducated Chinese masses. On July 20, 1905, a coalition of Chinese students, regular consumers, and merchants in the United States, Southeast Asia, and urban Chinese centers initiated a boycott against American goods and services to protest the heavy-handed treatment of Chinese by the U.S. Immigration Bureau. As early as January 1900, the Chinese ambassador to the United States, Wu Tingfang, had threatened such a possibility.[50] The boycott's organizers had awaited the outcome of Chinese attempts to renegotiate the Gresham-Yang Treaty (1894) for more respectful treatment of exempt Chinese and Chinese residents in the United States. When these efforts failed and Congress instead passed the exclusion laws in perpetuity in 1904, boycott leaders and the press called for the protests to ensue in urban areas in China and Southeast Asia, with widespread support among average Chinese. As noted by a student in America, E. Ling Soon, "If it is justifiable for America to exclude Chinese, then it is not only just but should be expected of China to exclude the products of American factories."[51] The demonstrations continued for months and ended fully only with the devastations of the San Francisco earthquake in 1906. Although the economic impact was minimal, as China was not a major trading partner of the United States, the boycott signified an emerging Chinese nationalism that identified Americans as a chief imperialist threat.[52]

The boycott presented the United States with a foreign relations quandary. Its Open Door policy in China had failed, for other powers had refused to limit their spheres of influence and sought business advantages that increasingly infringed on Chinese sovereignty, and America's efforts to present itself as a friendly power were undermined by resentments against the exclusion laws. Between 1905 and 1908, war between America and Japan seemed highly possible. Japan was emerging as a serious competitor in the western Pacific, a challenge underscored by its military victory over its far larger, European neighbor Russia in 1905 even as the United States was realizing that its newly enlarged naval capacities could not defend its recently acquired colony of the Philippines in case of Japanese attack. Both were competing for greater shares of the Chinese market and feared moves by the other to block their access. American construction of the Panama Canal (1903–1914) threatened Japan, whereas Roosevelt and his advisers feared that Japan could attack and take the Philippines.[53] Even though exclusion had been a thorny issue in Sino-American relations since the 1880s, in 1905 Roosevelt had particular motivation to make friendly gestures.

The excessive Boxer Indemnity presented opportunity to do so. Its imposition underscored American aggression on and exploitation of an already weakened China. Even before the final papers were signed, the U.S. government already knew the indemnity was set too high and would significantly impede China's ability to develop its economy and infrastructure and further stymie its efforts to stave off the aggression of imperialist neighbors such as Japan and Russia. The U.S. government could not justify keeping the excess money particularly when China's survival as a nation was in doubt. Certain influential sectors of American society and Chinese themselves publicly campaigned for the return of the funds and criticized the inequitable and unfriendly relationship between the two nations that the indemnity represented.

In June 1905 Roosevelt's secretary of war, William Howard Taft, delivered a speech charging that the United States had been "unjust" to Chinese. Although traditional exclusionists on the West Coast protested loudly, pointing to high levels of Chinese immigration fraud, business leaders chimed in about the damage to American interests inflicted by exclusion. Along with other members of the Open Door constituency, they pointed out that without admitting Chinese laborers, the United States could take steps to advance its economic and political influence by focusing on civil treatment for Chinese already resident in the United States and legally exempt classes. Even the emergence of Chinese nationalism could facilitate American influence under the motto of "China for the Chinese" coined by pundits in the United States. Viewing Chinese self-strengthening as "synonymous with the Westernization of China," America could extend its influence through "moral and material participation in that progress" without the appearance of coercion.[54] The belief that modernization would lead Chinese to adopt American ideas and methods led the United States to make considerable investments in educating Chinese as a "more subtle and strategic policy than using gunboats to open China to American influence and commerce" in ways that would not antagonize Japan.[55]

The idea of using the Boxer Indemnity remission to fund education "strongly appealed" to missionaries working in China and to educators such as "the dean of American missionary educators," Arthur Smith, and influential business and political leaders. Smith conferred with Lyman Abbot, prominent editor of the foreign affairs journal *The Outlook*, about using Boxer Indemnity funds for educational purposes. Abbot's son, Lawrence, brought this idea to Root, who arranged an appointment with Theodore Roosevelt.[56] Smith met with Roosevelt in 1906 and raised the specific issue of funding to educate Chinese, hoping to channel some resources to American Protestant colleges in China with the goal of "creating an influential body of Chinese leaders of American education." Returning excess funds from the Boxer Indemnity in the form of fellowships allowed the United States to dispense money it could not justify demanding or keeping while bolstering American claims to an international moral high ground as well as "a feeling of cultural superiority and a desire to help a backward ward along the path of progress."[57]

Chinese diplomats also lobbied for the return of Boxer funds to China. Key representatives now included several former CEM students who were personally inclined to value Western education and assumed leading roles in framing the next program to systematically bring Chinese students to the United States. Liang Dunyan and Tang Shaoyi helped to negotiate the Boxer Indemnity Fellowships during stints in Washington, DC, between 1905 and 1908. Although the Chinese government would have preferred the money be invested in industrial projects and modern banks, Presidents Roosevelt and Taft, their respective secretaries of state, and certain members of Congress prioritized American needs with the view that funding Chinese students would cultivate U.S. influence on China's future leadership class and foster access to Chinese markets.

Educators also favored recruiting students, mindful of the role they had played in organizing the 1905 boycott and the abolition of the Confucian-text-based official examination system. As the main groups to have established Western-style institutions of higher learning in China, missionaries hoped to gain greater influence with the waning of traditional learning. In February 1906 President Charles Eliot of Harvard had argued that the boycott would come to an early end if his institution offered full scholarships to Chinese. This idea seemed borne out when in 1907 Yale, Cornell, and Wellesley set up scholarships for ten men and three women and six hundred candidates turned out to compete in the exams for them in Nanjing.[58] Edmund J. James, president of the University of Illinois, wrote in a memo read by President Roosevelt that

China is upon the verge of a revolution. . . . The nation which succeeds in educating the young Chinese of the present generation will be the nation which for a given expenditure of effort will reap the largest possible returns in moral, intellectual, and commercial influence. If the United States had succeeded thirty-five years ago, as it looked at one time as if it might, in turning the current of Chinese students to this country, and had succeeded in keeping that current large, we should to-day be controlling the development of China in that most *satisfactory and subtle* of all ways,—through the *intellectual and spiritual domination* of its leaders.[59]

Open Door advocates claimed that the indemnity program would benefit China but also the United States, through a critical mass of American-educated Chinese leaders: "They will be studying American institutions, making American friends, and coming back here to favor America for China in its foreign relations. Talk about a Chinese alliance! The return of that indemnity was the most profitable work Uncle Sam ever did. . . . They will form a force in our favor so strong that no other government or trade element of Europe can compete with it."[60] America would compete for advantage in China but under the guise of advancing Chinese causes.

Some Chinese believed that study in the United States would benefit China, as articulated by W. W. Yen in 1905:

> [W]e are to be the interpreters and expositors of America to our own people. . . . I think we are able to bring to our own people a knowledge of the American people that no amount of explaining in books or by Americans themselves could accomplish. We constitute a bridge across the Pacific Ocean over which American education, American ideals, American machinery and manufactures, and all that is best of America pass to the Flowery Kingdom. We constitute the strongest link in the bond of friendship between China and the United States, strong because it is based on intellectual and disinterested reasons.[61]

President James of the University of Illinois argued that the United States was now the most "natural" country for China to send its students to in light of growing jealousy of Japan's rising power. He urged Roosevelt to send an educational commission "so that the two countries would become united in sympathy and friendship."[62] Roosevelt let himself be persuaded "to view educational work as a civilizing force among this backward race" by April 1906 and spoke of this intent in his annual address in 1907.[63]

Amid the struggles between the Open Door constituency and exclusionary forces, Roosevelt switched sides to ease the enforcement of exclusion. He directed the Immigration Bureau to respect the entry rights of exempt classes of Chinese through administrative reforms by executive order. He reformed the bureau in 1906 by removing "the notoriously racist" Victor Metcalf, then secretary of labor and commerce, and installing a new secretary who was instructed to "do everything to prevent harshness being done to merchants and students" while still strictly enforcing exclusion against laborers.[64] These shifts in presidential priorities contributed to improvements in how the Immigration Bureau handled Chinese student cases. By 1907, rather than requiring time-consuming interrogations and the gathering of additional evidence, immigration officials were to approve entry of Chinese students based on assurances issued by U.S. consular officials abroad—usually within a day of arrival.[65] According to Erika Lee, after 1910 it was ordered that students and teachers were to be investigated only while aboard ship and not landed and held in confinement at places like Angel Island unless there was some issue that arose with their case. Exempt Chinese such as merchants and their family members could have their documents preinvestigated to avoid more protracted delays.[66] Most students spent relatively little time at immigration stations, in contrast to the hardships endured by most other Chinese seeking entry under other statuses, who could be confined for anywhere from two weeks to two years.

However, developing processes to facilitate the entry of exempt Chinese without subjecting them to the hostility faced by suspected laborers and other banned classes took some time. Not until 1911 were procedures standardized for the issuing of passports, and Chinese students continued to face harassment by officials. In 1917 the official in charge of student affairs at the Chinese legation in Washington complained to the Ministry of Education that there were still "countless" cases of students being detained, which required the official to go to San Francisco to personally help them.[67] As described by Chen Wen-hsien, however, the U.S. courts also tended to distinguish between Chinese students and laborers. For example, in *U.S. v. Chu Shee* (87 Fed. 312 (1898)), the court ruled that the children of laborers did not assume their father's status if lawfully admitted as students. The courts also protected students from deportation if they had "temporarily engaged in manual labor while attending school" or had worked in a laundry. In the 1920s Chinese student status became even more closely aligned with that of other students, and further from that of co-ethnic Chinese, as supervision of their cases gradually shifted from the field offices to be handled in Washington, DC, along with those of other international students.[68]

Anecdotal accounts suggest some immediate improvement in immigration experiences for Chinese students, including that of Song Ailing's younger sisters, Qingling and Meiling, who arrived in 1907 as students and did not encounter the same kind of delays as their sister. Chinese students began arriving in greater numbers and from a broader range of backgrounds, including non-Christian households, with the encouragement signified by the Boxer Indemnity Fellowships. The experiences of Jiang Menglin (Chiang Mon-lin, 1886–1964)—president of Peking University, minister of education, and chair of the Joint Committee for Rural Reconstruction—illustrate these new patterns. Unlike the Songs or Kong, whose families had converted and attended missionary schools, Jiang's father educated him to participate in the traditional examination system leading to a career as a Chinese official. As his family moved around to escape various outbursts of unrest, Jiang attended a hodge-podge of establishments, including the family clan school, bilingual institutions such as the Sino-Occidental School in Shaoxing—where he learned about Western science, modern history, and the Japanese and English languages, and Zhejiang College in Hangzhou. In 1905 he passed the first tier of the examination system, but rather than embarking on the once prestigious career of official service, he decided instead to enroll in the entirely English-language Nanyang College to prepare himself to study in the United States. Although he failed to win a provincial scholarship, his father agreed to pay for his studies abroad. Jiang left for America to study at the University of California at Berkeley and arrived in San Francisco in August 1908. Under the new policies, he was landed within a day. Despite this relatively benign experience, Jiang commented, "The first thing I had felt on landing was the power of the state through the instrumentality of the immigration officials and police."[69] This statement contrasts markedly to what is an otherwise lightheartedly humorous account of cultural misunderstandings and moments of enlightenment. Jiang received his BA degree in pedagogy and continued for a PhD degree from Columbia University under the mentorship of John Dewey en route to his illustrious career in China as a prominent educator and government official responsible for developing modern educational institutions and managing Chinese relations with the United States.

Ameliorating Exclusion: Sino-American Collaboration through Educational Exchange

Chinese students closely observed shifts in their position in the United States. The Boxer Indemnity Fellowships converted vocal critics of exclusion into enthusiastic believers in America's disinterested friendship for Chinese even though many students still encountered some difficulties when they attempted to enter the United States and in their day-to-day living circumstances and courses of study. Just as the Boxer Indemnity Fellowships and newly enforced respect for the exempt classes showed that some Americans distinguished Chinese by individual capacities and caliber, so too could Chinese delineate friendly and supportive Americans from those immersed in their own ignorance and prejudices.

In 1909 In Young reflected on the recent changes in the status of Chinese students and the possibilities for Sino-American friendship. "In spite of the unjust Exclusion Laws and many other undesirable treatments which the American people give us, the relation between China and the United States is founded upon intimate terms." In Young noted the differences between Americans who shamed and insulted Chinese through overenforcement of the exclusion laws and those friendly to Chinese, "the true types of Americans, for they are the ones who differentiate the lower and upper classes of our people." In Young referred to the Boxer Indemnity and the "magnanimity" of friendly Americans it reflected. "We feel grateful toward the hearty welcome which American colleges and universities have extended toward us. The many privileges and opportunities which are opened to us for a higher education are worthy of the true Christian spirit of the Americans." Despite the travails of exclusion, the Boxer Indemnity remission persuaded those who benefited the most—students, merchants, and diplomats—and who were willing to accept the notion of American friendship even in the face of America's exclusion of working-class Chinese.[70]

In 1908 the *Chinese Students' Monthly* published an editorial titled "American Hospitality and the Chinese Students," which described Roosevelt's instructions to Congress "that the United States government should do everything within its power to help the education of Chinese students" and noted the wisdom of this strategy for "the influence of foreign educated students in China had been very strong in moulding the public opinion of the Empire," as manifested through tastes for foreign goods that had improved markets, and knowledge of foreign countries that had "reduced the possibility of friction and rupture in the relations of China and other nations." The editorialist predicted the arrival of more students to the United States under such encouragement from political and business leaders and of "prominent educators such as the heads of the different large institutions of learning whose sympathetic appreciation of the educational needs of China and whose willingness to help others have led to the founding of several Chinese scholarships in their universities and colleges."[71] This new form of international generosity marked the United States as more sincere in its outreach to China than other imperialist powers.

Another student editorialist, writing under the initials C.C.W., viewed America as "different from other civilized nations," saying that it "has aimed almost exclusively at a better understanding based on commercial opportunities" in contrast to others bent on "territorial robbery and self-aggrandizement," such as Japan. The student looked to aid from "civilized nations [to] help China to free herself from outside interferences," particularly "the United States [which] has always refrained from ravenous ambitions." This affirmation of America's supportive disinterest stemmed from its recent generosity, for "few can doubt the high esteem China has for the United States as a nation standing forward for justice. America's recent refunding of the overcharged Boxer indemnity speaks volumes for her in the heart of every Chinese."[72] Despite the failure of the Open Door and the imposition of exclusion, the United States was seen as a practitioner of "fair play." An alliance between America and China would "have a three fold significance: speedy reforms, a great market for America, and a real open door for the world." Facilitated by the "square deal" of the Boxer Indemnity Fellowships, "the coming of these students will help considerably in removing the unfortunate prejudices of our American friends. . . . False ideas about peoples can only be corrected by the intermingling of representative types of these peoples, which intermingling enables them to get acquainted and learn from such acquaintances that, after all, there is little difference in human nature."[73] Chinese students would be able to vindicate their individual value and abilities and demonstrate the capacities of Chinese for civilized behavior.

Student Counternarratives to Exclusion

The bilateral political value attached to educating Chinese expressed through funding for the Boxer Indemnity Fellowships produced the contradictory outcome that, even in the throes of the exclusion period, Chinese were among the most numerous international students in the United States. Universities and colleges in the United States established scholarships specifically for Chinese while national and provincial levels of Chinese government bureaucracies began offering competitive scholarships for study overseas. The highly visible successes of returned students motivated even Chinese without scholarships to use private funds to study abroad.

The United States began returning the Boxer Indemnity to China in 1908. Some of the money was used to establish Tsinghua College in 1909 as a preparatory school run "in the American way, with American personnel and an American curriculum."[74] Before the first Tsinghua students graduated, the Chinese government held competitive exams to select scholarship recipients. Some in these first two cohorts of Boxer Fellows, including the linguist Zhao Yuanren (Yuen Ren Chao, 1892–1982), had already studied in the United States but returned to compete for the prestigious scholarships. Other luminaries included Song Ziwen, Hu Shi (1891–1962), and the rocket scientist Qian Xuesen (1911–2009). From 1912 until 1929, Tsinghua College sent a steady flow of students to the United States. Funding permitting, students went every year so that by 1929, when the Chinese government reorganized the college and ended the practice of sending all its graduates to the United States, 1,268 Boxer Fellows had been selected.[75] Overall, Chinese student numbers increased steadily from 1900 to 1927, partially in response to greater incentives to go to America to study but also because of rising levels of xenophobia in Japan—the previous destination of choice for foreign study.

The Qing reestablished the Chinese Educational Mission to coordinate student affairs in America. As it had in the 1870s, it sought to ensure practical applications for study abroad and issued regulations in 1909 stipulating that 80 percent of those receiving funding study technical fields such as engineering, mining, or agriculture. Of the first cohort sent that year, forty-three of forty-seven were in scientific or technical fields.[76] After the fall of the Qing, central government control diminished and more students moved toward social sciences and humanities, but technical disciplines were still popular. From 1909 to 1929, nearly one-third of Tsinghua graduates studied engineering, more than the social sciences and humanities combined. Together with natural sciences and agriculture, engineering accounted for about half of all students.[77] Hu Shi and Song Ziwen were prominent exceptions to this emphasis on sciences and technology but played significant roles in the emergence of Western higher education systems in China.

Estimates of Chinese student numbers are unreliable through the 1920s because neither the Chinese government nor American institutions kept systematic records. Y. C. Wang and Weili Ye estimate that in 1906 there were about 300 Chinese students in the United States; in 1911, roughly 650; and by 1925 and 1926, an estimated 1,600.

Most attended schools in the East and Midwest, with much smaller numbers in the West and South.[78] Starting with the 1923–1924 academic year, the YMCA-organized Committee on Friendly Relations among Foreign Students began tracking international student numbers by working through advisers for foreign students on campuses across the United States. According to their counts, as illustrated in table 2.2, China was among the top senders of students to the United States through World War II.

International attendance at Columbia University's Teachers College illustrates patterns of the interest of American universities in facilitating the studies of Chinese and Chinese focus on particular institutions. During the 1920s Asia, and China specifically, sent more students than any other region at 25 percent from China and nearly 50 percent from Asian countries. Committed to international education, Teachers College provided prestigious Macy scholarships, which covered living costs, travel, and tuition. Chinese received these in the highest numbers. Between 1923 and 1928, 174 foreign students received full-tuition scholarships, with 49 going to Chinese, 11 to Indians, 9 to Russians, 8 to Turks, and 7 to Germans. There were 272 Chinese, 23 Indians, 50 Russians, 21 Turks, and 30 Germans studying at the college

TABLE 2.1. Chinese Students in the United States, 1903–1945

1903	1909	1910	1911	1914	1918	1921	1943	1945
50	239	292	490	830	990	679	1,191	1,972

Source: Wang, *Chinese Intellectuals*, 158.
Note: The numbers are incomplete as the government had a hard time tracking self-supporting students until after 1943.

TABLE 2.2. Number of International Students, by Major Sending Countries of Origin, 1923–1947

Country	1923–24	1930–31	1934–35	1936–37	1939–40	1942–43	1944–45	1945–46	1946–47
Canada	684	1,313	936	986	1,592	1,194	852	1,613	2,676
China	**1,467**	**1,306**	**787**	**1,519**	**691**	**784**	**823**	**1,298**	**1,688**
Cuba	139	150	149	261	217	267	314	579	585
France	126	143	88	89	76	186	115	109	517
Great Britain	255	615	281	263	352	423	255	276	499
India	231	195	118	68	62	54	73	197	786
Japan	708	987	878	1,713	191	43	45	38	60
Mexico	198	325	161	159	178	358	364	510	681
Philippines	591	890	417	337	217	89	116	86	395
Puerto Rico	181	246	185	318	507	574	593	866	1,235
Total	6,897	9,806	5,860	7,342	6,670	8,056	7,542	10,341	16,176

Source: Excerpted from Institute of International Education, "Table Showing Comparison of the Number of Foreign Students in the Colleges and Universities of the United States during Recent Years," *Twenty-Eighth Annual Report of the Director* (New York: Institute for International Education, 1947), 97–99.

Note: For the years 1932–33 and 1937–38, the figures for Asian students also include "students born in the United States of Oriental parentage."

during these years. This program seems to have borne fruit, with its graduates assuming key positions in the educational systems of their own countries as presidents, deans, and professors, and in government ministries. By the end of the 1920s, over 200 Chinese alumni of Columbia University were working in Chinese institutions of higher education.[79]

American efforts to recruit Chinese students successfully diverted emphasis away from Japan as a preferred site for foreign training in conjunction with the worsening of Sino-Japanese relations. Japanese had become more xenophobic in the belief that the 1905 Russo-Japanese Treaty was "grossly unfair." Japan's incursions into Manchuria also discouraged Chinese from traveling there, and Chinese hostility to foreign dominance quickly switched from America to Japan. The number of Chinese students in Japan dropped quickly from a peak of thirteen thousand in 1905 to under four thousand by 1910. Although closer proximity and lower costs ensured that the number of Chinese students in Japan remained greater than the number in the United States, American-educated students seemed to attain higher levels of success.[80]

American degrees conferred benefits in the Chinese job market. Y. C. Wang described inequitable salary structures for editorial staff at the Commercial Press, the leading publisher in China:

A Chinese college graduate with some experience received $80 dollars a month and was provided with a desk three by one and a half feet in size, whereas a graduate of a Japanese college was paid $100 to $200 and was allowed a desk three by two feet. Those who had graduated from Japanese imperial universities received $150 and were permitted a desk four by two and a half feet, in addition to book shelves, a rattan chair, and a crystal ink well; and graduates of western colleges received monthly salaries of $200 and were provided the same physical perquisites as the Japanese graduates. At the apex of the scale were the graduates of Harvard, Yale, Oxford, and Cambridge, who received $250 per month and were supplied with a custom-made desk in addition to the standard perquisites. According to eyewitness reports, this scale was rigidly practiced regardless of the ability of those employed.[81]

The Commercial Press represents one extreme of favoritism toward American-educated Chinese, but by the 1910s and 1920s there were many examples of such success. In Beijing in 1910, Wang tallied eighty-two Western-trained people, with half a dozen as board presidents or vice presidents and others working as councilors to boards, professors in government colleges, or directors of government departments. In the Republican era, Western-trained Chinese gained even more prominence. For example, out of the twelve members of the cabinet of the first elected president, Yuan

Shikai (1859–1916), ten had studied abroad: two in Japan and eight in Western nations such as England, Germany, and the United States, including one CEM student.[82]

The attempt to modernize China's government and institutions advanced the careers of the foreign educated, as suggested in table 2.3. The Chinese government was a chief employer of returned students, so much so that in the "Vocational Opportunities and Problems" section of Tsung-kao Yieh's survey of Chinese students in the Midwest in 1934, 27 of 41 respondents expressed concern that "People with exceptional training are often left out while others less well equipped secure better jobs" or that "I would like to get government work, but lack political pull."[83] By 1939 an astonishing 71 percent of those considered most prominent in China had studied abroad. Of these, about 36 percent had studied in the United States. This represented a sharp rise for American-educated Chinese from the 9.5 percent of 1916 but also a steep decline in the Japanese-educated from 33.7 percent in 1916 to 15.4 percent in 1939. A table compiled in 1931 by J. P. Chu showing the "Training Received by the 750 Leading Men in China," drawing on two versions of *Who's Who*, gave a total of 578 with "Modern Education," including 382 educated abroad (168 in the United States and 139 in Japan) and 196 educated in China. Of the 750, only 172 had received the "Old Education."[84]

The professional prominence of foreign-educated Chinese resulted in part from China's lack of its own institutions for modern education, and many of the returned students ended up working to develop and expand the infrastructure of Chinese higher education. In 1917, of 340 returned students, 39 percent ranked education as the most important field of employment,

TABLE 2.3. Educational Background of Listees in *Who's Who*, by Country of Study and Selected Years (in percent)

Country of Study	1916	1923	1932	1939
China	50.5	47.5	31.2	29.0
Japan	33.7	29.5	20.3	15.4
United States	9.5	12.9	31.3	36.2
England	1.6	2.0	3.2	6.4
Other	4.7	8.1	14.0	13.0
Subtotal	49.5	52.5	68.8	71.0
Total percentage	100.0	100.0	100.0	100.0
Total number	380	689	591	638

Source: Wang, *Chinese Intellectuals*, 177.

followed by government at 32 percent.[85] In the eyes of one former president of Tsinghua University, the transformations enacted by Western-educated Chinese were fundamental in developing modern China:

> It does not seem possible to give an adequate estimate of what the students as a whole have done for their country.... it has been entirely due to their efforts and influence that the country is being modernized.... [What] will stand out as a monument to their achievement and influence is the change ... from a monarchy to a republic, from an absolute despotism to a popular democracy, from an antiquated conservatism to a modern liberalism.[86]

As observed by Wang and others, foreign education came to define a certain class of Chinese elite. "There is little doubt that during these years almost all self-supporting Chinese students came from well-to-do families, and many of them were relatives or close friends of one another."[87] In the *Chinese Recorder*, Mei Hua-chuan described them as "a new factor—I had almost said a new class."[88] A host of powerful families illustrates the emergence of this new, interconnected set of national leaders who shared foreign education.

Just as multiple generations of American families came to China as missionaries, multiple generations of Chinese journeyed to America as students. The Song family was perhaps the most prominent example. Zeng Laishun, the CEM English tutor, taught his sons English and sent them as part of the program to the United States, and many CEM graduates found ways to give their children educations in the West as well. Alfred Zhaoji Shi (Sze Sao-ke, 1877–1958), the first Chinese graduate of Cornell University, had accompanied his elder brother, who was a member of the Chinese legation of 1894. During the next ten years, seven members of the Shi family would study in the United States. Shi went on to a prominent diplomatic career of his own and became related by marriage to V. K. Wellington Koo (Gu Weijun, 1887–1985), a future Chinese ambassador to the United States who received his PhD degree from Columbia University. Leading Chinese officials, such as Li Hongzhang and Grand Secretary Sun Jia'nai, systematically sent family members as well.[89]

Not all American-educated Chinese were so enamored of Western civilization. In contrast to famously Westernized Chinese such as Zhao Yuanren, Jiang Menglin, and Hu Shi, scholars such as Mei Guangdi (1890–1945), Chen Yinke (1890–1969), and Wu Mi (1894–1974) believed that Confucian tradition held the elements needed to modernize China, particularly in the vital area of "public morality."[90] However, amid China's tumultuous, wholesale experimentation with new political, social, and cultural forms, such cultural conservatives were but a small voice against the storm of those denouncing Confucianism as the source of China's decline and failure to modernize. By the 1920s and 1930s, many government bureaus were filled with returned students applying their foreign training in specialized bureaus such as the Ministries of Transportation and Finance.

The usefulness of American-educated Chinese resonated in the United States as well. In 1921 the businessman Robert G. Cook praised "the desirability of securing the goodwill of the Chinese businessmen, particularly while they are traveling in or through America. Such first-hand contact is necessary in the establishing of international goodwill and reciprocation of kindly feeling toward the people." Cook argued that "the best American in China is the Chinese student who has been educated in America and returns with an absorption of American ideals, and, together with the sterling qualities which make the Chinese a lovable people, such contact will make the Chinese Republic a greater people than they have ever been." Moreover, "the Chinese business man has a wonderful reputation in America. He is considered (1) truly informed, (2) painstakingly careful in his business, (3) and as an industrial worker whether he is a coolie or a great business man."[91] Stephen Duggan observed that six of ten members of the Chinese cabinet in 1925 had studied in the United States, "a source of pride on the part of Americans."[92] On a selective basis, the United States had many reasons to admit particular kinds of Chinese.

By 1931 even the Immigration Bureau regarded Chinese students with approbation.

> One pleasing feature of the immigration question concerning Chinese has to do with the body of students who are in attendance at our institutions of learning. The students who have come from China are almost invariably of a fine type, earnest and intelligent, who eagerly embrace the opportunity to secure advanced instruction. After the termination of their courses, many request and are granted permission to remain for a longer period in order to gain practical experience along the line of their studies, so that they may be better fitted to apply their knowledge upon their return to China.[93]

These numbers and the prominence of so many American-educated returned Chinese suggest not only the success of American outreach but also how well the programs and opportunities made available suited the agendas of Chinese. American-educated Chinese such as Kong Xiangxi would indeed go on to wield great influence in China, but not by spreading Christianity. Kong gained fame and fortune in part through his marriage to Song Ailing, which helped him to become one of the richest men in China through a succession of important positions in the Nationalist government of his brother-in-law, Chiang Kai-shek, as minister of commerce, industry, and finance. Kong's visible success, and that of many other American-educated Chinese, demonstrated how a certain degree of Westernization and U.S. credentials could fortify prospects in China in ways that fostered stronger personal and political ties between the United States and China, although not always to the advantage of Americans. As chapter 3 will explore, Yung Kuai would be joined by extensive ranks of other Westernized Chinese who quickly gained leverage in deploying their bicultural capacities to advance *Chinese* agendas with the institutionalization of student exchanges with the United States.

CHAPTER 3

The China Institute in America

Advocating for China through Educational Exchange,

1926–1937

In 1919 Meng Zhi (Paul Chih Meng, 1901–1990), a seventy-second-generation descendant of the Chinese philosopher Mencius (372–289 BCE), enrolled in Davidson College in North Carolina, an experience he viewed through the lens of historical perspective: "Although the college had sent missionaries to China, it had not seen a Chinese before."[1] Undaunted at being the only Chinese on campus, Meng emphasized the influence gained from his pioneering role: "My Americanization started at Davidson. My many Davidson friends, I dare to think, were a little bit Sinified in return by me." Meng's preparation for acting as a cultural ambassador in America had begun during his childhood, with English lessons from a missionary at his Beijing home and study in two institutions modeled on Philips Andover Academy: Nankai Middle School in Tianjin and Tsinghua Junior College in Beijing. Despite a brief imprisonment for protesting Japanese imperialism in China during the May Fourth Movement, Meng received a prestigious Boxer Indemnity Fellowship to study in the United States. He remained at Davidson for two years, honing what became a lifelong proclivity for identifying and building connections between Chinese and Americans. While in China he had converted to Christianity, persuaded by the commensurable values between Confucianism and Christianity, and while studying at Davidson he had observed similarities between the rural communities of the Shenandoah Valley in Virginia and those in Shandong Province in northeastern China. He went on to attend Columbia's Teachers College, following a long line of prominent, Westernized educators such as Hu Shi, Jiang Menglin, and Guo Bingwen (1880–1969),[2] who all wielded considerable influence in representing Chinese interests in the United States even as they shaped China's modern educational establishment in emulation of American models.[3]

Although not as well-known, Meng played an instrumental role in developing Sino-American partnerships, particularly around the education of Chinese in America over the course of his nearly forty-year career as director of the China Institute in America (1930–1967) (Huamei Xiejinshe, literally Society to Advance Sino-American Cooperation).[4] As a student, Meng had developed an extensive resume of leadership positions in an array of Chinese student and American international education organizations, such as the Chinese Student Christian Association (CSCA), the Nankai and Tsinghua alumni groups, and the YMCA-affiliated Committee on Friendly Relations among Foreign Students. The institutionalization of Chinese studies in the United States accompanied both a shift in Chinese government control over such programs and the growing conviction on the part of liberal missionaries and internationalists that their efforts should be concerned not only with extending American influence overseas but also with providing more balance in Sino-American relations and acknowledging Chinese sovereignty in forging their own path to modernity, albeit with the assumption that this would emulate American democracy and Christianity. To this end, in 1926 a board of Americans and Westernized Chinese used a second remission of Boxer Indemnity funds to establish the China Institute, with the goal of educating Americans concerning Chinese culture and contemporary events and managing Chinese student affairs to maximize acquisition of technical, scientific, social science, and economic expertise. Meng's bicultural proclivities and networks ideally suited him to direct this project. He skillfully deployed his position to cultivate organizational connections among American educational, missionary, philanthropic, and State Department circles to position himself and the China Institute as visible and effective advocates for Chinese students and political causes during the 1930s. He fostered not only greater awareness and support for Chinese but also material contributions from Americans toward student well-being and success.

Meng's career in international education and cultural collaborations occurred amid China's struggles to establish itself as a modern nation and the increasing institutionalization of international education in the United States. This kind of idealism coexisted uneasily with the imposition of the most restrictive American immigration laws in 1924 and the rejection of Wilsonian principles of self-determination, particularly by the rising powers of Japan and Germany but also by colonial regimes suppressing independence movements throughout the world. Meng undertook to serve Chinese students in their quest to acquire skills, knowledge, and support in the United States for national betterment, even as he sought to represent Chinese perspectives to growing audiences of increasingly sympathetic and informed Americans persuaded to support Chinese national rejuvenation and modernization. During the 1930s American hopes centered on the Nationalists under the leadership of Generalissimo Chiang Kai-shek and his American-educated, Christian wife, Song Meiling, after the success of his campaign to reunify China in 1928 ended the disarray and regionalism of the Warlord Era (1916–1928). Chiang and his wife projected a vision of Chinese modernity—culturally, politically, and economically—that inspired confidence in many Americans that China had finally begun its long sought conversion to democracy and Christianity. In advancing Sino-American cooperation around the mutual benefits of educational exchanges, Meng worked with both American and Chinese government agencies such as the Ministry of Education and Department of State, along with a host of nongovernmental groups such as the Institute for International Education and CFRFS.

The China Institute's emergence as a major player in international education circles in the United States reveals the growing agency of the Chinese government over both domestic and international education programs and funding that in many ways displaced missionary and U.S. government priorities. Such exchanges became more synchronized to Chinese plans for national economic development even as aspirations of extending American influence overseas were hampered by domestic racial discrimination that undermined the well-funded efforts of organizations such as the CFRFS and IIE. Meng Zhi was a deeply valued and significant collaborator in such internationalist efforts to facilitate the coming of Chinese students to the United States. His extensive professional and personal contacts with these programs situated him to influence the U.S. Department of State when it started cultivating international education as a soft diplomatic strategy during the mid-1930s. This symbiotic relationship around the education and training of Chinese intellectuals in the United States enabled Meng to lobby for increasing levels of support, resources, and status from both private and public American agencies on behalf of agendas set by the Chinese government. By the 1930s, educational exchange not only served to promote American causes in China but effectively channeled Chinese efforts as well in claiming obligation and resources from the United States.

Fostering Nationalism through Study Abroad

Despite the efforts of missionaries and educational groups to facilitate their studies, the shadow of exclusion permeated every aspect of Chinese student experiences in the United States and in many cases heightened their consciousness of being Chinese and the need to use their educational advantages to benefit China. They were keenly aware that they experienced additional harassments when attempting entry and in daily life compared with other international students, driving home the low status of Chinese in general and suggesting hypocrisy in American outreach to Chinese. Efforts to court Chinese by respecting the entry rights of the exempt classes and funding education through the Boxer Indemnity Fellowships could not completely compensate for the indifference and casual racism of most Americans.

Not only did Chinese students remain invested in their futures in China, many also felt responsible for improving American impressions of their homeland and fellow Chinese.

Before Theodore Roosevelt's efforts to press for administrative immigration reforms in 1908, the exclusionary treatment of students, merchants, and even diplomats in disregard of their legally exempt status contributed to the 1905 anti-American boycott and discouraged Chinese students from studying in the United States. In 1907 F. C. Yen had observed in the *Chinese Students' Monthly*, "To all of us, the most trying time is when we first land our feet in this country. . . . Instances have occurred time and again that some students have, during such times of trivial trouble, given up all their ambitions and actually returned home. . . . the difficulties of gaining admission into this country are always in dread of [*sic*] more or less by every newcomer."[5] Just as adverse conditions in Japan had discouraged Chinese students, difficulties in the United States made competitors like England, Germany, or France more attractive places for study abroad.

Exclusion and its underlying foundation of anti-Chinese hostility bound students to their fellow Chinese despite differences of class, native place and dialect, and economic prospects. Most students could not communicate with working-class Chinese because they spoke different dialects, and a minority seemed to blame the so-called coolies for poorly representing Chinese culture and civilization. For example, Chen Hengzhe (1890–1976), who studied at Vassar and became the first female professor at Peking University, described the "long-queued, ignorant San Francisco workers" in a 1915 letter to a friend.[6]

However, greater numbers of Chinese students identified with their less privileged compatriots. Weili Ye observes that in the *Chinese Students' Monthly* run from 1906 until 1931, "none of the articles emphasized the class differences between the students and the resident Chinese; some even identified the three major groups of Chinese in America, the laborers, the merchants, and the students, as one entity."[7] In his memoir, Jiang Menglin recounted humorously his visits to San Francisco's Chinatown and his fractured attempts to communicate, proudly referring to laundrymen in small towns as "my countrymen."[8] Many students echoed Jiang's identification with fellow Chinese, complaining of indifference and discrimination in the United States. In 1907 one writer explicitly linked the students' situation to that of Chinese workers and small business owners. In "When the Chinese Exclusion Act Will Be Repealed," C.C.W. defended Chinese laborers against standard justifications for exclusion by pointing out that the Chinese laundry worker could charge more "because he washes cleaner and irons better," while domestic servants earned more than their non-Chinese counterparts. In 1909 members of the Eastern Alliance of Chinese students set up a general welfare committee to help working-class Chinese in Boston and New

York by soliciting resources from merchant groups and political organizations to offer citizenship classes.[9] Rather than turning a blind eye to events off campus, Chinese students were acutely aware of the low status conferred on Chinese in general, while on college campuses, both international and American-born Chinese students mingled and participated in the same organizations, such as the Chinese Students Alliance and the Chinese Students Christian Association.[10]

Living in the United States provided daily reminders of the low racial status of Chinese regardless of their class or cultural capital. On a regular basis, Chinese students were refused rooms to rent and service in restaurants, stores, and barbershops, and they found it difficult to mingle with white Americans. For example, in 1920 the noted sociologist Chen Da recalled his inability to get service in a restaurant in Oregon, whereas in Seattle he was followed by a car whose passengers shouted "John Chinaman! Chin! Chinaman!"[11] Churches and college campuses provided friendlier environments, but Chinese were nonetheless often mistaken for laundry or restaurant workers or Japanese.

As they arrived in greater numbers, Chinese students created their own organizations for advocacy and mutual support. In 1901 students in UC Berkeley founded the Chinese Students' Alliance. At its peak in 1910, its membership comprised two-thirds of Chinese students in the United States, including American-born Chinese, and was divided into regional subgroups representing the Midwest, East, and Pacific Coast and held annual summer conventions. Many of its officers, having experienced the experiments in civic engagement the organization offered, became prominent leaders in China. V. K. Wellington Koo, for example, studied at Columbia from 1906 until 1912 and was a founder of the Eastern Alliance. He was also active in campus sports and government and was even elected to the nine-member representative board at Columbia. Koo had originally planned to train as an engineer but was pulled into politics through his experiences with campus affairs and elections. Even before receiving his PhD degree, he was recruited into the administration of China's first elected president, Yuan Shikai, and later would become ambassador to the United States for the Nationalists.[12] In 1905 the Chinese Students' Alliance began publishing the *Chinese Students' Monthly*.[13] In 1907 then editor-in-chief Wellington Koo described the publication's purpose: "For the members of the Alliance ... [as] a center of its interest and a symbol of its activity; for the body of Chinese students at large ... as a bond that unites them all; for our people in China, it shall supply a source of useful information; and for the people of the West, it shall act as an agent to present ... the 'other side' of the numerous 'Chinese questions.'"[14] The Chinese Students' Alliance hoped to foster nationalism over native-place ties and downplayed regional differences by adopting English as its official language. This decision made the publication available to the approximately two-thirds of subscribers who were not members—mostly Americans and Europeans hoping to learn more about contemporary Chinese affairs from its coverage of constitutional developments in China.[15] Even as Chinese students organized themselves in the United States, they remained critical of the discrimination they encountered and preoccupied with events in China, priorities that they publicized to Americans to raise awareness and sympathy.

Cultural Internationalism and the Emerging Infrastructure of International Education

The patriotic agendas of Chinese students faced mixed prospects as rising tides of nationalism in the first decade of the twentieth century doomed the Open Door policy and set the world's major powers on the path to open conflict.[16] Amid such competitive war mongering, a group that Akira Iriye has described as liberal expansionists, who would evolve to become cultural internationalists after World War I, paralleled the efforts of Chinese students in promoting international educational exchanges and understanding in the name of fostering world peace. Missionaries, educators, business interests, and powerful philanthropists emphasized cultural approaches to promote peaceful international relations.[17] In the words of Liping Bu, "The educated elite were especially interested in promoting international cultural understanding via educational exchange as ways to shape people's world outlook and international goodwill. They believed American democratic values and practices were crucial for the maintenance of world peace." This coalition emphasized "human contact and cultural understanding between different nations," agendas developed through funding and organizing institutions to support international education.[18] Private entities such as the Cosmopolitan Clubs, IIE, CFRFS, and National Association of Foreign Student Advisors laid the foundations of American educational and cultural outreach, whose principles and practices would be absorbed by the Department of State when it undertook cultural diplomacy in greater earnest during the late 1930s. Their ambitions to promote greater international understanding while spreading American influence often fell short of fulfillment because immigration conditions and domestic race relations marred foreign student experiences of American democracy.

To extend U.S. influence by educating future leaders of foreign nations required not only that international students come to study in the United States but that they have positive experiences of American society, industry, and political systems if they were to return to their respective homelands favorably inclined toward the United States. The total number of foreign students coming to the United States rose quickly in the 1900s, doubling after 1904 to reach 2,673 from seventy-four countries by 1913.[19] By the 1923–1924 academic year, when the CFRFS became the first organization to track numbers systematically each year, there were 6,897 international students, of whom 1,467 were Chinese. By 1946–1947, total numbers had reached 16,176, although Chinese numbers remained relatively steady at 1,688. See table 2.2.) Despite the growth of international education programs, however, nonwhite students and particularly Chinese continued to encounter problems not only when entering the United States but in their daily lives and studies.

International education organizations evolved to address some of these issues. For example, the Cosmopolitan Club movement aimed to arrange social contacts between Americans and visiting students. The first club was founded at the University of Wisconsin in 1903 and included both domestic and international students. It became a national organization in 1907 under the name Association of Cosmopolitan Clubs of the United States and the motto "Above all nations is humanity." Although programs varied from campus to campus, the overall goal was to develop in the world "the spirit of human justice, cooperation, and brotherhood, and the desire to serve humanity unlimited by color, race, nationality, caste, or creed, by arousing and fostering this spirit in college and university students of all nationalities."[20] Chinese played active roles in this organization. After arriving to study at Cornell in 1910, Hu Shi not only was active in the Chinese Students' Alliance but also joined the Cosmopolitan Club and served as president from 1913 to 1914.[21]

Cosmopolitan Clubs attempted to ameliorate the social isolation faced by Chinese and other nonwhite international students. Harry Edmonds, an intercollegiate YMCA secretary, started the New York branch after a chance encounter with a Chinese student on the steps of the Columbia University library in 1910 made him realize the lonely lives of such visitors. Edmonds's casual "Good morning!" was met with profuse thanks from the student, who replied, "Do you know that you are the first person who has greeted me in the three weeks I have been in New York?" Edmonds began to wonder how many other students encountered and felt alienated by such indifference. A few days later he and his wife personally invited a dozen students from different backgrounds to dinner at their home, setting the precedent for other prominent families, such as the Andrew Carnegies and Cleveland Dodges, to invite foreign students into their homes as well. Edmonds later established New York's Cosmopolitan Club with funding from John D. Rockefeller.[22]

Christian groups provided organizational support and resources to Chinese students as a form of outreach and facilitation. In 1906 John Mott of the YMCA and the World Student Christian Federation helped six Chinese students organize the Chinese Student Christian Association of North

America, which became the only organization comparable in size to the Chinese Students' Alliance.[23] The alliance and CSCA cooperated to some degree and even shared some members as the latter did not require its members to be Christian. CSCA held Bible classes and other religious meetings while advocating social service from its members.

In 1911 the International Committee of the YMCA in conjunction with the Student Volunteer Movement formally organized to facilitate international student studies in general through the CFRFS. At that time the CSCA already had about eight hundred members.[24] The CFRFS's aim was "to promote sympathetic and helpful relations between Americans and the foreign students—especially those coming from the Orient, the Near East, and Latin America; to influence the character, spirit, and attitude of the future leaders of these Oriental and Latin American nations; and to bring the educated young men and young women of these different lands under the best influences of the Western Christian nations."[25] The earliest stages of its work focused on Chinese students studying abroad and in China. On the West Coast it developed port-of-entry services for Asian commercial, educational, missionary and even diplomatic delegations to buffer the exigencies of exclusionary bureaucracies. It also solicited support from business interests to hold receptions for these delegations.[26] The CFRFS undertook to coordinate journeys for Boxer Fellows within the United States, while in China YMCA secretaries helped arrange passports, steamer tickets, and accommodations and offered advice about dress, appearance, and American customs. In San Francisco CFRFS secretaries greeted new arrivals and helped them through the immigration process. CFRFS representatives accompanied students to their schools and arranged gatherings with Americans.[27]

Starting in 1914 the CFRFS provided financial support to the CSCA to publish the *Chinese Christian Student Monthly* and to hire a Chinese secretary, a position filled at one point by Meng Zhi. According to the 1940 issue of the CFRFS publication *Unofficial Ambassadors*, of the annual CFRFS budget of $24,631.12, $2,150 went to the Chinese section.[28] Anson Phelps Stokes, Jr., chairman of the CFRFS Administrative Board, explained the motivation to commit so many resources to Chinese students. The growing influxes of foreign students in the 1910s provided "obvious opportunity for disinterested service" for all young people who "needed guidance, friendship and many services." Students from Asia were particularly good targets for such outreach because they "had made contact with America first of all through the missionary enterprise so that on coming here they would naturally welcome service by Christian organizations. Many were practicing Christians whose faith, both for their own welfare and for that of the world-wide church, should be nourished and developed."[29] The CFRFS was a pioneer in offering "the great secular services which now give educational information, counsel and hospitality to foreign students." With pride, Stokes's report noted the CFRFS's early support for the CSCA, many of whose past executive secretaries or officers are "now well known in the life of China," demonstrating the effectiveness of this outreach strategy.[30] The CFRFS's support enabled the CSCA to weather the economic downturns and political turmoil in China better than the Chinese Students' Alliance, which did not survive the 1930s.

Following the model of assistance to the CSCA, the CFRFS helped other students organize Christian associations according to national and regional origins for Japanese, Filipinos, Koreans, Indians, Russians, and Latin Americans to help with adjustments to American society and "to foster ecumenical fellowship." Such outreach to students was both an opportunity and a challenge as they were expected to become Christian leaders in their homelands but also because of their personal exposure to conditions in the United States. "The students' existential experience of racial discrimination generated their strong criticism of American racist practices both at home and abroad." The CFRFS aimed to help these students to develop nationalism, political liberalism, and ameliorate their experiences of American racism.[31]

The CFRFS eventually extended its service programs and social activities to aid all international students, building on the programs developed for Chinese. The assistance provided included "port-of-entry service, personal visits, group meetings, faculty advising, summer conferences, home hospitality, and the emergency fund." In the 1930s the group reorganized into four services that became its main programs after World War II: Port-of-Entry Service, Student Summer Conferences, Hospitality Program, and Emergency Fund Program, which had come into operation with the Chinese Revolution in 1911.[32] When the revolution cut off funding for Chinese students, local YMCAs extended help to prevent their departure and appealed to university administrators for financial assistance.[33] As with the disbanded CEM in 1881, American supporters of Chinese students rallied to raise funds and resources to enable them to continue their studies, acts of benevolence that would be repeated and expanded when the many future instances of upheaval in China imperiled student success in the United States.

The year 1919 witnessed the founding of the nongovernmental international education organization that would attain the broadest reach through its close ties to wealthy corporate philanthropists and State Department insiders: the Institute for International Education. Three members of the Foreign Policy Association founded the secular institute. Through regular lunch meetings at the Columbia University Club, which regularly brought together lawyers, professors, magazine editors, and former diplomats to discuss internationalist affairs during the isolationist 1920s, former secretary of state Elihu Root, Columbia University president Nicholas M. Butler, and City College professor Stephen Duggan (1870–1950), with support from the Rockefeller and Carnegie Foundations, established the IIE to promote America's international role and stature. The ultimate agenda of promoting America's foreign influence is apparent in the original name proposed by Duggan, the Institute for International Relations, which was shot down by Root, who pointed out that this was "encroaching on the domain of the State Department" and suggested a broader scope of action than was feasible given funding limitations. Duggan readily agreed to the more precise title.[34] The IIE provided professional services for international educational programs including administering fellowships for foundations and governments, generating educational information for foreigners and for Americans going abroad, coordinating international education and training programs, and advocating to the State Department on behalf of international students. Duggan served as the first director, a position he filled for the next thirty years, and was later succeeded by his son, Lawrence.

The IIE brought together international higher education programs, foundations, and industrial leaders. Root and Butler had served as the first and second presidents of the Carnegie Endowment for International Peace, which the steel magnate Andrew Carnegie (1835–1919) had established in 1917. Inspired by Carnegie in 1889, the Standard Oil magnate John D. Rockefeller (1839–1937) donated to found the University of Chicago and supported medical research and hospital construction, establishing the Rockefeller Foundation in 1913 under the leadership of his son John D., Jr. (1874–1960). Besides supporting internationalist causes, during the first half of the twentieth century Rockefeller philanthropy benefited China more than any other foreign country in the form of programs in science, medicine, and the arts, particularly the China Medical Board founded in 1914, which assumed financial responsibility for the Peking Union Medical College in 1915.[35] In parallel with missionary groups, the Rockefeller Foundation would fund many projects benefiting the Westernization of Chinese educational infrastructure, including aid to Chinese students in the United States.

Duggan was the staunchest of internationalists, with widely expressed beliefs in the power of education to promote international peace, social change, and progress, but also American influence abroad. He described exchange students as being chosen for showing "evident elements of leadership and in the course of time they nearly always become leaders. In most cases I have found them occupying positions of influence.... I was never visited by one who was not pro-American and using his influence to make our country better appreciated by his own people."[36] The IIE directed its efforts at educating foreign elites so that they could more effectively bring back American democratic traditions to their home societies. Because they were experiencing "cultural renaissance" during the 1920s and 1930s, East Asia and the Middle East were of particular interest. China's revolutionary upheavals drew the attention of American educators as an opportunity to enact greater transformations.[37] Duggan's commitment to international affairs and his influence with both philanthropists and State Department authorities positioned him to wield considerable influence in shaping the contours of what would become federal government policies regarding international education as a tool of America's foreign relations outreach.

Duggan's influence is apparent through his successful interventions to advocate for international students with various government agencies, particularly in immigration and employment matters. For example, the Quota Act of 1921 began subjecting international students in general, not only Chinese, to adverse immigration restrictions that resulted in some even being turned away. Historically, immigration laws had not numerically restricted entry by students, an exemption dating back to the 1882 law for Chinese and reiterated in the immigrations laws of 1917, 1924, and 1952 as well as the Gentlemen's Agreement with Japan in 1908. The Barred Zone Act (1917) privileged students along with other useful types of migrants: "government officers, ministers or religious teachers, missionaries, lawyers, physicians, chemists, civil engineers, teachers ... authors, artists, merchants, and travelers for curiosity or pleasure ... their legal wives or their children under sixteen years of age" even as it banned immigration by most other natives of "the Continent of Asia west of the one hundred and tenth meridian of longitude east from Greenwich and east of the fiftieth meridian of longitude east of Greenwich," an area of the world extending from Indonesia to Turkey.[38] As the United States became increasingly isolationist after World War I, however, the Quota Act imposed numerical limits on the numbers of immigrants from Europe and applied these quota restrictions against students despite the temporary nature of their visits. Definitions of student status and documentation requirements for entry also became more severe.

The entry experiences of Chinese students thus came to approximate more closely those of their non-Asian counterparts, and distinct from those of nonexempt Chinese. In 1920 the Immigration Bureau had centralized the handling of all student cases, including those of Chinese, in Washington, DC, and away from bureaucrats at local points of entry such as Angel Island in San Francisco Bay. After 1921 other international students faced additional scrutiny and even rejection when attempting to enter, a worsening in entry conditions that led Duggan to intervene to work out procedures and principles with the Immigration Bureau to minimize unpleasant experiences. He proposed a nonimmigrant visa for students along with procedures such as bonds guaranteeing their behavior and departure on completion of their academic programs and suggested guidelines for reliable documentation such as diplomas certifying graduation, proof of admission to approved American universities or colleges, and verification presented at the end of each academic year of continued enrollment. He also urged the Immigration

Bureau to allow students to remain as long as they were enrolled in academic programs and that they be allowed to bring spouses and minor children.[39] The U.S government largely accepted Duggan's suggestions, and the port-of-entry services first established by the CFRFS to assist Chinese were extended to a wider pool of international students.[40] Ironically, although international student numbers declined during the early 1920s until entry conditions could be sorted out, Chinese numbers remained steady because Chinese were already under such severe scrutiny and restriction.[41]

The Johnson-Reed Act of 1924 alleviated this crisis by defining students as "nonquota immigrants" whose entry would not be counted against the quotas used to limit immigration and settlement by national origin. However, more constrictions applied. A "bona fide student" had to be someone "at least 15 years of age and who seeks to enter the United States solely for the purpose of study at an accredited school, college, academy, seminary, or university" accredited by the secretary of labor, who required regular reports on student progress. Students were expected to leave after graduating and could not work in factories to support themselves.[42] In a comprehensive summary published in 1930 by the IIE, Ruth Mitchell provided guidelines for prospective students and advisers for foreign students premised on their temporary but not permanent residence.[43]

International education advocates contended with other fires, domestically and internationally. In 1911 the YMCA had acted to raise funds to support Chinese students who lost their funding from home in the conflagration of the revolution. When war in China again cut off student funds in 1927, emergency financial assistance was institutionalized through the Committee on Emergency Aid to Chinese Students, support that was extended to all foreign students in 1932. Wars in China in 1937 and again in 1948 also mobilized American financial aid to Chinese students.

A different kind of crisis erupted on September 1, 1932, when the secretary of labor issued regulations that foreign students could not engage in "any gainful occupation" whatsoever or would face deportation. The IIE and CFRFS protested against these labor policies, complaining that poor international students were being handicapped and that only the wealthy could come to the United States. They also pointed out that foreign students took jobs domestic workers could not perform, such as teaching languages. In 1934 these protests produced some changes—students could work a limited number of hours to support themselves, and port-of-entry processes became somewhat easier.[44]

Organizations such as the IIE and CFRFS worked systematically with government agencies to produce conditions to make international students feel welcome in the United States, an agenda that helps to explain an advertisement for the American Mail steamship line that appeared in the 1935 issue of *The Handbook of Chinese Students in the U.S.A.*:

Continue your American sojourn until you step ashore in China! The good opinion of American institutions that you have gained during your stay in America will continue as you return to China on one of the world-famous President Liners sailing from Seattle. It is an ideal and a pleasure to show our Chinese passengers true shipboard courtesy—an inviolable company rule.[45]

That an American company advertised to Chinese assuming their enjoyment of their time in the United States contrasts distinctly with how we have understood Chinese American experiences during the exclusion era. The student class of Chinese was intended to value their encounters with things American and to bring this appreciation home to spread to their fellow Chinese as future leaders and harbingers of modernity. To prepare them for such vital roles in achieving American foreign policy goals, they had to experience an America that presented at least an appearance of hospitality and egalitarianism. Such strategic considerations situated Chinese students very differently in America's racial and socioeconomic hierarchies from the outcast, working-class Chinese inhabiting Chinatown communities, advantages that nonetheless did not shield them from American racism or the understanding that race and nationality bound them to their less educated compatriots. Arguing for the inclusion of Chinese students and intellectuals into the framing of Asian American history, Chih-ming Wang advances the concept of "transpacific articulation formed and shaped in the dynamic interplay of colonial agitations, multiplex immigrations, antiracist and anti-imperialist struggles and the lures of the American Dream." Asian American identity "must be complemented by an understanding of Asia's transpacific desire and agitation, at once frustrated by America's imperial presence and inspired by its promise of modernity."[46] These contradictory relationships simultaneously beckoned Chinese to study in and emulate America even as its racial exclusions affirmed their commitment to building better futures in China.

Chinese Autonomy and Western Learning

The institutionalization and expanding reach of international education in the United States coincided with rising tides of nationalism in China and the Chinese government's growing control over domestic and study abroad programs. With leadership from Western-trained and respected advocates such as Hu Shi and Meng Zhi, among hosts of others, Chinese priorities for education gained ground in China and internationally, and particularly in the United States. Liberal missionaries were complicit in these shifts with their growing ecumenism and intensifying conviction that their role in China was not to proselytize but to help Chinese pursue their own version of modernity. This deference to Chinese sovereignty and self-determination emerged from growing respect and affection for Chinese people and their struggles, but also in response to the shockwaves of nationalist fervor sweeping through China.

In 1909, during the last gasp of the Qing, China had but twenty-four institutions of higher learning with a total of 4,876 students, who were taught by "a large number of foreign professors." After the Chinese Revolution of 1911, the instability of a frequently changing and incompletely established series of government administrations did not impede efforts to expand and modernize China's educational infrastructure. For example, President Yuan Shikai, who attempted to install himself as emperor, invested in education. Some of the earliest measures required imposing greater control over schools established by missionaries or other foreign entities.

Anti-imperialist anger had exploded in 1919 when the United States ignored the opinions of Chinese in signing the Treaty of Versailles, which endorsed the transfer of sovereignty over Shandong Province from Germany to Japan. The May Fourth Movement overran campuses throughout China, with thousands of college students, including many attending missionary schools, attacking a selfish and untrustworthy America that had betrayed Chinese and its own ideals of self-determinism voiced by President Woodrow Wilson.[47] Hu Shi spearheaded the cultural movement to popularize vernacular literature in order to liberate and mobilize the greater masses of Chinese while shedding the vestiges of Confucianism, which received blame for China's inability to modernize and self-strengthen. Such protests characterized the 1920s, as university students closely monitored the actions of campus administrators and education authorities to ensure that their decisions furthered the causes of democracy and modernization for China rather than personal gain or politics. After the fragmentation of the warlord era, 1922 saw the implementation of a new educational system "patterned after the American system." Chinese educators who had returned from the United States formed the private Federated Educational Association of China, which passed a resolution adopted by the Ministry of Education.[48] Government investments in education produced rapid increases in the number of students and universities: in 1925 there were thirty-four public and thirteen private universities, mainly emphasizing the natural and social sciences.[49] The Anti-Christian Movement and the Restore Educational Rights Campaign of 1924 brought the Christian colleges under greater regulation in the belief that "education should have been an integral part of national sovereignty and the primary function of education was to inculcate patriotism." The Chinese government required Christian colleges to formally register, place more emphasis on Chinese learning, and stop requiring courses in religion. Under these pressures, the Christian schools consolidated into thir-

teen Protestant and three Catholic colleges and universities whose proselytizing functions diminished considerably.[50]

The May Fourth protests fanned the flames of a long-brewing crisis in
the American missionary establishment. The challenge of whether and how
to integrate Chinese aspirations and beliefs into Christian efforts to convert
Chinese resonated with debates dating to the era of the Jesuits, whose efforts to assert commonalities between Confucian traditions and Christian
beliefs had fueled the Rites Controversy that culminated in the forced withdrawal of the Jesuit order from China in 1773. In the twentieth century the
question of whether Chinese culture should be considered equivalent to
that of Christianity again divided the missionary community. Although
missionary fundraising reached a peak in 1921, with the highest numbers of
missionaries sent abroad that year, the emphasis on conversion was losing
steam in some quarters, replaced instead by acceptance of Chinese commensurability. At one extreme, liberal Christians came to believe that the
purpose of educational facilities should be to help Chinese forge their own
path to national rejuvenation, and not conversion, a view explained by William Ernest Hocking of Harvard in *Rethinking Missions* (1932), which drew
on the findings of the "Laymen's Foreign Missions Inquiry" funded by the
Rockefeller Foundation. This syncretism, seemingly an utter betrayal of the
proselytizing priorities for missions in China, led to the expulsion of prominent Christians such as Pearl Buck from the Presbyterian Missions Board in
1933 and a rapid depletion of fervor for missionary causes more generally.[51]

Education reformers had forced some of these shifts through efforts to
tailor higher and international education to national priorities. American
educators and American-educated Chinese convened a conference in 1924
that recommended adapting existing educational programs to the needs of
Chinese national development, including restricting Chinese students to
specialized graduate studies and redirecting use of the first remission of
Boxer Indemnity funds away from study in the United States toward fostering scientific and technical training in China.[52] This nationalist program of
educational reform produced a spate of institutional changes such as greater
regulation of the Christian colleges, establishment of the China Foundation, and restructured use of Boxer Indemnity funds to develop educational
facilities in China.[53]

The May Fourth–inspired protests also led some American leaders to
make an effort to mend fences. Senator Henry Cabot Lodge wrote to Secretary of State Charles Evans Hughes in May 1921 suggesting the United States
remit the remainder of the Boxer Indemnity to China in emulation of its
first successful effort in 1908. The State Department backed Lodge's proposal, but disputes in Congress regarding the priorities, timing, and method
of the second remission delayed the vote until May 1924, when it passed

under the urging of "witnesses [telling] the House that American Education was helping to create a republic similar to the United States in China."[54] A key stumbling block had been congressional concern to prevent the Chinese government from gaining control of the funds. Paul Monroe at Teachers College, Columbia University, developed the solution to resolve this impasse between national governments during a visit hastily arranged in 1924. Monroe was a leading advocate of international education who sat on the IIE Administrative Board. He worked out a plan acceptable to both China and the United States that "focused the returned money on student fellowships, the building of a National Library, and the strengthening of science education in China."[55] Monroe produced the template for the China Foundation for the Promotion of Education and Culture, which was to administer the funds through an executive board composed of both Americans and American-educated Chinese for the purpose of "a closer cultural and educational relationship between China and America."[56] Despite objections by the Chinese government to American representation on the board, Congress had insisted on this constraint. The transparency of American efforts to turn this "gift" to self-advantage and to retain control inspired great resentment among Chinese, who proved indifferent and even hostile to the second Boxer remission in marked contrast to their gratitude for the first.[57]

Established on September 17, 1924, the China Foundation was to distribute funds "devoted to the development of scientific knowledge and to the application of such knowledge to the conditions in China, through the promotion of technical training, of scientific research, experimentation and demonstration and training in science teaching and to the advancement of cultural enterprises of a permanent character, such as libraries and the like."[58] The foundation's first board was made up of ten Chinese and five Americans, including Premier Yan Huiqing (W. W. Yen), V. K. Wellington Koo, Jiang Menglin (then president of Peking University), Zhang Boling (then president of Nankai University), Hu Shi, the highly sympathetic John Dewey, Paul Monroe, J. E. Baker of the Chinese Ministry of Communications, and Charles R. Bennett of the International Banking Corporation in Beijing. Zhou Yichun, the first Chinese graduate of Teachers College and a former president of Tsinghua University (1913–1918), was the first executive director.[59]

After loosely reunifying China through the Northern Expedition (1927–1928), the Nationalists under Chiang Kai-shek managed to restore the highest levels of centralized control since the fall of the Qing, although their hold on many parts of China was still tenuous. The Nationalist government further tightened regulation of educational institutions and international study, with efforts in the latter focusing on graduate study of greatest use to modernizing the Chinese economy and educational systems. Even as it imposed greater restrictions on foreign study, the regime valued educational exchanges as enhancing ties with the United States while providing critical training needed for China's development. With Hu Shi as their representative, the Nationalists immediately tackled restructuring the board of the China Foundation to install more members trusted to work on behalf of Chinese agendas. Over congressional objections, the reconstituted board then redirected use of foundation funds, which now included both Boxer remissions, to divert resources away from study in America and toward strengthening domestic educational infrastructure. After 1929 no longer would all Tsinghua graduates receive fellowships for study in the United States. Instead the funds were used to transform Tsinghua into a world-class university with up-to-date science and engineering facilities. The Nationalists gained leverage over all international students, whether privately or publicly funded, by requiring exit permits issued through the Ministry of Foreign Affairs to apply for passports, any sort of government funding or support, degree recognition, and jobs on return. The Ministry of Education determined how many students could depart in particular fields and allocated 70 percent of government funds to those in the sciences, agriculture, engineering, and medicine, with partial fellowships to encourage self-funded students to do the same.[60] Responsibility for tracking Chinese students in the United States and administering scholarship funds would fall to the newly established China Institute in America, also funded by the second remission of Boxer Indemnity funds.

The "nonpolitical and nonpartisan" China Institute was incorporated May 1926 with the purpose of promoting "closer cultural and economic relations." The first board of trustees included Guo Bingwen, Yale-in-China educator Edward Hume, Stephen Duggan, Nationalist representative Ernest Moy, and Paul Monroe.[61] As the institute evolved to become a key advocate for China and Chinese students, Monroe and other colleagues such as Duggan would be powerful allies and supporters. Although Guo Bingwen served as the first director, Meng Zhi assumed leadership in 1930 and became the individual most associated with its programs and influence. Through his student activities, Meng had already established networks among leading American-educated educators, including Hu Shi, and the leaders of Christian and international education organizations in both China and the United States when he was hired to reorganize the institute into a self-funded organization, direct cultural education programs, and serve as the Chinese government's liaison to Chinese students in America. Meng carried out these responsibilities with inspiration and dedication until his retirement in 1967 and played no small role in facilitating the growing U.S. support for China during World War II and the Cold War.[62] As indicated by the title of his memoir, *Chinese American Understanding: A Sixty-Year Search*, Meng fully embraced his personal and professional mission of promoting Chinese and American commensurability and collaborative activities.

His almost lifelong commitment to promoting friendships with Americans did not prevent Meng from perceiving the discrimination faced by Chinese in America. In his account of arriving in America at early dawn in September 1919, Meng observed: "We were immediately self-conscious at being Orientals. This feeling was aggravated by the immigration inspector. Chinese were herded to an isolated spot on deck and lined up for a physical examination. We were the last passengers to be released." Meng, however, also believed that it was possible for Chinese and Americans to interact on more equal terms. After the trials of immigration proceedings, he found that "the warm welcome showered upon us by friends and fellow countrymen once we were cleared immediately made us feel at home." Despite experiences such as being refused a room by the YMCA in Los Angeles, Meng would pursue the optimistic belief throughout his career that improved relations between Chinese and Americans were indeed attainable.[63]

Meng's professional influence built on the many leadership roles he had assumed as a student in both Chinese and international education organizations. In 1924 he served as general secretary of the CSCA and as Chinese secretary for the CFRFS, positions that required him to keep in touch with Chinese students throughout North America. Over the course of three years, Meng traveled 92,000 miles, visiting North American university campuses between stints editing the *Chinese Christian Students Monthly* and the CSCA yearbook.[64] By the time he completed his studies in 1927, he had fielded job offers to work at the China Institute from Guo Bingwen and Stephen Duggan, and at the Chinese YMCA from John Mott. Before deciding, he followed the advice of his former mentors Zhang Boling and Mei Yiji, both prominent university presidents in China, to travel for nine months in China and Europe with funding from the International YMCA to research the conditions of Chinese students.[65] By the time he returned to the United States to assume leadership of the China Institute, Meng had seen at first hand the extent of China's political and economic quagmire and the full range of Chinese student situations in both North America and Europe.

Meng assumed leadership of the China Institute in 1930 and undertook to get it on an independent financial footing as funds from the Boxer Indemnity were to be devoted to institutions in China. Under his leadership the institute took over disbursement of fellowship funds and services to students in the United States when the Chinese Education Mission in Washington, DC, shut down in 1933.[66] Meng solicited grants and the support of wealthy American supporters to finance the China Institute's activities alongside funding from China. For example, in 1944, when Meng decided the China Institute needed its own headquarters, he appealed to Henry Luce, who purchased the townhouse at 125 East 65th Street that still houses the organization today. As he had previously, Meng embarked on another

FORMAL OPENING OF CHINA HOUSE

On the table are exhibits of Chinese students' group life in the United States. The picture of some of the guests and the Student Council members was taken the evening of December 1, 1944.

FRONT ROW LEFT TO RIGHT: *Dr. P. W. Kuo, Miss Lillian Dong, Mme. Wei Tao-ming, Dr. Hu Shih, Mrs. Henry W. Luce, H.E. Ambassador Wei Tao-ming, Miss Catherine Lee, Mrs. Chih Meng, Dr. Lee Fah Yih;* BACK ROW: *Mr. Chih Meng, Mr. Henry R. Luce, Mr. Hanson Huang, Mr. James Ling, Mr. Edwin Kwoh, Miss Julia Liu, Mr. J. Y. Yen, Mr. Shelley Mark, Mr. Eddie Toy, Mr. Max Zung.*

Figure 3.1. Formal opening of China House, December 1, 1944. The publisher, Henry W. Luce, purchased this building outright at Meng Zhi's request. They stand together in the back row at the far left. Renowned scholar and popular speaker Hu Shi stands in the front row, fourth from the left, next to Mrs. Henry W. Luce in the center and Chinese ambassador Wei Daoming. Reproduced with permission of China Institute of America, courtesy of Harvard University Imaging Services.

extensive set of travels to look up fellow Tsinghua students and to study the problems of Chinese students in the United States so as to be better able to formulate policy. Meng visited 288 schools and universities in forty-six states over the next three years, gaining a greater knowledge of Chinese student conditions that, together with his extensive networks and reputable standing, made him a highly effective advocate for China and Chinese students.[67] The China Institute assumed responsibility for Chinese students in the United States, in parallel with the IIE's services to other international students. Meng used his close associations with Duggan and Monroe to promote broader awareness of conditions affecting Chinese students, which enabled him to swiftly mobilize support in times of crisis. As did the IIE, the China Institute began tracking student numbers, issued an annual directory, published guides regarding government regulations and practices, and intervened as necessary with government agencies for accommodations and changes of bureaucratic practice to facilitate student studies. Perhaps most important, under direction from the Chinese government, the institute allocated fellowships and other funding resources, with priority placed on students in the sciences and technology who maintained respectable academic standing. The Chinese government implemented more structure and systems guiding Chinese study programs in the United States during the 1930s, with the goal of ensuring greater returns on this investment in developing human resources. The contradictory coexistence of expanding services for international students alongside ongoing discrimination and segregation ensured that Chinese students had improving opportunities for study in the United States, including easier immigration experiences and the possibility of employment, even as they continued to feel alienated from American society.

Nurturing Nationalism Overseas: Chinese Students in 1930s America

A Chinese internationalist, Meng Zhi shared the vision of American counterparts such as Stephen Duggan and Paul Monroe that Chinese students should be able to experience the best of American civilization's democratic culture and social order, albeit for different reasons. Meng hoped to help the students train and acquire knowledge to help China's development by learning from the United States. However, he also faced the challenge that apart from their academic programs, most Chinese students continued to experience unfriendly and inequitable treatment by a majority of Americans. For example, the poet Wen Yiduo had arrived in the United States in 1922 with the goal of studying Western arts to "absorb the best in Western culture in order to create a new Chinese culture." Contrary to these aspirations, he remained quite isolated during his three years in America, later explaining "that his withdrawal from American society was a deliberate decision to avoid racial humiliation." In letters home he commented on racism in the United States: "In America only white people are respected. The colored people (here the yellow, black and red people are called colored) are barbarians." Rather than becoming an advocate for China's Americanization, Wen developed pointed criticisms, producing the poem "The Laundry Song" to capture the perspective of a laundry worker.[68] A decade after Wen's stay, Chinese students still regularly experienced unfriendly and discriminatory interactions with Americans.

During the 1930s indifference to Chinese still prevailed, as captured in a survey of 125 midwestern students conducted by Tsung-kao Yieh in 1932 and 1933, revealing the limited impact of programs enacted by the Cosmopolitan

Clubs, the CFRFS, and the IIE. Yieh's PhD dissertation, "The Adjustment Problems of Chinese Graduate Students in American Universities," focused on understanding Chinese student perspectives.[69] Unlike earlier publications, which focused on giving guidance to studying in the United States or how to improve the services offered, Yieh's findings resonated with a 1933 study run by Adelaide T. Case of Columbia's Teachers College for the YWCA appraising the work of the International Student Committee. Case identified the key problem as the "lack of genuine friendship and understanding on the part of Americans" for foreign students and limited opportunities for international and domestic students to interact socially and gain "deeper understanding."[70] Yieh's survey confirmed the limited impact of missionary and internationalist agendas and revealed the profound nationalism and sense of connection linking Chinese students to their troubled homeland. Although very high percentages of Chinese students complained of discrimination or the lack of meaningful interaction with Americans—with 81 percent encountering problems in "contacts with persons outside the university"; 79 percent "social and recreational contacts"; and 77 percent "contacts with American students"—their most significant concerns stemmed from financial difficulties (89 percent) and the ongoing Sino-Japanese conflicts (90 percent) (35). Chinese students remained more preoccupied with problems in China than with the possibility of life in the United States.

By the early 1930s mistreatment on entry was not a significant issue, with a total of only thirty-six complaints listed. The students understood that educational exchanges were meant to cultivate stronger international relations but that restrictive U.S. laws and unfriendly government bureaucracies operated in contradiction to these goals. However, the most frequently cited source of offense concerned class rather than race, for "immigrants are measured in terms of money rather than factors which foster international cultural relations." Only eleven complained about the "many details [that] delay landing." Although some legal changes had recently been made, "the common practice of discrimination against foreign students, and particularly Oriental students, which received its fullest expression in the Act, has tended to be continued" (104–5).[71] Despite these difficulties, the students seemed deeply appreciative of the opportunities at American educational institutions, particularly their democratic and scientific emphasis and the "excellence" of teacher qualifications, buildings, and organizational facilities (95–97).

Yieh's survey unpacks the tenuous financial position of most Chinese students. Distance and war interfered with the arrival of funds from both family and government agencies, while foreign student status sharply limited job options. The China Institute aimed to buffer some of these fluctuations. Oscillations in rates of exchange diminished the value of Chinese student resources. The currency in use by Chinese, Mexican silver, fell in value from a 1931 exchange rate of 5 for each U.S. dollar to only 3 to 1 in 1934

(41). Students also found it harder to find jobs because employment offices did not help foreign students and immigration restrictions "discriminate against the foreign student" (37–38).[72] However, only three students complained that their student status prevented a search for jobs, and only two about the requirement of returning to China (104–5).

Chinese students knew that they had some important American advocates who tried to reform conditions to improve their situation. "A number of the most prominent educators in the United States" linked the "problems of adjustment for the foreign students in the United States" to "the probable increase of racial and national prejudice" while criticizing "the injustices to the foreign students and the complications resulting from the operations" as aspects of "the strained relations with their countries of origin" (105–6). For example, the 1933 restriction on foreign student job options received sharp criticism in the *New York Times*. "The withdrawal from needy foreign students of the privilege of working their way through school in traditional American fashion has been denounced in the strongest terms by many leading educators," whose ranks included Nicholas Butler of Columbia, Cloyd H. Marvin of George Washington University, William John Cooper, commissioner of education in the Interior Department, and John H. MacCracken, associate director of the American Council on Education (106).[73] Advocacy on the part of some prominent Americans nonetheless did not mitigate indifference in everyday lives.

A minority of the students, just under a third, admitted to being Christian, but their religion seems to have exacerbated their maladjustment. Yieh observed that Christian students experienced *greater* feelings of alienation through starker "contrasts between the actual situation found and the idealization that has been built up prior to coming to the United States." One Christian student recalled: "When I was in China I had religious interests. I went to church every Sunday and was interested in various religious meetings. . . . In America, however. . . I am a stranger. . . . Sometimes I go to church but I do not feel as if I should be there. The church people are cordial to me but they do not treat me as one of their group. . . . Much worse than the church is the life in the social circles. Many places I cannot go" (43–45).[74] As feared by internationalist Christian leaders, Chinese impressions of the United States actually diminished after arrival.

Generally adverse conditions included complaints about rooming situations, prejudiced landladies, and difficulty getting into dorms (61–63). Yieh's survey subjects widely registered their embarrassment at "America's racial discrimination" and "movies derogatory to Chinese life." Of the eighty-one complaints about experiences off campus, fifty involved prejudice of some sort (71–72). The largely male student population, at seventy-nine out of ninety, referred to many instances of difficulties interacting with American women, which Yieh ascribed to "race discrimination" (73–74). Yieh recorded seventy-seven complaints of problems involving contacts with American students, which included forty-three complaints that "American students take an indifferent attitude toward us" (77).

An American staff member of the Chicago International House shrewdly observed the divide between institutional efforts to foster American and Chinese friendships and the token and ultimately alienating consequences of programs that provided few opportunities to develop real relationships. Referring to the occasional events at which "foreign students and other scholars from abroad" were invited to dinners or banquets and asked to speak, the commentator noted that these superficial efforts did not provide "frequent contacts to make possible real friendship between American citizens and foreign citizens" and left the foreign students feeling as if they were "being made exhibits before American organizations" (74–76). Chinese students understood that friendly interest directed toward them as "exhibits" nonetheless did not gain them true acceptance or standing in the United States, experiences that affirmed their connections to and futures in China. Such racial divides reinforced their attachments to China and Chinese efforts to deploy international students to advance national development.

Advocate for China: Meng Zhi and the China Institute in America, 1930–1967

As the Nationalists had gained control over use of Boxer Indemnity funds, the China Institute in America by and large served Chinese government objectives despite its official slogan of "promot[ing] a closer educational and cultural relationship between China and the United States." The influential American internationalists, philanthropists, and missionaries with whom Meng collaborated regularly were fully supportive of his efforts to represent Chinese interests and realities in the United States, for, as a *New York Times* article commented in 1926, Sino-American relations had been imbalanced by the greater "penetration effected by American business, by medical, educational and other philanthropies like the Rockefeller Hospital and School, and Yale in China," along with the Ford motor car and American movies, while "the dissemination of Chinese ideas and knowledge and culture has made little gain" in the United States.[75] Not only did the China Institute coordinate and serve Chinese students and encourage their studies in science, technology, and other fields useful to China's development, it also developed and propagated programs to educate Americans about Chinese society and contemporary affairs for "the stimulation of general interest in America in the study of Chinese culture."[76] The institute found willing American partners to advance such agendas in internationalist organizations such as the IIE, American Friends of China Society, Institute of Pacific Relations

(IPR), National Committee of Chinese YMCAs, and CFRFS.[77] It acted particularly in close parallel with the IIE, with the two organizations cross-referencing the other's activities in their respective *Bulletins* and publicizing the same information about immigration, scholarship, and academic procedures, but with the China Institute targeting Chinese specifically.

An early China Institute program was the Chinese educational exhibit for the Sesqui-Centennial Exposition in Philadelphia in 1926, which presented to "the American public the idea of the continuity of Chinese culture, of the rapid progress in modern education, and the evolution of a new Chinese civilization as a result of contacts with the West," and which won a Grand Prize from the International Jury.[78] After this early success, the institute implemented a series of regular programs that provided educational materials and classes to train American teachers about China, such as a speakers series about literature, archeology, economics, and educational conditions; a roster of traveling lecturers; assistance to libraries and universities to amass scholarly collections; and monthly publication of the *China Institute Bulletin* starting in 1926, which provided information for Chinese students about scholarships, application procedures, and immigration requirements along with updates about conditions in China.[79] Like the *Chinese Students' Monthly*, the *Bulletin* served non-Chinese readers as well by generating reports and opinions about Chinese affairs. Hu Shi was one of the China Institute's most popular speakers. As described by Stephen Duggan, "He is a splendid scholar, a great philosopher and a thorough Democrat. A fascinating talker and very approachable, he became a prime favorite with the American people and in great demand to make Commencement addresses and after-dinner speeches."[80]

Meng encouraged American investments in and commitments to Chinese education and students. In 1931 he published an article in the IPR journal *Pacific Studies* that depicted America's benevolent influence on China through study abroad programs. "The American Returned Students of China" presented a glowing account of the fruits of Sino-American cooperation in this area while overlooking conflicts. According to Meng, "Perhaps, in the history of international relations, no one nation of such magnitude as China has ever been culturally affected by another nation of a very different background to such an extent and so immediately." While noting the small numbers of Chinese who studied in the United States between 1881 and 1906 who were discouraged by the "anti-Chinese feeling and propaganda . . . then raging on the Pacific Coast," he noted that the Boxer remission and the Open Door policy "dispelled the ill feeling toward the United States engendered in China by the Exclusion Act" without any mention of the 1905 anti-American boycott. Meng described the depth of American involvement in preparing Chinese to study in the United States, through a total of about fifty schools in China, almost all of which had at least one American teacher.

The institutions sending the most students had been founded with the aid of Americans, including St. John's, Tsinghua College, and Beiyang. Although Meng acknowledged that as yet it was unclear "whether American education is entirely beneficial to Chinese students and through these students to China," he also emphasized "China's appreciation of American culture and her good will toward America" and the two-way translating role performed by American-educated Chinese. Meng affirmed America's positive influence on China, for "today America is recognized by the Chinese people as their best friend among the nations." America's youthful vigor was beneficial, for "China seems to be going through a second childhood. She is like an aged person whose habits were formed many years ago, but who is rejuvenated by changing circumstances and new ideas and who experiments with new toys, some of which are made by her own hand. During the second childhood of China, American education, through a large number of American returned students, plays an important part."[81] Meng's beguiling portrayal of how such a young but modern and democratic nation could mold and benefit a civilization as aged as China would motivate many Americans to support and protect the students seen as the chief vehicles for conveying such critical influence.

Through the *Bulletin*, the China Institute publicized educational conditions and options for Chinese but also the development of educational infrastructure in China and the goals of the Chinese government for education and China's modernization. For example, the article "Chinese Engineers" (1936) reported survey results of 105 engineers and their hopes for placements for "practical training either at their schools or in industrial and commercial establishments" such as Northrop, Douglas, Sun Shipping, Bethlehem Shipping, Du Pont Rayon, General Electric, and Westinghouse.[82] The *Bulletin* also explained that the Ministry of Education issued "certificates-for-studying-abroad," and that from 1929 until 1938, 7,454 had been dispensed. Of these, 1,845 students went to the United States, 706 to France, 600 to Germany, and 597 to England. The *Bulletin* did not mention how many went to Japan, America's old competitor.[83]

Meng and the China Institute interacted regularly with sympathetic internationalist organizations such as IPR (1925–1962), which provided a forum for representatives of countries around the Pacific to discuss problems and relations for the purpose of developing policy suggestions promoting Wilsonian liberal democracy throughout the world. The Rockefeller Foundation was a key financial backer for the IPR, many of whose members were elite representatives of business and academic communities from their respective countries, including prominent Asian studies scholars Owen Lattimore and Karl Wittfogel. Meng and other Chinese were active participants. For example, Y. S. Tsao, president of Tsinghua University, contributed "A Challenge to Western Learning: The Chinese Student Trained Abroad—

What He Has Accomplished—His Problems" in the IPR's *News Bulletin* in 1927, questioning "whether the Chinese student trained abroad is able to construct afterwards a structure nobler and statelier than what he has torn down."[84] Considering China's struggles even for territorial unity at the time, this view does not seem unduly pessimistic. China's modern fate, as conveyed by the capacities of its Western-educated elites, concerned internationalists from around the Pacific.

The intensifying crisis of Japanese encroachments on China provided Meng with many opportunities to campaign for American sympathy. Through editorials in newspapers, radio broadcasts, and constant speaking engagements, Meng publicized China's dire situation.[85] In 1932 he authored *China Speaks: On the Conflict between China and Japan*, demanding an end to "Japanese interference," and he remained an outspoken critic throughout the 1930s, engaging publicly with Japanese advocates.[86] When the Sino-Japanese War broke out openly in 1937, Meng provided a regular stream of information about the impact of the Japanese invasion on Chinese universities and their 50,000 students, 8,547 of whom were enrolled in American-sponsored institutions. He also noted the prominent role of "American-trained teachers and leaders" at the other schools. As China's universities and colleges withdrew and reestablished themselves in the Nationalists' wartime base in Sichuan, Meng ensured that the plight and perseverance of Chinese students remained well within public view in the United States.[87]

As chapter 4 will explore more fully, war raised the stakes of American "friendship" for Chinese, with the conflict against Japan, rather than China's imminent disappearance by invasion, compelling more concrete expressions of American goodwill. World War II provided an opportunity to test the degree to which Westernized Chinese efforts to cultivate American support would bear fruit. As Yieh had observed in concluding his study of his fellow students in 1934, "if the student is to carry home with him many benefits from his studies in America, then he must not be too susceptible to indiscriminate bias. The Chinese graduate students should feel the responsibility of representing China in America, and of interpreting Chinese ideals and attitudes to America." Americans had to match Chinese efforts, for "if anything can be done at all, it will be done not by the students alone.... The good will of both America and China is involved in the cultural contacts between representatives of the two civilizations. If the ground is sterile, the seed of good will does not grow."[88] The crucible of war would test such claims and assertions of Sino-American friendship.

CHAPTER 4

"A Pressing Problem of Interracial Justice"

Repealing Chinese Exclusion,

1937–1943

On March 31, 1938, the popular daily adventure comic *Terry and the Pirates* showcased the dramatic transformation of its villainess, Dragon Lady, into a compelling heroine as she delivered this rousing speech to a mob of Chinese bandits: "No one has ever accused the Dragon Lady of drum-beating patriotics—but at this moment the soil of China is being ravished by an invading horde. . . . it is no matter of individual feelings, but the preservation of your racial heritage. . . . I entreat you, men of war, to follow me—and throw your bravery against the iron heel of the Foreign transgressor!"[1] This greedy and manipulative pirate queen redeemed herself by proclaiming her Chinese nationalism and leading fellow descendants of Ghengis Khan to ally with the strip's blond, all-American protagonists, Terry Lee and Pat Ryan, in combating Japanese aggression against their homeland. Dragon Lady's metamorphosis graphically illustrates how the shared struggle against global fascism consolidated the transformation of Chinese into sympathetic fellow human beings who shared key American values: love of country, valor, and freedom. Successive international conflicts—World War II, the Chinese Civil War, and the Cold War—further eroded the racialization of Chinese as fundamentally alien and inassimilable while underscoring their value as political and strategic resources in the all-out struggle against fascism and then communism. The imperatives of wartime alliances required that Americans grant Chinese more equitable ideological and legal standing along with greater access to naturalization and immigration rights, aid and support as refugees, and employment and settlement options in the United States. Through war, Chinese gained acknowledgment and institutional recognition of affinities shared with Americans, key steps in their transformation from yellow peril outcasts into model immigrants of color.

Across the 1930s the rise to power of militarists in Japan superseded the efforts of internationalists and organizations such as the IIE and IPR to foster world peace through cultural exchanges and personal contacts. After Japan seized Manchuria from China and turned it into the puppet state, Manchukuo, in 1931, Manchukuo became Japan's northeastern base for the outright

Figure 4.1. *Terry and the Pirates: Redemption of the Yellow Peril.* These three panels depict the reformation of the Oriental villainess, Dragon Lady, from a greedy, backstabbing, biracial adulteress (January 23, 1937) into a valuable and ingenious ally transformed by patriotism for China (March 30 and 31, 1938). Reproduced with permission. *Terry & the Pirates,* characters, names and related indicia are trademarks of and copyright © Tribune Content Agency, LLC.

conquest of China, which began under the pretext of the Marco Polo Bridge Incident on July 7, 1937. Japanese forces that had been massing for months swiftly moved south, claiming the eastern third of China, including its most developed industrial and agricultural regions, and forcing the Nationalist administration of Chiang Kai-shek to retreat to its wartime capital in Chongqing, in the inland province of Sichuan. The massive shift in population, along with the transfer of higher education facilities and personnel, caused great hardship but also generated considerable sympathy around the world.[2]

Westernized Chinese such as Meng Zhi added their voices to the growing cacophony of protest against the Japanese invasion, persuading both private and public Americans to contribute support to Chinese students in the form of funds for tuition and living expenses, legal employment, and recusal from military service. As the United States officially joined forces with China after Pearl Harbor, the forces compelling even greater acknowledgment of Chinese equality intensified, requiring the repeal of Chinese exclusion and the conferring of citizenship rights. At the forefront of the campaign for Chinese rights stood Madame Chiang Kai-shek, the most visible symbol of how well Chinese could embody American ideals, and a potent wielder of Chinese influence over Americans in her own right.

Becoming Human: America's Chinese Friends

Milton Caniff's 1938 story line not only evoked recent headlines but also captured long-simmering strands of China and America's "special relationship" and expressions of mutual admiration that had coalesced through Chinese struggles to rejuvenate and modernize a homeland that was weak yet still bore the remnants of a once mighty cultural heritage. The feminine face of this transfiguration, characterized by valorous struggle, concerted nationalism, and highly effective communication with Americans, was personified by the very real and highly empathetic person of Madame Chiang Kai-shek, earlier known as Song Meiling. The wife of China's leader, the Generalissimo, the American-educated, Methodist Madame Chiang came closest to fulfilling the long-held hopes of both missionaries and educators that their considerable investments in proselytizing and teaching Chinese might finally produce the long-sought transformation of China into a modern, Christian democracy modeled on the United States. With World War II she also served as a compelling example that Chinese should no longer be barred from citizenship and should receive more equitable entry rights.

During the 1930s Madame Chiang played her part in improving American impressions of China alongside the publicity efforts of Meng Zhi and his roster of speakers and publications. She was featured constantly in the publications of the China-born son of missionary parents, media mogul

Henry R. Luce. Luce was an outspoken internationalist and friend of the Chiangs who made frequent appearances in his popular magazines, *Time* and *Life*, with Madame Chiang featured repeatedly as one of the "Ten Best Dressed Women in the World." Although not enough to compel official American intervention, or even to halt sales of U.S. steel to Japan, newsreel footage presented American movie audiences with regular coverage of Japan's growing encroachments in China, simultaneously popularizing the images of beleaguered yet brave Chinese and villainous Japanese. Madame Chiang's political clout grew with her reported role in resolving the 1936 Xi'an Incident, in which Chiang Kai-shek was kidnapped by one of his warlord supporters seeking to force him to cooperate with the communists. Credited with brokering the agreement leading to her husband's release, Madame Chiang joined her husband on the cover of the January 3, 1938, issue of *Time* as "Couple of the Year."

China and Chinese had another influential advocate in the author Pearl Buck (1892–1973), whose best-selling, Pulitzer Prize–winning novel, *The Good Earth* (1931), movingly portrayed a multigenerational Chinese peasant family's struggles for survival set against a backdrop of the natural and political turmoil besetting contemporary China.[3] The high-budget MGM epic based on the book (1937) featured extensive footage shot in China and starred the Academy Award–winning actress Luis Rainer as O-Lan, the patient and long-suffering wife whose labors and loyalty held the family together. The child of missionaries and raised in China, Buck claimed incomparable authority when she wrote over thirty novels and nonfiction accounts about China and Chinese people while actively contributing to public discussions of Asian culture, immigration, women's rights, and child welfare through articles and personal testimony, winning the Nobel Prize in Literature in 1938. She founded organizations such as Welcome House (1949) to facilitate adoptions of Asian and mixed-race children and the Pearl S. Buck Foundation (1964) to combat child poverty in Asia. Together with her husband Richard Walsh, of the John Day Publishing Company, Buck produced abundant materials featuring humanizing and sympathetic representations that called on Americans to aid the rest of the world and particularly Chinese. With the Japanese invasion of 1937, Chinese students cut off from support from home presented immediate and sympathetic causes for Americans to act.

"Symbols of Understanding":
"Permanent Peace" through International Student Exchange

International education gained legitimacy and government backing over the course of the 1930s.[4] The Department of State began adopting aspects of the internationalist vision of Stephen Duggan, Elihu Root, and Andrew

Carnegie by funding and implementing government programs to facilitate international educational and cultural exchange. These federal projects launched with the Conference for the Maintenance of Peace held in Buenos Aires in 1936 at which the United States signed cultural agreements with some of its Latin American neighbors. These kinds of cooperation became institutionalized with the establishment of the Division of Cultural Relations in 1938 to encourage and strengthen "cultural relations and intellectual cooperation between the United States and other countries."[5] Although the efforts were initially focused on Latin America, Chinese also received a share of attention and resources in the form of programs and funding for students and technical trainees in conjunction with private and government agencies in the United States. As described by Akira Iriye, "governmental support for, and sponsorship of, cultural internationalism would inevitably affect the nature of the movement. Officially sanctioned and promoted, cultural internationalism would become an aspect, an agent, of foreign policy."[6] Internationalists gained clout and government support even as their initiatives became subsumed by State Department agendas.

After the Marco Polo Incident marked the official outbreak of hostilities between China and Japan, Meng Zhi spearheaded fundraising efforts and turned his considerable networks and publicity savvy to sound the alarm about how China's crisis had cut off support to Chinese students in the United States. The China Institute *Bulletin* regularly reported on the devastating impact of the war on Chinese students. For example, in December 1937 schools in Shanghai suffered $10,942,242 in material damage, and a leading missionary school, St. John's University, relocated to escape Japanese bombings and was trying to reorganize its students and staff. Others were less fortunate, with "scores of primary school students" dying in Japanese air raids in Taicang, Jiangsu. The *Bulletin* expressed outrage about Japanese attacks on civilians: "These innocent students were attending their classes when the raiders rained bombs on their school."[7] As China's universities and colleges withdrew from Japanese-controlled territories along the coast and reestablished themselves in the Nationalist-held interior, Meng ensured that the plight and perseverance of Chinese students remained constantly in view of the American public.

The buildup of general American sympathies for Chinese, in conjunction with the China Institute's institutionalized cooperation with organizations such as the IIE, CFRFS, and IPR, enabled Meng to secure considerable American public and private resources and finances for Chinese students cut off from their funding from home. His close ties to students quickly alerted Meng to the crisis. Aided by Roger Greene and Edward Hume from the China Foundation board, he solicited emergency relief from American organizations such as the Rockefeller Brothers' Fund, the Strong Foundation, and some missionary groups while also seeking high-level help from the U.S.

government. Through Stephen Duggan, Meng gained an interview with Secretary of State Cordell Hull. Although Hull had no resources to allocate, Meng's personal acquaintance, Eleanor Roosevelt, arranged for him to meet Lauchlin Currie, a special assistant to the president who channeled funding through the newly created Bureau of Intercultural Relations. Although established to provide scholarships for Latin American students, the bureau was able to grant about $500,000 to Chinese. As more funds were needed, Meng followed Currie's advice to approach Song Ziwen, Madame Chiang Kai-shek's older brother and the Chinese foreign minister in Washington, DC, who arranged to match the American contribution.[8] After some negotiating around Nationalist mistrust for the avowedly "apolitical" Meng, the Committee on Wartime Planning for Chinese Students in the United States was formed in 1942. This committee ultimately aided 987 students, "who constitute[d] an important source of personnel and leadership" for China but were trapped in the United States.[9] By the end of World War II, 4,700 Chinese students had received assistance from these organizations.[10]

World War II had consolidated the centrality of Meng and the China Institute in the managing of Chinese student affairs. During the 1941–1942 academic year there were about 1,200 Chinese in the United States, of whom 211 were trainees. The China Institute disbursed fellowships from the Division of Cultural Relations of the Department of State (158); the Chinese Committee on Wartime Planning (114), the Tsinghua Foundation (33), and the China Foundation (12).[11] From the perspectives of both the Chinese and American governments, the China Institute in America was the central node for organizing Chinese student affairs, as indicated by an IIE guide for foreign students, issued in 1945, that directed Chinese to it as the clearinghouse for information about fellowships, lists of accredited institutions, and information about health insurance policies.[12]

In conjunction with the IIE, the China Institute also addressed the legal problems of international students who suddenly found themselves stuck in the United States without funding, restricted from working to support themselves, and subject to the U.S. military draft. Meng worked with Duggan to develop guidelines adopted by the Immigration Bureau and Selective Service to make accommodations in 1942. International students gained the right to seek full-time employment with permission from the Immigration Bureau, and nonresident students would not be subject to the draft. The China Institute served as a contact for prospective employers wishing to hire Chinese. Even industries with classified positions could hire Chinese students who had first been cleared by the Departments of War and the Navy.[13]

Meng Zhi also worked with the Chinese government to develop protections in the United States. In a 1942 letter to Song Ziwen, Meng informed the minister that although Chinese students were unlikely to be drafted, legally they could be. With Chinese government documentation, deferrals were possible for "those specializing in technology and other lines of work related to defense" and for "qualified Chinese students whose studies, research, or field work are related to China's national defense." Meng recommended, however, that for others whose work was only remotely connected to "any immediate needs in China, perhaps it is beneficial that they should be drafted into some kind of war work."[14]

Meng Zhi became an active partner with the U.S. State Department's newly established Bureau of Cultural Affairs, an entity developed with significant input from international education advocates and experienced China hands, Americans such as missionaries and scholars with long experience of the country.[15] The State Department had extended the bureau's programs to China in late spring 1941, after the provision of Lend-Lease aid to China, in part at the urging of Roger Greene, a China Institute board member, former consul general in the Foreign Service, and twenty-year resident director for the Rockefeller Foundation's China Medical Board. The Department of State had also consulted faculty in Chinese studies from several universities, including George Cressey of Syracuse, Woodbridge Bingham at Berkeley, John Lossing Buck and others at the University of Nanjing, along with Hu Shi, who was then serving as the Chinese ambassador. Throughout the short existence of the China section (1942–1949), which received an initial budget allocation of $150,000 from the Emergency Fund in January 14, 1942, Greene served as an ongoing consultant.[16] Wilma Fairbank, wife of the leading Chinese historian John King Fairbank, worked as a divisional assistant and praised the program as "a pioneer effort" that was "an experiment in the unaccustomed field of governmental cultural activity. It was also the first such official program to be tried outside the Western Hemisphere. It was a direct forerunner of the present-day technical assistance programs."[17] With their extension into channeling educated and skilled Chinese toward on-site training programs in major American companies, the educational exchange programs that had once served internationalist goals for world peace became integrated with industrial interests as well, as will be examined in chapter 5.

The Bureau of Cultural Affairs relied extensively on the established Chinese networks of its administrators and staff, existing connections that aligned its programs closely to those of international education and missionary groups. For example, Ben Cherrington, formerly of the YMCA, was the first director.[18] According to Fairbank, this personnel "brought close private connections with them ... and was a great strength," including Greene's associations with the Rockefeller Foundation and the missionary-founded American Bureau for Medical Aid to China, journalists and American exchange students, and John Fairbank's extensive academic circles. The bureau coordinated closely with the thirteen Christian colleges, such as Yenching, Nanjing, Ginling Women's College, and Lingnan.[19]

Of the many private institutions that the bureau worked with, however, the Chinese Institute in America "was one of the most important," reflecting the symbiotic relations between American cultural diplomatic efforts and Chinese programs for international education and training.[20] The Bureau of Cultural Affairs consulted Ambassador Hu Shi and accepted his advice that owing to travel difficulties, it might be better to aid Chinese students already in the United States rather than to recruit new students in China. The bureau also assumed that many resident recipients of such aid had held government office and planned to resume their positions on their return to China. In the late 1930s Chinese and Americans had partnered in implementing new programs to bring economically and strategically valuable Chinese selected by the Nationalist government to come to the United States for advanced workplace training in relevant fields, an expansion of international education programs that produced an even larger population of potential "model immigrants" resident in the United States with the unanticipated outcomes of the Chinese Civil War. Exigencies of America's wartime alliance with China would force the issue of citizenship and immigration rights for Chinese, although partially masked under the guise of sentimental attachments to educated, Westernized, and Christian representatives, chiefly represented by Madame Chiang Kai-shek.

America's Ideal Chinese: Madame Chiang Kai-shek

As described in chapter 2, Song Meiling was the youngest of three daughters of the wealthy, American-educated, Methodist businessman and ardent Nationalist supporter Charles Jones Song. She had come to America at age ten to study with her older sisters, and she received her undergraduate degree from Wellesley College at the age of nineteen. After returning to China, Song Meiling had to relearn Chinese but soon readjusted to life in cosmopolitan Shanghai from the base of her family's home in the International Settlement.[21] She and her sisters mingled in wealthy and influential circles with prominent Nationalists and a variety of expatriate Americans, including missionaries, businesspeople, and writers. Song Meiling occupied herself with a variety of charitable causes, seeking worthy outlets for her Christian values and American education. Through her marriage in 1927 to Chiang Kai-shek, who had converted to Christianity in order to marry her, she took on a role that placed her on the international stage as America's key hope for a democratic and Christian China. Madame Chiang Kai-shek was viewed as full partner in the modern coupling in governing China by implementing highly visible modernization projects during the 1930s.

After Sun Yatsen's sudden death in 1925, Chiang assumed his place as leader of the Nationalists, largely through his command of the Whampoa

Military Academy and its corps of officer graduates. A year after marrying Song Meiling, he managed to loosely reunify China through the Northern Expedition, in part by working with communist forces. This accomplishment, and Song Meiling's place by his side and role as adviser, chief interpreter, and communicator to Western powers, suggested that China was moving concretely toward a Christian and democratic future. As argued by Karen Leong, "With her command of the English language and her international status as 'China's First Lady,' Madame Chiang embodied not only China, but also Sino-American unity against Japan. . . . American acceptance of Madame Chiang as an educated, modern, beautiful and Christian Chinese woman"[22] did much to persuade Americans that the Nationalists were following an American-style path to democracy and capitalist development. Together the Chiangs promoted the New Life movement for the "moral regeneration" of Chinese through the promotion of the four Confucian values of propriety (*li*), righteous conduct (*yi*), honesty (*lian*), and integrity and honor (*qi*). More substantively, the Nationalists established the National Resources Commission (NRC) in 1932 to centralize control of China's economic development under the relatively autonomous authority of an educated, professional elite. Experts, not politicians, developed a series of five-year plans coordinating resources and development on a host of fronts: industry and commerce, agriculture, infrastructural planning and construction, taxation, communications, and education and training abroad. The NRC generated lists of required technical and industrial expertise that shaped government decisions about programs for study and training abroad. Despite this grand show of activity, however, Chiang Kai-shek never established full control of either Chinese territory or finances, although China gained enough stability to persuade many Americans that the Chiangs were the leaders that would direct China into its modern era.[23]

Madame Chiang also contributed prolifically to the outpouring of positive depictions of China's struggle for modernity. In 1940 and 1941 she authored two books, *This Is Our China* and *China Shall Rise Again*, published through the well-regarded private firm Harper & Brothers and featuring many photographs of her work among Chinese women and children. Some of her writings targeted Christian audiences, such as the slim monograph *I Confess My Faith* (1943), which was issued by the Board of Missions and Church Extension of the Methodist Church. Madame Chiang's byline appeared on reports published in many American media outlets and appealed to Americans on behalf of China from her position as a modern, educated woman. *We Chinese Women: Speeches and Writings during the First United Nations Year by Mayling Soong Chiang (Madame Chiang Kai-shek)*, jointly published by the Chinese News Service and the John Day Company in 1943, featured reprints of articles that had previously appeared in the *New York Times Magazine*, such as "East Speaks to West," and the *Atlantic Monthly*'s

"China Emergent." It also included the text of her message broadcast from Chongqing on June 13, 1942, "To My Alma Mater: To America," when she received a "Doctor of Laws" degree at the sixty-fourth commencement of Wellesley College.[24] Evoking her time in the United States and the deep influence of her education there, Madame Chiang called for the people of America to use their advantages to aid Chinese. "By marshaling all your power and influence to see to it that America helps to confer upon all races the freedom, the justice and equality that American herself enjoys. You would thus also help me because this is the vision I have held out to our people." This appeal gained potency from Madame Chiang's reminders of all that she shared with the American people. "I am not speaking figuratively when I say that I am with you in spirit today. I often recall with abiding affection my happy college days and you my friends whose problems and ideals I shared."[25] These evocations of common history, experiences, and commitment to democracy and freedom made Madame Chiang a charismatically brave symbol of how resonantly educated and Christian Chinese could be like Americans, not only in friendships forged through times of war but also for employment and even citizenship in the United States.

Madame Chiang attained a new pinnacle of celebrity through her triumphant speaking tour of the United States in 1943, which was coordinated informally out of the White House. A little over a year after America's official entry into World War II after the Japanese attack on Pearl Harbor, Franklin D. Roosevelt and his staff took advantage of a visit by Madame Chiang Kai-shek to the United States for medical treatment to arrange a national speaking tour to promote support for its Chinese ally. The tour began on February 18, when Madame Chiang became the first Chinese national and only the second woman to speak before the combined houses of Congress.[26] The eloquence of her evocations of China's struggle for survival, her personal ties to America, and the depths of friendship between Chinese and Americans beguiled this audience of seasoned politicians, drawing thunderous applause even as she used the occasion to request more military aid for China. Average Americans shared Congress's enthusiasm. In New York Madame Chiang displaced a boxing prizefight to speak before an audience of 17,000.[27] Geraldine Fitch described her reception in ecstatic terms:

> The Madison Square Garden appearance of China's First Lady . . . was the event of a lifetime. Madame Chiang herself . . . has rightly captivated the hearts of the American people, and I think has accomplished in one visit what centuries of formal friendship between China and America could not do. She has made Americans realize that the Chinese are like us: our differences superficial, our similarities fundamental. Restauranteur and laundrymen (and none better) the American people knew, but now they know there are the educated, the cultured, the beautiful, the tolerant, the Christian in China as well.[28]

Such spectacles and a rash of publicity transformed Madame Chiang into a popular celebrity who drew crowds into the streets waiting to catch a glimpse of her.[29] Her fundraising tour of the United States made stops in Boston, Chicago, and San Francisco, climaxing on April 18 at an appearance at the Hollywood Bowl before an audience of thirty thousand, the first time the great outdoor venue had filled since Pearl Harbor.[30] David O. Selznick, producer of *Gone with the Wind*, developed a pageant titled *China: A Symphonic Narrative* to showcase China's quest for modernity visualized as a progression toward Westernization accompanied by a score commissioned from MGM composer William Stothart and performed by the Los Angeles Philharmonic Orchestra.[31] At the climax of this musical and dance extravaganza, Madame Chiang walked onstage to speak about contemporary China's resistance against its Japanese invaders and its commitment to modernize as a democracy. Through personal example, Madame Chiang demonstrated that Chinese could mirror Americans in ways that reflected intelligence, beauty, and patriotic courage. Newspaper accounts celebrated her eloquence, courage, beauty, and glamorous, exotic outfits. Even as she courted American financial and military support of Nationalist China, Madame Chiang would also serve as the foremost example of why Americans should remove the immigration laws racially targeting Chinese and acknowledge their equal footing so that they could stand alongside Americans as authentic allies and welcome friends.

Threading the Needle of Immigration Reform: "Justice for Our Chinese Allies"

In her person and self-presentation, Madame Chiang exemplified the reasons that America should repeal its discriminatory immigration laws, which presumed the racial inferiority and incompatibility of Chinese. Wartime exigencies compelled this move, as Japanese propaganda cited the Chinese Exclusion Laws in urging Chinese to break with America and join Japan in a race-based alliance. On the heels of Madame Chiang's warmly received speaking tour, the Citizens Committee to Repeal Chinese Exclusion, including prominent pro-China leaders such as Richard Walsh, Pearl Buck, and the former medical missionary and recently elected Republican representative from Minnesota, Walter Judd (1898–1994). The committee swiftly acted on the general embrace of Madame Chiang to press for the repeal of the Chinese exclusion laws as a necessary "war measure."[32] Building on the January 1943 abrogation of extraterritoriality rights in China, which had been a significant irritant invoking international power imbalances and American racism, these advocates presented repeal as critical to maintaining U.S. friendship with China by gesturing to equal treatment.[33] Against the entrenched but now minority forces of southern segregationists, West Coast exclusionists, isolationists, and organized labor, the committee strategized how to thread the needle of immigration reform that would allow for repeal.

As analyzed by Fred W. Riggs in *Pressures on Congress* (1950), the Citizens Committee skillfully handled legislative processes that swung the tide of immigration restriction back toward a liberalizing path, albeit quite narrowly defined, to achieve its goal of wooing Nationalist China by making largely token gestures of greater equity for Chinese.[34] Over the long term, however, the passage of repeal became a harbinger of a steady trend toward immigration reform mandated by the growing importance of international considerations in what had previously been handled primarily as domestic matters of economic protections, racial segregation, and national security against unwanted aliens. The extremely circumscribed rationales used to press for repeal laid the foundations for conceiving and implementing immigration controls that would not only enable the first significant reform of immigration laws since the Johnson-Reed Act of 1924 but also set the United States on a path toward more general transformations in which criteria of family reunification, individual merit and economic contributions, and political compatibility would replace those of race and national origin as chief considerations for entry and citizenship.

Building on wartime exigencies but also increasingly widespread popular acceptance of acculturated, educated Chinese and growing discomfort with social Darwinist constructions of essentialized racial differences, the Citizens Committee acted strategically through a small number of key legislators and public figures to pursue a limited reform agenda tailored to overcome resistance based on principles of racial segregation, protection of labor interests, and opposition to new immigration in general. The committee recruited prominent sponsors such as former presidential candidate Wendell Wilkie,[35] historian Owen Lattimore, and social worker Bruno Lasker willing to publicly back the cause of repeal, published stories promoting the practical and idealistic rationales for granting equal status to Chinese, and throughout, carefully emphasized that the measure stemmed from motivated American citizens. Representatives of China remained ostentatiously silent in public on the matter. For example, throughout her speaking tour, Madame Chiang refrained from mentioning the issue, although Martin J. Kennedy (D-NY) sponsored a version of the repeal bill on the day of her speech to Congress, which he dedicated to her. On the weekend of May 15, 1943, just before a House committee convened to discuss repeal, she hosted a dinner party including "crucial members" that later acted as enthusiastic advocates for repeal, including Ed Gossett (D-TX) and Warren Magnuson (D-WA)—the sponsor of the bill that would eventually pass.[36]

Repeal's numerous supporters in Congress proposed a variety of measures that reveal a spectrum of visions for immigration reform, including

Judd's overly ambitious vision of entry quotas and citizenship for all Asian nations, while others sought narrower measures such as extending entry quotas only to allied Asian nations or admission only for the Chinese wives of U.S. citizens. To garner sufficient votes to pass, the measure had to strike a balance between foreign and domestic demands. On one hand, the Chinese government had to be assuaged that its citizens had gained equitable conditions for entry and residence. On the other hand, the bill had to promise limited impact to appease those Americans concerned about restricting labor competition and racial integration. It would be the Magnuson bill that offered an attainable balance between narrowly framed reforms that nonetheless accomplished foreign diplomacy goals by calling for changes benefitting *only* Chinese. Repeal abolished the Chinese exclusion laws, granted naturalization rights only to Chinese, and placed Chinese on the same quota entry basis as other countries legislated with the Johnson-Reed Act of 1924. This gesture toward equitable treatment would allocate Chinese an annual quota of only 107, compared with Britain's quota of 66,000. Even when admitted on the same basis as other nationalities, the numbers of Chinese entering each year would be miniscule. As observed by Stephen Duggan, "Surely a population of 135,000,000 could absorb 110 persons annually without dangerous consequences!"[37]

Moving toward this symbolically momentous, yet practically inconsequential, reform generated debates and witness testimony that scrutinized the influence of domestic racial inequalities on America's foreign relations, how best to manage "minority problems," the possibility of Chinese assimilability and contributions to America, how "racial equality" might be introduced to immigration laws without triggering a flood of arrivals from Asia, and whether Chinese would be content with symbolic quotas. The twenty-one-member House Committee on Immigration and Naturalization, chaired by Samuel Dickstein of New York, convened over seven days in late May and early June the most extensive set of hearings, with fifty-one witnesses drawn from many representative groups, many carefully vetted by the Citizens Committee to advance the cause of repeal.[38] Representative A. Leonard Allen (D-LA) led the opposition in repeating concerns that changing immigration laws would undermine domestic workers and exacerbate America's "minority problems." These testimonies and discussions mapped out compromises and rationales that would later be deployed in campaigns that produced the Hart-Celler Immigration Act of 1965: if the United States were to claim a position of leadership in the world, it could no longer restrict entry based on presumptions of essentialized differences between races and nationalities; once-excluded nationalities and races, however, could be admitted with minimal impact because their numbers could be tightly limited and screened for those with potential to make the greatest contributions.[39]

Advocates of repeal, including many church and missionary groups and internationalists, emphasized its necessity as a "war measure." Layered onto these political rationales were admiration for Chinese war efforts; hopes of fostering economic cooperation and American advantages after the war; perceptions of strong similarities between Americans and Chinese; calls for immigration restrictions to consider individual merit over racial heritage; praise for examples of enlightened, assimilable, and economically contributing Chinese; and criticisms of the illogic and injustice that the meanest of Europeans might gain entry and American citizenship, whereas exemplary and talented Chinese, such as Madame Chiang Kai-shek, could not. These affirmations of American affinity and appreciation for Chinese could be expressed through highly limited immigration reforms that gestured toward equal treatment in admitting very small numbers of only Chinese, and not any other excluded groups, a gesture that "experts" on China nonetheless reassured the House committee would be acceptable to the Chinese government.[40]

The repeal hearings reveal that beliefs in essentialized racial differences, and inequalities, had lost ground. Rather than evoking the inferiority, racial incompatibility, and unfair economic competition presented by Chinese and "Orientals" in general, and the dangers inherent in racial mixing that had compelled Asian exclusion, opponents of repeal predicted intensification and expansion of the problems of integration, coded as "social equality," for different races. Representative Allen aired such concerns openly:

> We have in this country a serious minority problem, occasioned by people having been brought here against their will, decades ago. . . . We in the South have had a lot of trouble with that problem. . . . Are you not afraid that if we let down the bars and let orientals [sic] generally come into this country, that we will have not only one minority problem, but perhaps several.

In response, the witness so questioned, the Reverend John G. Magee of St. John's Episcopal Church in Washington, DC, affirmed his belief in both the merit of individual Chinese and compatibilities between Chinese and American civilizations while revealing his disdain for those Chinese already resident in the United States. "I think it would be an education for us to have some Chinese of the best cultural background in our midst, for the United States will occupy a new position in the future of the world. The Chinese in this country are mostly the descendants of coolies" (20). By enacting immigration reforms that admitted better kinds of Chinese, Congress could remove the embarrassment of exclusion while improving the caliber of Chinese in the United States. Although not all the witnesses espoused this differentiation of Chinese by class, future versions of immigration laws would come to enshrine this kind of selection principle.

Long-standing views regarding segregation and racialized conceptions of citizenship and national belonging came to the fore in Allen's exchanges with the scholar and Indian independence activist Dr. Taraknath Das (1884–1958), a lecturer at City College in New York and a naturalized citizen.[41] Das criticized American immigration policy by noting that "an ignorant street-sweeper from England" could become a U.S. citizen but not Dr. Sun Yatsen, the "George Washington of China," or Chiang Kai-shek, Rabindranath Tagore, or Nehru. He quoted the eminent historian Arnold Toynbee's observation that "the so-called racial explanation of difference in human performance and achievement is either an ineptitude or a fraud." When questioned about the link between the "racial equality being claimed for immigration reform" and "social equality" within the United States, Das affirmed his belief in the "philosophy of social equality" and the right of Jews, Negroes, and American Indians "to even become the President of the United States" because "the political right and social right go hand in hand" (41).[42] This statement enraged Allen, provoking him to angrily question whether Das thought that "we should dine with those of the Ethiopian race and accord to those people every social privilege?" (40). Das played into Allen's hands by asserting that "it will do a man honor to dine with a man like Booker T. Washington, or Dr. Carver, as President Theodore Roosevelt did." Allen, the leading voice of segregationists on the committee, jumped on this response. "I thank you for giving your views. You have done your cause more harm than anybody else."[43] The bulk of other testimony and views of other committee members, however, would reveal that the sands were shifting away from Allen's presumption of American commitments to a racially differentiated and segregated society.

The efforts of internationalists—missionaries, educators, business interests, and so forth—capped by China's devastating wartime sufferings and sacrifices and the widespread effects of anti-Japanese propaganda had rendered opposition to Chinese entry on racial grounds impolitic in 1943. Traditional opponents of Chinese immigration, such as organized labor groups and veterans associations, carefully couched their reservations as stemming from economic considerations rather than race-based antagonisms. For example, L. S. Ray, the acting executive secretary of the National Legislative Committee of the American Legion, expressed admiration for Chinese war efforts but conveyed his belief that repeal would not significantly affect Chinese morale and that the subcommittee needed to be mindful to protect jobs for returning soldiers and sailors (168). Ray emphasized that the American Legion opposed repeal on economic but not racial grounds and wished to offer material aid but not admission (174), a view largely shared by S. E. Wilkins, representing the Veterans of Foreign Wars (176), and Lewis G. Hines of the American Federation of Labor (183).[44] Those who opposed repeal on openly racial grounds, such as Agnes Waters, the DC representative of Crusading Mothers of Pennsylvania and National Blue Star Mothers, who cited "the invasion of the Asiatic race," Kipling's comment that "East is east and west is west and never the twain shall meet," and her belief that "practically all of the Chinese are Communists and when they come in here, they come in here to ruin this country," was quickly silenced by committee members, some of whom asked that her testimony be stricken (184–86).

The Congress of Industrial Organizations (CIO), represented by Kermit Eby, changed its position altogether. Citing the history of organized labor's support for Chinese exclusion, Eby noted that under wartime circumstances, the CIO was asserting "leadership which places public interest above group interest" and would support the Federal Council of Churches and Catholic churches in opposing "discrimination of people on the basis of their racial origin" and an appeal to "the abstract concept of justice" (97–98).

Other testimony echoed such idealism and pragmatism in international affairs. Senator Mary Farquharson, a past state senator in the state of Washington representing the Women's International League for Peace and Freedom, proclaimed: "We are shocked to hear a statement such as was made here this morning that certain races are degenerate, certain races are immoral. . . . the Chinese should not be judged on the basis of race or nation, but on the individuals." On more practical considerations, "we think immigration and naturalization laws in an interdependent world are of extreme importance if something is to be worked out that will not end in another war," and "we are convinced that our self-interest cannot be considered apart from the self-interest of other nations" (88). Other witnesses testified to the need to remove racism from American laws. For example, Frank Campbell, pastor of the Methodist Church in Neoga, Illinois, described exclusion as "the grossest insult our country has ever tendered a friendly nation" (7–8).[45]

One of the most famous of internationalists, Pearl Buck, testified as well. Buck cited her extended experiences of living in China for four of her five decades to claim authority in stating, "I know the Chinese people, I know how they live." She stressed the high caliber and commensurability of educated Chinese with Americans. "Her people have high standards of ethics, of business ethics; we know that in our country" (68). However, it was not possible to appreciate the best of Chinese, for "Literate Chinese, great scholars, brilliant young men and women, famous Chinese citizens, were all held inferior to the most illiterate peasant of Europe." Buck attacked the foolishness of the exclusion laws. "We have excluded not only Chinese coolies; we have excluded Chinese of the highest quality and attainment by our total exclusion laws. It is the injustice of the total exclusion that hurts the Chinese, the humiliation it puts upon them as a people," that was "more than injustice. It is a denial of our democratic ideals" (70). When baited by Allen to speak about broader reforms and "social equality among all the races," Buck carefully limited her projections to the situation of Chinese (72–73).

Remaining focused on repeal as a necessary wartime measure to maintain America's alliance with China, Buck avoided these traps and continued to emphasize that "the Chinese people are extraordinarily like us . . . in our democratic traditions, and in the way we behave and in our feelings toward family, and our realisms, and our practical qualities, and I attribute it to the fact that their country is so much like ours" (75).

Buck was far from alone in identifying with Chinese and asserting their suitability for U.S. citizenship. Madame Chiang's triumphant speaking tour capped off years of positive publicity in underscoring exactly how deserving of entry quotas and citizenship rights select Chinese could be. As put by the Methodist Reverend Dr. Lloyd Worley, "We feel a particular kinship to China because it happens the Generalissimo and Madame Chiang Kai-shek are co-religionists of ours." However, Worley noted, even though she was "one of the great women of the world and . . . an outstanding Christian woman," Madame Chiang could not receive U.S. citizenship (88). Will Rogers, the comedian and representative from California, described the embarrassment he and others in the House felt when "Mme. Chang [*sic*] Kai-shek spoke before the House of Representatives. Listening to this well-poised, highly educated world leader, an exquisite woman of great charm and wide intelligence, I want you to know that many of us sitting in the House felt embarrassed to remember that by the laws of this country, this woman was legally not good enough to apply for citizenship in the United States, if she had wanted to; but we exclude her purely on the basis of race."[46] In a radio debate about repeal, Representative Walter Judd scored points by concluding with outrage, "Our exclusion of the Chinese on a racial basis also violates the finest traditions and the moral sense of the American people. Under our present laws, Hitler is admissible to our country and eligible for citizenship—Madame Chiang Kai-shek is not!"[47]

The contradiction between the generalized racial discrimination embedded in the Chinese exclusion laws and the accomplishments attributable to outstanding, individual Chinese provided potent arguments for repeal. Witness after witness testified to their personal friendships and admiration for Chinese, emphasizing the many attributes they shared with Americans that would make them ideal citizens. Dr. Arthur Hummell, chief of the Asiatic Division of the Library of Congress, described Chinese as "a socially democratic people" who lived in "a classless society." He claimed that "the Chinese is perhaps the most individualistic man in the world" and that "their ideals are very much like our own, in fact, more like our own than the ideals of some European nations that we know. There is nothing in their system of government that is antagonistic to ours" (24). Hummell stressed that if repeal took place and exclusion was replaced by a quota system, "if there are 107 to come in, most of them would be merchants, scholars, teachers, or students. I should not worry a bit about labor" (24). According to the

Reverend John J. O'Farrell, a Jesuit from New York, "The Chinese have consistently shown themselves to be an industrious and law-abiding group of people, and their offspring have contributed to the good of the community as far as racial barriers and prejudice allowed. Being democratic in spirit they have more in common with the American spirit than some other more-favored groups" (30–31). With such an impressive view of Chinese, it is little wonder that the Reverend Thomas B. Cannon, a fellow Jesuit, described repeal as "a pressing problem of interracial justice" (54).

The few Chinese Americans who testified also underscored the high economic value of the right kinds of Chinese. Dr. Min Hin Li, a resident of Honolulu, U.S. citizen, and past commander of the Hawaiian American Legion, testified that he served as an example that "the Chinese can be assimilated."[48] He described the upward mobility of Chinese in Hawaii, where "professional men have come forth from the rank and file of sons of former plantation laborers, and are today surgeons, physicians, dentists, lawyers, architects, and experts in Government agricultural experiment stations." In Hawaii men such as himself were in the ranks of veteran's organizations and served in both elected offices and the civil service (208–10). Chinese had become entwined into the fabric of everyday life in Hawaii as leaders and stalwarts of the economy.

The theme of Chinese usefulness and assimilability ran through other testimony. Paul Yee, an electronics engineer working in the War Department in Washington, DC, and a third-generation "American-Chinese," addressed fears of "coolie labor" by pointing out that many Chinese were in fact "specialists" with "special faculties." He described two Chinese engineers working as technical trainees for Westinghouse in special electronic work on "some of the most important secret radar work today, radar and radio equipment." The two top men in the RCA research laboratory were technical trainees from China. Yee pointed out that an annual quota of 107 could be used to bring in those with such developed skills while underscoring the assimilability of Chinese such as himself, noting that although he looked Chinese, he was actually American (203–4).

Witnesses testified that repeal was a necessity for building stronger international relations, a required building block for world peace, even as they sought to limit immigration reform to symbolic numbers. The Reverend O'Farrell described repeal as "a sane and workable internationalism based upon those necessary principles of international justice and charity, the only real guarantee of international peace," but he was also careful to distinguish it from the "racial equality" of repealing the laws without permitting "unlimited immigration" by Chinese. O'Farrell stressed "that fundamental equality of nations could be demonstrated by assigning, say, a quota of 100 or more a year, to the Chinese people" (30–31). According to the earlier testimony of Reverend Magee, "enlightened Chinese" understood sovereign rights of nations to control admission to borders and did not expect mass labor migration that would disrupt the U.S. economy (15–16). In a letter to Eleanor Roosevelt, Theodora Chan Wang, president of the Chinese Women's Association in New York, echoed these views and expressed opposition to laws that "would invite an influx of workers, from any nation, who would inevitably disrupt our labor balance, or otherwise disturb the economic equilibrium of this country" while supporting "certain measures which should be adopted now . . . that should token recognition of our equality in the newer, freer order of democracy." Laws that admitted "a limited number of Chinese" who "would be accorded the same welcome, and the same privileges being granted the Hebrew, the Negro, the Slave, and the numerous divers [sic] races who yearly seek refuge on our shores. It matters little if the maximum is 100, or 50, or even 10, so long as that privilege exists and can be made known to those in the conquered areas of China" (6–7). This willingness to accept limited concessions paved the way for an otherwise momentous shift in rationales regarding how America should enact immigration controls.

Navigating through this maze of heated and entrenched sets of fears and aspirations, Representative Judd applied a keen political instinct to forge acceptable compromises from the various constituencies debating repeal. Judd had extensive missionary credentials, having served as a traveling secretary for the Student Volunteer Movement and for ten years as a medical missionary in China (1925–1931, 1934–1938). Determined to gain a better platform to press for American support for China's war against Japan, he ran for office and was elected to the House of Representatives in 1942. Despite his deep convictions about the necessity of breaking America's isolationist stance, particularly with regard to nations in Asia, Judd was not nearly as concerned for domestic conditions of racial inequality, considerations that he often compromised in the process of skillfully negotiating symbolic gestures toward his foreign policy ends in ways acceptable to segregationist and labor interests. He proved to be exactly the facilitator needed to break the impasses around repeal of the exclusion laws.

Judd testified late in the hearings, and as a seasoned missionary, his authority on the subject of China and Chinese views was unquestioned. He proclaimed stirringly that repeal "would restore confidence. It would rekindle the fires of hope in the hearts of a billion Orientals who want to be with us, if they are sure it is for their freedom, too. It would invigorate and galvanize them into more active effort and resistance, as no amount of pronouncements or Atlantic Charters, or even of planes and guns, can do" (145). He also warned that delays and half-hearted measures would lead Chinese to lose confidence in American friendship: "China has always had this profound, almost pathetic faith in America. She wants to continue to have it. But such factors as the above have made her begin to doubt. There is such thing as a breaking point" (145). However, Congress had before it a readily implemented solution: "The most dramatic and helpful thing imaginable would be a removal by Congress of the discrimination in our immigration laws against the Chinese" (147).

Judd's proposals for immigration reform addressed a plethora of objections in ways that would echo in later legislative efforts. A pragmatist, he was willing to make compromises that achieved his foreign relations priorities even in ways that fell far short of the ideals being claimed. For example, although he had originally conceived repeal as granting citizenship rights to all nations, he withdrew this effort in recognition that the Magnuson bill, with its limited focus on Chinese, conveyed American friendship for China while acknowledging the concerns of opponents regarding economic competition, increasing influxes of immigrants, particularly from Asia, the specter of more "minority problems," and strongly felt enmity to Japan. Judd originated the idea that Chinese immigrants, unlike those from Europe or the Western Hemisphere, could be tracked by race rather than citizenship or place of birth, so that those from other areas such as Hong Kong or Latin America would be charged "to the quota of the country from which their immigrant ancestors came" (148–49). This racial categorization would resolve concerns raised by the American Federation of Labor "because there would be no possibility of Asiatics getting in by using other Western Hemisphere countries as stepping stones." Judd concluded, "We could thus remove all discrimination and stigmas from our immigration laws without increasing the total number of immigrants and by admitting less than 500 Asiatics per year" (150). Although Chinese would still be racially stigmatized in being tracked by racial ancestry rather than nationality, Judd claimed that they would be content to enter under the same quota system as other countries, even if the Chinese quota was tens of thousands fewer than that of favored nations like Great Britain. Ignoring the millions of Chinese who had migrated to Southeast Asia and elsewhere, Judd claimed that "it is not that many want to come to this country; it is that they want the right for persons of their race to come. Chinese have not been people who go out and encroach on their neighbors. They have not been a migrating people. It is equality they want. And equality under the formula is 107" (150). He also argued that repeal would diminish the specter of "race war" by acknowledging the due resentments of both Chinese and Japanese at American racism. "If the Chinese or the Japanese had been excluded on an economic basis, they would not have objected; they resented being excluded on a racial basis, the pigment in their skin. They rightly resented being branded as biologically inferior" (151).

Judd summed up the many reasons for offering this low-impact gesture of equality to Chinese. He described how the United States had lagged behind Russia in expunging extraterritoriality claims, and he urged the committee to take further action by passing legislation "to remove the stigma and at the same time check loop holes that might allow Oriental laborers to come in that would be harmful to American standards of wages and living." Repeal rested as well on moral grounds for "men are created in rights before the law" and should be considered "as individual human beings, not by the race to which they belong." Moreover, the United States had economic needs for Chinese markets, and "China, if free and friendly, will have tremendous needs for technical assistance, new developments and industries, engineering, machinery, roads, railways, and so forth. To have the inside track in helping develop the tremendous markets of Asia, and in helping satisfy those markets, can come nearer to being to us after this war what our own West was after the previous wars, than any other place in the world." He support for repeal was "not starry-eyed sentimentalism and idealism; it is good hard sense" (152). Judd concluded with the powerful observation that in the thick of war, "we can have our prejudices, or our sons. If we must have our prejudices now, then I am compelled, out of concern for my country to warn that we cannot escape sending out our sons to die later" (155). As had Buck, Judd attributed Japanese enmity to the insult of the 1924 law: "The single, most important cause for our being at war with Japan is the Exclusion Act of 1924" (77, 163). Unless the United States amended its offensive immigration laws, new foreign wars would certainly ensue.

Of all the supporters of repeal, Judd was the only one whom Allen found to acknowledge his fears of a future invasion of "orientals." "I believe you have been perhaps the only witness who has frankly stated the bigness, shall I say, of the proposal facing us. I think it is your opinion that it is an oriental question, not a Chinese, not a Korean, and not a Japanese question, but an oriental question" (156). Judd's grasp of the big picture in turn made Allen trusting enough to ask his opinion regarding the necessity for removing part of the "wall against orientals" that had stood for sixty-one years. Judd affirmed the need to repeal exclusion but stipulated that immigration quotas and citizenship could be granted only to Chinese. Allen immediately understood that what Judd proposed were "gestures" that would not significantly increase the numbers of Asian immigrants (157). Judd emphasized that he did not think "it would be economically wise to take in 10,000 Chinese or other orientals in here every year" and asserted his belief in the wisdom that "the quota principle was based on the desire to keep the United States predominantly of the peoples which founded it" (160). As chapters 5 and 6 will describe, Judd contributed significantly to immigration reforms during the 1950s that gradually brought Asians into more equitable standing with whites, but through token measures that continued to privilege ties to Europe while screening Asians for their capacities to contribute to American agendas.

Congress had to strip away discrimination from American immigration laws but worked out mechanisms to do so that would minimize disruptions to domestic concerns about racial differences and securing borders against unwanted immigrants. For example, the imposition of a small quota enabled Chairman Dickstein to dismiss concerns about economic competition by pointing to the small numbers of Chinese who could enter. Judd's strategy for allocating Asian quotas by race, regardless of place of birth or citizenship, also provided reassurance that larger immigration flows from elsewhere would not result. When questioned by Allen as to whether an "oriental" born in Hong Kong could then come under the large British quota if exclusion were lifted, Dickstein drew on Judd's proposed solution to respond that "the bill could very easily be drawn so as to have the Chinese quota apply to all Chinese no matter where they live" (171–72, 227). In 1952 the McCarran-Walter Act applied this racial tracking even more broadly by imposing the Asian-Pacific Triangle caps on entry.

In the end the subcommittee voted 8–4 in favor of advancing the bill, although the most outspoken critics, such as Allen, did not attend the meeting and were not allowed to vote by proxy.[49] Although no recorded vote was taken on repeal, Riggs's tallies from the House and Senate subcommittees show the bill had thirty-three supporters in the House committee, twelve opponents, and eleven abstainees, and six supporters on the Senate committee, three opponents, and one abstainee.[50] On October 11, 1943, President Roosevelt added his voice to the call for repeal, calling the effort "important in the cause of winning the war and of establishing a secure peace." Of Chinese exclusion, he commented, "Nations, like individuals, make mistakes. We must be big enough to acknowledge our mistakes of the past and to correct them."[51] Roosevelt emphasized idealistic principles but also the political expedience of repeal: "We can correct a historic mistake and silence the distorted Japanese propaganda." Noting the quota of 107 Chinese immigrants per year, Roosevelt stressed that there would be little economic impact but great benefits. For example, naturalization rights to these limited numbers of Chinese "would operate as another meaningful display of friendship" not only during times of war but for the future "in days of peace." Congress passed the bill, which Roosevelt signed on December 17. Under wartime conditions, the racist legislation was quickly repealed and replaced by a law only moderately less so. Considerable differences between Chinese rights of entry and permanent status and those of Europeans remained.

Quickly, and chiefly justified by political exigencies, Congress enacted repeal of the Chinese exclusion laws in ways that bore negligible economic and demographic costs as a symbolic gesture of friendship and racial parity with Chinese. The long-suffering resident Chinese American community barely benefited, either in significantly increasing levels of immigration, particularly of family members, or in naturalizations to citizenship. They had served primarily as the unwelcome "coolie" counterparts to the desirable educated Chinese that properly framed immigration laws could select for admission. As anticipated, the number of Chinese remained low at 117,629 in 1950, an increase of only 40,125 from the 1940 population of 77,504.[52] However, in the long run, as feared by its opponents, repeal indeed acted as a harbinger of further immigration reforms. Although specifying only Chinese, repeal established congressional approval for the principle that Asians should have equal citizenship and immigration rights. Other Asian allies, Indians and Filipinos, also gained entry quotas and naturalization rights in 1946, with racial restrictions on citizenship removed altogether in 1952, permitting even the formerly hated Japanese to become Americans. Slowly but steadily the inequities built into the quota system fractured as well through passage of successive, small-scale laws that permitted greater Asian immigration in the form of war brides, refugees, transnational adoptees, normalization of status, and students, culminating in the general overhaul of 1965.

World War II and America's turn toward international responsibilities had fostered this momentous shift, although the full implications were not yet fully acknowledged by its supporters. Another unanticipated consequence of America's alliance with China was the presence in the United States of far greater numbers of potential immigrants of precisely the high individual caliber and economic value that supporters of repeal had claimed in their portrayals of deserving Chinese. Starting in the mid-1930s, the State Department had undertaken international education and technical trainee programs as a form of foreign relations targeting chiefly Latin American countries but also China. Federal resources turned toward bringing thousands of carefully selected intellectuals and students to advance their technical and economic expertise on the premise that they would return to guide Nationalist China's recovery and modernization after peace resumed. These careful arrangements fell apart, however, with the unanticipated victory of communist forces in China's Civil War, a disaster that stranded this elite group in the United States, leaving them poised to become a highly visible and symbolically potent group of racial-minority, model immigrants whose outstanding individual trajectories demanded further immigration reforms.

CHAPTER 5

The Wartime Transformation of Student Visitors into Refugee Citizens, 1943–1955

IN 1948 THE AUTHOR C. Y. LEE (Li Jinyang, b. 1917) was renting a single room over a Filipino nightclub in San Francisco, eking out a living working under the table as a writer and editor for hire at two Chinatown newspapers. He had arrived in 1943 to study literature at Columbia University but switched to the MFA program at Yale. When he received his degree in 1947, the Chinese Civil War (1945–1949) prevented his return to China, and he had no choice but to overstay his student visa and work illegally. He had been liable for deportation when one of his stories won first prize in a *Reader's Digest* contest. Lee presented this honor at his next immigration interview in hopes of gaining another deferral of deportation. To his surprise, the officer offered him permanent residency instead. Lee remained in the United States legally, gained citizenship, and continued a prolific literary career culminating in publication of the best-selling novel *Flower Drum Song* in 1957, which became the basis for the popular and colorful tale of Chinese American integration featured in the successful Rogers and Hammerstein Broadway musical (1958) and Universal Studios movie (1961).[1]

Lee's route to citizenship reveals how World War II and the Cold War had dramatically improved the possibilities for Chinese students to resettle permanently and become Americans. Most likely, Lee's specific change of status became legally feasible through the Displaced Persons Act of 1948, which gave the attorney general powers to adjust the status of a nonimmigrant present in the United States before April 1, 1948, to that of permanent immigrant if found to be "a worthy applicant" showing "long presence in the United States and a good moral character."[2] Along with Chinese American residents who through military service and employment in wartime industries gained access to mainstream jobs, higher education, residential dispersion, family reunification through the War Brides Act, and citizenship, students also gained better options for lawful employment, family reunification, and extended legal residency. Lee was among the thousands of Chinese who continued to arrive in the United States during World War II as students and through other forms of cultural, educational, and now technical exchanges. The State Department's growing investment in cultural diplomacy, organized under its Bureau of Cultural Affairs and later funded through the Fulbright Act of 1946, brought in significant new groups, including greater numbers of professors, government representatives, and technical trainees who presented an even more accomplished array of Chinese to America, including brilliant scientists like Li Zhengdao (T. D. Lee), Yang Zhenning (C. N. Yang), Wang An, and Qian Xuesen.

At the war's end, with the many ties so developed with the Nationalists, in addition to the considerable military and economic aid conferred during the war, the U.S. government hoped that Chiang Kai-shek would remain in power, even if in alliance with the rising force of the Chinese Communists under Mao Zedong's charismatic leadership. Efforts to broker cooperation, by no less an authority than General George C. Marshall, failed to reconcile the two sides after their decades of enmity and fundamental differences. Despite the concerted assertions of friendship and support for the Nationalists under conditions of war, Roosevelt and many informed members of the State Department were keenly aware of the corruption and incompetence besetting their former allies and were prepared to allow the Chinese Civil War to take its course as it became apparent by late 1947 that the far more disciplined Communists would win. The administration even issued the China White Paper in 1949 explaining this decision.[3] The abrupt descent of the Iron Curtain and the rapid onset of the crisis mode of the Cold War changed these plans and launched the China Lobby of Nationalist supporters—including many former missionaries, business leaders, and anticommunist, former internationalists—into strident activity against American acknowledgment of the newly established People's Republic of China. This influential, albeit minority, group traced its origins to Song Ziwen's efforts to generate pressure on Congress to allocate military and economic aid to China in 1940. The Korean War (1950–1952) confirmed fears of Communist Chinese expansionist aspirations, and the question of "Who lost China?" became a key driver of McCarthy-era paranoia that destroyed the careers of many of the experts on China who had held realistic criticisms of the Nationalists and supported cooperation with the PRC.[4] For the next three decades, the American government would be forced by the vocal China Lobby to act as global protector of "Free China," Chiang Kai-shek's fiercely anticommunist but violently authoritarian administration on Taiwan.

In this newly bipolar world, thousands of Chinese students, trainees, visitors, and diplomats fell between the cracks of these two unacceptable choices for "home" and found themselves stranded in America with limited options of where to settle even as their educational training and work experiences made them valuable commodities in the intensifying competition for world supremacy economically, militarily, and in the race to space. Old expectations that they would return to China and contribute to its

Figure 5.1. Li Zhengdao (*left*) and Yang Zhenning. Courtesy of Emilio Segrè Visual Archives, American Institute of Physics.

modernization were no longer practical. Nor did the relocation of the Nationalist government to Taiwan entice those with no previous connection to the undeveloped frontier island or those critical of Chiang Kai-shek. For example, I. M. Pei had visited Taiwan in 1954 to fulfill a commission from the United Board for Christian Higher Education in Asia to design the campus of the newly established Christian school, Tunghai College, and Luce Chapel. Whereas this local architectural landmark using innovative techniques in reinforced concrete still stands, Pei chose not to remain and returned to the United States to become a U.S. citizen and founded his firm I. M. Pei and Associates (now Pei, Cobb, Freed, and Partners) in Boston in 1955, from which he pursued an internationally lauded career that included major buildings such as the Kennedy Library in 1964. Like Pei, C. Y. Lee and most other Chinese students had planned to return to China after completing their studies but found themselves transformed by war into stateless refugees remaining under tenuous legal terms in America, with limited legal rights of residency or employment under existing immigration laws. Established attitudes and practices of sympathy and encouragement for students, compounded by new consideration that this highly strategic population should not be forced into Communist hands, led Congress to act swiftly to pass laws that provided financial support for them to remain and complete their studies and then seek jobs, and eventually to become Americans permanently when it became clear that Communist control of China was stabilizing. Motivations to accommodate educated and trained Chinese, particularly in the fields of science and technology, had grown with the addition of technical trainee programs that heightened the economic caliber of Chinese persons visiting the United States during the 1940s.

"Exporting Know-How in Human Containers": Technical Trainees in World War II

By World War II, most Chinese training and studying in the United States specialized in particularly useful fields such as the sciences and technology.[5] As described in chapters 2 and 3, from the outset the Chinese government had encouraged acquisition of practical learning, a priority maintained through the 1920s and 1930s and expanded with the addition of technical training programs that placed carefully selected Chinese engineers, technicians, scientists, and other government officials to gain practical experiences and exposure to advanced technology in American industrial research centers and worksites eager to employ inexpensive, skilled workers. Such programs served the purposes of both governments while advancing the careers of the individual participants.

As early as the late 1920s, international education programs had expanded to include work-study projects that brought skilled and educated trainees to work temporarily in the United States to gain more practical experience and exposure to cutting-edge research. The Bureau of Immigration and the Labor Department had begun allowing some European university graduates admission with nonquota visas to work temporarily in American industrial plants to prepare them to introduce new technologies when they returned home.[6] In 1927 Joseph Bailie's Institute for Technical Training placed Chinese in positions with the Ford Motor Company.[7] In 1936 such programs included Chinese engineers, technicians, scientists, and civil and military personnel who trained in American industrial and commercial establishments such as DuPont Rayon, General Electric, and Northrop.[8] Despite the full onset of the Sino-Japanese War the next year, the Nationalists continued sending technical trainees in preparation for postwar reconstruction, which would require thousands of economic and technical experts whom they hoped to have educated and trained in the United States.[9] Wilma Fairbank observed that the Nationalists drew on long traditions of distinguishing scholars from soldiers in privileging "persons with education and advanced technical skills" as "a vital resource for the management of the postwar renaissance which shimmered in the unknown future" so that students and intellectuals remained on university campuses while "unlettered farmboys and the urban proletariat" were sent to fight the war against Japan.[10] Such priorities meant that students and trainees continued to receive government support to come to the United States during World War II and through the last stages of the Chinese Civil War.

Programs for trainees arriving directly from China overlapped with those for international education in 1938 when the National Resources Commission and the Ministry of Communications entrusted the China Institute with the task of recruiting railway, highway, electrical, radio, and other engineers from among students in the United States for six months of practical training in Chongqing.[11] However, as war prevented these graduates from returning to China and legal restrictions prohibited them from seeking employment in the United States, Meng Zhi found a solution in which "some of the advanced students can be employed to render definitely useful services both to China and the United States during their enforced stay" by filling American needs for trained technical workers and giving Chinese additional work experiences that would better prepare them to help rebuild China once they returned home.[12] Although these programs extended the residence of students in the United States, their priorities remained closely bound to China's anticipated economic needs.[13] By January 1945 the China Institute and the Committee on Wartime Planning had placed 516 former students in such positions.[14]

The U.S. government and the Nationalists cooperated extensively over technical trainee programs. For example, an early duty of the Bureau of Cultural Affairs was to place trainees selected by the Nationalists in field stations for the Department of Agriculture, Tennessee Valley Authority, Bureau of the Census, Library of Congress, and Division of Tax Research of the Treasury Department, and in war industries such as aircraft companies, electrical manufacturers, locomotive works, steel companies, and other engineering and scientific firms.[15] Once trainees had been selected on the Chinese side and their desired training designated, U.S. counterparts would arrange placements in appropriate workplaces.[16] Selected from the best of Chinese technocrats by university presidents, government officials, and faculty, the participants in these training programs also benefited the United States by providing highly skilled labor during wartime shortages.[17] As Paul Yee had testified before the House committee debating repeal in 1943, the top researchers at Westinghouse and RCA were Chinese technical trainees.

William Kirby's case study of the first thirty-one engineers sent in 1942 illustrates these dynamics. This "first and most selective group" represented various divisions of the NRC, such as the Central Machine Works, Hydroelectric Power Bureau, Central Electrical Manufacturing Works, Mining

Bureau, and Economic Research Bureau. Each received several internships over a two-year period in organizations such as Monsanto, Westinghouse, RCA, Du Pont, the Tennessee Valley Authority, U.S. Bureau of Reclamation, and U.S. Steel. After their training, these men all pursued careers that took them to considerable heights in China, Taiwan, and the United States. Twenty-one remained in China, three moved to the United States, and seven went to Taiwan. Those in the PRC achieved "substantial careers in technical work" until the Cultural Revolution. Of the three resettling in the United States, one became a shipping magnate and multimillionaire while the other two became "project engineering managers for multi-national companies." The seven that went to Taiwan in 1949 attained the most success, with one becoming a wealthy financier, three serving as presidents or chairmen of major state-run industries, two receiving cabinet assignments as ministers of economic affairs, and one becoming premier. During World War II several thousand Chinese engineers came to the United States through NRC sponsorship, with some funded by Lend-Lease funds, including future Chinese American computer entrepreneur and innovator Wang An.[18]

American private and public organizations partnered in such programs. The International Training Administration (ITA), based in Washington, DC, was another key participant. This "private, nonprofit service organization" provided much of the coordination between American industries and "the many hundreds of technical trainees coming from abroad for first-hand experience in factories and business establishments" through 113 separate training programs.[19] In 1944 and 1945 more than three thousand trainees from China arrived for both military and technical training in fields ranging from aeronautical engineering to telecommunications in over 350 U.S. companies.[20] The most ambitious such program brought more than a thousand Chinese technical personnel as part of the Lend-Lease agreement in 1945 through arrangements made by the China Supply Commission and the U.S. Foreign Economic Administration.[21] In 1946, in marked contrast to the Chinese Educational Mission in 1881, more than a thousand Chinese cadets trained at the U.S. Naval Training Center in Miami.[22] Concerned that these trainees should have positive experiences of America to share on their return to China, the Bureau of Cultural Affairs commissioned the China Institute to arrange social gatherings to make them feel welcome. Echoing earlier efforts by the Cosmopolitan Clubs and the CFRFS, local committees in larger cities such as New York, Philadelphia, Baltimore, and New Haven organized opportunities for trainees "to meet and mingle socially with members of the communities in which they are living."[23]

Despite these concerted efforts by American institutions to help China, Nationalist authoritarianism and efforts to exert political controls threatened to upset this mutually beneficial collaboration. Fairbank described the conflicts that arose when Minister of Education Chen Lifu[24] sought to impose "thought control" on students in the United States by directing their funding, sending agents to supervise them, and forcing them to join party organizations such as the Nationalist Youth Corps. The Sino-American alliance was strained further with U.S. awareness that Chiang Kai-shek was hoarding munitions and his best troops to fight the Chinese Communists rather than committing fully to the ongoing battles against Japan. In 1944 even prominent educators such as Jiang Menglin and Mei Yiji, along with anyone hoping to study abroad, were forced to submit to the Central Training Corps for political indoctrination and instruction that included military drilling and rifle practice.[25] These measures provoked a boycott against Chinese students by American institutions, which in turn endangered the $4.8 million in Lend-Lease funds that Song Ziwen had arranged to fund 1,200 Chinese trainees. Under such insistent resistance in the United States, the Nationalists relented and lifted the indoctrination measures by the end of the year so that the exchange programs could resume.[26]

Such disagreements about the parameters of educational exchange did not prevent the CFRFS from trumpeting the growth in international programs. Understandably, American business interests were also enthusiastic supporters, as indicated by this quote in *Flying* magazine: "It will have the nation for its campus, the factories and business offices of the United States for its classrooms, and crack students from all over the world for its pupils." On behalf of the Indian government, M. S. Sunduram, an Indian educational liaison officer, sought to replicate Chinese benefits and arranged similar training for several hundred fellow Indians in the fall of 1945.[27] Paul Kramer has criticized such programs, observing that international education organizations "fastened and often subordinated pacifist idioms to projects in the expansion of U.S. corporate power through the training and familiarization of foreign engineers, salespersons, and administrators in U.S. techniques and products for potential export."[28] The practical aspects of such programs would grow in the aftermath of World War II, which had made acceptable the hiring of foreign graduates from American institutions into employment in the United States. Technical training programs shifted the agendas for international education from shaping the future leadership of other nations to providing skilled workers for domestic purposes.

Educational, technical, and cultural exchange gained even greater institutional legitimacy and resources when Truman signed the Fulbright Act (Public Law 79–584) into law on August 1, 1946, authorizing the sale of surplus military property abroad to fund educational and cultural exchange programs with foreign allies. Under the Department of State's Bureau of Cultural and Educational Affairs, China and the Philippines were two of the first twenty-three countries targeted for this kind of partnership in 1947.[29] Although the China program lasted only a year before the Communist victory shut it down, the priority it received illustrates China's importance to America's postwar goals for international leadership.

Other Chinese professionals, particularly faculty and government officials, also visited the United States in growing numbers. In May 1941 the Chinese Ministry of Education had begun issuing regulations granting sabbatical leaves to college professors. The U.S. Bureau of Cultural Affairs facilitated faculty exchanges as part of its brief. According to Y. C. Wang, such exchange programs were so popular that "during the war and immediate postwar years, the presidents of all major Chinese universities visited the United States, and many remained there for a number of years. By glancing through the bulletins of the China Institute in America during those years, one can find almost the entire *Who's Who* among China's Western-educated elite." Between 1945 and 1947 about four hundred senior NRC officials paid visits. Perhaps the most visible visitor was the warlord General Feng Yuxiang, who went in 1946 to study "irrigation problems" and received more than $130,000 for a stay of less than two years. Wang compares this vogue of going to America in the late 1940s to the "Chinese exodus to Japan in 1905 and 1906," noting that both occurred right before the fall of Chinese regimes.[30] Programs for visiting faculty and government officials continued to operate even as Nationalist defeat became inevitable through 1948, bringing even more elite Chinese to the United States.

Postwar International Education

Through World War II and the anticipated expansion of American influence abroad with the war's end, both public and private agencies concerned with international education and other forms of cultural exchange sought and realized increasing numbers of foreign students, which doubled from a total of 7,542 during the 1944–1945 academic year to 16,176 in 1946–1947, and almost doubled again by 1950–1951 to reach 30,462. Chinese student numbers grew as well over the same time period, rising from 823 to 3,549 in 1949–1950 despite the Chinese Civil War.[31] In 1948 the 2,710 Chinese students enrolled in 405 colleges and universities in all but three states across the nation were the second largest contingent of foreign students, exceeded in number only by Canadians.[32] In the reconfigured world, international educational exchange was presumed to have a critical role.

The Fulbright Program embodied many of these ideals. J. W. Fulbright, the longest-serving chair of the Senate Committee on Foreign Relations, anticipated great outcomes from exchange programs in progress for global humanity. "Civilization is what educational exchange programs are all about. They are concerned with increasing man's knowledge of science and the arts. But they are primarily concerned with increasing man's understanding of himself and of the national and world societies in which he lives."[33] The United States fostered such exchanges to improve international relations throughout the world.

> The national purpose . . . has been "to increase mutual understanding between peoples of the United States and the people of other countries; to strengthen the ties which unite us with other nations by demonstrating the educational and cultural interests, developments, and achievements of the people of the United States and other nations, and the contributions being made toward a peaceful and more fruitful life for people throughout the world; to promote international cooperation for education and cultural advancement; and thus to assist in the development of friendly, sympathetic, and peaceful relations between the United States and the other countries of the world."

Alongside outright grants of economic aid and military assistance, the United States aimed to help less-developed states advance economically to become more fully integrated partners in the capitalist and democratic alliance against the communist world. By training foreign elites who would lead their homelands to collaborate with the United States, the State Department pursued a relatively cheap means of cultivating international influence. The 1952 and 1953 Committee on Foreign Relations found that "the exchange of persons programs were the most effective and, at the same time, among the lowest in cost."[34] In these projects for advancing American aims overseas, Chinese students retained central roles.

Meet the USA: Chinese as Exemplary International Students

In preparation for the anticipated surge in international student numbers with the end of World War II, the IIE published an important guide in 1945 to orient foreign students to life in the United States that reveals many of the assumptions and aspirations it shared with the State Department for such programs. The author was a Chinese, Ching-kun Yang, who had received a PhD degree from the University of Michigan and was teaching at the University of Washington. *Meet the USA* had originated as a handbook Yang wrote for Chinese students that came to the attention of Stephen Duggan, who commissioned Yang to make an English-language translation jointly published by the IIE and the Department of State. The IIE's annual report for 1946 proudly proclaimed *Meet the USA* as "the outstanding publication during the current year" and promoted it to a general readership of Americans besides visiting students. Duggan introduced the book by acknowledging that although many of its examples, including the chapter on "Racial Discrimination," addressed difficulties specific to Chinese, it had general relevance for all foreign students, and "United States teachers and students" could benefit from learning about how a foreigner viewed their home.[35]

Yang's authorship of *Meet the USA* and its contents reflect the centrality of Chinese student experiences in framing American international educational programs. They were considered exemplars of the kinds of difficulties foreigners might encounter in America but also models of how visitors should handle the opportunities and challenges of fully appreciating and transforming U.S. society. The guide sought to mitigate experiences of discrimination by emphasizing America's progress and desire to become a more equitable democracy. To this end, the IIE frankly acknowledged that the United States harbored racist elements but sought nonetheless to persuade visiting students that Americans and American democracy still deserved their respect. Yang's guide allocated Chinese students key roles in advancing racial equality and intercultural understanding as cultural bridges who could inform ignorant but open-minded Americans through the right kinds of activities and attitudes while in the United States. Signifying the IIE's trust in the judgment of its foreign collaborators, Duggan insisted that Yang had received carte blanche to write the handbook according to his own vision and had produced "a searching analysis of American civilization and culture" capturing "all phases of our life: political, economic, social, cultural, and industrial." Duggan positioned Yang as a sympathetic outsider aware of America's shortcomings but also infused with admiration for its ideals in noting "the most friendly nature" of Yang's criticisms, which were "suffused by a loving enthusiasm for the American dream." By reading *Meet the USA*, Duggan promised, American readers would acquire "an increased but chastened pride in [their] country" as seen through the eyes of a Chinese visitor.[36]

Apart from its ideological sinews, *Meet the USA* provided a general orientation with chapters about American geography, demography, democracy, constitutional rights, achievements of the common man, and problems of democracy and industrialism, in addition to practical advice concerning preparations for departure, school selection, getting "From Pier to Classroom," "Understanding America by Participation," media such as newspapers and movies, etiquette and customs, and estimated costs of recreation and travel. The appendices provided suggested readings about American history and life, tables of accredited institutions, agricultural colleges, engineering colleges, commonly used academic terms, distances between main cities, a national map, and a list of IIE publications (vii).[37]

Yang frequently discussed the great American bugaboo of racial discrimination but portrayed such inequalities as being under attack and soon to dissipate. In "Unity in Diversity," he claimed that with conquest of the "wild continent ... tolerance gradually became an American characteristic" even though "colored races and new immigrants from Europe ... were frequently slighted and were called Chinks, Wops, and many other uncomplimentary names" on arrival. Despite the passage of time and some improvements in this situation, Yang admitted that "racial prejudice can be encountered almost anywhere in the country. The Negro problem is still a very serious one" (4–5). Nonetheless, because "the white citizen" was paying attention, such problems were diminishing. For example, African Americans had made many political and economic inroads, particularly in New England, since the U.S. Civil War. And yet, in the South, "serious discrimination in social and economic life confronts the American Negro today, and his full status as a citizen is still to be attained" and fought for by liberal leaders (37–38). Enlightened Americans recognized their nation's shortcomings and were working to move closer to their constitutional ideals.

Yang also scrutinized hostility to Chinese and included an abbreviated history of exclusion and other anti-Chinese laws and violence (4–5). In the 1940s Chinese students still faced difficulty renting rooms and sometimes ran into hostile immigration officials who suspected them of being laborers (86, 129). Yang stressed that anti-Chinese hostilities were also regional in nature. "The West coast is the headquarters of discrimination," but Chinese met with "fair treatment" in the South and there had "never been any violence" in the Midwest; only "a minority that is dying out" believed out of ignorance that Chinese could only do laundry, restaurant, and domestic work and were incapable of social progress. While the majority might "harbor social discrimination," they did not hate Chinese. The well-educated "know our shortcomings but they realize our virtues, and admire our ancient and great civilization. They have high hopes for the future of China and are strongly opposed to the general attitude of prejudice." Pointing to improving conditions, Yang credited enlightened Americans for their support during World War II when "they were the main force in winning sympathy for China, in sending help, and in abolishing laws inimical to the Chinese" (130–31).

Yang's acknowledgment of American racism accompanied assertions that conditions were improving but placed responsibility on Chinese for changing negative impressions. Education would provide the solution to America's racial problems: "What constitutes the real 'melting pot' of the Americans are the 240,000 schools" (6). He offered suggestions for how Chinese students might use their presence in America to further racial equality and mutual understanding. In "Etiquette and Customs," Yang provided advice about winning American friends and making a good impression. While American teachers and friends praised "the good manners and good behavior of Chinese students," they harbored "dislike of excessive politeness and formality." Yang advised his readers that "Americans love humor, as do the Chinese, and it will help in social gatherings to tell a few Chinese jokes and stories" (124).[38] Yang urged Chinese to adjust to their circumstances and display the attributes preferred by white Americans.

In "Racial Discrimination," Yang concluded that "racial prejudice is not directed exclusively against any one race but is general." Despite perceptions that "the Europeans may soon be assimilated into America's social structure, while the color of our skin makes assimilation more difficult," eventually the problem would be resolved because "a long time is required to harmonize the interests and patterns of living of various races within a nation" and "American leaders today are still campaigning for the harmony and unity of all races." Chinese could play their part in advancing the cause of racial equality by attempting to "make contact with Americans whenever possible." Yang urged Chinese students to observe American customs, particularly concerning cleanliness in their rooms and especially food. There should be no cooking in rooms, no food waste in the wastepaper basket, and no loud noises from talking and playing mahjong. He advised that "the most effective way of mitigating racial prejudice against us is by informing Americans about China and Chinese culture" and cautioned against responding to hostility or ignorance with resentment. Progress required that "one of the parties takes a magnanimous attitude and gives the other fellow a chance to understand him, [so] the vicious cycle may start to break." Over time and shared experiences, Yang asserted, Chinese would gain better standing in the United States. He pointed to the successful repeal of the exclusion laws as an example of how "liberal American leaders" were working to correct the mistakes of the past and to improve relations with China, in part based on shared wartime struggles against Japan (129–32).

Yang's guide sought to advance Sino-American relations by accompanying its critique of racial problems in the United States with examples of improving conditions and strategies for how Chinese students could help build mutual understanding and acceptance. His solution required, however, that Chinese bear the chief burden for extending the hand of friendship in familiarizing themselves with the cultural and social mores of Americans and serve as cultural translators for the growing ranks of Americans who were uninformed but interested in the shared goal of racial equality for all. Yang's representation of domestic race relations, and his projections of the improving state of democracy in the United States, bolstered the vision of the IIE and the Department of State for educational and cultural exchanges that enhanced the foreign influence of the United States and situated it as a global leader. Even as *Meet the USA* acknowledged racism in the United States, it insisted on the commitment of Americans to democratic ideals while giving Chinese and other international students responsibility for teaching them greater appreciation for foreign cultures and persons.[39] Although an unintended outcome, *Meet the USA*'s advice about becoming effective cultural brokers also showed Chinese strategies for becoming good American citizens. Perhaps no other Chinese students demonstrated the ready translatability of educated, acculturated Chinese students and representatives into model American citizens better than the brilliant linguist Zhao Yuanren (Yuen Ren Chao, 1892–1982) and his wife, the cookbook author Zhao Yang Buwei (Buwei Yang Chao, 1889–1981).

Becoming American: The Meandering Path to Citizenship of Zhao Yuanren and Yang Buwei

Zhao Yuanren was something of a Renaissance man whose studies, career, and travels with his wife Buwei engaged with a wide range of Chinese and American collaborations around educational and cultural exchange in ways that revealed how well Chinese could intermingle with Americans and claim equal standing among them. Zhao made many trips to America, first as a student and then as a professor, highly regarded scholar, and representative for educational affairs on behalf of the Nationalist government. He wielded expertise in musicology, philosophy, mathematics, physics, acoustics, and linguistics along with an adeptness for languages in speaking several Chinese dialects along with German, French, and a smattering of Greek, Latin, and Japanese as well as full fluency in English with enough skill to use it to craft puns and jokes. In 1910 Zhao had placed second out of seventy successful candidates who competed for the first round of Boxer Indemnity Fellowships. He achieved his BA degree in mathematics from Cornell in 1914 and a PhD degree in philosophy from Harvard in 1918. He created the first pronunciation system for Chinese using an alphabetic script, *Guoyu romazi*, but also taught physics and mathematics at institutions such as Cornell and Tsinghua before taking up his main interest, linguistics, in earnest.[40] In a famous early "love match," for which both broke engagements arranged by their families, he married Yang Buwei in 1921. Buwei came from a wealthy Nanjing family, had studied at the McTyeire School, and received a medical degree in Japan. When she and Yuanren met, she had already worked as a principal at a girl's school and founded her own hospital. As a couple, the Zhaos were readily mobile, self-assured, and highly personable breakers of racial barriers in demonstrating through personal example how skillfully and smoothly Chinese could interact with American elites.

In 1921 Buwei gave up her professional pursuits to accompany Yuanren when he returned to America to teach philosophy at Harvard at the invitation of his former teacher, William E. Hocking. This was the first of many journeys across the Pacific, for as a couple, the Zhaos seemed to move easily between China and America, unencumbered by discriminatory immigration restrictions or authorities. Despite the exclusion laws, nowhere in Yuanren's copious autobiographical writings and Buwei's well-known *Autobiography of a Chinese Woman* is any mention made of difficulties entering the United States, a transition for Chinese usually associated with tremendous anxieties about extended incarcerations in port facilities, grueling interviews by skeptical immigration officials, onerous evidentiary requirements, and the looming threat of being turned back.[41] The couple returned to China where Yuanren conducted linguistic fieldwork throughout the country on behalf of Academia Sinica accompanied by Buwei, who collected recipes. They came to America again in 1932 when Zhao headed the Chinese Educational Mission in Washington, DC. Their final journey to America took place in 1938, with Zhao invited to teach at the University of Hawaii, then Yale, and then Harvard, employment stints that carried them through the end of World War II. The *Autobiography*'s account of their many smooth passages between China and America and their ready access to white American society, employment, and homes presents a Chinese family that had already attained full acceptance in the United States.

Even as a young man, Zhao had shown his aptitude for an American life. Of her husband's second homecoming, Buwei wrote: "When Chao Yuenren returned to China in 1920, he did not return sincerely. He got a leave of absence from Cornell to have a look at things, possibly to get his freedom, and would return to his job in America in a year's time. He had been thoroughly Americanized and wanted to live in America." Referring to Zhao's facility with languages, Buwei linked patriotism and national identity with individual capacities to speak in foreign tongues. "He came back with an English-speaking and American-feeling mind." According to these standards, Buwei remained essentially Chinese. "The reason why I am so thoroughly Chinese is because I speak nothing but the Chinese language. I have tried to speak Japanese and English and German, but whatever language I speak comes out Chinese in spirit. Anyone who wants to learn Chinese grammar can profit by studying the kind of English I speak."[42] The couple's banter regarding how and where to locate their home, in their travels and in their cultural preferences and core values, suffuses the two popular books they coauthored for American audiences, *How to Cook and Eat in Chinese* (1945) and *Autobiography of a Chinese Woman*. The former was the first bestselling Chinese cookbook written for non-Chinese and is still widely used today. Building on its success, Pearl Buck encouraged Buwei to write *Autobiography of a Chinese Woman*, which offered a humorous account of Buwei's childhood and the Zhaos' marriage, family life, and many travels.[43]

Published by Richard Walsh's John Day Company with Buwei Yang Chao listed as official author, these charming guides to Chinese American life and culture nonetheless bear the hallmarks of Zhao Yuanren's wit and showcase his facility with English and love of verbal puns. The preface to each volume acknowledges Buwei's limited English-language capacities and describes Yuanren's role as "translator" for his wife's handwritten Chinese accounts. The two occasionally disputed her version of events, in which case their oldest daughter, Rulan or Iris, was called in to mediate, as recorded in the occasional footnotes. Although it is difficult to know the exact extent to which Zhao Yuanren shaped the books' contents, they are filled with wordplay such as in the description of the third-floor flat in Cambridge, Massachusetts, which they sublet from Professor William McDougall, who also lent them a "very welcome mattress."[44] Zhao's verbal adeptness enlivened *How to Cook and Eat in Chinese* with engaging descriptions of Chinese cooking techniques and philosophies and coined the now common and highly evocative terms "potsticker" and "stir-fry." The *Autobiography* observed racial inequalities in the following manner: "Some American friends said that we should not live with colored people. I did not understand what they meant until I learned that yellow and red were not colors, but that black was." Despite such admonitions, the Zhaos decided to live in an apartment sandwiched between two black families who helped them with babysitting.[45]

Together these books presented Chinese culture and people accessibly and intimately, giving Americans, on the one hand, their own fluency and familiarity with Chinese foods and cooking techniques while providing, on the other hand, beguiling examples of compatibilities and equivalencies between Chinese and American peoples. Through these books, the Zhaos presented a persuasive case that not only are Chinese and Americans not so different, but Americans could acquire some Chinese ways and Chinese were socially adept and capable of becoming American with charmingly Chinese characteristics.

How to Cook and Eat in Chinese conveyed to Americans that such culturally specific skills could be learned and readily shared by all. Buwei had come to write the cookbook with the encouragement of faculty wives whom she had befriended while volunteering for charity events in New Haven. She was an authoritative yet accessible teacher, acknowledging that she had learned to cook only while a student in Japan pining for familiar dishes. She encouraged readers by noting that if she could learn to cook Chinese on her own, then so too could Americans, with her guidance. *How to Cook and Eat in Chinese* drew on the many recipes she had collected while accompanying Yuanren on his linguistic tour of China. The cookbook brought Chinese culture directly into American homes and rendered Chinese ingredients and cooking techniques comprehensible and reproducible by Americans in their own kitchens. As proclaimed in the cover blurb, the recipes "haven't a spoonful of anything in them that you cannot get right here in the United States; but they are true Chinese dishes." The guide's success reflects how readily Chinese culture could be domesticated and adopted by average Americans, an act of absorption advanced for Chinese people with the publication of Buwei's autobiography just two years later.

The *Autobiography* translates Chinese people into Americans on several levels. As discussed earlier, it depicts the Zhaos' many travels and their extensive experiences of bicultural education, family life, professional experiences, and the ready compatibility of Chinese and Americans. Through anecdotes, use of language, and humor, it underscores the attractiveness of the Zhaos and their Chinese American family life and ready engagement with persons and things American. It ends on an ambiguous note, however, with the completion of World War II and the unanswered question of whether Chinese so acculturated and well adapted to life in the United States should not simply become Americans and relinquish the goal of returning to China.

The *Autobiography* contains many instances of how well Chinese and Americans worked together and shared values. A particularly vivid example recounts the Zhaos' life in New Haven, where Yuanren assumed a temporary teaching position at Yale before moving onto Harvard. According to Buwei,

> I soon found myself a natural part of the community with surprisingly little self-consciousness. So far as social life went, Yale might as well be a Tsing Hua University or an Academia Sinica, . . . When I watched Leonard Bloomfield think on his feet, which he did by tilting his head and looking at the left front corner of the ceiling, I immediately recalled Li Fangkuei doing exactly the same thing when he lectured in Nanking. And no wonder, since Li had been Bloomfield's pupil in Chicago. (295)

Through the lens of Buwei's experiences, American places and people could be readily overlaid and mapped onto Chinese ones. Chinese seemed able to absorb American ideas and even personal mannerisms just as easily as Yuanren and Buwei moved through American society. As intellectuals and cosmopolitans, they embodied the possibility that Chinese could be at home among white contemporaries. When the Zhaos departed New Haven in 1939, they sent cards to all their new friends and acquaintances to thank them "for having added for us one more place in the world returning to which will always be like returning home" (301). Unlike most other Chinese of their generation, the Zhaos could identify with and feel comfortable in the United States even as they longed for their other home in China.

At the end of the *Autobiography*, the Zhaos are undecided about where they have the strongest ties and where they should go. During the war they had been unable to return to China, but despite their longing for family and home, they found plenty to keep them occupied and content in the United States. Each time a letter arrived, the family had debated. "Should we go back? Had we better go back? How were we going to go back? . . . Pearl Harbor put an end to these sentimental gestures to ourselves. Whether I was glad or troubled—probably I was both—there was nothing further to do about it. A family like ours would have to remain abroad for the duration"

(310). Being stranded in America seemed to cause little hardship, with Yuanren readily finding employment teaching at elite institutions. When the war did end, the Zhaos were staying at a friend's cottage in the Green Mountains of Vermont. As soon as the radio announcers declared Japan's surrender, they celebrated with thoughts of going home. "We felt like driving clear across to China. But instead, we drove to New York to see [our friends] T'ao Mengho and Hu Shih to celebrate" and then to Washington, DC, to visit one of Zhao's old Harvard schoolmates. The trip affirmed the many ways they belonged in America, for they encountered many sites saturated with fond memories: two different buildings occupied by the Chinese Educational Mission, which Yuanren had frequented first as a student and then as director, the Lincoln Memorial, and the amphitheater behind the Tomb of the Unknown Soldier, which "reminded me of the open-air Amphitheater in front of the Sun Yat-sen Mausoleum of Nanking." The family—father, mother, and four grown daughters—discussed going home. Through their constant travels, this meant different things for various family members, including "our hotel in Washington," "Walker Street and the fall term" in Cambridge, and the ancestral houses in "Lanchia Chuang and Yenling Hsiang" in China. Yuanren was torn between completing his linguistic tour of China or remaining to publish his translation of *Through the Looking-Glass*, while Buwei contemplated a traditional life surrounded by children and grandchildren or retaining her active rounds of social and charitable events in the United States. The family seemed poised to return to China but never did. "Yuenren resigned from Harvard. We packed up our things in wooden boxes to ship to China. But at our silver wedding, nearly ten months after V-J Day, we were still having our family picture taken in a Boston studio" (see fig. 5.2). The *Autobiography* concludes with the Zhaos still in America but thinking that they will return to China (316–18).[46]

Publication of *How to Cook and Eat in Chinese* and *Autobiography of a Chinese Woman* came at a juncture when war and other international pressures magnified the many practical reasons for accepting Chinese as U.S. citizens. The Zhaos, and particularly Yuanren with his work as linguist, translator, teacher, and educational representative and his mastery of languages, exemplified literally how well Chinese could operate as cultural bridges but also as fully fluent Americans. Why, then, was it Buwei and not Yuanren who was invited to be the featured protagonist of the *Autobiography*? With general audiences as their targets, Buwei was perhaps the more appealing subject as a woman associated with Chinese cooking and motherhood. Americans had demonstrated their appreciation for Chinese women through the large audiences for Buck's *The Good Earth* and its heroine, the long-suffering O-Lan, and the celebrity of Madame Chiang Kaishek. Yuanren's ventriloquism in showcasing his wife Buwei as the spokeswoman illustrating the compatibilities of Chinese and Americans built on

Figure 5.2. Zhao family portrait taken in 1946 as they were deciding between their two homes, America or China. In back, *left-to-right*: son-in-law Peiyong; daughters Nova, Bella, Lensey, and Iris (Rulan); son-in-law Xuehuang. Front, *left-to-right*: Buwei and Yuanren. Purdy Photographers, Boston.

established sympathies and embrace of Chinese women as wives, mothers, and preservers of Chinese tradition, even as he positioned Chinese for consideration as U.S. citizens.

The Zhaos remained in the United States and became American citizens in 1954. Zhao Yuanren took a faculty position at UC Berkeley, and daughter Rulan became a professor of musicology at Harvard. China's turmoil, but also their own outstanding capabilities, American opportunities, and their own inertia and attachment to a place that had come to feel like home led them to remain and sink deeper roots. As the next section will describe, that they had the option to do so resulted from congressional decisions to provide financial support but also legal status for Chinese visitors who had become refugees with the outbreak of the Cold War in East Asia.

The Strategic Value of Educated Chinese

Like I. M. Pei, the Zhaos, and C. Y. Lee, the majority of Chinese present in the United States at the end of World War II as nonimmigrants, whose ranks included students, government officials, consular representatives, tourists, businesspeople, sailors, journalists, priests, and some very wealthy refugees, had not planned to stay until forced to do so by the ascent of the Communists in China. An estimated five to twelve thousand, many with close affiliations with the Nationalists, lost their anticipated futures, contacts with family and friends, funds, employment, and a place they could claim as a permanent home, despite their considerable expertise and experiences.[47] The intensifying global conflict and their demonstrated economic and political value provided the U.S. government strong motivation to find ways to help them remain on the American side of the growing political divides.

By early 1948 State Department authorities realized the inevitability of Nationalist defeat and prepared to switch tracks, with some experts on China advocating that the United States cede support for the Nationalists and deal instead with the incoming Communist government. Chiang Kai-shek and the Nationalists proved tenacious, however, in holding on to American protection. As described earlier, the outbreak of the Korean War extended the crisis of the Cold War to Asia, situating Taiwan and the off-shore islands of Jinmen (Kinmen or Quemoy) and Mazu (Matsu) into critical nodes in the defensive perimeter developed to contain communist expansion. In this time of crisis, the staff and trustees of the China Institute again took the lead in working with the Committee for Advisors of Foreign Students and the IIE to lobby "the leaders in the American Government and the State Department" concerning the immediate problems facing Chinese students cut off from funds, with limited means of legal employment to support themselves and no homes to which to return. The long history of American education of Chinese students made helping them, in the words of leading missionary Robert Speer, "so clear a duty, and so rich an opportunity" in the face of their loss of China. Moreover, from a strategic perspective, the State Department hoped that its old goals of educating China's future leaders in order to extend American influence might still be viable, with the hoped for demise of the Communist regime.

In March 1948 Congress had approved an initial allocation of $500,000 for Chinese student support from the aid-to-China program of the Economic Cooperation Administration (ECA) primarily to support those in the technical and scientific fields aligned with ECA goals.[48] A July 1949 congressional report described the Chinese Student Emergency Aid Program as serving both humanitarian and political goals:

> The immediate purpose of this legislation is a humanitarian one—to provide urgently needed financial assistance to Chinese students in the United States. From the standpoint of the long-range foreign policy of the United States, however, there is an equally compelling reason for assisting these men and women. These students have had an opportunity to observe and experience the democratic way of life. Thus, because of the traditional position of scholar-leadership in Chinese society, they are in a unique position to exert a profound influence on

the future course of their country. There is no question but that it is in the interest of the United States to assist these individuals who can play such a vital role
in shaping China's future.[49]

Aided in the House by Representative Walter Judd, Meng Zhi and his allies
repeatedly and successfully urged Congress to direct aid originally intended
for the Nationalist Chinese to the cause of Chinese students stuck in America. Judd sponsored HR 4830 requesting that the 81st Congress authorize the
secretary of state to allocate four million dollars for "necessary expenses of
tuition, subsistence, and return passage to China for selected citizens of
China to study in accredited colleges, universities, or other educational institutions in the United States." This measure, PL 327, passed on September
29, 1949, with sponsorship from William Knowland in the Senate.[50]

As Chiang Kai-shek fled to Taiwan in fall 1949, along with about two million soldiers, bureaucrats, and the chief art treasures of the imperial palace,
the United States was prepared to let China's political realities take their
course. Despite the already considerable allocations from Congress, the
China Institute estimated that a total of ten million dollars was needed for
an estimated 3,800 stranded students.[51] Taking its advice along with that of
the Committee for Advisors of Foreign Students, Congress allocated this
amount through the China Area Aid Act of 1950 (PL 535, Title II, passed June
5, 1950), by providing a further six million dollars from unexpended China
ECA funds to cover tuition, living costs, transportation, and medical care for
both students and trainees. Those completing programs could seek employment with approval of the Immigration Bureau. Eligible applicants included
students resident in the United States "not less than one year"; research scholars and teachers; Chinese citizens now in Free China, and Chinese citizens
outside China and outside the United States. The China Institute *Bulletin*
provided instructions for how students and researchers could apply.[52]

Over the next seven years, 3,517 Chinese students and 119 scholars received this congressional funding. The Division of Exchange of the Department of State funneled these funds through the administrations of 572 authorized universities and colleges. The Chinese Student Aid Program ran
until June 30, 1955, when most of its beneficiaries had completed their programs, many to the level of master's and doctoral degrees. About eight million of the original allocation of ten million dollars had been used, and the
remainder was diverted to other programs.[53]

Another major legislated shift allowed some Chinese with temporary statuses to work legally in the United States, with fewer able to gain legal permanent status. As discussed earlier, the Displaced Persons Act of 1948 enabled about 3,645 Chinese already resident in the United States, such as C. Y.
Lee, to apply for permanent status and remain.[54] On June 16, 1950, a second
refugee act gave them opportunity to adjust their status to stay and work

under stipulated conditions. The China Area Aid Act of 1950 "authorized and directed" the Commission of the Immigration and Naturalization Service "to promulgate a general regulation permitting Chinese students to take jobs for as long as they remained in the country," even after the completion of their studies. These measures contrast sharply with exclusion-era harassment of nonexempt-class Chinese who were presumed to be illegally resident and lived under constant fear of deportation. To underscore the relative privilege of Chinese students and distinguish their separate trajectories in contrast to working-class and Chinatown Chinese who bore the brunt of such hostility, Rose Hum Lee labeled them "the stranded students."[55]

When the refugees in question included individuals with the abilities of Nobel Prize–winning physicists Li Zhengdao and Yang Zhenning, computer entrepreneur Wang An, architect I. M. Pei, and rocket scientist Qian Xuesen, the eagerness of the U.S. government to provide fulfilling employment in the United States and prevent their departure for Communist China is completely explicable. Li Zhengdao was only 30 and Yang Zhenning 34 when they jointly received the Nobel Prize for physics in 1957, the same year the Soviet Union beat the United States by sending Sputnik into space. The desperate competition for technological superiority in the military and space technology rendered the scientists and technicians sent to train and study by the Nationalists useful and necessary human resources for the United States. The utility of such highly talented and capable Chinese scientists would prompt newspapers to argue that U.S. immigration laws should be amended because without recourse to special measures, a scientist like Li Zhengdao would have been forced to return to China. As one editorial argued on behalf of Chinese scientists, "But they come from a country and an area of the world against which our immigration and naturalization laws discriminate.... Surely, in this instance, there is evidence of the need to drop our quota system based on national origins and replace it with one which judges applicants on the basis of equality and desirability instead of race and colour."[56] In turn, the dramatic political transformation of their homeland motivated many Chinese students and intellectuals to remain in America. When seeing off the literary scholar Wu Ningkun at the docks of San Francisco in July 1951, Li Zhengdao explained his own decision not to return to China by saying, "I don't want to have my brains washed by others."[57]

Wang An presented another compelling case for the granting of U.S. citizenship to educated and technically skilled Chinese. Wang arrived in the United States in June 1945 as a technician with the NRC after gaining his degree from Jiaotong University and working in Guilin for a couple of years. To get to America, he had to fly across "the hump," stayed in Calcutta for about a month, then traveled by U.S. transport vessel through the Suez Canal to arrive at Newport News, Virginia.[58] With the unfavorable turn in the Chinese Civil War, he decided to stay to study for a PhD degree at Harvard

University. He began a small computer firm, but during the mid-1950s he and his wife Lorraine were still resident aliens. "In the mid-1950s, however, the People's Republic of China intimated that it was going to demand the repatriation of those Chinese students who had stayed in the United States after the Revolution. We were contacted by American government officials, who, in a warmly appreciated gesture, offered us the chance to become American citizens." Wang An had some reservations about this conversion of status, although it offered him stability and security. "I was ambivalent about giving up my Chinese citizenship. While I disliked what was going on there politically, China was still my birthplace. Nor did I think that America was a utopia [referring to McCarthyism].... Still, it seemed to me that America had the best system—as a nation we do not always live up to our ideals, but we have structures that allow us to correct our wrongs by means short of revolution."[59] Wang became an American on April 18, 1955, and went on to build one of the world's leading computer businesses during the 1980s.

Incentives to liberalize U.S. immigration laws to accommodate such outstanding economic and technical contributors paralleled American losses of such valuable persons, as illustrated most painfully by the case of rocket scientist Qian Xuesen. In 1949 and 1950 about a thousand Chinese had returned to Communist China, 637 at U.S. government expense. Such departees were not necessarily communists or leftist sympathizers, but simply Chinese patriots or those who could not imagine never seeing their home and families again. Despite such nonpolitical motives, the United States changed its policy in January 1951, and Chinese "with certain types of technical training" were banned from leaving. That year, the Immigration Bureau issued 150 detention orders and seemed to decide on a case-by-case basis whether those requesting to depart possessed critical skills and knowledge. Those considered particularly strategic, most notably Qian Xuesen, were forcibly detained. A Boxer Fellow, a highly regarded faculty member at Cal Tech, and a founder of the Jet Propulsion Laboratories, Qian had gained U.S. citizenship in 1949 but had hoped to visit his parents in China. Despite Qian's marriage to the daughter of a highly placed Nationalist official, the FBI suspected him of communist sympathies based on some early student friendships and forcibly removed him from the SS President Cleveland in Honolulu and placed him under house arrest for five years, canceling his security clearances and preventing him from conducting research. Under such conditions, Qian became hostile to the United States and open to invitations to return and work in the PRC. In a POW exchange negotiated in 1955 by Chinese foreign affairs officer Wang Bingnan, Qian was at the top of the PRC's list. He returned to China, where he founded the national missile program. The loss of Qian stands as the most potent example of American mishandling of skilled and experienced Chinese.[60]

Despite such incentives to liberalize U.S. immigration laws, through 1965 conditions shifted only moderately in response to the changed international landscape and domestic pressures, reflecting the entrenched power of restrictionist conservatives in Congress. As mentioned earlier, the Displaced Persons Act enabled more than three thousand resident refugee Chinese to regularize their status. In 1952 Congress passed a new general immigration law that retained the discriminatory national origins quota system despite Truman's presidential veto. The McCarran-Walter Act, at the urging of Walter Judd, introduced significant, albeit largely symbolic, acknowledgments of Asian entry rights such as granting quotas to Asian countries, permitting nonquota immigration by close relatives, and removing the racial bar on naturalization. Ethnic Asians faced tiny quotas—China's was 105—and an absolute cap of 2,000 on the Asian-Pacific Triangle tracked Asians by race in order to severely limit Asian immigration overall. The McCarran-Walter Act emphasized economic priorities with at least 50 percent of each nation's quota reserved for first-preference applicants defined as persons with special skills needed in the United States, such as "college professors, chemists, meteorologists, physicians and surgeons, dentists, nurses, veterinarians, engineers, tool designers, and draftsmen," although Chinese chefs could qualify for this category. Under these highly constricted conditions, employers gained the authority to petition on behalf of first-preference Chinese nonimmigrant-status employees to gain permanent residency.[61] Other measures benefited Chinese refugees, with one provision allowing deportable aliens resident before June 26, 1950, to apply for stays of deportation through December 24, 1957, enabling those with temporary visas such as Chinese students to extend their stays.[62]

Gaining permission to remain in the United States, even as first-preference applicants, still pitted Chinese against the tiny, "hopelessly oversubscribed" immigration quota.[63] Chinese adjusting their status under the Displaced Persons Act became chargeable to the quotas set in 1952.[64] By 1957 this quota was mortgaged until 2036. Unaware of the highly constricted availability of quota slots, many nonimmigrant Chinese applied to change their status to permanent resident, were denied, and thus became liable for deportation. Procedural changes did, however, allow "qualified first-preference immigrants to remain in the United States while awaiting their quota numbers," most of whom were working at large corporations or at colleges and universities.[65]

Such problems underscored the incapacity of the McCarran-Walter Act to permit resettlement by educated and skilled people seeking employment in the United States but also revealed a growing institutional will and adaptability to find ways for such useful individuals to make America their home. Cold War politics, and the fear that capable scientists and technicians might fall into the communist camp, also motivated such accommodations. As will be discussed at greater length in chapters 6 and 7, successive presidents from Truman to Johnson used refugee legislation to demonstrate the shortcomings of the McCarran-Walter Act and press for liberalization of immigration law.[66] While the Refugee Relief Act of 1953 (RRA) would allocate two thousand visas for the admission of Chinese and three thousand for Far Eastern refugees, it would also enable several thousand Chinese residing in the United States on or before August 7, 1953, to become eligible for adjustment of status to permanent residence and citizenship.[67] Despite such stopgap measures and irregular routes to citizenship, many Chinese students and their stateless compatriots faced the quandary of having only temporary permission to remain in the United States legally.

These legal and economic shifts did not completely ameliorate decades of anti-Chinese discrimination. Despite the celebrated successes of Chinese such as Li Zhengdao, Yang Zhenning, and I. M. Pei, many highly educated Chinese found themselves confined to the same service industries constraining their less educated, Cantonese co-ethnics, as observed by sociologist Rose Hum Lee: "Many of the stranded were forced through circumstances to accept employment with Chinese employers as waiters, kitchen helpers, cooks, clerks, etc. Others have engaged in the same kinds of enterprises the sojourners operated: restaurants, curio shops, chop suey supplies, truck farming, poultry raising, and so on."[68] Even as the percentages of Chinese employed as professionals and technicians rose from 1940 to 1970, Chinese also remained overrepresented in service work, at 19.6 percent in 1970.[69]

Even the most prominent of "stranded scholars" experienced discrimination. Yang Zhenning held a prominent faculty position at Princeton's Institute for Advanced Study but harbored such significant doubts about the United States that he delayed naturalizing until 1964, despite having spent most of his adult life in America. He still felt considerable pride in his Chinese ancestry and was reluctant to relinquish ties to the country where his father still resided, and he was keenly aware of American hostilities to Chinese. "I learned, as time went on, that the early history of Chinese in the United States, *our* history, was drenched in unspeakable prejudice, persecution and massacres." Yang cited the various Chinese exclusion acts and how they had "reduced the Chinese community in the United States to a warped, isolated, and despised pool of exploited bachelor laborers, which it still was when I came to the States in 1945." Despite his educational credentials and high status, Yang personally experienced discrimination. In 1954 a housing developer refused to sell him and his wife a house on the grounds that their race might affect his overall sales. Yang consulted a lawyer, who advised that the case had little chance of success in court. Yang required another decade to come to terms with the place of Chinese in America, but during the optimistic years of the Kennedy administration, he finally decided to become a U.S. citizen with the understanding that "I knew that America had been most generous to me. I had come very well equipped, but America had allowed me the opportunity to develop my potential. I knew there was no country in the world that was as generous to immigrants."[70] Yang understood the trade-offs in becoming an American: his considerable individual capacities put him in a position to gain citizenship and the optimal research conditions offered by American capitalism despite the keenly felt imperfections of its democracy. His educational and professional attainments had not shielded him from the kinds of harassments and obstacles besetting less fortunate Chinese, and he well understood the challenges that all Chinese, be they world-renowned scientists or obscure laundry workers, confronted in making lives in America.

Yang Zhenning's experiences notwithstanding, World War II and the Cold War significantly changed ideological and institutional practices of immigration and citizenship affecting Chinese, with broader consequences. As feared by its opponents, repeal of the exclusion laws did indeed open doors to a widening array of immigrants, with more Asian allies, Filipinos, and Indians gaining naturalization rights and immigration quotas in 1946. The United States also found itself obliged to do something about the hundreds of thousands of refugees left homeless and stateless by the war and its reconfiguring of national boundaries and alliances. Through war, politics and pragmatism came to trump race as criteria for who should be considered good candidates for U.S. citizenship. As refugees, Chinese students, intellectuals, and government representatives became even more compelling candidates, not only because of American sympathies for their wartime allies, educational attainments, and ready employability, but also because of their shared political causes and capacities to contribute to America's Cold War efforts against communism. Such considerations facilitated the transformation of student visitors into refugee settlers and citizens, although legal conditions restricted the numbers who could make this transition. In 1956 the Committee on Educational Interchange Policy issued a report assessing congressional aid to Chinese students and described this shift in goals: "In retrospect, certainly, both humanitarian and national interests were well served by our national policy towards Chinese students in the United States in the difficult years from 1948 to 1955." The students had earned their degrees and many had become self-supporting, but the following problems remained: finding "satisfactory employment"; "the almost insoluble task of bringing their families from China"; and above all, "a satisfactory adjustment of their immigration status is a paramount preoccupation." During the 1950s solutions were available but highly limited because of the tiny immigrant quotas for Chinese.

For some it may be possible to shift to permanent residence status under provisions of the Refugee Relief Act of 1953; others, by marriage to Americans or by private legislation, may achieve a preferential status as quota immigrants. . . . [However,] unless Congress enacts further legislation . . . [many] may find themselves in a sort of legal limbo for years, technically subject to deportation because their student visas have long since expired, but, as long as China remains Communist, never to be forced to return.[71]

This growing receptivity to Chinese immigrants, selected on the basis of individual capacities for self-support, political correctness, and economic contributions rather than race and national origins, would frame the minor shifts in immigration law and procedures enacted in the decade that followed, leading up to the 1965 Hart-Celler Act, in support of new global realities and America's international ambitions. Much of these struggles played out across the largely new terrain of refugee aid and relief.

CHAPTER 6

"The Best Type of Chinese"

AID REFUGEE CHINESE INTELLECTUALS AND
SYMBOLIC REFUGEE RELIEF,
1952–1960

THE MARCH 5, 1956, ISSUE OF *LIFE* MAGAZINE devoted nine pages to the seven-year Romeo and Juliet saga of Chinese lovers kept apart, not by feuding families but by the inhumanity and irrationality of America's immigration laws. "The Agonizing Odyssey of Two People in Love" movingly recounted the tortured romance of P. C. and Grace Li and their protracted, international quest to reunite, complete with lavish photographs of the loving couple both together and apart. Their separation began in 1948, when Li left their home in Shanghai for what was intended to be a two-year master's degree program at Columbia University. Their plans derailed when the Communist victory forced Grace to flee to Hong Kong. Although, with her bilingual abilities, she quickly found a job, her husband was unable to join her after finishing his MA program because he had never been a legal resident of the British colony. Nor could Grace obtain a visa to visit him in the United States because the American consulate assumed, correctly, that once admitted she would stay. The Lis began seeking alternatives, including applying for a student visa for Grace to attend Columbia. Each visa application required a raft of paperwork and tense interviews, with the American consulate taking months to decide each case. In the meanwhile, the Lis grew desperate. Learning that it was easier to obtain visas to visit Europe, where she hoped it might be more feasible to gain legal admission to the United States, Grace journeyed on her own to London, Paris, and Amsterdam and in each city applied in turn for permission to enter America. Consular processes for each application again took months. While in Europe, Grace finally learned that the student visa she had sought in Hong Kong had been denied. Meanwhile her husband had begun a PhD program that allowed him to remain in the United States despite being a stateless alien. Eventually both the London and Paris consulates turned down Grace's visa applications after noting her husband's residency in New York.

This adversity forced Grace to take another desperate step. She applied for a visitor's visa to Canada in order to at least be on the same continent as her husband. When asked, however, she lied and stated that he was in Hong Kong, knowing that the truth would lead to another denial. She arrived in Montreal late in 1953, bringing the couple a mere 325 miles apart. Li boarded a train and the two managed a scant two-week interlude together. Their next effort to meet, however, ran afoul of Canadian immigration authorities, who picked up Li with the warning that his alien status did not guarantee his right to return to the United States, a requirement for visiting Canada. Once again, national sovereignties and lack of legal standing kept the pair senselessly apart, and Li returned to New York alone.

The Refugee Relief Act of 1953 provided measures for their reunification. Stateless residents such as Li could apply for permanent resident status, and several thousand refugee visas became available to ethnic Chinese. Grace quickly applied for one of the latter and fulfilled the arduous requirements of having a clear political history, a documented record of flight from communism, a U.S. citizen sponsor who would guarantee she would not become a public charge, and prearranged employment in the United States. By the time she had completed all these procedures, it was 1956 and Grace Li lacked only one piece for her application to be complete, a reentry guarantee from another government in case she was deported from the United States. *Life* magazine published its account just as the Lis had learned that the Canadian government was not willing to provide the needed assurance.[1]

The publicity and attending sympathy for the Lis pressured both the legislative and executive branches of the U.S. government to find a solution. Senator Herbert Lehman (D-NY) and Representative William McCulloch (R-OH) sponsored private bills to waive the reentry requirement in Grace's case. The Office of Refugee and Migration Affairs (ORM), which ran the Refugee Relief Program (RRP) under the directorship of Pierce J. Gerety, evaluated its options to bring a successful resolution to the case without the appearance of favoritism. The ORM's advice to Grace was to go to Taiwan, from which she held an endorsed passport, where she might apply for her reentry documents. Amid concerns that this plan would take too much time and that available visas were running out, the Costa Rican ambassador to Canada chivalrously offered his government's services in providing the guarantee, if Grace were to go there to apply.[2] After almost a decade of solitary journeys through Hong Kong, England, France, Holland, and Canada, Grace Li traveled to Costa Rica, where she was finally able to complete the paperwork needed to reunite with her husband. On June 18, 1956, she boarded a plane in San Jose bound for New York, having finally fulfilled the many legal requirements needed to join P. C. Li in America.[3]

The P. C. and Grace Li story illustrates the humanizing of Chinese immigrants that occurred during the 1950s, not only in compassionate media accounts but also in legislative and bureaucratic processes that sought to facilitate the immigration of selected, sympathetic, employable refugees whose moving stories and meaningful lives in the United States furthered foreign policy agendas in Asia while pressing the need for immigration reform in America. The Lis' moving tale captured the confluence of desperation, exile, politicized exigencies, and migration opportunities that befell Chinese with the establishment of the PRC and the new sense of responsibility on the part of Americans to provide aid. Although a deeply submerged subtext of the Lis' story, the Cold War divide and competition for the loyalties of foreign allies compelled significant transitions in the positioning of Chinese as welcome and sympathetic immigrants to America, U.S. humanitarian responsibilities to fellow anticommunist peoples, and the production of propaganda seeking to enhance American influence abroad.[4]

A tale such as the Lis' required careful management because a happy ending could demonstrate America's commitment to friends in Asia along with the racial democracy within its borders, whereas prolongation of an unhappy separation underscored the inequities and inadequacies of U.S. immigration laws and the highly limited aid allocated to Chinese refugees. This chapter explores how refugee relief programs furthered the transformation of Chinese into welcome and valued immigrants with shared political and economic values, whose limited numbers and symbolic value in the war on communism enabled not only the warm reception of readily assimilable, educated new immigrants but also redemption for resident Chinese Americans. The growing understanding that Chinese would never arrive in such numbers so as to constitute a tidal wave of "coolie" invaders helped dissipate yellow peril fears and motivated programs to normalize even the beneficiaries of the "paper son" system of immigration fraud.

Refugee policy operated in contradiction to the restrictive and racially discriminatory quotas imposed by the McCarran-Walter Act (1952) and the Johnson-Reed Act (1924).[5] The practice of allocating differential quotas based on national origins—a thin mask for racial preferences—proved a constant aggravation and barrier to post–World War II efforts to build alliances with recently emerging African and Asian nations whose minimal quotas underscored their lack of welcome in the United States. Through refugee admissions and soft diplomacy programs featuring cultural tours, exchanges of experts, and the recruiting of international students, the State Department deployed mobility and exchanges as a means of fostering American friendships with newly strategic global partners. These measures worked not only to increase nonquota immigration by allies restricted by minimal quotas but also to demonstrate that admitting more Asians, albeit in symbolic numbers, would not significantly affect America's demographic and cultural core. They also showed that immigration laws could be calibrated to select for the most valuable and sympathetic kinds of immigrants of color to enter the United States. Admitting an attractive, employable couple such as the Lis presented America in a good light while adding to its store of well-educated, readily assimilated ethnic professionals. Of such racially marked Americans, Christina Klein commented, "Although they are not exclusively foreign, their partial foreignness makes them worth assimilating into American society, because it legitimates the nation's claim to be a 'nation of nations.'"[6]

Between 1944 and 1960 the cumulative numbers of Chinese entering under nonquota statuses constituted a significant rebuke to the inequitable quota system, which had first been implemented in 1921 and applied to Chinese in a slight improvement over the Chinese exclusion laws with the repeal of 1943. Although Chinese gained rights to citizenship by naturalization, the immigration quota was but a token gesture toward equal standing, a status affirmed in the controversially limited overhaul enacted with the McCarran-Walter Act. From 1944 until 1960, 8,781 Chinese were quota admissions while 23,433 were nonquota. Of the nonquota admissions, the biggest group were wives of U.S. citizens at 16,985; 6,862 came under the 1953 Refugee Relief Act; 3,514 through the 1957 refugee law; and 1,492 arrived as "Other classes."[7] That such greater numbers came under nonquota statuses illustrated the inadequacy of the existing system, a problem underscored by the hodge-podge of refugee legislation used to admit Chinese on an ad hoc basis.

Refugee admissions of Chinese became a means of advancing U.S. diplomatic agendas in East and Southeast Asia, applying pressure for immigration reforms, and opportunities to demonstrate the limited consequences of removing race-based discriminations from immigration controls if enacted to restrict numbers while selecting for preferred categories. Even as the Eisenhower and Kennedy administrations pressed for such reforms on the basis of humanitarian and political exigencies, they also entwined economic considerations to select for the most useful and productive Chinese to be among the only somewhat less limited numbers granted refugee status into the United States.

Across the 1950s, Chinese gained growing rights of entry and permanent settlement through claims on refugee status conferred with the sharing of American political values and causes that nonetheless limited the numbers of those who could enter to a few thousands, burdened by additional constraints intended to minimize their economic and demographic impact through requirements that each refugee have sponsors and pre-arranged employment, in addition to bearing their own costs of travel. As demonstrated through the activities of the State Department and Central Intelligence Agency (CIA)-funded refugee relief organization, Aid Refugee Chinese Intellectuals, Inc. (ARCI), these strategic admissions addressed several agendas, perhaps the least of which was humanitarian relief. The United States conveyed support for "free" Chinese on Taiwan and elsewhere in Southeast Asia, while rehabilitating its reputation for racist segregation and immigration laws. International outreach demanded that Chinese be made to feel welcome and at home in America, even if the structures for refugee aid limited their numbers and attempted to screen for their educational and economic credentials. This method of showing American acceptance of Chinese minimized their impact by narrowing the range of those admitted to those bearing the most desirable traits, a tactic that nonetheless demonstrated how immigration reforms might be enacted.

Cracking the Quota System

Even as the refugee laws provided exceptions to and a critique of the quota system, they further naturalized the use of economic criteria in selecting those receiving visas. The first refugee law, the Displaced Persons Act of 1948, set aside 30 percent of its visas for agricultural workers—a measure that aimed to limit the entry of Jews—followed by preferences for "professional or highly skilled persons."[8] Although this law did not provide visas for Asian refugees, section 4 permitted displaced persons present in the United States before April 1, 1948, to adjust to permanent immigrant status. As observed by Mae Ngai, applying such selective criteria "was an important move that introduced into immigration policy the idea that American economic preferences should determine the selection of immigrants—an idea that seems in retrospect ungenerous when applied to people rendered homeless and stateless by war but which idea quickly became naturalized as an assumption of immigration policy."[9] Ngai notes that such "economic nationalism" contradicted humanitarian principles of refugee relief but helped to mitigate the opposition of restrictionists who sought to minimize the impact on the United States of immigration from non-Western parts of the world. The employment conditions featured in the allocating of visas allowed formerly unwelcome immigrants to be portrayed as contributing materially to the United States. Such considerations shaped choices facilitating the access of certain kinds of Chinese to gateways into America while fortifying gates against those thought likely to become public charges.

In spite of calls to reform immigration laws, such fears of "minority problems" and unacceptably large influxes of immigrants led Congress to resoundingly pass the McCarran-Walter Act retaining the national origins quotas, even overriding Truman's presidential veto.[10] Nonetheless, the McCarran-Walter Act made some provision for new admissions of political refugees in granting the executive branch authority to parole refugees into the United States. Admitted on a temporary basis, such parolees could gain permanent residency and citizenship only by vote of Congress. President Kennedy authorized the parole of 15,111 Chinese between 1962 and 1966, a significant influx compared to the small numbers of Chinese able to immigrate since the early

1880s but relatively low compared to the 32,000 Hungarians admitted in 1956 and the 200,000 Cubans between 1960 and 1962.[11] Moreover, almost a quarter of the Chinese parolees had professional or technical training.[12]

Although allowing slight increases in Chinese immigration, these limited measures nonetheless fueled pressures for further reforms as applications for refugee visas far outnumbered those available and the small regular quotas quickly became "hopelessly oversubscribed."[13] These limitations led to a proliferation of private bills proposed in Congress, as had been filed on behalf of Grace Li, increasing from 429 in 1945–1947 to 4,797 in 1953–1955 and 2,810 in 1955–1956, forcing Congress to vote on thousands of individual cases in the absence of a more rationally framed immigration law.[14] In a precursor to the brain-drain crisis erupting in the mid-1960s, tens of thousands of Chinese and other Asians arrived as students, particularly in engineering and the sciences, readily found employment, but faced considerable hurdles when trying to regularize their legal status (see chapter 8). Even the wealthy former minister of finance and foreign affairs, Song Ziwen (1891–1971), a Boxer Fellow, graduate of Harvard and Columbia, and brother to Madame Chiang Kai-shek, had such limited options that he contacted the State Department asking whether he could qualify for a refugee visa, having arrived as a diplomat and needing to regularize his status.[15] Such cases enabled successive presidents from Truman to Johnson and congressional reformers to use refugee legislation and programs to press for liberalization of immigration law.[16]

The ostensibly nongovernmental organization Aid Refugee Chinese Intellectuals illustrates State Department enactment of these entwined priorities. ARCI emerged in 1952 for the stated purpose of identifying and aiding educated, anticommunist Chinese refugees in Hong Kong to reestablish new lives. Despite claiming private status and humanitarian agendas, ARCI was a creature of the China Lobby that received most of its funding covertly from the Department of State and as such operated almost entirely to implement U.S. government projects. ARCI's programs thus reveal the considerable cynicism shaping American relief efforts for Chinese refugees, thereby providing the most explicit illustration of how American anticommunism during the Cold War remade the terrain of Asian immigration by emphasizing foreign policy goals and economic pragmatism in ways that repositioned Asians as model immigrants.

Aid Refugee Chinese Intellectuals, Inc.

With the end of World War II and the rapid onset of civil war in China, Hong Kong's population had increased convulsively from 600,000 in 1945 to 2.5 million in 1951.[17] Although part of this rapid growth consisted of returning residents, the great majority were newcomers in flight from the war but also from the relentless southern progress of Mao's forces. Successive waves of refugees descended on Hong Kong, numbering in the range of fifty thousand per year through 1957, imposing on the colony enormous challenges around providing adequate housing, employment, utilities such as water and electricity, and schools.[18] Although European refugees received far more attention and resources, Hong Kong bore the highest degree of pressure from the Cold War's uprooting of peoples. In 1955 the State Department estimated there were 1,700,000 escapees and refugees from communism, with 200,000 in Germany, 35,000 in Austria, 11,000 in Italy, 20,000 in Greece, 2,000 in Turkey, 740,000 in all other Western European countries, 1,000 in the Middle East, and 670,000 in Hong Kong.[19]

Racism and geopolitics complicated the provisioning of aid to Chinese refugees in Hong Kong. European refugees received the bulk of assistance from the United States and the United Nations High Commission on Refugee Relief (UNHCRR). By definition and aid provided, the Asian refugee problem barely existed in comparison. Moreover, the Nationalist/Communist divide suspended Hong Kong's refugees between competing agendas, which complicated efforts to resettle them or implement other kinds of relief measures. Although accommodating of the status quo until ready to reclaim the territory, the PRC regarded Hong Kong as falling under British rule illegitimately. The Chinese who had fled to Hong Kong were therefore not refugees as they remained on Chinese soil. Governments and other international agencies, such as the United Kingdom, that acknowledged the PRC had to respect this assertion. The British and colonial authorities feared upsetting the Chinese government by allowing the politicization of the presence of refugees in Hong Kong while the Nationalist and U.S. governments sought to use the "voting with their feet" aspect of refugee movements to embarrass and undermine the legitimacy of the PRC. They sought as well to mobilize Chinese intellectuals so that they might work toward the cause of Free China, or the remnants of Chiang Kai-shek's Nationalist government based on Taiwan.[20] Acting under constraints imposed by Hong Kong authorities, the State Department conducted refugee programs by working through established voluntary agencies such as the Church World Service, Lutheran World Federation, and National Catholic Welfare Service. Unlike the Christian organizations, which had extensive legacies of humanitarian outreach, ARCI had been created solely to address the Cold War Chinese refugee crisis, revealing Department of State and CIA priorities and manipulations in East Asia.

ARCI's operations and governance were strongly influenced by the abrupt cessation of access to the many institutions and programs Americans had established in China. In particular, missionary and educational organizations such as the YMCA, United Board of Christian Colleges in China, and China Medical Board, with their long histories of great investment in educational and medical infrastructure in China, were suddenly sundered from these programs even as the United States embargo cut off trade. The severing of official relations forced these organizations and the individuals who ran them to seek new outlets for their ambitions and resources, not always successfully. Some "China hands" became staunch advocates for the Nationalists in their exile on Taiwan and vocal critics of any move to acknowledge the legitimacy of the PRC while seeking other Asian societies in which to construct new schools and other structures conveying American influence. Many of these Nationalist sympathizers became active in organizations such as ARCI, which not only enacted State Department agendas but carried out many programs intended to aid Chiang Kai-shek. Key ARCI administrators and staff were prominent members of the China Lobby, which operated nearly simultaneously its successful Committee of One Hundred campaign which kept the PRC out of the United Nations until 1971.[21]

Recovering ARCI's origins has been like peeling away the layers of an onion in which widely publicized representations masked more deeply hidden agendas. The best-known accounts credit former medical missionary and member of the House of Representatives Walter Judd for leading a private American relief organization assisting educated Chinese refugees. This thin mask shielded the China Lobby's political efforts to restore Chiang Kai-shek to power on the mainland by directing the most elite of refugees in Hong Kong to Taiwan. The State Department's support of these programs, along with implementation of the East Asian branch of the Refugee Relief Program, obscured the CIA's fielding of an intelligence outpost in Hong Kong. At its core, ARCI was conceived by a Chinese American Nationalist operative, Ernest Moy (1894 or 1895–1958), who witnessed the Chinese refugee crisis in Hong Kong and acted in part to relieve the distress of the most educated but also to ensure that their skills and talents were put to use for anticommunist, and particularly Nationalist, causes.[22] Despite the varying agendas funneled through ARCI's programs, its backers and staffers shared convictions that the Cold War had rendered the mobility of Chinese intellectuals of critical and strategic importance.

Correspondence archived with the family papers of ARCI's Far Eastern representative, George Fitch, and his wife Geraldine reveal Moy's early warnings concerning the crisis facing educated Chinese refugees in Hong Kong and his efforts to publicize the issue and help them find stable homes and useful employment. Although he falls in and out of the historical record, we know that the American-born Moy had joined the Nationalists as a teenager during one of Sun Yatsen's campaigns in the United States. He journeyed to China in 1928 and worked in various capacities on behalf of the Nationalists, primarily in various news services and as a representative at China-related events on the East Coast during the 1930s, including China Institute in America programs. In 1946 the Chinese American journalist

Figure 6.1. Ernest Moy with Chiang Kai-shek, 1957. Moy is on the right. ARCI Collection, Box 22, Letters from Hong Kong and Taiwan, January–June 1957. Courtesy of Hoover Institution Library & Archives, Stanford University.

Flora Belle Jan described receiving help from Moy, then director of the Shanghai Headquarters of the War Area Service Corps, in arranging rent-free lodgings at a club for Allied Forces.[23] By 1950, however, Moy was in Hong Kong and personally witnessed the tripling of the city's population and the desperate plight of hundreds of thousands of barely housed, under-employed refugees. As chair of the Service Committee for the American University Club of Hong Kong, Moy had been trying unsuccessfully to find jobs for some of the educated refugees.[24]

Moy returned to the United States to work as a foreign correspondent in Washington, DC, and immediately sent a memo to the State Department dated October 10, 1950, that mapped out many of the projects that ARCI would eventually undertake. He detailed the plight of Chinese intellectuals in Hong Kong and the potential usefulness of trained, skilled Chinese to the American economy as "professionals and technically trained, English-speaking, anti-Communist Chinese" or "elsewhere where we may need people of the knowledge and skills they possess." In addition to resettle-ment, he also suggested using these displaced intellectuals to establish "a publishing center in Hong Kong" to counter the rise in communist propa-ganda and a "guerilla-aid center" for those on the mainland.[25] Finding the State Department unresponsive, Moy contacted Geraldine Fitch in March 1951, hoping to use her missionary networks to recruit support from the Committee for Free Asia. Geraldine had married into the multigenera-tional, missionary Fitch family, and her China-born husband, George, had worked for decades in American service organizations in Asia, including the YMCA and the United Nations Relief and Rehabilitation Administration. Both Fitches were fervent members of the China Lobby throughout the 1950s and 1960s, with Geraldine publishing *Formosa Beachhead* (H. Regnery, 1953), advocating for Chiang Kai-shek, and criticizing State Department policy. At this juncture Moy's project failed to spark George Fitch's interest, although Geraldine continued to correspond with Moy to offer encouragement and suggestions. For the rest of the year, Moy reported to Geraldine regarding the roster of individuals and organizations with established interests in Chi-nese affairs that he had contacted, including B. A. Garside of the American Bureau of Medical Aid for China (ABMAC), Kong Xiangxi, and the United Board of Christian Colleges in Asia. He received vague promises of assis-tance from the China Institute for resettlement efforts in the United States and from the International Rescue Committee (IRC) for setting up Hong Kong offices. Otherwise, many well-known China hands and anticommu-nist leaders, such as John Leighton Stuart, Albert C. Wedemeyer, Claire C. Chennault, and Charles Edison, turned down Moy's offers to lead "the pro-posed committee to aid refugee Chinese intellectuals."[26] Not until Novem-ber 17, 1951, was Moy able to write triumphantly to Geraldine that "Con-gressman Judd has agreed to head the relief project!"[27] With Judd on board, and then the Fitches and a cluster of close associates (Christopher Emmet,[28] Garside, Oram, Liebman), ARCI quickly became a reality and incorporated by February 1952.

Of the four key individuals associated with ARCI who published mem-oirs or biographies—Judd, Garside, Fitch, and Liebman—Marvin Liebman was the only one to write frankly about ARCI's covert activities.[29] He con-cludes in hindsight that ARCI received its operational permissions so quickly because of CIA interventions. Although its influence on ARCI functions is understandably poorly documented, the CIA provided $50,000 in seed fund-ing, channeled through the Eli Lilly and Kresge Foundations.[30] Harold Oram, who fundraised for a range of left-liberal, anticommunist CIA front organizations, probably acted as liaison, and at least two agents, Travis Fletcher and later Halleck Rose, served as staff in the Hong Kong office.[31]

Initially ARCI's core mission was to relocate some twenty-five thousand "intellectual" Chinese refugees stranded in Hong Kong and funnel them to aid Chiang Kai-shek's mission to retake the mainland. Through its special relationship with the State Department, ARCI not only received U.S. government support for its assistance to Taiwan but gained preferential consideration for the refugees that it sponsored when opportunities later arose to enter America through the Refugee Relief Program.[32] The State Department reinforced ARCI's emphasis on aiding elite Chinese with contractual language recognizing "the special need for assisting educated and experienced Chinese refugees stranded in Hong Kong to reestablish themselves in places and positions where they can once more become self-supporting and productively engaged in the specialized skills and professions for which they have been trained."[33] From the outset neither ARCI nor the Department of State intended to alleviate the suffering of the mass of refugees in Hong Kong, but only that of Chinese considered most useful to American aims.

Drawn from an incestuous collection of former missionaries and trenchant China Lobbyists, ARCI's New York executive committee reflected how the outcomes of the Chinese Civil War and the Cold War divides in Asia had warped and transformed the aspirations and objectives of educators, proselytizers, and internationalists. They remained deeply committed to abetting and shaping China's modernization into a democratic nation through its educated elite, a dream abruptly shattered with Chairman Mao Zedong's victory and entrenchment of power on the mainland. The founding of the People's Republic had permanently separated them from the considerable infrastructure of schools, hospitals, churches, and other outreach programs that they had constructed over more than a century of dedicated service. The proximity to their ultimate goal of a Christian and democratic China, as wrought through the leadership of the Methodist Generalissimo and Madame Chiang Kai-shek, and its sudden, abysmal collapse, render somewhat explicable the fanatical devotion of the China Lobby to supporting Chiang's aggrandized claims to rule China from Taiwan.

Originating in the World War II drive to procure American funds and equipment for the Nationalists, the China Lobby had received its name in 1949 from members of the New York Communist Party. On the American side, China Lobbyists included former missionaries, scholars, businessmen, and many of the key players in ARCI, such as Representative Walter Judd, publicists Harold Oram and Marvin Leibman, publisher Henry Luce, and staffers B. A. Garside and George Fitch, who worked closely with Nationalist representatives such as Song Ziwen and Kong Xiangxi through the 1950s and 1960s to ensure that Congress allocated economic and military aid to

Taiwan and prevent political recognition of the PRC. Motives of the China Lobby members ranged from genuine concern for Chiang Kai-shek to desire for a presidential election issue against Democrats in 1948 and 1952. Some members, such as George and Geraldine Fitch, genuinely believed in "the importance of a special relationship between Americans and Chinese based on missionary endeavor and Washington's turn-of-the-century open door policy of equal commercial opportunity and territorial integrity." Every China Lobbyist harbored fears of communist takeover and its impact on economic relations, converted Christians, and the struggle against the Soviet Union. China Lobbyists were willing to brand any opponents of Chiang Kai-shek as traitors to the United States. According to Nancy Bernkopf Tucker, "They toiled to make support for Chiang and loyalty to the American government synonymous; in time, they succeeded," enough to keep Nationalist Taiwan in the UN seat for China and block membership of the PRC for more than two decades.[34] The effectiveness of the China Lobby complicated Department of State agendas in East Asia in which Chiang Kai-shek was a necessary, albeit untrusted, foil for the PRC who had to be reined in from excessive military action.[35] Through 1955 ARCI's operations, and particularly the Taiwan office, remained bound to the flawed vision that Chiang could retake the mainland and that Chinese refugee intellectuals could be channeled into his struggles to do so.

ARCI convened its first executive meeting early in 1952 at its New York headquarters with an executive committee reuniting many Nationalist supporters, including Judd, Emmavail Luce and Leslie Severinghaus, Elizabeth Luce Moore, Mansfield Freeman, Oram, Garside, and George Taylor, along with several Nationalist advisers such as Taiwan foreign minister George Yeh, V. K. Wellington Koo, Meng Zhi, and Academia Sinica president Hu Shi.[36]

The executive committee's first action was to confirm Moy's account of conditions in Hong Kong by sending Father Frederick A. MacGuire, head of the Department of Foreign Missions of the National Catholic Welfare Conference, and James Ivy, then associate director of the Committee for a Free Asia, another CIA-backed organization, to survey the situation.[37] Drawing on their report, the first ARCI board mapped out the organization's goals, strategies, and structure but drew largely on Moy's ideas for strategic resettlement of useful refugees, a language institute to produce propaganda materials, and higher educational facilities. ARCI mounted a fundraising campaign, established offices in Hong Kong and Taiwan with local advisory boards, and recruited an Educators Advisory Committee consisting of college and university presidents. In this tripartite organization, the executive board in New York set overall policy, raised funds, and publicized ARCI's cause; the Hong Kong office registered Chinese intellectuals and their families, developed programs to provide residential and employment help, and processed paperwork for migration abroad as opportunities arose; while the Taiwan office made arrangements to resettle refugees in Taiwan by lining up jobs and accommodations and negotiating with the Nationalist government for the documentation and security clearances needed to bring ARCI's registrants to Taiwan or elsewhere. Despite Moy's initial founding role, Judd, Oram, and Executive Director Garside made key operational decisions and coordinated with State Department authorities in Washington, DC.

ARCI's fundraising strategies mirrored State Department efforts to mask political agendas under the guise of humanitarian concern and identification with Chinese and their plight in Hong Kong. ARCI's campaign drew on established views of educated Chinese as sympathetic and commensurate with Americans in making its appeals to a general public. This campaign launched with a lavish gala dinner at the Plaza Hotel in New York on April 28, 1952. Oram recruited support from "the leading scholars, educators and intellectuals of this country" along with "leading . . . businessmen, churchmen, writers, scientists, technicians, governmental leaders, heads of other China aid organizations" to produce "a guest list of high enough prestige to fully impress the press, the public, and our potential source of funds, with the importance and urgency of our program."[38] ARCI's promotional materials celebrated the bonds shared by all free, educated peoples, declaring that "the mind of man is the essence of our common humanity, free men must stand together against Communist tyranny which limits freedom of thought and inquiry and starves and crushes the mind."[39] Although a key target of the campaign, the immigrant genius Albert Einstein, did *not* sign on, the evening brought together other celebrity intellects such as Arthur Schlesinger Sr. and Arthur Scheslinger Jr., Robert Oppenheimer, Thornton Wilder, ten Nobel Prize winners, Carl Jung, Walter Gropius, Bertrand Russell, and John Dos Passos.[40] The evening featured speeches by Walter Judd and the former assistant secretary of state for Far Eastern affairs and current head of the Rockefeller Foundation, Dean Rusk, whom Oram directed to emphasize the "solidarity that exists between all men of good-will regardless of their language, color, or location" and to celebrate the "inherent pledge of the intellectuals of the Free World standing together against all the foes of Freedom."[41] Rusk's speech stressed the benefits of saving Chinese. "We are compelled by self-interest not to lose their contribution to the intellectual life of the world community, for none would be a greater loser than we ourselves." Many of ARCI's future publicity campaigns featured this list of "sponsorship of the highest character," which appeared in full-page ads in the *New York Times* and the *Washington Post* alongside evocations of destitute yet heroically freedom-loving Chinese: "Save one Chinese family from slowly starving to death in Hong Kong"; "Your gift of $350 will save one Chinese for freedom"; "Send $350 to enable the resettlement of one family—family group which thought enough of freedom to hazard the agony of exile rather that bow to Communism."[42] ARCI managed to raise about $250,000 of its $1 million goal from foundations, private donors, and some government grants. The year 1953 would, however, prove to be the high point of its fundraising efforts, and ARCI soon become chiefly dependent on covert funding from the Department of State.[43]

Throughout its existence, ARCI would remain attentive to cultivating publicity for its refugee relief efforts in fulfillment of State Department goals to advertise American support of politically sympathetic Chinese while obscuring the staunchness of its ties to Chiang Kai-shek's Nationalist administration and the limited nature of assistance proffered. The magnitude of Hong Kong's refugee problem dwarfed not only American desire to help Chinese but also the limited willingness to provide them with new homes in the United States. Hong Kong would be left largely to cope on its own, managing to channel the drive and energy of its new residents into the economic miracle that took off in the 1970s, for most other countries, including Taiwan, were also hostile to additional Chinese settlement that might include some communist agents. International humanitarian pressures elevated the cause of refugees alongside potent critiques of America's racial segregation, forcing the United States to demonstrate concretely its commitment to human rights and racial equality. Chinese refugee relief projects served both purposes, even when enacted as symbolic gestures during the 1950s and 1960s. Nonetheless, up to thirty-two thousand refugees were able to immigrate, accompanied by flurries of positive publicity that facilitated the breakdown of the exclusionary regimes that had once sharply delimited the American possibilities available to Chinese.

Cold War Inhospitality

Despite its claims of humanitarian relief and long-standing concerns for Chinese, ARCI's leadership had never intended to address the full scope of the refugee crisis in Hong Kong. ARCI's executive director, B. A. Garside, summarized the organization's chief objective: "to save, for future service to China, a few thousand of the key Chinese intellectuals stranded in Hong Kong." The executive committee hoped to accomplish this end by moving most of its registrants to Taiwan while helping a few to establish themselves in Hong Kong or elsewhere. ARCI never aimed "to provide relief for the much larger number of Chinese in Hongkong who have had a little junior college training, but did not fall within the category of present or potential leaders."[44] The narrow scope of this agenda reveals both ARCI's and the State Department's disregard for the suffering of the bulk of Chinese refugees but reflects continuities with old habits of privileging Chinese students and intellectuals as the most likely to wield national influence. Almost immediately, however, ARCI's mission foundered against the impossibility of identifying "future leaders" by advertising for refugees to register themselves and overcoming the complexities of constraints on international migration, even to locate them in Taiwan to work on behalf of the Nationalists much less other parts of the world historically hostile to Chinese immigration.

Many legal challenges barred efforts to resettle Chinese refugees from Hong Kong as demonstrated by the Grace Li case. Refugees needed passports and other forms of documentation that governments were reluctant to provide. Refugees also needed to find countries willing to accept them. Taiwan seemed the most likely option but was willing to receive only limited numbers of even educated refugees, fearing infiltration by communist spies and additional pressure on the island's poorly developed economy. Many Southeast Asian countries and the white settler nations of Canada, the United States, and Australia were hostile to settlement by Chinese, and the last three had legally restricted their immigration. International agencies seeking to aid refugees in Hong Kong had to contend with the limitations imposed by colonial authorities fearful that local relief efforts or overtly anticommunist efforts might anger the PRC.[45] Despite these multiple obstructions and challenges, ARCI attempted to implement its political plan, with results that perhaps predictably fell short of its original vision.

From the outset ARCI's Hong Kong office registered too many refugees whose leadership potential was hardly predictable. The office had been established in March 1952, and its first act was to issue a call inviting Chinese intellectuals to register for resettlement aid. By only requiring two years of college or its equivalent, this initial enrollment produced a roster of about twenty-five thousand registrants who together with dependents totaled around seventy thousand refugees that ARCI committed itself to resettle or assist. George Fitch, who supervised both the Hong Kong and Taiwan offices, was left to bemoan the "vast flood of refugees whom we could never hope to assist."[46]

In internal documents ARCI's leadership and staff were explicit in their emphasis on aiding educated Chinese while dismissing their working-class counterparts. In a letter to Garside in 1956, Fitch expressed frustrations that so many ARCI registrants had been turned down by the FBI and Taiwan's Ministry of National Defense for visas and passports as security risks. "It is exasperating in the extreme.... On the other hand hundreds of coolies have been passed through simply because they have relatives over in the States."[47] Garside echoed Fitch's views, stating bluntly that "students are more desirable than cooks, waiters and truck gardeners" as recipients of aid from ARCI.[48] Moreover, ARCI aimed chiefly to channel selected registrants to Taiwan in support of Chiang Kai-shek's campaign to retake the mainland, as summarized by Garside: "I think it fair to say that most people here have been thinking of Taiwan as the principle point of resettlement of Hong Kong refugee intellectuals. The whole basis of our plea to the American people is that these people must be saved for service to Free China."[49] To this end, ARCI emphasized close, almost sycophantic cooperation with the Nationalists, a priority made clear in the selection of George Fitch as the Far Eastern representative. Hired in September 1952, Fitch had retired after many decades of service with the YMCA in China and Korea and several years at the United Nations Refugee Relief Association. The Fitches were personal friends of the Generalissimo and Madame Chiang Kai-shek, with the latter having attended Wellesley with Geraldine.[50] Fitch was tasked with a delicate balancing act, for "he had to be able to maintain good relations with three governments out there, that of China, of Hong Kong, and agencies of the United States; plus skill in not producing reprisals from Communist forces; and at the same time have the work coordinated with the ARCI Board in New York, Washington and a few other cities."[51] Fitch possessed unassailable political credentials, at least from the Nationalist perspective, and had established working relationships with many other Nationalist officials, such as Vice Minister T. H. Zheng, who would chair the Leadership Project; new staff member C. C. Zheng, who had formerly worked as comptroller of the Ministry of Education and as a professor of economics and banking at the University of Taiwan; and Dr. Han Liwu, who served as chairman of the advisory board.[52] This close relationship produced programs that sought to directly channel ARCI registrants for service to the Taiwan government.

ARCI's New York leadership and Taiwan staff remained enamored of the Nationalists even though ARCI objectives were so often blocked by the very government they were trying to assist. Resettlement required extensive cooperation from various Nationalist government agencies, which often prioritized local matters of security and economic constraints over ARCI's attempts to resettle useful refugees in Taiwan to support them. ARCI could not relocate refugees without passports issued by the Taiwanese government, a process requiring approval from the Security Bureau, which initially required Chinese refugees to apply in person for passports in Taiwan and whose security checks moved slowly, only to reject many. After constant negotiation and consultation with Nationalist authorities, the first ARCI registrant arrived in Taiwan only in November 1952, after a delay of several months, and resettlement remained disappointingly slow for the duration of ARCI's active existence.[53] As observed by ARCI executive committee member George Taylor in May 1952, Chiang Kai-shek "still has the view that the intellectuals are dangerous people and should be controlled in thought and deed, but he sees some of the big political issues involved in taking the initiative away from the Communists and he has his eye on the technicians and industrialists."[54] Fitch lamented in December 1952 that "everyone with whom I have talked, from the G'imo on down, has shown nothing but favorable interest and a desire to be helpful, but the fact is that it is still just as difficult to bring in anyone from Hongkong as it was six months or a year ago."

The Nationalists were also reluctant to accept more educated refugees into an economy with a shortage of white-collar and professional jobs and housing as well as relatively low pay scales. As will be discussed in chapter 8, the Taiwanese government encouraged college-educated youth to go abroad for graduate study. Registrants frequently resisted moving to Taiwan because the Hong Kong staff often could not provide them with specific guarantees regarding employment, locations, salary amounts, and accommodations.[55] Despite their dire circumstances, the most able of ARCI's registrants frequently found other options for themselves, as Fitch noted with some disappointment that "there is a larger proportion of the class of people whom we most desire, who have either managed to gain a livelihood in Hongkong and prefer staying there to accepting the very low pay and uncertainties of life in Taiwan, even though their positions in Hongkong may not bring them an adequate income."[56] Unexpectedly, refugees had their own preferences, and agency, in shaping their future options.

ARCI's two most effective resettlement programs, the so-called "440 Specials" and the Leadership Training Project, funneled several hundred registrants prescreened for political orientation and security purposes directly into training programs and employment in the Nationalist military and public administration offices, all at considerable expense to ARCI, or the State Department. ARCI built dormitories, a dining hall, toilets, kitchens, and a library for these programs, as well as paying the Nationalist government $65 each per year for food and incidental costs.[57] A British colleague in the Hong Kong office, Ernest Nash, complained openly that such measures did not constitute relief when the ARCI New York board had refused to fund other local measures, such as a proposal to provide capital for the startup of small businesses or small-scale factories.[58] Nash correctly pointed out that ARCI's programs fueled local perceptions that it was an "anti-Communist organization" which should "quickly be outlawed by the Hong-kong authorities." ARCI did not employ Nash more than a year, although Fitch remained.[59]

As the limits of resettlement in Taiwan became clear, ARCI sought alternative destinations elsewhere in Asia and South America, possibilities lamented by Fitch. "If they are sent to Timor or Southeast Asia, it would undoubtedly be a fine humanitarian service; but most of such intellectuals would probably never be available again to serve the cause of Free China, either in Taiwan or on the China Mainland."[60] ARCI remained bound to help those it had registered, even when new homes were not readily available. Ultimately ARCI did not pursue the Timor plan and assisted over fourteen thousand registrants and their families to resettle in Taiwan. Only about three thousand of these were direct beneficiaries of ARCI's strenuous efforts to match registrants to jobs and gain clearances from the Security Bureau. The other eleven thousand found their own way, managing with the help of relatives and friends to find employment, homes, and the necessary documents, but still turned to ARCI for travel funds and resettlement expenses. Most of the rest made homes in Hong Kong or resettled in the United States even as the Department of State more fully co-opted ARCI operations to its own ends of enacting the Refugee Relief Program to admit symbolically potent but numerically low numbers of Chinese refugees into the United States.

The Domestic Face of Refugee Relief

Fast on the heels of the McCarran-Walter Act, the Eisenhower administration and congressional immigration reformers moved to pass the Refugee Relief Act of 1953 as a temporary measure to widen America's immigration gates. The RRA allocated 214,000 nonquota refugee visas, chiefly designated for Europeans including 2,000 for Chinese and 3,000 for Far Eastern refugees, again at the insistence of Congressman Judd, who pointed to the need for America to cultivate better ties in Asia by acknowledging its share of the global refugee crisis. The RRA addressed opponents' concerns about economic competition and security by requiring extensive political and economic vetting of applicants, who had to demonstrate their opposition to communism, prearranged employment in the United States, sponsorship by a U.S. citizen willing to provide assurances that they would not become public charges, and reentry guarantees from their place of residence in case of deportation from the United States. The law prioritized "Persons whose services or skills are needed in the United States," and the parents, spouses, and minor children of U.S. citizens.[61]

As demonstrated by Grace Li's experiences, such extensive requirements—framed to protect U.S. domestic interests—severely complicated the enactment of the RRA and undermined the image of humanitarian aid to refugees it was meant to convey even if, several years after lawful arrival and residency, refugees could then apply for citizenship. America's version of refugee resettlement sought to minimize providing for their well-being once in the United States. Nonetheless, this law enabled several thousand Chinese already residing in the country on or before August 7, 1953, such as Grace's husband P. C. Li, to adjust to the status of permanent residents. In addition, 2,777 Chinese refugees gained entry for the first time.[62]

Congressman Judd's concerted championing of China as critical to American foreign policy reverberated with State Department views of the region, particularly concerning the loyalties and actions of overseas Chinese. In early 1954 Hong Kong public affairs officer Arthur Hummel authored a secret memo titled "Overseas Chinese." He estimated that there were ten million overseas Chinese, twelve million including residents of Hong Kong.

"Their importance is disproportionately great . . . because of their ethnic solidarity and their heavy concentration in skilled crafts and commerce. Although this minority group is not organized and is for the most part essentially apolitical, it continues to regard mainland China as its 'homeland' and, upon occasion, has responded to political developments in China." Hummel outlined U.S. objectives as minimizing the influence of the PRC first by encouraging assimilation of overseas Chinese in their countries of residence. Another measure involved pressing the Nationalists "to establish closer contact with the Chinese communities outside mainland China and Formosa, and to take steps to win their sympathy and their support" even though "the objectives of the U.S. Government and that of the Government of China vis-à-vis the overseas Chinese are not completely identical."[63] This struggle to channel the loyalties of overseas Chinese was waged in part through the enacting and publicizing of U.S. relief efforts for refugees. Judd noted disapprovingly that some of the Far East refugee visas had been issued to Japanese, who "were not originally intended to be beneficiaries of the Act" because the stakes for Asian refugee relief had been to cultivate connections to overseas Chinese.[64]

A total of about 2,500 ARCI registrants would resettle in the United States under refugee relief measures undertaken in 1953, 1957, and 1962. Although far fewer in numbers than the approximately 14,000 that went to Taiwan, their impact in the United States was much greater. The domestic settlement of Chinese refugees helped to demonstrate that limited liberalizations of immigration law could improve foreign relations while minimally affecting the demographic composition and economic competitiveness of the United States, in part through propaganda emphasizing the contributions and ready integration of refugees chosen for their skills and educational background. The State Department's United States Information Agency magnified such claims through publicity campaigns that conveyed both U.S. sympathies for Chinese abroad and reassurance to Americans that these new influxes of Chinese strengthened the United States, having been vetted for their political beliefs, work ethic, economic contributions, and family stability.[65]

Refugee admissions of Chinese functioned in distinct contrast to the deviance and fraud associated with the working-class, single men of the Chinese exclusion era who had been defined by race and by law as outsiders to the United States. Unlike the pervasive antagonism and policing of "paperson" passport applicants, the public relations aspects of the refugee program required that the United States appear sincere in its efforts to aid refugees by applying liberal definitions of the Refugee Relief Act's terms, exhausting all the allocated visas, and ensuring ready integration of the refugees once admitted. As educated and relatively Westernized Chinese, ARCI's registrants seemed more likely to fulfill these agendas. ARCI's Hong Kong and

Taiwan offices were readily turned to implementing the Refugee Relief Program, despite Fitch's grumbling that registrants brought at so much cost and effort to Taiwan were being encouraged to leave. As will be discussed at greater length in chapter 7, coordinated publicity campaigns accompanied America's programs for refugee relief, promoting the image of deserving Chinese families fleeing to freedom, whose economic capacities and shared political orientations vanquished outmoded beliefs that racial differences determined fitness for American citizenship.

Unlike ARCI's board and staff, the State Department easily relinquished the troubled program of resettling ARCI intellectuals in Taiwan to direct them to the United States.[66] Apart from a few dogged Nationalist supporters such as the diplomats Everett Drumright and Karl Rankin, other State Department officers, U.S. presidents, and the National Security Council were but reluctant allies of Chiang Kai-shek, concerned more about restraining him from attacking the mainland even as they sought to build the prestige of Free China on Taiwan. The educated and skilled Chinese thought so useful in Taiwan could make equally great contributions to the economy of the United States. With this pragmatic understanding, the State Department pursued the foreign relations goodwill that would emanate from allowing symbolic numbers of such Chinese to enter the United States.[67] The Refugee Relief Program turned ARCI into even more a creature of State Department prerogatives with the hiring of new staff to implement the complicated visa application procedures—which required interviews, processing paperwork, and arranging passports, sponsors, reentry permits, and employment in the United States. When the Taiwan office shut down altogether in mid-1956, the weight of ARCI's operations shifted completely to Hong Kong and almost entirely served State Department agendas.

Travis Fletcher was the CIA's man in Hong Kong, ostensibly hired to handle the complex paperwork, documentation, and personal narratives required by U.S. consular officials deciding whether applicants were qualified for refugee visas.[68] To simply qualify, applicants had to document a two-year history of political activities and travels, a sponsor in the United States, employment, and reentry guarantees. Those fulfilling these requirements still had to stand in line for the few thousand visas allocated to East Asians. The Hong Kong consulate ended up approving several thousand more applicants than there were available visas, leaving on the books compelling cases for further allocations of aid and entry visas. In fulfillment of these responsibilities, ARCI gave Fletcher ideal cover to interrogate recent arrivals about conditions on the mainland and to recruit possible agents for activities in Southeast Asia.[69] Frederick LeClerq served as director of resettlement services in New York and managed the American end of the Refugee Relief Program by tracking down employers and sponsors for ARCI applicants. Staff at the Taiwan office cooperated reluctantly and inefficiently, preoccupied with the failure of their mission to aid the Nationalists and the contradiction of redirecting registrants resettled with such difficulty in Taiwan to the United States.[70]

The Imperatives of Refugee Relief

Despite support from the White House, many congressional representatives, and a broad swathe of Americans sympathetic to the plight of refugees whose relatives and friends were otherwise denied entry by the quota system, the Refugee Relief Program got off to a rocky start. Immigration restrictionists, claiming security concerns, insisted on the appointment of Scott McLeod to run the program. Under his leadership, visa approvals trickled out, hampered by the slow development of procedures and paperwork and close screening of political sympathies and qualifications for refugee status. In Hong Kong, for example, the American Consulate did not receive clear instructions for processing visa applications until mid-1954, a year after the law had passed. Press criticisms and constituent protests fueled administration concerns about a public relations fiasco if the full allotment of refugee visas were not distributed before the program expired in December 1956. In June 1955 Pierce J. Gerety was appointed deputy administrator of the Bureau of Security and Consular Affairs to run the program.[71] Although McLeod remained director in name, Gerety assumed administrative responsibility for the program, and the rate of visa acceptances accelerated.[72]

These politics delayed the issuing of visas in Hong Kong, where the consulate lacked guidance regarding the proper procedures and paperwork. Obstacles particular to Chinese included the requirement that applicants hold reentry permits in case of deportation from the United States. The Taiwan government was reluctant to provide these, forcing ARCI staff to negotiate with London so that the Hong Kong colonial authorities would provide them instead.[73] This hurdle cleared in August 1954 so that ARCI could proceed. Nonetheless the first ARCI registrant, Dr. Patrick Lieu, a 1943 graduate of Ohio State University and former U.S. naval officer, and his family did not arrive until January 1955.[74] ARCI staffers and the State Department made the most of such publicity opportunities and ensured that a bevy of journalists waited in greeting when the Lieus landed at San Francisco on the *President Wilson* on January 7, 1955.[75]

ARCI staff and their State Department liaisons agreed that as educated intellectuals, their registrants enhanced America. As LeClerq wrote to Fletcher, "we all want to have the best type of Chinese resettling here."[76] LeClerq understood clearly that refugee relief concerned not just humanitarian outreach but selecting for those kinds of people who would advantage the United States. Early in 1956 he asserted that "one of the intentions of the Act was that the immigrant should be a real asset to this country's economy or culture."[77] Gerety, who ran the Office of Refugee and Migration Affairs, shared ARCI's goal of selecting for the "best type of Chinese," although the means to do so was not straightforward. He shared with Congressman Judd complaints by "people such as Bishop Ward of the Methodist Church that better educated and more intellectual Chinese had had difficulty in getting sponsors and were being crowded out of the benefits of the Act in some instances by Chinese being sponsored to work in laundry establishments and restaurants." Nonetheless, Gerety observed that "it would probably be impossible to write up language with respect to 'selection' such as giving preference to English-speaking Chinese or high school graduates." The main mechanism available was to give preference to "all of the agency endorsed cases," a method Judd agreed seemed the most workable.[78]

ARCI's emphasis on Chinese intellectuals was shared with the Refugee Relief Program, the Department of State, and the Central Intelligence Agency, underscoring the limited nature of American commitments to improving immigration conditions for Chinese. Walter Judd's legislative career is emblematic of this highly constrained form of friendship and humanitarian outreach, manifested in both his advocacy of greater symbolic equity for Chinese in the form of citizenship rights, immigration quotas, and refugee visa allocations alongside simultaneous support for severe numerical restrictions, racial tracking, and preferences for educated and employable individuals.[79]

ARCI provided a partial solution for privileging the admission of educated refugees. From the beginning, its registry of refugees had screened for the "better" kinds of Chinese, and ARCI applicants received greater consideration from the consulate general in Hong Kong.[80] Halleck Rose was specifically commissioned "to cut through red tape and expedite any urgent matters" on ARCI's behalf while serving as director of "Special Projects" in the Office of Refugee and Migration Affairs in Washington, DC.[81] ARCI's budget supervisors at the International Cooperation Agency (ICA) arranged "for ARCI registrants to be given preference on the ground that they would be more of an asset to this country than the average applicant."[82] Such favoritism applied even in cases of registrants applying to enter the United States as service workers due to constraints in arranging suitable jobs for educated refugees. ARCI staff attached notes to the visa office in the many cases where "the applicant is being offered a minor job, such as grocery clerk or houseworker [but was] actually a well educated person."[83]

Efforts to direct refugee visas to educated Chinese did not ensure appropriate jobs for those with higher levels of skills and attainment. In the United States LeClerq encountered many difficulties finding professional and technical jobs for the most qualified of ARCI registrants because employers were understandably reluctant to hire engineers or teachers without the chance to interview them first. LeClerq settled for unskilled and service-sector jobs to process more registrants with sanction from ARCI leaders.

> I recently discussed with Mansfield Freeman and Ernest Moy the possibility of bringing in our registrants in quite minor capacities such as waiters or food checkers in Chinese restaurants. There has been a natural reluctance on the part of employers to take on refugees "sight unseen" in the professions for which they are qualified. Our chief object therefore should be to bring them in under any category, even the lowliest; once here they would be able to find positions more suitable to their attainments.[84]

LeClerq justified service work in the belief that educated Chinese would attain upward mobility, either for themselves or by the next generation. Despite the "large number of assurances made in behalf of persons coming in as household, restaurant, and shopworkers," LeClerq noted that they "are really highly educated ... [and that] if such applicants had a fairly good education they could considerably better themselves here." He predicted that the progeny of these educated immigrants would go on to greater attainments and cited the example of one Mr. Choy, who "has two highly successful establishments in New Jersey and a son graduating from Yale this coming year and who intends to take up a medical career."[85]

ARCI's roster abounds with examples of registrants whose children became successful. For example, Evelyn Hu-Dehart's father received a degree in mathematics from Peking University and worked as a banker before ending up as a refugee in Hong Kong. There he worked as a translator for the U.S. Information Agency and registered with ARCI. In August 1959, with Rose acting as associate director, the Hu family received its visa to come to America and departed aboard a chartered Pan Am flight routed through Guam. Despite ARCI's publicity regarding the great aid and comfort afforded its registrants, apart from their entry visas, the Hu family fended for itself in America, with Evelyn's father working in a library shelving books and her mother as household maid struggling to put their three children through public schools in Palo Alto, California. ARCI's bet on the Hu family's eventual success paid off, however, with Evelyn attending Stanford University on scholarship, eventually earning a PhD degree in Latin American history from UT Austin, and becoming a professor at Brown University. Her brother studied at Princeton and became a successful Silicon Valley engineer, while her sister attended UC San Diego and the University of Michigan and ascended to become a vice president at Costco.[86] Even if they did not join the professional classes, importing educated immigrants was a successful investment that paid off as successive generations pursued schooling

Figure 6.2. Chinese refugees waiting to board a plane in Hong Kong chartered by Aid Chinese Refugee Intellectuals, Inc. (ARCI), in December 1958. To generate publicity, ARCI sought to make each departure a newsworthy event by having a large group depart on the same plane and by photographing the occasion. The banner reads "Good Luck and Happy Landings!" ARCI Collection, Box 1, "Chartered Flights." Courtesy of the Hoover Institution Library & Archives, Stanford University.

and joined middle-class ranks, providing compelling evidence not only of American magnanimity to Chinese but also of how well Chinese could become Americans.

Passport Fraud and Refugee Facilitation

The politics of refugee resettlement operated in direct contradiction to previously dominant efforts to enforce Chinese exclusion. The Cold War and U.S. foreign relations concerns required that refugee visas be granted as expeditiously as possible, demonstrating America's welcoming and race-neutral support for fellow anticommunists. In contrast, Chinese linked to exclusion-era immigration flows remained subject to intense scrutiny and hostility through their association with elaborate and largely successful, multigenerational systems of identity fraud based on citizenship claims through family relationships. The limited annual quota provided in 1943 had not changed Chinese dependence on the so-called paper son system.

After 1948 the crisis around Chinese illegal immigration compounded when the Immigration Bureau rationalized procedures by requiring Chinese to apply for passports at the nearest American consulate rather than first journeying to various immigration stations in the United States and being detained in ports such as San Francisco, Seattle, New York, Galveston, or Boston while waiting to learn whether they would be allowed to enter. Hong Kong became the chief site for Chinese applying for passports to enter as derivative citizens. The rapid accumulation of applicants and the extensive measures required to thoroughly investigate each case—including blood tests, multiple copies of family photographs, interviews of the applicant and supporting witnesses, and sometimes visits to homes and villages—generated backlogs of several years. State Department officials frequently referred to Hong Kong as the "fraud capital of the world" in correspondence with one another, an insider's joke that did not dispel fears that communist agents were using the paper son system to infiltrate the United States.

Everett Drumright, a long-term State Department officer, former head of Chinese Affairs, staunch Nationalist supporter, and fluent Chinese speaker, assumed the consul general's position in 1954 and immediately confronted responsibility for 117,000 applications, each of which required days of processing that had produced a backlog of four to twelve years.[87] J. Edgar Hoover himself had called attention to the security crisis represented by Chinese successes in immigration fraud. Between 1952 and 1955 over 1,200 Chinese applications were turned down, although far greater numbers gained admission.[88] In 1955 Drumright issued an urgent report asserting that almost all Chinese in America had entered illegally and that communists could use the paper son system, based on citizenship claims derived through birth in the United States and then parentage from a U.S. citizen father, to gain admission to the United States.[89]

Louis Goelz, who served as consul general in Hong Kong during the early 1960s, observed that fraud was "a very big problem in Hong Kong, and in all Chinese cases. A lot of fraud, of course, concerning citizenship and the issuance of passports, and passport applications." Goelz described the investigative strategies deployed by the consulate, which required the services of ten to twelve Chinese who acted as "informers and undercover investigators for us." These "outside men" helped the consulate try to find "briefing books" by raiding homes—measures that British authorities had explicitly forbidden to consular officials.[90] The most useful investigative tool had been developed under Drumright—a detailed listing of all the villages in nearby Guangdong and the surname groups inhabiting them. These concerted efforts suggest the frustration of U.S. consular staff and their determination to crack down on Chinese immigration fraud.

Rather than setting up new offices to manage refugee applications, however, the State Department lodged the new program in the same offices with the same staff as existing immigration affairs. Although additional consular officials were hired to handle the extra work, they were asked to evaluate applications from very different perspectives. Halleck Rose reported this contradiction to Pierce Gerety:

> We should never lose sight of the fact that the RRP and the regular immigration and passport program at the Consulate General at Hong Kong are directly opposed to each other in their objectives. We are seeking to facilitate the entry into the United States of qualified Chinese refugees and the regular program is, in effect, seeking to restrict Chinese immigration into the United States. The people working on the regular program have had so many fraudulent cases to deal with consisting of applicants for nonquota visas and American passports that they are convinced that every Chinese seeking to enter the United States is a fraud.[91]

In many instances consular officials accustomed to policing immigration fraud applied their regular investigative standards to refugee cases only to have their decisions overturned by authorities in the Refugee Relief Program seeking to emphasize the hospitality and liberality of the United States.

The Doris Low Chia case illustrates these contradictory aims. The U.S.-born Low Chia had traveled to China as a child with her parents in 1924. She returned to the United States in 1936 but moved back to China in 1947 after marrying a Chinese Air Force officer. After the PRC was established, they relocated to Taiwan where she voted in a Chinese election in 1951, thereby losing her U.S. citizenship. She filed for admission as a refugee under the 1953 act, only to have her application denied by an immigration officer who found that "none of the events which would qualify her as a refugee took place subsequent to the loss of her United States citizenship." The Office of Refugee and Migration Affairs circulated as a guideline its dissenting opinion that Low Chia had held Chinese citizenship from birth, according to the Republic of China constitution, and despite her birth in the United States. Moreover she had married and become the dependent of a Chinese Air Force officer and considered herself a Chinese national, as demonstrated by voting in Taiwan. The memo urged a generous interpretation of Low Chia's qualifications for refugee status for, "Apart from the facts of the case, the Refugee Relief Act provides for the applicant's only immediate possibility of re-entering the United States permanently, which she now wishes to do in order to give her two American citizen children (born in China prior to her expatriation) the benefit of an American education."[92] This convoluted reasoning, which found Low Chia to be a Chinese citizen for purposes of qualifying for a refugee visa but also a U.S. citizen in order to confer such status on her children, illustrates the RRP's expansive definition of refugees and its administrators' determination to admit more deserving Chinese.

The federal government's relative lack of security concerns pertaining to admission of Chinese refugees is signaled by a 1956 report filed by Representative Michael Feighan (R-OH), a restrictionist in immigration matters who would assume the mantle of leadership opposing the reforms of 1965 after the death of Representative Francis Walter in 1963. In 1955 Feighan had embarked on a seven-week inspection tour of East Asia scrutinizing implementation of the Refugee Relief Program. Consular officials in Hong Kong quavered at his likely criticisms of their handling of Chinese cases in the "fraud capital of the world." Despite their fears and the long history of the paper son system, Feighan's report took aim not at Chinese but at the "over 5,800 so-called 'White Russian' refugees" who had passed through Hong Kong from the PRC "without having any security check whatever made on them" and stated his intention to demand that Congress launch a full investigation into "this breach of security in laying open the countries of the free world to wholesale infiltration by communist agents."[93]

In contrast, Feighan praised refugee programs for Chinese, complimenting the U.S. voluntary agencies for "making a substantial contribution to the spiritual and material strength of the free world and to the cause of a just and lasting peace" and that they and the "victims of Communism in the Far East" that they served were "deserving of continued and expanded support by the United States government and the American public in general." Feighan also urged Congress to "provide a remedy for those provisions of the Refugee Relief Act of 1953 . . . which have proven to be senseless obstacles to the successful administration of the Act," to press for greater efficiency in approving refugee visas.[94] Feighan's report suggests that by 1955 Chinese refugees did not suffer from the taint of fraud, or even communist infiltration, that had shadowed other Chinese immigrants for several generations.

The FBI and Immigration and Naturalization Service (INS) also took steps to dispel the stigma associated with regular Chinese immigration, which involved dismantling the pernicious paper son system of fraudulent entries that had complicated processing of so many Chinese passport applications. Despite Drumright's alarming report, Chinese immigration in other ways had long posed little threat to the United States because the numbers were so low, with only about twenty-five thousand immigrants admitted during the 1950s and less than seventeen thousand the decade before, and consisted largely of family reunification cases and carefully screened refugees and first-preference workers.[95] In contrast, migration within the Western Hemisphere had become a far greater threat in the form of largely unsanctioned migration by Mexicans, estimated at 1.5 million in 1953 alone by Jules Edelstein, executive assistant to the leading immigration reform advocate, Senator Herbert Lehman (D-NY). In 1954 Edelstein had predicted that "millions of undesirables might come in from Latin America including, I suppose, Communists from Guatemala."[96] By the mid-1950s "Mexican immigration was rapidly emerging as the major concern," with heated disagreement between employers, labor groups, and the U.S. and Mexican governments about the *bracero* programs and the implementation of "Operation Wetback" in June 1954 under the command of General Joseph Swing to round up deportable aliens. That year the INS reported a record 1,035,282 apprehensions.[97]

While America's relationship with its neighbors to the south remain bedeviled by conflicts over migration and effective enforcement of restrictions, the INS took steps to dismantle its long-standing problem of Chinese immigration fraud. The Chinese Confession Program, "a procedure for an administrative adjustment of status," called on Chinese who had fraudulently immigrated to the United States to voluntarily disclose their false status and acknowledge *all* the names of their "paper" relatives, whether in the United States or still unused slots, in exchange for which the INS would attempt to adjust their legal status so they could legally remain.[98] Enacted in partial acknowledgment of Chinese American claims that "Chinese exclusion was the cause of Chinese illegal immigration," the confession program aimed to shut down the paper son system so that it could not be used by communist spies and to normalize the status of Chinese Americans who would then be able to integrate more fully, having shed their illegal status.[99] In practice this program terrified and divided the Chinese American community, which had been policed so stringently for decades by the very same government agencies suddenly calling on them to acknowledge their illegal entry, a deportable offense, and betray friends and relatives without any guarantees that doing so would secure their right to remain. By 1965, 11,336 Chinese had participated willingly, with 19,124 implicated in the confessions of others forced to do so as well, eliminating about 5,800 unused slots. Only about 13 percent of the Chinese American population of 1960 (237,292) had cooperated willingly or unwillingly, with most who did so remaining in the United States cleared of the shadows of exclusion, while most of those who had stayed silent were able to do pretty much the same. As observed by Mae Ngai, "The confession program served as a means of renegotiating the terms of Chinese Americans' citizenship,"[100] a necessary step before Chinese could be positioned as model immigrants. This move became possible in part because the number of Chinese immigrants would remain low while new laws added selection processes to privilege educated, usefully employable Chinese in the admissions process. Despite the low participation rates, the confession program enabled the INS to claim that the exclusion era's legacy of pervasive immigration fraud had been administratively dissipated, allowing at last for the full integration of Chinese Americans.

Refugee immigration mobilized Chinese American residents and community leaders as well. In March 1956 John F. Rieger, an assistant deputy administrator of the Office of Refugee and Migration Affairs, worked with Al Hausske, assistant coordinator of the Far East Consulate General, and Roland Kenney, Refugee Relief Program coordinator in the U.S. Embassy in Taipei, to help bring more than fifty Chinese chefs to work at the House of Chen restaurant under sponsorship by the Chinese Consolidated Benevolent Association (CCBA). Although visas were running out and the Taiwan government was reluctant to issue more passports, the opportunity for positive publicity and relations among Chinese Americans was too great. Rieger urged Hausske to work out the problems, noting that "the CCBA indicates it is planning a big public reception for the first arrivals so we should have, if possible, at least a score on hand." Rieger pressed the matter over Hausske's objections to uneducated refugees, writing on March 22, "I can only say, while appreciating the consideration brought forth in your letter, that cooks, bakers and other skills represented in the group of people included in this special project are skills which are needed in the United States and are in short supply according to the United States Employment Service." Rieger emphasized that, "as directed by the Act itself, persons whose services or skills are needed in the United States would have first preference in processing."[101] Despite the urgency attributed by the Office of Refugee and Migration Affairs, the case continued to malinger through the summer, with Hausske explaining to Rieger that his requested "priority for processing" in April ran into the problem that Far East visas had been used up and the Nationalist government was no longer willing to provide endorsed passports for the Chinese visa allotment. "The cases sponsored by CCBA and The House of Chen may very well be completely stalled." No less a person than Secretary of State John Foster Dulles, in a telegraph dated June 27, 1956, weighed in on the matter. "View visa issue House of Chen cases Department would be extremely embarrassed if no CCBA cases issued Section 4(a) (12)."[102] Under such pressures from the White House, there was no option but to find ways to admit the House of Chen chefs.

As illustrated by the cases of Grace Li, Doris Low Chia, and the House of Chen cooks, refugee admissions operated under very different imperatives than had exclusion-era Chinese immigration. The pressure was not to exclude but to facilitate entry, to display the opening of doors and provision of new homes in a flurry of publicity showing the sympathetic help of Americans to Chinese. In turn, the refugee programs reassured Americans by admitting small numbers of educated and at least readily employable Chinese, demonstrating that such pragmatically selected immigrants had minimal, and possibly even positive, impact on American society and economy. Against the backdrop of the Cold War, in which the movements of people and particularly those with valuable skills and visibility had become valuable propaganda tools deployed against the fearsome communist enemy, international relations concerns fueled the urgency to admit high-profile Chinese.

The case of the actress Li Li-hwa (b. 1924) required considerable manipulation. Described as "the leading Chinese motion picture actress in the Far East," Li had applied for a refugee visa in 1955. After she was interviewed on December 16, 1955, Hong Kong consular officials determined that her professional and financial success after relocating in 1947 disqualified her as a refugee. The report noted that she held savings of US$250,000 and net income in 1954 and 1955, "in excess of HK$500,000" and concluded that although she was anticommunist, she "can hardly be called an 'economic' refugee."[103] Noting her Jaguar, Cadillac, and estimated US$75,000 annual income, immigration officers in Hong Kong initially rejected her application. The visa officer, however, decided that Li Li-hwa "is not to be regarded as having re-settled here" despite her economic success. Pointing out that "considerable pressure is being brought to bear on prominent Chinese personalities in Hong Kong by the communists to return to China" and that "it was not the intent of Congress that persons' ability, diligence and talent should set to preclude refugee status[, it] is felt that Miss Li is in fact a political refugee."[104] The U.S. Information Agency also applied pressure confidentially for Li's admission as a refugee. Gerety received a visit from Frank Tribbe, general counsel of the U.S. Information Agency, who explained that Li "is willing to make propaganda pictures … at no expense … USIA believes that the granting of a visa to Miss Li for permanent residence in the United States, and her subsequent appearances in propaganda pictures would be of great value to the United States government." Tribbe urged that "the most liberal interpretation possible" be applied to her case. Unsurprisingly, in October 1955 the Refugee Relief Program accepted Li's qualifications for refugee status while the U.S. Information Agency arranged for Cecil B. DeMille to act as her sponsor.[105]

Li Li-Hwa arrived in the United States to great fanfare and first met De Mille in Hollywood as he touted his plans to feature her in his remake of *The Buccaneer* starring Yul Brynner. Li embarked on a national tour and met with Chinese community leaders in cities such as San Francisco, Chicago, and New York. In Washington, DC, she met with both Congressman Judd and Nationalist ambassador Tong Shen Kwong. Ultimately she did not appear in *The Buccaneer* and made only one American movie, *China Doll* with Victor Mature in 1958. After this brief flirtation with Hollywood, Li returned to Hong Kong, where she joined the Shaw Brothers Studios in 1960 and continued her successful Chinese-language film career, winning a couple of

Best Actress honors from the Golden Horse Film Awards.[106] Despite all the efforts to use her fame for the purposes of American foreign policy, Li Lihwa's brief time in America registered very little publicity.

The Growing Mandate for Refugee Relief

Despite its well-publicized activities, the Refugee Relief Program did not resolve the global refugee crisis and instead extended domestic debates about national obligations to expand the scope and targets for relief efforts. The program officially ended December 1956 without distributing all available visas. By May 1956 only nine thousand of forty-five thousand visas for escapees in Germany and Austria had been issued and they were not expected to be fully utilized, while refugees from less favored nations such as Latvia, Poland, other Balkan nations, and China held far more approved applications than allocated visas. In testimony before the Senate Judiciary Committee, Gerety had noted the "very bad, damaging psychological blow to the entire escapee program" that visas were available but would not be used. Eisenhower also urged reallocation of visas. "Despite the lack of action so far, there is some hope for passage of the Refugee Act amendments. The feeling is that in an election year, Congress may want to do something for voters interested in liberalizing immigration rules." Congress could pass a temporary law to do so without making changes "in basic immigration law" that the president had requested.[107] Such stopgap refugee measures helped immigration restrictionists stave off more general reforms.

After the Refugee Relief Act expired, Congress passed PL 85-316 in 1957 authorizing redistribution of the unused refugee visas with the following priorities in selection of refugees: "(1) the degree of professional, technical, or other skill, (2) hardships or persecution, (3) sponsorship in the United States, (4) ability to speak English, and (5) unification of close relatives." S. W. Kung commented that "evidently the act emphasizes immigrants with technical skills and aims at reuniting families in the United States."[108] These preferences predicted the terms of the Hart-Celler Act of 1965 and were feasible in 1957 in part because they did not add to the numbers of new entries already agreed on by Congress. This law enabled Chinese stymied by the oversubscribed quota to gain permanent residency through the attorney general's power to adjust the statuses of a "limited number" of skilled aliens present on July 1, 1957, who possessed approved first-preference petitions filed before September 11, 1957.[109] The Act of August 8, 1958 advanced a registry or amnesty provision for those who had entered prior to June 28, 1940.[110] This succession of piecemeal refugee laws and private bills, and their failure ultimately to address the magnitude of accepted visa applications from Chinese found to be deserving immigrants, underscored the failings of the McCarran-Walter Act and the pressing need to modify immigration restrictions to acknowledge individual merit and potential for contributions while disposing of the racial and national origins discriminations that remained.

Refugee resettlement in America extended ARCI's existence far beyond the two years originally envisioned by its founders and the scope of its goals for aiding Chiang Kai-shek. However, the organization could not shut down until it had removed more registrants from its roster and collected more of their travel debts. As early as August 1955, Garside had asked Hong Kong staff to establish how many registrants had been "integrated into the Hongkong economy" and no longer needed ARCI's help, but there still remained "5,928 registrants who have special skills, education, or professional experience."[111] In August 1956 B. A. Garside contacted the State Department's International Cooperation Agency hoping to shut down operations with the end of the Refugee Relief Program in December, but ARCI continued through the 1957 and 1958 redistributions of visas for "deserving applicants." In October 1958 Representative Judd wrote to Robert S. McCollum of the Office of Refugee Management Affairs in Washington, DC, concerning the limited numbers of refugee visas available to "the large number of deserving applicants," and especially ARCI registrants who would "make particularly valuable contributions to American life." In response, McCollum urged Judd to keep ARCI going until the five thousand remaining registrants on the rolls were resettled.[112] As will be discussed in chapter 7, ARCI registrants also benefited from the parole of Chinese in 1962 by President John F. Kennedy. When the Hong Kong office finally closed in 1960, only 241 registrant cases remained, involving 926 people.[113] During the 1960s Garside continued running the New York office, largely to collect on travel loans made to ARCI registrants to ensure that the State Department would recover its funds and to send registrants reminders to apply for citizenship as soon as they qualified.

The latter stages of ARCI's activities represented Chinese refugees as deserving immigrants and valuable additions to American society, as conveyed by Lawrence Dawson of the ICA to Garside in July 1958: "We ... are pleased to know that the United States is receiving such an increment of skills and education and are sure that all those associated with Aid Refugee Chinese Intellectuals must feel gratified in the knowledge that their efforts have been ... responsible for presenting these fine people with the opportunity to build a future for their families in honor and dignity." As refugees, Chinese had become "fine people" whose "honor and dignity" and right to have a "future for their families" was advanced and celebrated by the Department of State. Outreach to Chinese not only provided refugees with new homes and a chance at brighter futures with "honor and dignity" but in turn brought to America their "skills and education." American benevolence was justified with economic returns.

Perhaps the most widely published trait attributed to ARCI's registrants was their performance as committed capitalists, as demonstrated by their diligent repayment of travel loans extended by ARCI using State Department funds. Walter Judd's authorized biography emphasized their fiscal responsibility as an indicator of their suitability for life in the United States: "One dramatic index of their industry and integrity is their voluntary repayment of the travel loans which ARCI advanced to enable them to get to the United States. Of the $241,297 advanced in travel loans, they have to date repaid ... 96.3 percent."[114] The New York office remained open with the aim of collecting 100 percent of these loans, as Garside reported steady progress to the Office of Refugee and Migration Affairs. Although "a very small number" were causing difficulties, "in general we are very proud of the character and the performance of this group of new Chinese-Americans. Nearly all of them have faithfully made payments on their loans month after month, even though this involved serious financial hardships. At the same time, they have managed to give the best possible education to their children, and have gotten well-established in their communities." Despite considerable challenges and struggles, registrants fulfilled their fiscal responsibilities even as they raised another generation of similarly upstanding Americans, as illustrated by the example of one C. C. Wong. "During the first few years he was in America he had rather serious difficulties finding employment which would give him sufficient income to provide for and to educate his family. But with the passage of time he has become well-established, educated his children, met all of his obligations, and shown himself to be an American citizen of whom we can all be proud."[115] This narrative became the standard circulated by ARCI: not only would the Chinese they had carefully selected repay their debts, they would prevail over initial difficulties to find decent jobs, educate their children, and become model citizens.[116]

Former Hong Kong consul general Louis Goelz summarized the changes in attitude toward Chinese as immigrants more generally that took place during the 1950s and early 1960s. Despite having administered the consulate in the "fraud capital of the world" during the early 1960s, he seemed largely sanguine at the high levels of illegal immigration and his limited success in stemming it just a decade after the security crisis identified in the Drumright Report. Rather than a high-stakes battle over national security, Goelz seemed to regard the paper son system as something more akin to a game. "They won more often than I did, of course. But it was still an interesting challenge." Moreover, he did not perceive illegal immigration as a reason to dismiss Chinese altogether as human beings or as acceptable immigrants. When asked his feelings about the paper son fraud, Goelz responded, "Chinese are very nice people once you get to know them." Living and working among Chinese people had changed his views of them, for not only did he like them as people, he admired their drive and capacity for success. "They started out with nothing, and wound up with everything." Goelz recalled one former employee who received a refugee visa and departed with his wife of one month and only $100. He arrived in America where relatives gave him a job raising flowers in South San Francisco. "Today that same local employee is a multimillionaire. He got involved in real estate in San Francisco, and made a fortune."[117] Such celebratory accounts served to vindicate decisions to admit more Chinese by demonstrating how easily they became high-achieving, capitalist Americans.

By the early 1960s Chinese could be protagonists in the kinds of tales of immigrant striving and success that enshrine America's core values even as they mask the considerable difficulties and sense of displacement experienced by many Chinese refugees of this era. Although the United States provided political sanctuary and freedom, employment, educational opportunities, and the easing of segregationist discrimination, many refugee Chinese found their unexpected settlement in America to be a form of exile involving separation from family and friends, downward mobility, and an unresolved quest for social and cultural belonging even though conditions had improved greatly since the exclusion era. Even the great Hu Shi, intellectual heart of the May Fourth Movement, former president of Peking University, and Chinese ambassador to the United States, could find employment in the United States only as curator of Princeton University's Gest Library.[118] The American life of the beloved Chinese writer Zhang Ailing (Eileen Chang, 1920–1995) illustrates such tormented trajectories. Zhang arrived in America through the Refugee Relief Program as a Chinese celebrity employed by the U.S. Information Agency in Hong Kong. Born in Shanghai to a prominent but troubled family, she was educated in both Chinese and English and precociously published her first literary works to great acclaim in 1943 while still in her early twenties. Her emotional and ironic stories, precisely rendered, such as "Lust, Caution" and *Love in a Fallen City*, drew a wide readership in the last stages of World War II, despite her slow output and difficult marriage to a known collaborator, Lu Hancheng. Her avowedly apolitical, highly personal themes boded poorly for her future in Communist China, and by 1952 she had joined the flood of refugees desperately seeking sanctuary in Hong Kong. Zhang's fame and skills brought her a contract with the U.S. Information Agency, under which she translated American classics such as Hemingway into Chinese and wrote two English-language novels critical of Chinese communism, *The Rice Sprout Song* (1954) and *The Naked Earth* (1956). As had many other Chinese staff working for American agencies in Hong Kong and Taiwan, Zhang was among the first Chinese to receive a refugee visa in 1955. Despite the relatively fortunate circumstances of her arrival, American publishers were unappreciative of Zhang's talents and she never regained her former productivity or prominence as a writer. Zhang earned her living as a researcher at the Center for

Chinese Studies at UC Berkeley and died alone in a Los Angeles apartment, her body discovered by her landlord only several days after her passing.

Despite the relative welcome and privilege attending Chinese refugee admissions into the United States, the Refugee Relief Program was run to maximize positive publicity for the United States while minimally committing resources to aid resettlement, a form of help so limited that it required refugees to repay their own costs of travel to the United States. The program sought to select for Chinese refugees already equipped to make their own way—through their training and education, work experiences, and relatives and friends willing to provide support and employment. That the salvation of coming to America involved considerable downward mobility for many, as illustrated in the cases of Zhang Ailing, the Hu family, and the many former engineers and bankers who ended up working in Chinese restaurants, often disappears from this tale of American magnanimity.

To be sure, many Chinese refugees made the most of the limited opportunities available to them in 1950s America. Cecilia Chiang (b. 1919), the wife of a former Nationalist diplomatic officer, painstakingly started over again by establishing a restaurant. Long separated from the courtyards and many servants of her childhood home, in America Chiang learned to scrub kitchen floors as she struggled to make her business a success. With the help of a former San Francisco consul, Linsan Chien, as her manager and talented chefs, Chiang introduced Americans to a personalized selection of what she called "Mandarin" cuisine, a step up from the previously popular tastes for chop suey and egg foo young, on her way to a glamorous career as a celebrated restaurateur and hospitality consultant.[119] Abetted by growing interest in and receptivity to things Chinese, Chiang carved out a new life for herself as a capitalist entrepreneur in America.

Other refugees were not so adaptable. Despite the stability of life in the United States, many Chinese never regained their former standing or sense of purpose. The sociologist Betty Lee Sung observed in 1967 that "offhand, I can name an architect, a vice president of a finance company, a welder in an aircraft factory, a medical student, and a dental student who work regularly over the week ends as waiters or headwaiters in various Chinese restaurants." Education did not help "the intellectual and political refugees who once held high office in China" find comparable employment in the United States. As observed by Sung, "At first, these *émigrés* disassociated themselves from the 'overseas Chinese,' whom they looked down upon as laundrymen and restaurateurs. When they began to look around for means of earning a livelihood or investing their capital, they found that restaurants can yield a good living and handsome returns."[120] A decade later, in 1976, this generation of Chinese had not recovered their standing. "The problem of underemployment is greater than that of unemployment for the Chinese." Sung stressed that "when it comes to dire necessity, one accepts such work, even though the position may be far beneath the worker's qualifications." She noted, "When highly educated and skilled persons are admitted to this country but are hampered at every turn to practice their trade or profession, underemployment inevitably results," and she cited the examples of a former Shanghai plastic manufacturer working as a waiter, a former Hong Kong accountant working in a kitchen, or a former principal working as a grocer.[121] Zhang Ailing's blighted literary career is a tragic example of such lost destinies. The literary critic Dominic Cheung observed that if not for the political division between Nationalist and Communist China, Zhang "would have almost certainly won a Nobel Prize."[122] That Zhang Ailing immigrated to America and died in such obscurity is but one of the almost forgotten tragedies of this generation.

CHAPTER 7

"Economic and Humanitarian"

PROPAGANDA AND THE REDEMPTION OF CHINESE IMMIGRANTS THROUGH REFUGEE RELIEF

SEVERAL DIGNITARIES AND HIS FATHER greeted Eng Se-suey and his family when they arrived at the Chicago airport in the early hours of June 5, 1962. Mayor and Mrs. John Overbach, Nationalist China's consul general Frank Tze-tun Sia, David Lee of Chinese Refugee Relief (CRR) from Washington, DC, and Frank J. Eng turned out to welcome the forty-five-year-old, his wife, and three of four children on their way to Park Ridge, Illinois, to work with the senior Eng in his restaurant.[1] This humble "refugee from Communist China" received such a grand reception as the first arrival in the Kennedy administration's newly authorized parole of Chinese refugees from Hong Kong and as an indicator that U.S. openness to Chinese immigrants had expanded to include those joining family members who were also economically self-reliant even if not well educated. A recent surge of refugees into the port city, some forty thousand in May alone, had evoked widespread public and congressional outcries of sympathy and calls for aid to the already overwhelmed colony. The most dramatic response was the parole of several thousand into the United States, prioritizing family reunification, employment skills needed in the American economy, and the backlog of nineteen thousand approved applicants who had been denied visas earlier owing to the woefully inadequate immigration quota and refugee visa allocations for Chinese.[2]

Eng Se-suey's admission redressed several of these considerations. His resident father would provide employment in his restaurant, and the Engs could finally reunify after decades of separation. Eng Se-suey had first applied for an entry permit in 1955 after fleeing from Taishan County in 1953 when Communists confiscated his land. The annual Chinese immigration quota of 105 gave him almost no chance of joining his father until the parole program cracked open the gates for him as a refugee. Through a translator, Eng expressed joy on arrival in Chicago, describing it as "the happiest day of my life; my thoughts are about a new life in this country."[3] Eng's new beginning had a bittersweet ending, however. Frank J. Eng died within a week from liver cancer but at least had had the chance to see his son once again. Frank had come to the United States in 1916, before the birth of his son, and did not meet him until a trip to Hong Kong thirty-three years later, in 1959. The parole program intervened in time to permit them one last visit together, albeit a brief one.[4]

The poignant accounts of the Eng family reunion were no accident. By 1962 moving stories of the courage and humanity of deserving Chinese refugees had become a trope in American media accounts concerning Chinese refugees, immigration, race, and egalitarian access to the American dream. Cold War liberalism had reworked the potential of Chinese, not only as immigrants but as Americans who, in the conceptual framing of Ellen Wu, were becoming "definitively not-black" subjects starting in the 1940s through attribution of cultural traits such as family values, hard work, low crime rates, and self-sufficiency.[5] On behalf of Chinese refugees, State Department policies mandated the publicizing of sympathetic narratives such as that of the Engs to demonstrate simultaneously to both domestic and international audiences that the United States was acting as leader of the democratic world in its concern for all peoples, regardless of race, in providing refuge, succor, and opportunity for fellow enemies of communism. The Engs' well-publicized story allowed Americans to take pride in their generosity and benevolence while providing reassurance that, when properly handled, refugee admissions had few negative consequences in costs or disruptions to society. A stable family unit such as the Engs could be readily absorbed with prearranged employment and existing family and community ties that managed any other needs for adjustment. Refugee programs that had begun as foreign policy outreach in turn provided potent rationales for reform of domestic immigration laws.[6]

During this era politics and popular culture humanized Chinese in presenting them as deserving and welcome immigrants, even when unreasonable restrictions forced them to enter illegally. *Flower Drum Song*, the Rogers and Hammerstein musical (1958) and Hollywood movie (1961) based on C. Y. Lee's novel from 1957, was but one of the most visible renderings of Chinese as sympathetic, *potential* Americans, particularly when female and of the intellectual elite. The movie begins with a series of charming watercolors by the popular Chinese American painter Dong Kingman that visually track the journey of the heroine Mei Li from Hong Kong to San Francisco, where she enters America literally stashed in a crate and emerges covered with packaging material. Despite her father's warning that "we are illegal; it is unlucky to start in a new country by breaking the law," Mei Li expresses confidence in their American future by replying, "I will only break it a little bit." She later justifies their violation of U.S. immigration laws by pointing out the unreasonableness of the ten-year wait required for legal entry by otherwise faultless Chinese such as they (see fig. 7.1). Mei Li's illegal entry gains

Figure 7.1. Illegal immigrant heroine of *Flower Drum Song*. Moments after sneaking into America in a box, the protagonist's chief love interest, Mei Li, played by Academy Award–winning actress Miyoshi Umeki, with her father played by Chingwah Lee, consults a policeman for directions. Publicity still, Universal Studios, 1961.

emphasis in Hammerstein's reworking of Lee's novel, with the stage and movie versions transforming the father and daughter from southern Chinese who had entered *legally* as servants to an American general with aspirations of opening a restaurant into a professor "from the North" forced to sneak into America in a box.[7] This shift in class, place of origin, and mode of entry positively portrayed educated, northern Chinese refugees, even those present in the United States illegally, and compared them favorably to lower-class residents of Chinatown from Guangdong. To underscore the virtue and attractiveness of these new classes of immigrants, Mei Li, despite her modesty, proves so beguiling and readily adaptable to American life that she wins the heart of the protagonist, Wang Ta, scion of a wealthy, recently immigrated family, away from the glamorous, Cantonese nightclub stripper Linda Low, played by Nancy Kwan. Miyoshi Umeki's performance as Mei Li built on her Academy Award–winning role as the Japanese military bride, Katsumi, in *Sayonara* (1957) whose back-scrubbing devotion to her American airman husband played by Red Buttons established compelling and lasting images of the willing docility and servitude of Asian wives. Both Mei Li's illegal entry and Katsumi's tragic suicide because she is not allowed to accompany her husband to America challenged immigration laws to change in order to admit more such model Asian women into the United States.[8]

During the Cold War such public entertainments filtered practical imperatives to demonstrate U.S. concern for Chinese allies through symbolic gestures of aid, enacted in part by addressing the otherwise enormous East Asian refugee crises through the allocation of nonquota entry for an eventual total of about thirty-two thousand Chinese refugees.[9] Out of an estimated Hong Kong refugee population of 1.5 million in 1955, these lucky few had been prescreened, not only for their political beliefs but for their capacities to minimize their impact on the United States, and even for their potential to contribute economically and strategically. As idealized immigrants, the widely publicized merits of Chinese refugees advanced arguments that immigration laws should be reformed to admit both more Chinese and more refugees.[10] In the face of such needy yet useful subjects, who could so readily be integrated into the United States, should not a mighty democratic and capitalist nation admit just a few thousand more?

Such popular media representations of sympathetic and deserving Chinese refugees manifested national security and public policy agendas traceable to the White House and Department of State. As early as 1952 the loyalties of overseas Chinese residing chiefly in Hong Kong and Southeast Asia had become matters of utmost concern, which the State Department and various relevant agencies sought to channel away from Communist China through programs of cultural and educational exchange, cultural propaganda, establishment of higher education institutions in "free" Asia,[11] and selective and limited admission of refugees into the United States. The last stratagem required maximizing publicity and events in order to obscure what were in practice highly circumscribed programs for Chinese refugee relief and immigration. Compassionate portrayals of Chinese refugees thus abounded in media accounts and public debates during the 1950s and early 1960s and extended to enfold working-class but nonetheless worthy Chinese such as Eng Se-suey. The parole program in 1962 provided the exclamation point merging the display of American empathy for Chinese refugees with pressures for domestic immigration reforms, agendas enacted by the hastily assembled Chinese Refugee Relief organization headed by Anna Chennault (see fig. 7.2), the Chinese American widow of World War II Flying Tigers hero General Claire Chennault, with the backing of a board of politically prominent immigration reformers and Nationalist sympathizers. Newly arrived Chinese refugees served as living examples in public discussions demonstrating that individual traits such as employability and

Figure 7.2. John F. Kennedy with Anna C. Chennault, chairwoman of Chinese Refugee Relief. Kennedy met with Chennault in the Oval Office on June 2, 1962. Credit: Robert Knudsen, White House Photograph Collection. John F. Kennedy Presidential Library and Museum.

educational attainments alongside family reunification should supplant race and national origins as chief considerations for admission. Although general immigration reform did not take place until 1965, the events of 1962 shifted the terms of debate sharply forward.

Celebrating Chinese Humanity to Publicize
American Humanitarianism

World War II had shattered American isolationism, leaving in its wake a relatively young nation at the forefront of global leadership and harboring ambitions requiring greater openness to intercultural encounters and collaborations. Cultural and educational exchanges were growing and well-funded components of State Department programs. Passage of legislation such as the Fulbright Act (1946) and the U.S. Information and Educational Exchange Act of 1948 (PL 80–402), more popularly known as the Smith-Mundt Act, aimed to extend American influence abroad. As described by Kenneth Osgood, "The battle for hearts and minds was waged not just with words, but also with deeds—actions calculated to have an impact on public perceptions." The cultural Cold War mobilized on a number of fronts, including "covert operations; cultural and educational exchanges; space exploration and scientific cooperation; book publication, translation, and distribution programs; nuclear energy and disarmament; diplomatic negotiations; and the daily operations of foreign affairs personnel abroad."[12] To Osgood's list, one might add refugee admissions.

In 1952 the goals of internationalist organizations such as the IIE and the CFRFS had become U.S. foreign policy with the U.S. Information Agency promoting international programs of exchange in the belief that "personal contacts are a primary source of strength . . . and that face-to-face persuasion exerts a dominant influence."[13] The State Department arranged opportunities for these kinds of influential encounters through a range of programs offering Chinese greater opportunities to enter the United States, albeit for temporary visits. In May 1954 a Far East Public Affairs Officer recommended that "every effort should be made to liberalize the U.S. entrance restrictions against Overseas Chinese selected for travel grants in furtherance of USIS objectives" and that "provision should be made for a much wider exchange of Chinese students, teachers, leaders, and specialists among the countries of [Southeast Asia]." This officer suggested that Chinese Americans be mobilized to assist in Exchange of Persons programs.[14] Government-run exchange programs became a key component of soft diplomacy during the Cold War.

Refugee relief became another form of migration commanding State Department attention and publicity. In April 1954 the U.S. Information Agency issued a directive emphasizing "the critical importance of the Overseas Chinese in the present Far East pattern and their probable effect on future developments in terms of U.S. interests." Such strategic significance made it "a minimum essential that the Overseas Chinese be denied as an asset to world communism in general and to the Peking Regime" and be seen as choosing Free China and the United States instead.[15] Secretary of State John Foster Dulles supported such outreach as "a primary objective" in order "to keep constantly before its target audiences on the China mainland concrete and factual results of the negative and oppressive aspects of Communism." Unrest could be fostered with "knowledge that escape is possible, even for relatively few, and that efforts are being made to assure that escapees are well received and treated."[16] Not only should Chinese be encouraged to visit America, but a select few should be able to resettle permanently to show American support and investment in Chinese who might inspire others to defy communist control. For propaganda purposes, symbolic migration of a few, publicity-generating Chinese refugees advanced America's covert war against communism.

To this end, U.S. Information Agency programs grandly publicized the acceptance and smooth integration of Chinese refugees in the United States even though actual numbers admitted were low and never intended to address the full scope of the Asian refugee problem. In comparison to European refugees, who received the bulk of American attention and resources, relatively few Chinese gained admission. As Dulles admitted, "the [Far Eastern Escapee] program is admittedly small in relation to the total refugee problem." Being so limited in scale, the program focused on resettlement of "that small percentage of the bona-fide Chinese political refugees who are identified as being in groups or categories having special political or psychological significance" (1).

As with repeal, the U.S. government sought to wield great influence through symbolic gestures of concern. A 1957 memorandum circulated in the Bureau of Chinese Affairs acknowledged these limited ambitions. "The Far East Refugee Program of the U.S. Escapee Program is the most significant external refugee-aid program in the Far East and the only U.S. government refugee-aid program in Hong Kong which contains the largest single bloc of anti-Communist refugees in the world. . . . FERP seeks to achieve maximum psychological impact through relatively token assistance." Although the United State could not, and did not, aim to "shoulder the major burden of resettlement and assistance to the mass of 700,000 to 1,000,000 refugees in Hong Kong," it could publicize the $3.2 million spent since 1953 on housing, vocational and language training, job placement, resettlement aid, and medical aid through private voluntary agencies such as ARCI but also the many organizations that had long histories of missionary activities and investments in China. U.S. Information Agency stories stressed the historic depths of Sino-American friendship by highlighting government aid to "groups and individuals carefully selected from the mass of refugees (particularly the leadership echelon) in Hong Kong" in hopes of promoting Free China as a viable alternative to Communist China, and to advertise U.S. assistance to Hong Kong and to "the vitally important overseas Chinese communities." Such publicity aimed to undermine "Communist propaganda alleging that U.S. humanitarian interest in refugees is circumscribed by considerations of race."[17]

To overcome the charge of racism and segregation undermining claims of American democratic leadership, the U.S. Information Agency publicized stories that celebrated the compatibilities and sympathies shared by Americans and Chinese.

In 1954 Dulles had determined that the Far East Refugee Program (FERP) was "capable of producing useful material for possible exploitation through U.S. media" concerning "the repressive nature of Communist China" (3–4).[18] His memo included specific guidelines and themes to optimize propaganda goals, such as selection of humanizing "individual stories of refugees" to highlight the American voluntary agencies, many subsidized by the refugee program, that aided "selected refugees . . . to resettle, either through local integration in Hong Kong or through movement outward" (2). The sharply restricted scope of the program required that U.S. Information Agency officials maximize the generosity of U.S. refugee relief programs while downplaying its comparatively limited scale with the warning that "because the program activity directly financed by the Escapee Program is small, the statistical approach should be minimized in favor of individual story treatment" (4–5). Dulles cautioned against bringing up potentially damaging comparisons between the far greater resources benefiting Europeans compared to Asians and urged that the resettlement of European escapees from Asia receive little coverage. Instead, publicity should feature "hard news concerning the resettlement in the U.S. of Asians under the Refugee Relief Act" and emphasize their "parallel values" (5–6). He urged U.S. Information Agency staff to seek out "human-interest story materials" that would appeal to "both Asian and selected non-Asian audiences" that stressed "the resettlement stories of persons who formerly held positions of prominence on the mainland" (4–5).[19] As a State Department–funded organization, ARCI carried out directives from Harry Lyford, a public relations and publicity officer, to provide story ideas for "any newsworthy cases coming over."[20] Such propaganda projects portrayed Chinese refugees as welcome and readily assimilable in the United States, thereby highlighting that Chinese had opportunities in the free world.

Overseas Chinese with compelling stories received special attention. The case of deaf-mute Lau Wen-ngau, "one of China's best-known track and field stars," arose in June 1955. Lau was already in the United States, having arrived in 1950 as a visitor to run in the Boston Marathon. When he sought a way to resettle permanently, his case came to the attention of the Office of Refugee and Migration Affairs, which evaluated his application in light of information received from the U.S. Information Service in Hong Kong regarding his celebrity among overseas Chinese. Richard McCarthy, the agency's director, warned that Lau's fate would make a considerable impression in swaying their support for either the United States or China. "If Lau is deported, [m]any people here would feel the United States handled the case of this handicapped athlete in heartless fashion. . . . On the other hand, if the

Communists could get hold of him, they would undoubtedly exploit his athletic fame and his treatment in the United States for propaganda purposes." Lau's prominence, and competition against the communist side for his loyalties, fed the decision to grant him permanent status.[21]

Emphasis on individual successes and human interest stories masked the limited aid given in the face of the great size and intractability of refugee problems in Hong Kong. In September 1957 the head of the Far East Refugee Program, Lawrence Dawson, summarized the challenges. Although new influxes had largely stopped, the approximately 1.5 million refugees in Hong Kong lived "under conditions ranging from poor to indescribably bad ... the problem is attracting increasing world-wide attention."[22] By targeting the newsworthy and most sympathetic refugees, the U.S. Information Agency aimed to magnify perceptions of American responsiveness to the plight of Chinese. At the same time, such selective measures served to admit primarily the most readily integrated of Chinese refugees and to persuade Americans of their ready assimilability.

News coverage of Chinese refugees during the 1950s underscored Chinese contributions and potential for Americanization, the generosity of Americans to Chinese, and the shared anticommunism of both. For example, a September 1955 *New York Times* article recounted the arrival of Mrs. Wan Ju Pan Chan, a widow, her son, and three other boys at Grand Central Station under the sponsorship of Mrs. Theodore Evans of Kent, Connecticut. Eighteen months earlier Mrs. Evans had applied through her church to sponsor them under the Refugee Relief Program under guidance from the Church World Service. The merits of their case were clear, as the boys were "all sons of Chinese college professors." In order to send them to the Housatonic Valley Regional High School in Falls Village, Connecticut, Mrs. Evans started working as an elementary school teacher while Mrs. Chan worked as a governess in the Evans home—a job somewhat relevant to her former career as a primary school teacher in Hong Kong.[23] This chain of mutual support reiterated well-worn tropes of American salvation of deserving Chinese.

During the 1950s the plight of overwhelming numbers of desperate Chinese refugees crowded into beleaguered Hong Kong became a standard set of images familiar to many Americans. For example, Peggy Durdin's *New York Times Magazine* feature "The Chinese Scroll Called Hong Kong" (1958) vividly illustrated the suffering and fortitude of refugees while emphasizing the stark contrasts between extreme wealth and poverty in the British colony. "Hong Kong is a center of free, untrammeled private enterprise.... It has a million Chinese refugees, in desperate need of help." The many photographs presented the main bridge crossing into the PRC at Lowu, a slum clearance project, contrasted with the luxuries of the Hong Kong Club. Durdin was emphatic in her descriptions of Chinese refugee suffering and perseverance.

Between two and three thousand refugees live in tall "resettlement" buildings where two or three families often crowd into a small room to share the rent of less than three dollars monthly. Hundreds of thousands will spend this and other winters in hillside shacks, caves, on streets, under staircases. Thanks to their tenacious hold on life and incredible energy—and the help of private relief agencies—some refugees earn an "adequate" living.

A model family had the father doing piecework at a factory and the mother embroidering at home, watching over "undernourished children" whose educational opportunities were limited. Durdin cautioned about the great local divides between the wealthy and the poor and the limited hope available to the latter, and issued an extended warning concerning the extent of Communist infiltration of Hong Kong organizations and local newspapers.[24] Unless the United States acted to give hope to Hong Kong's worthy but ill-fated poor, they could readily turn to the other side.

In January 1960 another *New York Times* article presented winter conditions. It offered estimates of the dramatic increase in Hong Kong's population from 1.7 million in 1948 to 3 million and even close to 4 million in 1960. The numbers were hard to pin down, as much of the migration was illegal and propelled even more by the cold winters of China, where, "peasants must work long hours with little more than rice gruel as their reward." After fleeing communism, they arrived in Hong Kong only to subsist in "shanty towns that straggle up the bare, brown slopes of Hong Kong's harborside hills, where a home is a hut of tinsheets, cardboard and sacking and congestion is so great that people sleep in shifts." The young suffered the most under such dire conditions for "more than 50,000 refugee children roam the streets and squatter areas without proper homes or families. Little bundles of rags in street doorways turn out to be sleeping infants."[25] Such voyeuristic accounts of Chinese anguish and endurance echoed tales of deprivation from the Sino-Japanese War and demanded Americans assume responsibility for alleviating the continued torment of Chinese. The humanity and worth imbued in Chinese refugees paralleled growing calls for immigration reforms in the United States—a campaign that gained urgency in part because changes in law were needed so that America could fulfill its obligations to less fortunate but worthy fellow members of the free world suffering for their anticommunist beliefs.

Kennedy's Campaign against the Quota System: Foreign Relations and Economic Nationalism

During the 1950s and early 1960s, improving views of once excluded groups such as Chinese, promoted in accordance with State Department agendas, fueled efforts for immigration reform. Pressure to replace the McCarran-Walter

Act began even before it had passed so resoundingly in Congress. Although the State Department initially supported the legislation, "because they make provisions for the admission of Orientals, especially Japanese, into this country and would therefore contribute to our foreign policy in the Far East," Eisenhower's White House communicated that it "strongly oppose[d] these bills" and asked the State Department to consider alternatives.[26] At issue were the McCarran-Walter Act's retention of the inequitable quota system, which all but shut out Asians and Africans, sharply limited southern and eastern European immigration, and provided inadequate entry measures for refugees. Enactment of the Refugee Relief Act in 1953 was in partial redress of the shortcomings of the McCarran-Walter Act.

John F. Kennedy's campaigns to legislate immigration reforms both as a senator and as president provide a window into the ideological and institutional conflicts that delayed substantive change until 1965. Deeply entrenched factional interests sparred across a congressional committee structure that allowed strategically placed restrictionists to block reform measures from reaching a vote.[27] Across the 1950s, a broadening array of ethnic, religious, missionary, educational, and industrial interests aligned against the McCarran-Walter Act's emphasis on race and national origins in support of considerations such as kinship relationships, shared values and politics, foreign relations, and economic utility. Despite such growing consensus regarding the need for comprehensive reform, congressional passage of a new immigration law was long delayed, revealing the depths of different views regarding how American borders should be regulated and the logjam of congressional processes.

Immigration reform operated at the confluence of the internationalist and civil rights agendas that became hallmarks of Kennedy's presidency. As a freshman senator in 1953, Kennedy supported the omnibus Lehman Bill, which "made the applicant's individual training and qualifications the test for admission" but did "not make over the face of America" by accepting numerical caps on admissions.[28] Other proposed modifications with resonance for the future included reallocating unused visa numbers from countries with large quotas to countries with visas mortgaged far into the future while granting some adopted children the same status as natural children and "restoring to professors eligibility for non-quota status if an American university requests their services."[29] A test of whether a modestly different set of principles for immigration restriction could pass in Congress, this effort failed, as would many others in the years to come. Kennedy would nonetheless continue to propose bills, maintaining his emphasis on removing the discriminatory national origins quotas and trying out other rationales in hopes of finding a passable solution. In July 1954 he contacted the chair of the Senate Immigration Subcommittee requesting action on bills that would "make a complete substitution for the McCarran Walter Act" for "the removal of discriminatory features," particularly by reallocating unused quota numbers to countries facing long mortgages, a tactic that could introduce more equity without increasing the overall cap already set.[30]

Representative Francis Walter (D-PA) staunchly led the defense of the status quo, leading Kennedy to seek his concurrence for shared principles of immigration control that could attract more bipartisan support. In 1955 Kennedy solicited Walter's cooperation in advancing a bill setting up a commission on immigration and naturalization policy modeled on the Hoover Commission "to review the operation of the McCarran-Walter Immigration Act and to recommend such changes as experience may show to be desirable." Kennedy acknowledged their differences even as he asked Walter to cooperate with this "desirable method of removing the issue from political and emotional arguments."[31] Through such attempts at negotiation, Kennedy contributed to minor reforms of immigration law that revealed principles by which increases or variations in admissions criteria might be tolerated by restrictionists, such as the reallocation of unused refugee visas in 1957, which permitted entry by more Chinese but only by working within the overall cap of 214,000 already set by Congress.

Reinforcing the calls for reform made by domestic lobbying groups, Nationalist government representatives repeatedly raised the issue in conversations with the State Department. In January 1957 S. H. Tan, minister-counselor of the Chinese Embassy, mentioned the recent parole of 32,000 Hungarian refugees to his counterpart at the U.S. Bureau of Chinese Affairs. Tan pointed out that there were about 24,000 Chinese refugees in Hong Kong and Taipei hoping to come to the United States. Only 2,000 had received refugee visas under the Refugee Relief Program, even though the Republic of China government had provided 4,500–5,000 passports making them eligible. Knowing that Congress was studying immigration reform, Tan urged his State Department counterpart to "make some sort of favorable recommendation to the U.S. Congress concerning the Chinese Refugees."[32]

Tan's request aligned with the sentiments of many Americans. In a speech delivered on January 31, 1957, Eisenhower called for reforms to the McCarran-Walter Act on behalf of those seeking asylum from communism and amendment of the quota system. He specifically cited the small quota allocated to Chinese, which prevented adequate aid to the "great many refugees [who] are in a desperate plight awaiting places to go for resettlement." The annual quota was only 105, 50 percent of which was mortgaged to Chinese already resident in the United States through 2036. For the next eighty years, only 52.5 spaces were available each year for Chinese refugees.[33]

Kennedy persisted in proposing reforms. In 1957 he presented S.2410 as a "comprehensive" immigration bill that combined "the best features of all the immigration bills introduced this year," such as admission of an estimated 72,000 immigrants in the next two years with provisions for nonquota admission of refugees, including orphans, and reallocation of 30,000 un-used visas from countries such as England to places like Italy and Greece. Kennedy claimed to have obtained "wide agreement on it among key mem-bers of both Houses," including Representative Walter, but it too did not come to a vote.[34] Motivated by the legislative deadlock, Kennedy tried to mobilize public enthusiasm for immigration reform by publishing the pamphlet *A Nation of Immigrants* in 1958 with the help of a ghost author, the prominent Harvard immigration historian Oscar Handlin.

Chinese Americans, alongside the many southern and eastern European ethnic communities facing low quotas, became increasingly vocal lobbyists for immigration reform. Shing-Tai Liang, president of the Chinese Consoli-dated Benevolent Association, wrote to Senator Kennedy on August 27, 1957, to comment on S.2792 and HR 8123, which called for the "exemption from deportation of aliens" who had arrived between December 22, 1945, and November 1, 1954, through fraudulent claims if "such misrepresentation was predicted upon fear of persecution, in the event of repatriation." Chinese Americans who lived under the persistent shadow of paper son fraud from the exclusion era took eager interest in measures that might provide relief from their pervasive fears of deportation. Liang urged that the measure's deadline be extended to before December 22, 1945. He noted the many "law-abiding persons of Chinese ancestry who are in this category" who had oth-erwise "lived exemplary lives and deserve to be accorded the benefit of the humane provisions of this Section."[35] The Chinese American community had gained enough standing and political savvy to lobby for laws that could erase its history of illegal immigration stemming from discriminatory and unreasonable laws.

Non-Chinese advocates for immigration reform pointed out that current laws inhibited the immigration of strategically useful individuals. Mark Damon of Cambridge, Massachusetts, wrote to Senator Kennedy describing the "several thousands of scientists and engineers, living in the U.S., whose skills and experiences are urgently needed in our defense work," but unable to settle due to "a minor immigration regulation." Damon referred specifi-cally to first-preference immigrants who were "aliens whose services are needed urgently in the U.S." but had started out as "non-immigrants." They faced many immigration hurdles despite, in some cases, having received high levels of security clearance for work on U.S. defense projects such as guided missiles, rocketry, and weapons systems fields. Damon blamed these complications for the "departure to Red China of several Chinese experts in radar and electronics."[36] Damon's letter echoed State Department reports that communist agents were "waging a ruthless terror campaign against anti-Communist Chinese refugee atomic scientists and technicians in the U.S." intended to force Chinese physicists and electronics, aviation, and engineer-ing specialists to go home.

Retaining Chinese scientists had gained urgency in 1957. Under the leadership of Chinese ambassador to Poland, Wang Bingnan, who had brokered the departure of Qian Xuesen in 1955, "psychological warfare" tactics included blackmail against those with families still in China through letters, phone calls, and personal visits demanding that Chinese scientists "place at the disposal of the Communist Government the special skills acquired in America." The International News Service described the students facing such concerted recruiting efforts as "the cream of the crop in China" that came to study after World War II, whose ranks had included Qian along with Li Zhengdao and Yang Zhenning.[37] On October 4 the Soviets had leapt ahead in the space race by launching Sputnik. Under such conditions, the valuable skills of educated Chinese, and their strategic importance in the severe technological and military competition of the Cold War, went a long way to rendering beliefs in essential racial differences and inequality shortsighted and even dangerous. Circumstances had changed so much that the very laws that used race to limit immigration and settlement in America had become foolhardy anachronisms when the cost might be losing the war for global freedom against the Soviet Union. Understandably, Kennedy responded to Damon, affirming his concurrence with the state of crisis and efforts for reform: "I am working on an Immigration bill which has just such a provision which you suggested."[38]

The racial repositioning of Chinese continued. In 1959 Reverend Peter Shih of the Chinese Christian Church of New England wrote to Kennedy, describing at length the hardships faced by Chinese refugees in his church and asking him to find ways to regularize their status. Kennedy responded with compassion: "I believe this is not merely a Chinese matter. It is a simple humanitarian gesture which is consistent with American traditions, and I hope that lawful status can be granted all residents of America who have proved their loyalty and usefulness to this country."[39] At least in Kennedy's eyes, their race and national origin should not prevent Chinese from receiving the same immigration and citizenship rights possessed by other Americans.

Against the growing drum beat for immigration reform, in March 1960 Representative Walter proposed refugee legislation of his own that he hoped would ameliorate the drive for broader changes. Walter's bill adopted long-standing proposals for permanent refugee laws that had no set expiration or numerical limits but used the UNHCR's narrow definition, which did not include the two biggest groups of refugee of the 1960s: Arabs who had formerly lived in Israel and Chinese living in Hong Kong or elsewhere. In effect, only European refugees would benefit. A host of refugee affairs activists protested, led by Msgr. Edward E. Swanstrom, executive director of Roman Catholic Relief Services and chair of the American Council of Voluntary Agencies for Foreign Service.[40] Walter's bill ultimately passed but left considerable scope for continuing calls for broader reforms. Chinese Americans grew in visibility in these campaigns, particularly with the long-delayed admission of Hawaii as a state and the election of Asian Americans such as Hiram Fong to Congress. As a senator, Fong (R-HI) joined the ranks of legislators demanding a racially more equitable system of immigration admissions in growing numbers through the early 1960s.

These unresolved struggles positioned the Hong Kong refugee crisis in 1962 as a strategic opportunity to air long-standing grievances against the McCarran-Walter Act, present the claims of deserving Chinese, and press for change. Louis Goelz, the American consul general in Hong Kong who presided over the parole program in 1962, observed that the measure "had a lot of urgency attached to it—I believe for political reasons but the idea was to issue as many Chinese visas as was possible." Many years of neglect, he said, had intensified the problems. A congressional subcommittee reported that an estimated 1.2 million refugees had entered Hong Kong since 1949—about one-third of the city's total population. About 40,000 to 50,000 had been entering each year—half legally and others "without control." Since 1953 only about 30,000 refugees had managed to move elsewhere—about 18,000 to Taiwan and 10,000 to the United States through 9,118 visas issued through the Refugee Relief Program and the 1957 Act.[41] In 1962 the sudden population growth had produced "some pressure being brought, mostly from California. There was political pressure being brought to bear against the White House, and the White House was responding to it. They wanted that program started, and they wanted it done as soon as possible." Through this maelstrom America's immigration gates widened considerably for Chinese because "most people in Hong Kong were refugees . . . and anybody who left the Mainland at any time who could qualify at certain dates and circumstances involved. Anybody could qualify."[42] Despite Goelz's generalizations, in practice the 1962 parolees were drawn from applicants already vetted to magnify American relief efforts while demonstrating the low costs and many advantages of domestic immigration reform.

The Refugee Crisis of 1962

Reports of a new Chinese refugee crisis started surfacing in March 1962. After several years of relative calm, during which only a trickle of new arrivals had been able to cross the policed border, suddenly daily influxes of about 250 started flooding into the port of Macao. Most of these new refugees possessed exit permits and spoke of food shortages in China. Initially Americans barely responded to this influx.

By May, however, the tide had turned toward crowded, familiar Hong Kong, which ignited U.S. concern. Alarm grew after May 1, when daily influxes surged to 1,000 to 6,000. The reasons for the recent deluge were unknown. "Most of the refugees are able-bodied young peasants from the surrounding region. Few have told stories of political persecution. Few have shown unusual signs of malnutrition or starvation."[43] Hong Kong attracted greater attention for several reasons. The World Refugee Year activities of 1959–1960 had directed attention to the high numbers of refugees struggling there. U.S. attorney general Robert F. Kennedy had made a well-publicized visit to the city in February that included visits to sites demonstrating American charity.[44] News that the beleaguered colonial authorities, already coping with an estimated 1.2 million refugees, were turning back all those that they could catch further inflamed public sentiments. Could the United States allow people who had risked their lives to escape to freedom be forced back into communism?[45]

The poster child for this latest publicity campaign was nineteen-year-old Lee Ying (see fig. 7.3), whose face besmeared with mud and tears broadcast her utter despair when forced to return across the border. On May 15, 1962, the *New York Herald Tribune* ran her photograph with the title "Red Past, Red Future" and the caption "Lee Ying, only 19, has to go home again. That's Red China, across the way from Hong Kong. Terror and misery from which she fled make up Lee Ying's future. But the British authorities, alarmed by a rising wave of refugees from Red China, send them back from Hong Kong. Lee Ying shows she faces a grim future." Reprinted widely on American front pages and fundraising brochures, Lee Ying's tragedy provided compelling fodder for Americans to respond to the latest Chinese refugee crisis.

Hiram Fong implored his fellow senators to take action, stating that America had a responsibility to undertake more of Hong Kong's struggle against Chinese communism "for to our shame we have been most derelict in the past." Citing a *Life* magazine editorial, Fong pointed out that the United States had accepted but 5,300 Chinese refugees since 1953, Taiwan only 14,000, Australia none, and Canada only close relatives and skilled workmen, while the "voices of charity in Latin America are silent." Even the UNHCR dealt only with Europeans, as did Walter's Refugee Law in 1960. Fong called on his fellow senators to pass reforms showing American leadership and to convince other nations to share Hong Kong's burden to "demonstrate that we are willing to give sanctuary to persons fleeing Communist tyranny no matter in what quarter of the globe it exists."[46]

Editorialists called for Congress to take action, linking the refugee crisis to America's flawed immigration system. On May 23 Max Frankel of the *New York Times* reported that in the past month alone, Hong Kong authorities had turned back 30,000 refugees, reiterating the recent steep rise in Hong Kong's population, which had nearly doubled to about 3,250,000 within the past decade from such emergency flows. Frankel made pointed criticisms of U.S. immigration laws that admitted so few Chinese each year.

Figure 7.3. "Red Past, Red Future." This title and image of the nineteen-year-old, weeping Li Ying appeared on the cover of the *New York Herald Tribune* on May 15, 1962, and was widely used to publicize the plight of Chinese refugees newly arrived in Hong Kong and forced to return to Communist China. Walter H. Judd papers, Box 185, folder 3, Hoover Institution Archives. Courtesy of Hoover Institution Library & Archives, Stanford University.

In response to such pressures, Congress contemplated some relief measures, ranging from Senator Hubert Humphrey's (D-MN) call to use the Food for Peace program to donate food, clothing, and medicine to Senator Philip A. Hart's (D-MI) more sweeping proposals to increase the Chinese annual quota and schedule Senate hearings by the judiciary subcommittee. Representative Walter initially resisted any new admissions of refugees, preferring instead that the United States provide aid by donating food surpluses and insisting as late as May 21 that more immigration was not a possible option: "We, of course, are in no position to absorb any significant number of these people."[47] He and others, such as Senators Karl Mundt (R-SD) and Humphrey, pointed to Taiwan as a possible alternative.[48] However, although Taiwan had offered to receive the refugees, neither Washington nor London saw it as a real solution. Taiwan had received "relatively small numbers of refugees" because security measures were "cumbersome and that of screening against Communist agents even more difficult" and its economy had no need of "peasants." However, other possibilities for resettlement were unworkable even if countries farther away were willing to accept Chinese refugees because their open doors would cause embarrassment for "the United States and most other Western nations that have laws that reflect a fear of a large influx of Asians." Canada had responded by deciding to admit a scant one hundred families. The lack of official response contrasted with high levels of general outcry, with the International Rescue Committee claiming a "very dramatic response" by the public, which had been "'far greater' than in the Cuban refugee program" of 1960.[49]

Under these circumstances of general sympathy for Chinese, on the evening of May 23 Attorney General Robert Kennedy officially authorized use of parole to admit 5,000 refugees.[50] The White House had gained Representative Walter's support for the details of how parole for Chinese would be implemented. At a press conference Walter announced that "preference will be given to those with the technical skills in greatest demand in the United States, and those with close family ties here. They will be drawn from a pool of 5,000 people who have been cleared for entry but who have waited many years for visas because of the small immigration quota for Chinese." He expressed approval for measures that emphasized "first-preference" qualifications and the existing backlog of cleared visa applicants that considered "skills that are scarce in the United States, plus sponsorship to guarantee support." Transportation costs were managed by requiring refugees to fund their own travel or get help from relatives or organizations. This version of refugee admissions incurred few expenditures on the part of the United States, apart from granting admission to a few thousand additional Chinese, and served as a rehearsal for how criteria for general immigration reform might shift away from national origins.[51] Walter predicted the program would start admitting Chinese within two weeks, a projection realized with the entry of the Eng Se-suey family on June 5.

Framed in this way, with minimal and possibly beneficial outcomes for the United States, the parole of Chinese quickly attracted a host of other supporters who could advocate wholeheartedly for this kind of low-cost humanitarian outreach. Senator Thomas Dodd (D-CT) insisted that "we in the United States must first recognize . . . our own responsibilities in the Chinese refugee problem. The . . . problem of refugees from communism is the collective responsibility of the free world, and . . . because of the great power and wealth of the United States in the free world community, this responsibility is pre-eminently our own." Although America had done its part in Europe, "in the case of the Chinese refugees in Hong Kong, I feel we have permitted the British administration to carry an exceedingly heavy burden."[52] For emphasis, Dodd submitted a resolution (S. Res. 346) along with the deputy majority leader, Hubert Humphrey, and Senators Paul Douglas (D-IL), Clair Engle (D-CA), and Mundt affirming the "generous and humane refugee policy" of British authorities in accepting 1.5 million refugees, despite the thousands then being sent back, as well as the decision to offer parole for 5,000 Chinese refugees, "giving preference to family reunion cases, to those who have already applied for admission to the United States, and to professionals, specialists, and skilled workers who can make a significant contribution to American society."[53] Mundt echoed support for more admissions under such selective restrictions, pointing out that in his home state of South Dakota resided "some distinguished Americans of Chinese ancestry; they are splendid citizens. So we would welcome additional members."[54] On May 25 Walter echoed Dodd's move in proposing his own bill in the House to admit already approved, first-preference applicants, limiting numbers and imposing employment selection criteria.[55] These measures would allow to enter the United States not the crush of recent refugee arrivals but refugees already resident in Hong Kong who had established their economic and political bona fides.

The parole of Chinese refugees provided a platform to press for general immigration reform. Senator Hart, known as the "Conscience of the Senate" and a leading advocate for both the Civil Rights Act of 1964 and the Voting Rights Act of 1965, assumed the mantle of leadership for advancing civil rights in border restrictions as well. Within a few days the Senate Judiciary Committee convened a Subcommittee to Investigate Problems Connected with Refugees and Escapees to discuss the problems in Hong Kong and Macao to proclaim American responsibility for aiding Chinese refugees, albeit in limited numbers and after careful screening, but also to praise the attributes of Chinese immigrants in a segue to calling for general reforms of immigration laws. Referring to letters from his constituents, Senator Hart launched the discussions by boldly stating that "the majority of Americans ... now believe the problem is one for all free people" and not just that for the government of Hong Kong.[56] Kenneth Keating (R-NY) described the situation as "one of history's most heartrending episodes in human misery" for which "there has been no exodus from freedom to tyranny" for the Hong Kong refugees from Chinese communism. Keating questioned whether "the free world [has] really lived up to its responsibilities in this area" and pointed out that "our immigration laws have discriminated against Orientals almost from their inception." In 1961 only one one-thousandth of all quota immigrants admitted had been Chinese, and U.S. refugee relief programs had provided little help for Hong Kong refugees. Keating urged that the United States take greater steps than a one-time parole, pointing out that some Chinese nationals had been deported from U.S. soil itself owing to lack of provisions to allow them to stay. These intractable problems required "an enlightened immigration policy and a more equitable refugee relief program."[57] Undertaking such reform measures could benefit more than America's domestic racial inequalities.

State Department representatives affirmed the foreign policy advantages of the parole in ameliorating discriminatory legislation of the past. Averill Harriman, assistant secretary for Far Eastern affairs, testified to the "good reaction from some of our Asian friends who live here in Washington." According to Harriman's informants, parole for Chinese "indicates a changed attitude toward immigration from Asian countries, and ... admitting more Asians or not discriminating against Asians in our immigration laws would improve our image ... among the Asian people."[58] In contrast, inaction produced negative responses. Senator Fong queried Richard Brown, director of the Office of Refugee and Migration Affairs, about reactions to the failure of Walter's limited refugee law in 1960 to admit Asians. Brown replied, "Quite candidly and honestly ... I think it had an adverse effect upon our image."[59] By 1962 limited measures of refugee relief were no longer adequate to mollify America's Asian allies in the face of permanent laws that treated them unfairly.

Chinese Refugee Relief

Beyond the one-time parole and flurry of accompanying publicity, the White House and State Department created a new organization intended to convey American concern for Chinese refugees at the highest levels of power, as well as the integration of Chinese Americans into U.S. democracy. Like ARCI a decade earlier, Chinese Refugee Relief swiftly came into being with a roster of high-powered backers listed on its masthead, such as honorary cochairmen and past U.S. presidents Herbert Hoover and Harry Truman, and a group of founding sponsors that included Eleanor Roosevelt; Chinese ambassador Jiang Tingfu; Representatives Walter, John W. McCormack

(D-MA), and Judd; Senators Douglas, Humphrey, Dodd, Keating, Eugene McCarthy (D-MN), and Fong; former Hong Kong consul general Everett Drumright; the author Lin Yutang; and Archbishop Paul Yu Pin.[60] Unlike ARCI, which operated under close CIA supervision to channel the mobility of Chinese intellectuals overseas, Chinese Refugee Relief functioned chiefly within the United States under the figurehead leadership of two Chinese American immigrants, Anna Chennault and the Washington businessman David Lee, who welcomed the Eng Se-suey family in Chicago and served as treasurer.

Attractive and ambitious, Chennault had had little interaction with Chinese American organizations or communities before agreeing to head Chinese Refugee Relief. After the death of her much older husband, she had moved to Washington DC and became a well-known political hostess. Despite her lack of community ties, Chennault eagerly provided the ethnically appropriate public face of this "private relief program" that prominently displayed Chinese American integration and support for Chinese immigrants from the highest circles of American leaders. The main image used to publicize CRR featured Chennault standing alongside Kennedy in the Oval Office (fig. 7.2).[61] CRR functioned primarily for publicity purposes, widely proclaiming its general goals of limiting public expenditures by asking "the American public to support a drive to feed, clothe, and resettle the refugees" in order "to show people who want to be free that we still care about them" but never fielding any staff to carry out such projects.[62] According to David Lee, Chennault raised some funds during trips to Taiwan but quickly lost interest in the organization.[63] CCR served as the platform that launched Chennault's career as a political operative supporting flexible agendas. After advocating for Chinese refugees on Kennedy's behalf, Chennault became a fundraiser for Nixon, acted as informal U.S. liaison to Vietnam, and shed her Nationalist ties altogether to facilitate improved U.S. ties to the PRC during the rapprochement of the 1980s. The practical aspects of selecting and moving key Chinese refugees to the United States fell to the International Rescue Committee, which Hugh Wilford describes as "heavily implicated in the covert network that bound the U.S. intelligence community to the émigré relief organizations of the early Cold War era," that took over functions formerly performed by ARCI.[64] ARCI's Hong Kong office had shut down in 1960, after Travis Fletcher's determination in 1958 that few among newer influxes of refugees were college educated and were therefore not relevant to ARCI's aims.[65] Chinese Refugee Relief, in the guise of Anna Chennault, assumed responsibility for performing American concern for a broader assortment of Chinese refugees. As CRR chairwoman, Chennault also served magnificently in providing public testimony that highlighted Chinese model minority traits that positioned them as exemplary immigrants shaped by values and cultural practices.

The publicity campaign extolling the virtues and compatibility of Chinese refugees as immigrants continued with the arrival of the sixth parolee, after the five members of the Eng family, on June 7, 1962. As movingly recounted in "13-Year Wait Ends in Joy for Chinese Girl," the twenty-three-year-old Deanna Chu was the last of her family of seven to come to the United States and the first parolee to come to the New York area. She reunited with her sisters and father at the Overseas Press Club in the company of William J. Vanden Heuvel, president of the International Rescue Committee. She had learned only four hours before departure that she would be admitted to the United States and was able to board a plane escorted by Vanden Heuvel who happened to be visiting Hong Kong. The pair landed in Philadelphia because of bad weather, and Vanden Heuvel drove Deanna to New York for her long-delayed family reunion, which was well attended by journalists despite how hastily the Office of Refugee and Migration Affairs had granted Deanna entry. As reported by the *New York Times*, "As Miss Chu emerged from the elevator on the tenth floor, her younger sister, Lillian, 21, ran toward her. They had not seen each other for six years. 'Lillian!' cried Miss Chu, as both erupted into tears and laughter." The last time Deanna had seen two of her other sisters was 1949 when they had left for the United States. The Chus were clearly deserving of American aid as the children of a former officer in the Nationalist Ministry of Communications who had made his way to the United States in 1956. The family were pleasingly Chinese with the necessary attributes for integration into the United States. "All four sisters at yesterday's reception wore traditional Chinese sheath dresses, with high Mandarin collars, but spoke softly to each other in British-accented English." Deanna had been paroled through the efforts of her sister, Dorreen, a writer for NBC's *Today Show* who had brought her situation to the attention of Vanden Heuvel, who claimed he had been able to expedite Deanna's case because family reunification was a priority in the parole program. Left unsaid was how moving a human interest story the Chu family reunion provided for newspaper reports.[66]

Seven months later the *New York Times* reported the arrival of the five thousandth parolee, Thomas Lee Ching, emphasizing his suitability to assimilate into American life. Lee conveyed a sense of settledness when asked about his future and employment, saying, "It doesn't make very much difference, we will be content to live in the United States from hand to mouth." Lee traveled with his wife and seven children and had worked for the Nationalist Foreign Affairs Bureau before the Communist takeover led to his flight to Hong Kong in 1949. During World War II he had worked as a translator with American Army and Marine units, and then as an English teacher and translator while in Hong Kong.[67]

Despite initial plans to parole only 5,000 Chinese, the U.S. consulate in Hong Kong continued accepting applications until December 31, 1963. A total of 1,558 other refugee visa recipients were already waiting to follow Thomas Ching. Referring to the tiny regular quota of 105, the *New York Times* account noted that "the special presidential order was a move to release the feeling of hopelessness that had settled over the crowded British possession and its packed crowds of refugees from Communist China." Such charity was not detrimental to the United States, for "the first priority is those with skills beneficial to the American economy. These would be professional persons primarily" followed by parents, spouses, and children of citizens and permanent residents, then siblings and married children of resident aliens. Nor were the parolees necessarily a permanent problem because Congress had yet to vote to allow them to apply for citizenship. In the end, the parole program provided admission and eventually permanent status for 15,011 Chinese.[68] Of the Chinese parolees, almost one-quarter had professional or technical training while 60 percent were relatives of U.S. citizens.[69]

The Reciprocal Damage of Immigration Selection

Despite the heartwarming stories of the Engs, Deanna Chu, and Thomas Lee Ching, the limits of parole and aid to Hong Kong's refugees received criticism in Asia. In *Asian Survey* Hu Yueh had commented on Taiwan's "token relief" efforts that "produce greater results in terms of political propaganda than in terms of relief." The only real assistance provided was transport to Taiwan, but as it benefited only 55,000, it fell far short of matching the scale of the problem.[70]

In the same vein, although the parole program in 1962 had been described in the American press as "a token effort to relieve the strain on the British colony,"[71] its intended beneficiaries were not so grateful. Officially colonial authorities had welcomed President Kennedy's authorization of parole, but in practice the program did little to alleviate Hong Kong's population pressures. "Informed sources" conveyed both official intentions to continue sending back as many refugees as could be caught and the "hope that the United States public will not expect Hong Kong to admit refugees to replace those going to America," for those entering the colony were estimated to be double to four times the numbers of those leaving. Responding to American emphasis on admitting those with skills and professional backgrounds, "Informed sources said that United States decision meant Hong Kong would lose persons with skills who could not be satisfactorily replaced from the present flood of refugees who are mostly peasants."[72] Enactment of the parole program through mid-June 1962 confirmed these worries about loss of skilled individuals. The Hong Kong government did not view emigration "as an over-all solution to the colony's refugee problem" because in the past it has tended to skim off the elite of Hong Kong's skilled and literate people. Most countries have restricted their acceptance of immigrants from Hong Kong to skilled workers or relatives of people already settled in the country. The vast majority of recent refugees from China have been illiterate peasants who would be acceptable to no country on the basis of the present standards. Any mass emigration of Hong Kong's skilled workers, many of whom have gained their proficiency here over the last ten years, would leave Hong Kong with a residue of untrained people capable only of the simplest manual labor. The industries that have made Hong Kong a self-supporting colony would quickly slow down.[73]

Although this article identified the Chinese Nationalist government on Taiwan as the chief target of such criticisms, U.S. policies reflected the same kinds of self-serving help that inflicted damage on Hong Kong's economy.

Within America, one-time refugee relief measures no longer sufficed to stave off demands for more permanent immigration reforms. The *New York Times* complained that "No arrangements . . . to provide relief for the migrants and remove some to Taiwan, the United States and Canada can be really effective, so potentially large is the problem and so small the help we proffer" unless Congress acted "to modify our immigration laws to give at least some minimal relief and perhaps to ease our conscience just a little."[74] The *Chicago Daily News* argued for the importance of Hong Kong and its strategic and humanitarian value in the war against communism. "Two things are clearly at stake here. One is the continued existence of Hong Kong as a British trading post—and as an eye and ear on the Chinese mainland. In human terms, however, the immediate concern must be for the thousands of starving people trying to escape from the hell their Communist masters have made." The *Richmond Times-Despatch* emphasized that "The United States . . . cannot afford to turn its back on the tearful and suffering Chinese who wish to escape to the free world."[75] Elected officials were prepared to take such actions. As Senator Hart reconvened the subcommittee on Hong Kong and Macao's refugee crisis, he urged passage of his proposal to admit fifty thousand refugees and received support from other legislators, such as Keating, who called for "an enlightened immigration policy and a more equitable refugee relief program" in order to resolve once and for all "the Hong Kong problem."[76]

From Temporary Parole to Permanent Reform

When the Senate subcommittee reconvened on June 7, the hearings focused on the need for permanent immigration reform to resolve long-standing refugee problems. The principles deployed in the parole of Chinese refugees, which had received such bipartisan support, provided the basis for discussing new approaches to border controls. Hart once again set the agenda by summarizing the Hong Kong situation in which about 19,000 refugees had already registered for visas but only 2,056 would be admitted through the limited parole program. He urged further action through support for S.3043, which would increase the Chinese annual quota to 5,335 and separately provide for admission of 50,000 refugees from around the world each year. This bill had twenty-five cosponsors in the Senate, many of whom had been founding sponsors of Chinese Refugee Relief. Hart promoted the bill's advantages as "eliminating the present law's discrimination against Chinese and nationalities of other Far Eastern countries" without fear that it would "open the floodgates of immigration."[77] The bill attempted to address a multitude of competing fears and priorities.

Fellow reform advocate Keating squarely tackled fears of economic competition in explaining his support for S.3043 by referring to constituent letters "asking why I wanted to bring more Chinese into this country when we already have an unemployment problem." He cited other correspondence from Hickey-Freeman Co. of Rochester, New York, a clothing manufacturer hoping to employ 150 Chinese. Keating ascribed "economic and humanitarian" motives to Hickey-Freeman, observing that "even in areas of unemployment, certain skills may be in short supply." That is, the United States could admit more immigrants if it selected those with abilities and training not available among Americans. Thereby the United States could kill several birds with one stone—help Chinese by admitting them in greater numbers, fill gaps in the U.S. economy's need for skilled workers, and ameliorate international impressions that America was undemocratic in discriminating by race and national origins in its immigration laws.[78]

Echoing the rationales given for the repeal of Chinese exclusion, an array of refugee relief advocates, many affiliated with religious organizations, testified to the need for solutions in the form of immigration reforms which would nonetheless have limited impact on the United States. James MacCracken, director of Immigration Services of the Church World Service, stated: "We...do not believe in irresponsible immigration into our country. We do believe that greater attention can meritoriously be paid to refugees, family reunion, and special skill categories." MacCracken noted that both President Kennedy and Representative Walter had affirmed these priorities "in their separate and important Chinese refugee immigration proposals" and called for permanent legislation addressing such needs.[79] The Most Reverend Edward E. Swanstrom, executive director of Catholic Relief Services of the National Council of Welfare Churches, affirmed America's humanitarian obligations abroad: "the lives of hundreds of thousands of human beings, made to the image and likeness of God, like ourselves, are involved and no human effort should be spared to find a solution to them. The nations of the free world met the test before, when over 10 million people found themselves displaced in Europe after the last World War and I am sure they can meet it again. Much of the leadership, however, will have to come from our own nation" (36).William J. Vanden Heuvel described widespread sympathy for Chinese refugees and refugees in general: "There was a real identity with the problem and a tremendous urge to help" (52, 54).[80] William W. Channel of the American Friends Service Committee pointed out that by addressing "one of the most dramatic refugee problems in the world today," the United States could "take advantage of the Chinese desire to work and make a better life for themselves." As "a courageous and industrious people," Chinese would "make their way if given a chance" (65–66). Channel affirmed Keating's claim that refugee relief could be both a humanitarian gesture and of economic benefit to the United States.

Chinese refugees themselves provided the most compelling evidence for why laws should be changed and more admitted. Deanna Chu was among the witnesses testifying on June 7 and described her family's substantial record of attainment in government and academics, leading Hart to respond "I wish we were going into the living rooms of every home in America" and declare "I would like to find anybody that would not wrestle with the proposition that this American society is not richer because you and your sisters are here" (57). The Chus demonstrated that refugees and their children did not necessarily become burdens on American society but welcome assets.

Some of the most compelling arguments for immigration reform were made by Anna Chennault, representing Chinese Refugee Relief. Chennault used her own example to argue the low costs of greater acceptance for Chinese as refugees and as immigrants: "I can tell you about the heart and mind of the refugee, for I myself and my 4 sisters were refugees from Japanese terror in China during World War II. I know the misery of physical privation of the homeless and the emotional privation of the forgotten. When I think of the refugee in Hong Kong, I can only pray 'There but for the grace of God go I.'" Chennault claimed that beyond material aid, what the United States could provide, inexpensively, was hope: "Other witnesses have told you of their physical misery. But for me, who has been a refugee, their most terrible misery is in the heart, for the most vital need of men is hope, and the refugee goes to sleep fearing that the world has no room for him and that his future holds no hope. But more than food, more than shelter, these good people need hope." She affirmed the effectiveness of America's programs for symbolic refugee relief in bolstering the resistance of Chinese to communist enticements. Further emphasizing the low costs of aiding Chinese refugees, she described the goals of Chinese Refugee Relief as being to "raise private funds through public solicitation" and working with "existing international nongovernmental refugee organizations such as church and social welfare groups." Claiming personal experience and expertise, Chennault presented aspects of the program that "we believe are essential to public understanding of this problem" and skillfully articulated qualities of the Chinese parolees that rendered them ideal immigrants: "Those who are now coming to the United States have been fully cleared as to security by agencies of the U.S. Government. . . . They represent the top level refugee group: businessmen, technicians, engineers, and others possessing specific skills. None of these refugees are coming here to be a burden on our relief agencies or to take jobs from American workers." Chennault stressed Chinese family and cultural values that made them stable, productive, and self-sufficient members of society.

> Nor will the children of refugees represent a problem to their communities. We Chinese-Americans can point with pride to the fact that because of the strong family bonds that characterize the Chinese people, juvenile delinquency is almost unknown in Chinese-American communities, and that Chinese-American citizens are not found on American relief rolls. Once this is understood, we believe that the American public will recognize that these people will make a lasting, worthwhile contribution to their communities and the Nation.

Economically, politically, and socially, Chinese parolees were compatible with American values, even embodying ideal cultural traits for an immigrant group. They could be admitted at little cost, financial or otherwise, to America and would work to earn their keep. After Chennault's own testimony ended, she introduced prime examples of such model immigrants: Eng Se-suey, his wife, and their two daughters.[81]

Chennault interpreted for Eng, conveying his appreciation for the opportunity of settling in the United States. "He is very happy and very grateful that he comes to America, a free country. . . . It was wonderful to leave the misery as a refugee and come into this country as a free citizen." Eng valued his chance to gain acceptance. "He also wants to express that his family and his children are growing up as Americans, and be good citizens to this country," and he expressed gratitude for the exercise of executive authority providing his salvation. "He said if not because of the emergency law, he still wouldn't be here today." Hart seized this opportunity to iterate the value of Chinese as immigrants: "I think that the more people in this country see the Engs and families like them, the greater the opportunity will develop for understanding and appreciating the need to improve the immigration attitude in this country." For emphasis, Hart referred to a White House reception honoring American Nobel Prize winners, whose ranks included fifteen immigrants, with the comment, "We need these people. We are the better because they are here" (92–94). The parole program in 1962, with its emphasis on family reunification *and* employment, had conjoined the once largely separate streams of working-class and petty entrepreneurial Chinatown Chinese with that of educated Chinese as sharing qualities of hard work, economic achievement, family values, and tremendous potential to contribute to the United States.

The Chinese American witnesses demonstrated the kinds of model immigrants and citizens that reformed immigration laws could admit, as observed by Senator Alexander Wiley (R-WI) in his compliments to Anna Chennault: "It has been a high privilege for me to sit here this morning and see this fine American citizen, Mrs. Chennault. We know what contribution she has made, what contribution her husband has made. I will agree with your sentiment that we are practically all of us sons of foreigners. And we can use more of this quality stuff in America" (97). To punctuate this call for Americans to do their part, even the newly arrived and far from well-off Eng Se-suey donated twenty dollars to Chinese Refugee Relief. Chennault explained, "He just told me, even he himself, a refugee, and they do not have much money. But he feels that he is now in this country, he is more fortunate than the rest, and he wants to do whatever he can" (104). In the face of Eng's generosity, how could better-established Americans refuse to support a cause with such low costs and such clear advantages?

Experts in Chinese refugee relief affirmed the high human value of even destitute Chinese not yet allowed to immigrate. Donald E. Anderson, director of the Lutheran Immigration Service, described a "typical" refugee, Mr. H., who was a 1937 graduate of Sun Yatsen University and had worked as chief accountant in a provincial government department. He and his family fled to Hong Kong in 1949, where they subsisted in a rented, 10x12 foot squatter hut. Mr. H. could not find employment as a bookkeeper, so his wife supported the family as a seamstress working on a secondhand machine at home surrounded by their children. Not until the machine broke down after four or five years did the family ask for help. Despite their poverty, "His hut was found to be neat and tidy, and his children clean and orderly. . . . Multiply this story of Mr. H. by the thousands, and it becomes possible to know the Chinese refugee. . . . His hardship, his poverty, and the almost insurmountable conditions surrounding him have not destroyed his integrity and dignity as a human being." America's inhumane and impractical immigration laws limited solutions for such deserving individuals and families. "If, for example, Mr. H., who is a desirable immigrant in that he has the will to work, the initiative to find ways to support himself and his family, and the dignity and integrity to become a good citizen, wished to emigrate, it would be almost impossible for him to do so." Understandably, the Lutheran Immigration Service Committee had voted on June 12, 1962, to support the "principles and objectives implicit in" immigration reform bill S. 3043 (107–9, 111).

Setting aside racial differences, Chinese American witnesses cited their cultural values in asserting the merits of Chinese immigrants. Irving Sheu Kee Chin, an attorney with Holtzman, Wise & Shepard in New York, presented the perspective of Chinese American communities. The American-born Chin was an impressive witness, having a BA degree from Yale, having served in the U.S. Air Force, then having graduated from Harvard Law School. He was president of the Chinatown Junior Chamber of Commerce, dean of the Chinese Christian Youth Conference of the East Coast, and legal counsel to the Chinatown Trade Association. Chin urged the subcommittee to increase the overall number of refugees admitted and the annual Chinese immigration quota while getting rid of racial tracking by the Asian-Pacific Triangle and emphasizing instead the adaptability and economic worth of Chinese:

> Once given the advantages of education and the freedom of opportunity as it exists in America, the modern Chinese integrates well into the American society while simultaneously contributing his talents toward American growth and progress. Thus the professions of medicine, law, psychiatry, teaching, engineering, and science are staffed with Chinese who are making their mark in the professional world. Engineers of Chinese ancestry now work in perfecting electronic defense projects and missiles for the protection of America as well as being involved on the space satellite program. (133–35)

Chin argued that admitting more Chinese would "give the opportunity to those refugees to produce some day another Albert Einstein or another Nobel Prize winning Chinese; to demonstrate beyond a doubt that the United States practices what it preaches about equality by putting democracy into action; to show that the melting pot theory is fact, not fantasy; and to prove that America is still the land of opportunity" (137). He cited Li Zhengdao and Yang Zhenning as examples of "how well the Chinese are integrating into the society and contributing to America's progress" and pointed out "that many of the refugees on the proposed first preference quota have professional skills and qualifications and will eventually be of service to the community" (133–35).

Chinese talents and skills would not only enhance the American economy, Chin claimed, their culture and values would impose little burden on the United States. "The strong family ties, inner control and discipline found in the Chinese family have been repeatedly hailed and cited for the nonexistence of juvenile delinquency. The respect for law and order coupled with the high degree of family pride and training are factors derived from the Chinese culture. The industrious family working together will also be characterized in the new refugees." Chinese values ensured the "absence of a need for public welfare or for the care of the aged" because "Confucian filial piety and respect for the elders" would guarantee "that there will be no public charges, no juvenile delinquency, no unemployment problem as these new immigrant Americans eagerly await the richest blessing of all—a new life" (133–35). Those admitted through family reunification would be provided for by their relatives. Chinese American organizations would raise funds toward their support in cooperation with Chinese Refugee Relief and not impose on public finances. Furthermore, Chinese lived in the United States in very low numbers: "I think once the American people realize how insignificant the group is, that even if you doubled the whole number of—double the number of people of non-Caucasian ancestry here, you will increase it to only 1 percent of the whole population." Hence there was no risk "that you are going to Orientalize America" (140).

Samuel E. Yee, an assistant city attorney representing the city and county of San Francisco and the Chinese American Citizens Alliance, criticized Walter's refugee law from 1960 for excluding Chinese and insisted on "the legal rights of all Chinese-American citizens . . . to secure to them equal economical and political opportunities and concurrently to continually reaffirm to them their correlative rights, duties and obligations as such citizens" (128). Yee noted improvements with the parole in 1962 but complained of its overemphasis on "professionals, specialists and skilled workers who can make a significant contribution to American society," requesting greater emphasis on family reunification in arguing that "paroled refugees with family ties in this country will be assured of temporary financial and material aid without the danger of becoming public charges" or "security-risk problems." Friends and relatives create jobs and assistance, he said, and he iterated the Chinese American community's support for S. 3043 (129–30). On behalf of George Christopher, the mayor of San Francisco, once the heart of the anti-Chinese movement, Yee introduced a letter of welcome for Chinese. Mayor Christopher offered the following guarantee: "We assure you that any Chinese refugees who may be legally admitted to the United States will be welcomed by the San Franciscans" (127).[82]

Chinese had been purged of their yellow peril threat when it became clear that the United States could limit their numbers to tolerable levels and impose restrictions so that they would not only not burden American society and economy but become readily integrated, economically contributing citizens instead. The United States could remove racially discriminatory criteria from its immigration laws, confident that selection measures could ensure that those who arrived would be assets to the United States. The stage was set for America to change its laws to start admitting more Chinese, albeit those best positioned to benefit the United States.

On June 18, Hart made another appeal to the Senate for support of S. 3043 by evoking "the plight of Chinese refugees [which] causes genuine concern and sympathy in the hearts and minds of all Americans" and the inadequacies of stopgap, refugee measures. The "Chinese parolee program is only a piecemeal approach to the situation. What we really need in the long run is an intelligent reform of our basic immigration law. Such action on the part of Congress would strike a greater blow for freedom, and would serve as a far more appropriate example for other nations to follow." What was needed, he charged, was a "bill [that] would remove the discriminatory clauses in the Immigration and Nationality Act of 1952, thereby raising the Chinese quota. It would also place on our books a permanent provision for the admission to this country of up to 50,000 refugees annually, from all parts of the world." Hart challenged his colleagues and President Kennedy to enable America to live up to its ideals before an attentive world. "This bill, Mr. President, would bring our present immigration concepts and practices more closely into line with our traditions and ideals, and add substantially to our good will throughout the world. . . . Our response to the needs of Chinese refugees is being observed by a waiting world. They want to see if we practice what we preach."[83] Despite these impassioned arguments, Hart's bill died in committee, and Congress would take yet a few more years to bring American immigration laws closer to the constitutional ideals he had invoked.

In 1962 Congress *did* pass a narrower law that partially ameliorated the situation of Chinese immigrants while enacting entry preferences with the greatest resonance and acceptability in Congress. Passed on October 24, 1962, Public Law 87–885 was subtitled "An Act: To facilitate the entry of alien skilled specialists and certain relatives of United States citizens, and for other purposes" and granted nonquota entry for those qualifying under the McCarran-Walter Act of 1952 as first-preference immigrants, or "aliens with special occupational skills," who had applied to regularize their status before January 1, 1962. Suddenly, PL 87–885 cleared the logjam of first-preference Chinese applicants awaiting quota slots and enabled them to regularize their status without the decades long waits imposed by the quota system. This law signaled Kennedy's intention to feature economic considerations when advocating immigration reform, a project he did not complete and which fell to Lyndon Johnson to oversee, but with far less conviction and understanding of relevant issues.

Despite the rhetoric brandished in Congress and State Department machinations through ARCI, refugee laws and processes were imprecise mechanisms to screen for Chinese immigrants with the greatest potential for economic contributions, as even those with marketable skills often could not find suitable employment though they enhanced the overall educational attainment statistics attributed to Chinese. Alongside refugee admissions, however, operated a more direct mechanism for the United States to recruit Chinese immigrants with the most useful skills and training, particularly in the science and technology fields. As chapter 8 will describe, American programs for international education had continued to expand after World War II, with the significant change that foreign graduates could now legally seek jobs in the United States, which for many served as a stepping stone to applying for permanent residency and citizenship. Despite their demonstrated desirability as employees, these educated workers ran afoul of the quota system, which by 1957 was already mortgaged until 2036. The pragmatism of enabling such usefully trained and experienced workers to regularize their status and remain in the country attracted widespread support, adding to pressures for immigration reform.

CHAPTER 8

Symbiotic Brain Drains

IMMIGRATION REFORM AND THE KNOWLEDGE
WORKER RECRUITMENT ACT OF 1965

IN 1951 YI-FU TUAN (B. 1930) ARRIVED in America to study for a PhD degree in geography at UC Berkeley. He would graduate to an illustrious academic career, moving inland to teach at several prominent universities before retiring from the University of Wisconsin at Madison in 1998.[1] Timing and politics were to his advantage, for the Cold War and America's alliance with Nationalist Taiwan—for which Tuan's father had worked as a diplomat—ensured that he enjoyed once unthinkable opportunities newly available with the dismantling of Chinese exclusion as an intellectual from the right side of the global political divide. Tuan's success derives only in part from his individual brilliance, for changing conditions in American society opened previously closed doors that allowed him to attain his full professional potential, as had I. M. Pei, Li Zhengdao, Yang Zhenning, and Wang An. During the 1950s, instead of having to return to China to work, Tuan could legally find a job in the United States while enjoying a broader array of intellectual and professional choices.[2]

At first Tuan had to assert his standing as an academic unburdened by his ethnic heritage. In contradiction to prevailing trends in the field, an influential graduate adviser suggested that he research Chinatown as a suitable dissertation topic. Appalled, Tuan elected instead to measure pediments in the Arizona desert, an unraced project comparable to those of his non-Asian classmates.[3] From quantitative geographer he evolved to found the field of humanistic geography and become celebrated around the world for his imagination and insights regarding the emotional interphase of humans with their physical worlds. Such a career trajectory had not existed for Chinese in America before World War II—those who managed to escape laundry and restaurant work to enter white-collar and professional employment were often bound to projects associated with their ethnic heritage. Tuan's many publications—monographs such as *Topophilia: A Study of Environmental Perception, Attitudes, and Values, Space and Place: The Perspective of Experience, Landscapes of Fear,* and *Cosmos and Hearth: A Cos-*

Figure 8.1. Yi-fu Tuan conquers the American West, 1954. Tuan in the Little Colorado Canyon researching his PhD dissertation, "Pediments in Southeastern Arizona" (1959). His younger brother, San-fu Tuan, took the picture. Courtesy of Yi-fu Tuan.

mopolite's Viewpoint—tackle ambitious terrains.[4] Tuan's pioneering body of work has expanded "concepts of geography beyond the physical towards the metaphysical, ethical, and aesthetic," exploring how "the meanings and processes of place—their material and symbolic qualities—as well as the range of peoples and social relations that continuously define and create social and spatial contexts" might be considered in humanities and social science fields as disparate as history, cultural studies, anthropology, and poststructuralism.[5] Tuan scrutinized the broad intersection of nature and culture in topics such as "environmental perception, symbolic landscapes, geographic aesthetics, environmental ethics, and cultural fantasy"[6] to produce revelations concerning "humans' emotional ties to place" that are now so pervasive, yet uncited, that a *Chronicle of Higher Education* article described his influence as follows: "The most flattering way of putting this might be to say that Mr. Tuan enjoys a rare kind of acknowledgement: He is so present that he is invisible, informing others at a deeper-than-footnote level."[7] Tuan's intellectual legacy speaks to the breadth of human experiences in ways that transcend race and ethnicity.

Nor does Tuan regard himself as participating in Asian American history. In *Who Am I? An Autobiography of Emotion, Mind, and Spirit*, he self-deprecatingly notes that the unlikely combination of being a "middle-class Chinese" and a "geographer" does not fit traditional narratives of ethnic biographical writing.

> A middle-class Chinese such as myself cannot offer the attractive and highly marketable theme of struggle and heroic climb from Chinatown poverty to suburban affluence. For I had no such struggle and climb. Chinese immigrants who were middle-class professionals have always been accepted and successful in the United States. And what is more boring than a story of unqualified success—from good student to well-paid engineer?[8]

Unmentioned in Tuan's account is the reality that Chinese Americans had only recently gained ready access to middle-class standing, much less mainstream acceptance. It is precisely because Tuan did *not* experience this mythologized ascent through ethnic immigrant struggle that his life and career illuminate how discourses of race and immigration had shifted in the mid-twentieth century. Tuan's path to success reveals how the Cold War, changing laws regarding citizenship and immigration, and shifting terms of racial inequality and international politics made it both possible and desirable for nonwhites such as Chinese to transition effortlessly into the middle-class mainstream.

Tuan was an early example of a migration flow that gained the label of "brain drain" by the mid-1960s. He was one of thousands of Chinese that arrived after World War II for purportedly temporary study in the United States who found legal employment and means to resettle permanently in what became a widely debated transfer of valuable, educated human resources from developing to industrialized nations. The student "side door" provided a reasonably reliable pathway to immigrate into the United States through the initially temporary, but numerically unlimited, route of entering legally as a student, finding employment, and remaining.[9] The most difficult step, sharply restricted until 1962 by quota restrictions, was conversion to permanent status. On behalf of such economically useful individuals, however, the Immigration Bureau, Congress, and the State Department made legal and administrative accommodations that permitted extensions of legal residency. This immigration flow built on the foundations laid by the roughly twelve thousand "stranded students" transformed by World War II and the Cold War into refugees who settled in America and the influxes of refugees admitted directly from Asia who had undergone efforts to screen for their educational, political, and employment qualifications. The international student immigration side door tapped even more directly into these economic preferences by admitting only those Chinese who could gain admission and means to finance education in the United States and find jobs with employers who could apply for their permanent status.

After World War II the Department of State, with congressional backing, expanded international education programs along with other forms of cultural and technical exchange. Student admissions were unrestricted by immigration quotas, providing a legal means of entry for far greater numbers of Chinese. As detailed in figure A.2, total student numbers increased from 7,542 in 1944–1945, to 25,464 in 1948–1949, 34,232 in 1954–1955, and 48,486 in 1959–1960. The number of Chinese students increased from about 1,300 to 10,000 across these years, while those from decolonizing nations such as India grew even more dramatically, leaping from only 73 in 1944–1945 to 6,813 in 1964–1965. International students began their journey to becoming American by earning graduate degrees, often in scientific, medical, or engineering fields, which enabled them to seek jobs legally, often with employers who could apply for them to gain citizenship. In this way, long-standing American investments in educating future leaders to enhance U.S. influence in China turned toward cultivating a valuable and skilled workforce to feed domestic economic development.

As with the stranded students, restrictive and inegalitarian U.S. immigration laws severely limited the abilities of even the most strategically specialized and educated workers from Asia to gain legal permanent residency. Alongside the politics of the international refugee crisis, economic and military competition against the communist bloc demanded capacities for technological innovation that exerted additional reasons to reform immigration laws. In the two decades after World War II, a succession of presidents working with congressional reformers and lobbying by a widening array of ethnic and religious organizations sought ways to modify America's discriminatory quota system and citizenship and employment practices to privilege the migration of economically useful, value-added elites. The Hart-Celler Act of 1965 enacted many of these priorities, accelerating and magnifying the brain-drain phenomenon even as it enabled unprecedented diversification of the American population through immigration.

Internationally, considerable consternation and alarm greeted this dramatic turn in the flow and settlement of international students in the United States. By the 1960s and 1970s, perceptions of a brain drain spurred global criticism for the loss of such precious human resources from developing nations and particularly to the United States. Those on the sending end re-garded America's long-term acquisition of their most educated elites as a cynical form of theft by the world's most powerful and wealthiest nation from the poorest and most aspirational. International education programs that had once provided training and experience for a leadership class to bring back modernity and progress to struggling homelands had turned into a system for the steady loss of such talented and cultivated individuals. From the perspective of the United States, accusations of brain drain im-peded its efforts to foster stronger international relations by training leaders of emerging nations and expanding capitalist partnerships overseas. How-ever, in the long term for economies that nonetheless managed to advance economically, a so-called brain drain was but one stage of an exchange of knowledge workers, part of a long-term circulation of technological innova-tions and economic formations that over time furthered the integration of the American capitalist powerhouse with the developing economies from which the knowledge workers originated. Starting in the 1970s Chinese knowledge workers returned in growing numbers, bearing not only their advanced degrees but additional training, experience, connections, access to capital, and industrial and entrepreneurial savvy that advanced the global-ization and sophistication of their homeland's economy in collaboration with that of the United States.

Nationalist Taiwan could be considered the chief sufferer of brain drain as a primary partner in the interchange of knowledge workers with the United States. Tracing back to the long-established international education infrastructure that emerged alongside the Boxer Indemnity Fellowship pro-grams (1908) and the Chinese Educational Mission (1872–1881), this com-plexly layered relationship channeled the migration circuits of educated Chinese who brought networks, cultural capital, and knowledge but also desperation to gain footholds in the United States. Although not an engi-neer or scientist as were so many of the brain-drain Chinese, Yi-fu Tuan em-bodied many representative qualities. Prior generations in his family had studied in the United States. In Tuan's case, this training helped his father gain connections and prestigious, if poorly paid, employment in the Na-tionalist foreign service. The Tuans prioritized study abroad, and during World War II his father's work in the diplomatic corps allowed Yi-fu to study first in Australia and then attend Oxford before coming to the United States for graduate study. Like other Chinese of his generation, however, Tuan faced limited options for a Chinese homeland, with neither Taiwan nor the PRC presenting attractive options for fulfilling employment or safe residence during the 1950s. As did thousands of other Chinese able to mus-ter the access and resources to do so, Tuan made his way to America, where he carved out a new life and a new home under increasingly favorable legal, institutional, and ideological circumstances.

Within the broader picture of domestic race relations and Cold War divides, the successes of educated Chinese provided proof of America's functioning democracy while contributing vital scientific and technical skills to its competition against the Soviet Union as well as vindicating the appeal and generative capacities of capitalist enterprises. "Free world" partners deployed exchanges of students, cultural representatives, technical and military experts, and other kinds of leaders as ways of affirming shared beliefs and convictions regarding political and economic ideologies. Despite widespread critiques of a brain drain as depriving developing nations of their most valuable human capital, the bodies, connections, technologies, and knowledge so circulated served to strengthen ties between the United States and Nationalist Taiwan. The mutual sharing of businesses and enterprises, along with the accompanying organizational and political practices and beliefs, furthered the integration of economic and political systems in both states, vividly illustrating how immigration laws and practices served to further foreign relations even as they fostered the greater numbers, acceptance, and visibility of educated Chinese as welcome immigrants in the United States.

The Strategic Foundations of Brain Exchange

As described in chapter 5, the Department of State had begun facilitating international education programs as an effective form of diplomatic outreach in the mid-1930s, particularly with Latin American neighbors and China. Even in the thick of World War II, it had expanded educational, cultural, and technical exchange projects in the belief that personal encounters and collaborations fostered stronger alliances while usefully training Chinese scientists, bureaucrats, and technicians who provided cheap, skilled labor in key industries. In particular the technical trainee program paired the needs of the Nationalists for greater technical expertise and experience with the hunger of American industries for skilled and inexpensive workers.

With the end of World War II, the number of students and trainees increased as educational exchange gained importance as a tool of foreign relations. The U.S. Technical Assistance Program continued to bring in Nationalist scientists and technicians despite the rapid onset of the Chinese Civil War and reached a peak of enrollment in 1949 with 3,916 participants, followed by 3,637 in 1950 and 3,549 in 1951. National Resource Commission application records suggest that approvals were facilitated during 1948 and 1949 to promote escape from China in the final stages of the Civil War.[10]

Despite their troubled alliance during World War II and the China White Paper in 1949 in which President Truman blamed Nationalist failings for their loss in the Civil War, the outbreak of the Korean War in 1950 saved Chiang Kai-shek on his last foothold of Taiwan. The island became an invaluable, unsinkable aircraft carrier holding the line against an expansionary People's Republic of China. As the U.S. Seventh Fleet began patrolling the Formosa Strait to ensure the survival of "Free" China, the maelstrom of recriminations concerning how the United States had "lost" China destroyed the careers of many of the foreign service officers and scholars most knowledgeable about the country, producing a severely limited capacity for the United States to deal realistically with the PRC.[11] During an era infested by Senator Joseph McCarthy and anticommunist paranoia, this purging of the ranks of the "China hands" allowed the China Lobby to emerge as an influential, yet minority, interest group that effectively leveraged Chiang Kai-shek's survival as a critical strategic issue for the United States.

Although the White House and Department of State held different priorities from the Nationalists, with the United States emphasizing containment of the PRC and Chiang Kai-shek claiming ambitions to retake the mainland, they collaborated amicably in the sending of Taiwanese students to America.[12] Along with other anticommunist allies, Taiwan benefited from programs funded by the Fulbright Act of 1946 and its successors such as the Act for International Development of 1950, which aimed "to aid the efforts of the peoples of economically underdeveloped areas to develop their resources and improve their working and living conditions by encouraging the exchange of technical knowledge and skills." More broadly, such programs sought to promote global capitalism and to guide economic development in developing nations to become more closely integrated into the capitalist free world and within the U.S. realm of leadership.[13] As early as 1952 and 1953 the State Department's Committee on Foreign Relations determined that "the exchange of persons programs were the most effective and, at the same time, among the lowest in cost" of programs for developing influence abroad.[14]

The Nationalists reciprocated American interests in the exchange of technical knowledge and skills and actively maintained pre–World War II programs to prepare and select students and government workers to acquire additional education and training in the United States. Beginning in the 1950s, a steady outflow of Taiwan's best-prepared and well-connected students came to an America with emerging capacities to provide them not only with education but also with jobs and chances to resettle permanently. Although they arrived with student visas mandating their return to Taiwan, most of those applying to study in the United States viewed it as a step toward remaining, with the knowledge that despite the restrictive terms of immigration laws, such relocations were quite feasible and in fact facilitated. The great numbers that accomplished this transformation, approximately 90 to 95 percent of Taiwanese students through the 1970s, reflects their desperation to escape from bleak conditions on Taiwan, the resourcefulness of migrants in expanding their available options, and the complicity of both the U.S. and Taiwan governments in enabling their resettlement despite official policies stipulating the temporary nature of student statuses.

Exile on Taiwan

The greater opportunities available to the stranded students and their brain-drain successors and the comparative ease with which they entered white-collar and professional employment have tended to mask the duress and losses sustained in their migration to America. Despite their student status and better access, they were nonetheless refugees unexpectedly cut off from China who struggled with the unresolved turmoil of lost homes and family members, the violent security regime imposed by the Nationalists, the ongoing instability and threat of communist invasion to Taiwan, and the limbo of legal but not yet permanent residency and employment in the United States. Nationalist-affiliated Chinese, here labeled the mainland Chinese, had fled to Taiwan in the late 1940s only to find themselves at odds with the already resident Taiwanese, some of whom had settled on the island centuries earlier but all of whom had experienced the relative stability and prosperity of Japanese colonial rule (1895–1945). The February 28 Incident of 1947 (Er'erba shibian), in which Taiwanese protested the corruption and disarray of Nationalist rule and demanded sovereignty, was followed by a military crackdown resulting in an estimated twenty thousand deaths and the imposition of martial law until 1987.[15] Such conditions provided powerful motivations for both mainland Chinese and Taiwanese to seek an alternative home, even as the United States offered greater possibilities for entry and settlement.

During the 1950s Taiwan's primarily agricultural economy held few prospects for the newly arrived mainlanders, many of whom were accustomed to living in China's most industrialized and developed cities. In 1954 the entire island had but one stoplight, in the capital city of Taipei, which was only for show and unneeded for the scant motorized traffic. Taipei had just one elevator—in the tallest, four-story building.[16] Although he stayed for less than a year before departing to study in the United States, Winberg Chai recalled his dismay at living conditions: "the constant humid heat, the hunger, the terrible pineapples, the fear that the People's Liberation Army would arrive any day and take over the island too."[17] Facilities for higher education were equally limiting. In 1949 there were only six institutions, with a total enrollment of 6,573—one university, two colleges, one teacher's college, and two polytechnic institutes, mostly left over from the Japanese colonial period.[18] After 1949 choice positions in government and industry were occupied by well-connected mainland Chinese, with few openings for Taiwanese or even the offspring of Nationalist officials.

These limited employment options augmented fears and anxieties about Chiang Kai-shek's brutal authoritarianism, which had also thwarted ARCI agendas in sharply constricting new refugee arrivals. Although most attention has focused on the White Terror crackdown against Taiwanese, Dominic Yang and Mau-kuei Chang argue that the Nationalists disciplined "not only . . . native Taiwanese political activists, but also . . . a large number of mainlander dissidents and alleged 'Communist spies' . . . all in the name of the sacred mission of mainland recovery."[19] They cite statistics that during the 1950s mainland Chinese were 40 percent of known White Terror victims while accounting for only 10 to 15 percent of the total population. Accordingly, they argue that "in early post-war Taiwan, the KMT may have purged and disciplined the migrant community with more rigor and intensity than it applied to native Taiwanese." Chiang Kai-shek fiercely sought out and crushed possible rivals for power. Yang and Chang argue that

> dissident intellectuals, influential provincial leaders, and rival forces within the KMT needed to be brought under tighter control and (re)indoctrinated with KMT ideology and the personal cult of Chiang Kai-shek. Therefore the hunt for "Communist spies" and suppression of political dissidents had a greater overall impact on civil war migrants than on the local population during the early postwar years.[20]

Chiang's ruthlessness in destroying potential challengers quashed U.S. State Department hopes of promoting a "Third Force" alternative for his leadership of overseas Chinese.

Yang and Chang underscore that the mainland Chinese were refugees who suffered the attending traumas and dislocations. In the early 1950s mainland Chinese displayed statistically significant, higher rates of crime, suicide, and mental illness. Anecdotal evidence depicts "the communal dislocation experienced by civil war migrants" with vivid accounts of personal losses emerging from the profusion of newspaper advertisements searching for lost relatives and friends (*sunren qishi*), underscoring the many incidents of family fragmentation and displacement in exile.[21] Taiwan's current prosperity and material affluence have obscured the fact that so many mainland Chinese "left China in such an intense and dramatic fashion that they were deeply traumatized by the brutality of warfare as well as vivid memories of Communist persecution. Many arrived in Taiwan literally with only the clothes on their backs."[22] As depicted with such clear-eyed tenderness in Bai Xianyong's short story collection *Taibeiren* (Taipei People) (1971), they remained deeply and dysfunctionally immersed in their own misery, nostalgia, and the black shadow of Chiang Kai-shek's implacable crusade for mainland recovery. And they became preoccupied with finding an escape.

Although now touted for its economic "tiger" miracle, Taiwan's first years under Nationalist rule emphasized a military and security buildup to the exclusion of developing economic and civic infrastructure on the island, despite copious resources channeled from the United States. Between 1951 and 1965 congressional appropriations for Taiwan totaled $2.5 billion, an average of $167 million each year. With U.S. aid, "profliga[te] Nationalist military spenders" presided over a military budget equaling 15 percent of GNP, with 85 percent of the government's total expenditures going to the military. One-seventh of able-bodied men entered the military rather than working in farms and factories, to the detriment of economic development.[23] By 1954, however, the Sino-American Mutual Defense Treaty and the tenacity of the Communist government led many mainlanders outside the government and military establishment to accept the permanence of the PRC and the indefinite loss of their Chinese homeland.[24] Chiang Kai-shek and his followers were slower to acknowledge these new realities but turned more systematically to economic development in the late 1950s.

With no roots in island society, and under American pressure not to repeat their record on the mainland, the Nationalists eventually put through sweeping agrarian reforms that had been beyond their capacities on the mainland. Inheriting a huge cache of confiscated Japanese properties, the government implemented a highly centralized plan of industrialization and development across the island under advisement from American experts. Some 40 percent of all capital formation on the island derived from U.S. aid and contributions of material goods. Rapid economic growth ensued based on export-oriented small local businesses and educational progress.[25] Under such conditions the Nationalist government maintained its policies of actively encouraging study overseas as a crucial strategy to acquire more technical and economic expertise. From the relatively undeveloped base of Taiwan, study abroad also served to funnel intellectuals into meaningful pursuits until the island's economy advanced enough to provide appropriate employment. In 1971 a Ministry of Education officer explained: "The Kuomintang rule could not contain such potential intellectual elements, particularly those dissident ones, in this small island, not only socially and economically but also militarily and politically."[26] Until Taiwan's economy could develop sufficient industrial and technical sophistication, unemployable college-educated workers were potentially more of a security threat than a resource and better sent away to gather more skills and training elsewhere.

As they had during the 1930s, the Nationalists imposed rigorous conditions on students seeking to study overseas, requiring political indoctrination, demonstrated English-language abilities, proof of admission, and ability to fund tuition and living costs. Starting in 1955 applicants had to pass screenings by the Security Bureau and extensive testing imposed by the Ministry of Education. The selection criteria included graduation from a four-year or junior college, completion of a year of military service for male students, and passage of tests held annually by the Ministry of Education, with automatic denial of visas in cases of failing the Test of English as a Foreign Language (TOEFL) exam. Students had to demonstrate either full scholarships from American institutions or evidence of possessing the US$3,000–4,000 needed to cover tuition, room and board, and other expenses. According to Charles Kao, this screening process meant that "the Chinese government, paradoxically, has sent the cream of its college graduates abroad. Precisely because of the high quality and good background, these students can easily adapt themselves to the new environment and consequently have less inclination to return." Such circumstances led one famous scholar to joke that the Nationalists should only send students who failed in the exams and keep those who passed.[27] Building on older patterns of emphasizing sciences and engineering, students in the 1950s clustered in these fields, but as the areas of expertise most likely to provide scholarships and employment after graduation in the United States.

The Student Side Door into America

The impressive career of Chang-lin Tien (1935–2002) illustrates the fierce determination and established methods that mainland Chinese deployed to gain entry to and settlement in America. His once affluent family had lived first in Wuhan and Shanghai but lost their fortune in the flight to Taiwan in 1949. Tien's father died a broken man, leaving behind a family of twelve living in a one-room home. Tien worked his way through high school and studied at the prestigious National Taiwan University. He applied to 240 schools in the United States and received a full fellowship from the University of Kentucky. Although he had to borrow money to fly to Seattle in 1956 and endured a seventy-two-hour bus ride to Louisville, Tien received his MA degree within one year and continued on to earn his doctorate in mechanical engineering at Princeton and become a professor at Berkeley—rising through the ranks to become full professor, department chair, vice chancellor of research, and eventually the first Asian American chancellor of a University of California campus.[28] His outstanding professional achievements exemplify the parameters of brain-drain immigration even as they mask the considerable obstacles he overcame as a refugee. His ability to transcend family poverty and displacement to study in the United States illustrates how international education pathways relocated from China to Taiwan and expanded so that many less talented students, both mainland and Taiwanese Chinese alike, could also immigrate by claiming student status.

Jack Peng also used the student side door to resettle in the United States. Peng first entered the United States in 1949 as a teenage dependent accompanying his father, who worked for the United Nations. On turning eighteen, however, Peng lost his dependent status, whereupon he "realized that going to school was the only way to stay in America." During the 1950s and early 1960s, he attended college and graduate school in electrical engineering and physics in order to maintain the right to remain in the United States, although quota restrictions prevented him from acquiring citizenship.[29]

In the quadruple biography *Beyond the Narrow Gate*, Leslie Chang traced the paths of her mother, Mary, and three of her classmates from Taiwan's most elite girl's high school, Beiyinu (Taipei First Girl's School), class of 1955, who came to America to study, marry, have children, and make new lives. All four came from well-connected families and had parents and even grandparents who had studied in America. Of the four, however, only one, Margaret, followed the path of attending college, studying science, and coming to the United States for graduate school.[30] The others arrived through less prestigious methods. Dolores arrived with her mother on a temporary visa as a dependent of a diplomatic representative but then was able to gain permanent residency status. Another classmate, Suzanne, had poor grades but transferred to a small Catholic school that her father, the minister of overseas Chinese affairs, arranged to have accredited. From there Suzanne won a scholarship to another Catholic school, this time in America (77–78).[31]

Chang's mother, Mary, was an orphan who arrived through a scholarship arranged by Archbishop Yu Bin, formerly of Nanjing, who had testified in support of repeal in 1943. Although a student at Beiyinu, she had poor grades and used family contacts to gain entry as a student. A great-aunt, the wife of a Nationalist general being held captive on the mainland, knew Yu Bin, who was stationed in New York, where he used his networks to arrange scholarships and admission to Catholic schools for Chinese to study in the United States. According to Chang, "On one of his trips to Taiwan, my mother and a younger cousin spent a day with his entourage, following him from function to function. By the end of the day, my mother had her scholarship" (77). Mary received an associate's degree from Marymount Junior College in Virginia in 1958, married another Chinese from Taiwan who worked in insurance, and had a successful career as a realtor in Hartford, Connecticut (81–83). Lilly Levin was another indifferent student who came to America with the help of Yu Bin.[32] Strikingly, none of Chang's Beiyinu quartet admit agency in making the choices and taking the actions that led them to come to America. Arrangements were made, and they ended up in the land of opportunity almost as if by happenstance, tumbleweeds blown haphazardly across the Pacific and taking root in the United States. The routinized systems funneling such unmotivated migrants emerged out of long-standing traditions of cooperation between Chinese Nationalists and Americans on behalf of Chinese students.

Starting as early as 1947, Yu Bin facilitated the immigration of about four thousand students from Taiwan, Hong Kong, and Macao through the 1960s. Chang interviewed Father Chan, the staff member chiefly responsible for student affairs. Chan not only arranged scholarships and admissions, he also greeted students when they arrived in San Francisco, helped send them to their various schools, taught them about American foods and slang, and organized summer employment in the Catskills. Decisions about where to send students depended on the availability of scholarships. Because Mary Chang requested help late, she ended up at a less desirable two-year institution. Many other women studied nursing because such scholarships were more readily available. Yu Bin's office worked with over three hundred Catholic colleges, including St. John's, Fordham, and St. Francis in New York; Seton Hall in South Orange, New Jersey; the Manhattan Boy's School; and St. Vincent Girls' School (92–95, 99).[33]

Government exchange programs also provided passage to America. For example, the U.S. Embassy created a Taiwan Youth Committee intended to supplement its economic and military programs by funding about nine hundred university youth to visit America each year, of whom 90 percent did not return. This situation created a quandary, for the program was intended to cultivate goodwill, but embassy staff worried that denial of visas might produce "antagonisms of varying degrees toward the United States."[34] The United States also made considerable investments in educational infrastructure in Taiwan, an estimated $55 million on school buildings and equipment and on instruction techniques. This investment was considered fruitful because the Aid for International Development program helped 2,400 Chinese, most of whom were young students, teachers and professionals who came to hold "important positions."[35] As a well-known friend to the Nationalists, Representative Walter Judd was contacted by many Chinese in Taiwan and Hong Kong about scholarships at American universities and access to Economic and Cultural Affairs funds.[36]

Between 1950 and 1965 an annual average of about 2,000 students, many in the sciences and engineering, arrived as nonquota entries to the United States to attend institutions throughout the country.[37] During the 1954–55 academic year, there were 2,553 students, a number that had increased to 20,770 in 1982–1983.[38] High percentages of Taiwanese college graduates traveled abroad for graduate study, with a high of 47.8 percent in 1955 down to a low of 9.4 percent in 1975. Most of those arriving as students ended up remaining during the 1950s, 1960s, and 1970s. Between 1950 and 1969, 22,319 students left Taiwan to study but only 1,346 returned, or 6.5 percent.[39] According to U.S. government statistics of Chinese students arriving and leaving between 1962 and 1969, 15,959 arrived and only 486 went back, for an approximate overall return rate of just 3 percent (see table 8.1).[40]

Many of the Taiwanese students who had legally entered, studied, found jobs, and established families resided in the United States in a state of legal limbo until reforms in immigration laws in 1962. A succession of stopgap laws and procedural measures helped them extend their stays, although often through stays of deportation that provided only temporary permission to remain. Some of the stranded students, such as C. Y. Lee, were able to convert their status with the Displaced Persons Act of 1948 and its amendment in 1950 as already resident displaced persons. The next available option occurred with the McCarran-Walter Act (1952), which gave first preference to those applying for citizenship through their employers. Although the miniscule annual quota produced a wait of about three decades, one-time measures such as PL 85–316 (1957) and PL 85–700 (1958) responded to the launching of Sputnik to help first-preference applicants to remain. The 1957 law enabled Chinese stymied by the oversubscribed quota to gain permanent residency through the attorney general's power to adjust the statuses of a "limited number" of skilled aliens present on July 1, 1957, who possessed approved first-preference petitions filed before September 11, 1957. PL 85–700 continued to help first-preference immigrants by providing them with nonquota status if they possessed petitions approved by the attorney general before July 1, 1958.[41] The Act of August 8, 1958, advanced a registry or amnesty provision for those who had entered prior to June 28, 1940.[42] The necessity for such stopgap measures to admit highly qualified, educated, and technically trained workers applied pressure for immigration reforms, as did the increasingly unmanageable increase in private bills sponsored by congressional representatives on behalf of thousands of deserving individual immigrants.[43] Finally, in October 1962, PL 87–885, "An Act: To facilitate the entry of alien skilled specialists and certain relatives of United States citizens, and for other purposes," opened the gates in granting nonquota entry for all those that had applied to regularize their status before January 1, 1962, as first-preference immigrants under the McCarran-Walter Act.[44] Although barely noted elsewhere, this law pointed to major shifts toward economic priorities that would become permanent with the Hart-Celler Act of 1965.

These routes to citizenship privileged those with strategically useful skills. The chemical engineer Edward Huang recalled obtaining his citizenship status through an established back door in the late 1950s. The process involved getting his employer to send a letter to a particular official in the State Department describing Huang's work as "vital to national security," whereupon his application would be approved.[45] C. C. Tien, a civil engineer and brother of Chang-lin Tien, planned to return to Taiwan when his temporary visa expired, although his employers wished him to remain. America's competition with the Soviet Union facilitated his resettlement. "You

TABLE 8.1. Number of College Graduates from Taiwan Going Abroad for Study and Returning from Abroad in Selected Years

Year	1951	1955	1960	1965	1970	1975	1980	1985	1988
Number of college graduates	1,013	1,591	4,628	7,118	16,959	24,564	32,360	36,885	40,205
Number going abroad to study	340	760	643	2,339	2,056	2,301	5,933	5,979	7,122
Number returning	17	34	47	120	407	569	640	1,350	2,296
Percent going abroad	33.6	47.8	13.9	32.9	12.1	9.4	18.3	16.2	17.7
Percent returning	5.0	4.5	7.3	5.1	19.8	24.7	10.8	22.6	32.2

Source: Sun Chen, "Investment in Education and Human Resource Development in Postwar Taiwan," in *Cultural Change in Postwar Taiwan*, ed. Stevan Harrell and Huang Chun-chieh (Boulder, CO: Westview Press, 1994), 103. The figures are from Ministry of Education, *Educational Statistics of the Republic of China*, 1989.

know what happened? *Sputnik*. The Russians shot *Sputnik* up into space, and Congress was panicking. They passed a bill called 'First Preference.' Anyone with an advanced degree in engineering or science could apply for permanent residence." The laws passed in 1957 and 1958 directly benefited skilled workers such as Tien, who was among the first to apply for this opportunity with his company's sponsorship.[46] Others would have to wait for general legislation to account for their legal residency and employment in the United States, which did not confer permanent status. For example, Jack Peng had just passed his PhD orals in physics while attending the University of Georgia when Lyndon B. Johnson signed the Hart-Celler Act into law. Suddenly Peng's life became much simpler, although he had managed to remain in the United States for over fifteen years with only temporary residency rights.

> President Johnson's immigration act stipulated that if you have special skills, you could get a higher preference level. So the physics department head wrote a letter of recommendation for me, stating that I did have the special skills to qualify. Because of that, I could move up to first preference instead of fifth, as petition[ed] for by my brother, and earn my permanent residence, so that within five years, I could become a citizen.[47]

Peng's pathway to citizenship reflects the shift toward prioritizing and facilitating immigration by knowledge workers based on employment, principles of immigration selection that have since gained general acceptance as rational standards for entry and settlement in the United States. This dramatic shift came only after decades of constant and mounting pressure for immigration reforms that would discard the national origins quota system.

Opening the Gates

As described in chapter 7, the push for immigration reform had been a protracted, deeply contested, and long-delayed process. As early as 1944 White House officials such as Immigration Commissioner Earl Harrison and his successor Ugo Carusi had called for greater attention to the "international implications" of immigration laws in pressing for reforms.[48] By 1950 a coalition of Jews, Catholics, liberal Protestants, left-leaning Democrats, and ethnic organizations were pressing for abolition of the national origins system in favor of one emphasizing individual merit, as argued in William S. Bernard's *American Immigration Policy: A Reappraisal* (1950).[49]

These campaigns informed the significant reforms enacted through the Hart-Celler Act. Hart would continue to propose bills that aimed "to eliminate the provisions which discriminate against certain nationality and racial groups" and facilitate family reunification while increasing the overall immigration quota by 100,000 to 250,000. Support was mounting for such measures—S.4030, for example, had the endorsement of twenty-five senators and the backing of Senator James Eastland (D-MS), the powerful chair of the Judiciary Committee, which oversaw immigration legislation. Hart particularly emphasized his goal for "an immigration statute that will select the best immigrants without prejudice because of race or nationality."[50] Although S.3043 did not pass, Hart would try repeatedly with bills reiterating nearly the same terms.[51]

Disappointing immigration reformers, John F. Kennedy did not propose general immigration reform during the first two years of his presidency despite receiving from the Bureau of Security and Consular Affairs a proposal for immigration legislation with seven main provisions drawing on ideas and bills developed during the 1950s. The State Department's agenda in May 1963 addressed a mixed bag of priorities and sought to improve access for groups facing inequitably small opportunities to legally immigrate while retaining overall caps on entry, prioritizing skilled workers, and addressing foreign policy concerns for refugees. The proposal suggested mechanisms such as the redistribution of unused quota numbers to first-, second-, and third-preference applicants, which included employment considerations; broadening the definition of refugees to make more Asians admissible; the elimination of the Asian-Pacific Triangle; nonquota status for immigration within the Western Hemisphere; and the imposition of visa fees to help cover costs.[52]

Vice President Lyndon Johnson, in his capacity as president of the Senate, assessed for Kennedy the kinds of immigration reform that might pass in Congress in 1963. The legislature echoed many of Hart's and the State Department's priorities and supported replacing the outdated and meaningless national origins system with a preference system that emphasized the skills of the immigrant and their relationship to American needs; family relationships between immigrants and relatives already here; and priority of registration. In particular, Johnson's outline recommended that "especially skilled or trained workers" need not arrange for jobs before coming because this was inhibiting useful immigrants from applying for entry.[53] Such terms would greatly improve immigration conditions for Chinese, considerations informed in part by lobbying from both Nationalist and Chinese American advocates.

As they had since the 1943 campaign for repeal, but with growing clout, Chinese American community leaders pressed for immigration reform. Lim P. Lee, a well-connected community leader and Democratic activist in San Francisco, corresponded regularly with the White House deputy press secretary, his fellow Californian Andrew Hatcher.[54] Lee conveyed community criticisms of discriminatory immigration laws, such as the Asian-Pacific Triangle, which led to the turning away at the border of the biracial Canadian writer Wayson Choy, an event decried in Chinese American newspapers.[55]

J. K. Choy, an assistant vice president of the San Francisco Federal Savings & Loan Association, wrote directly to Kennedy reminding him of promises made while he was a senator criticizing "the most blatant discrimination" of the McCarran-Walter Act and of proclamations made as president that "there is no place for second class citizenship in America." Choy summarized the ongoing impact of the Chinese exclusion laws even after their repeal and asked Kennedy to amend the laws so that dependents of Chinese who had entered fraudulently could regularize their status. Choy acknowledged that these paper son immigrants were not being deported to Communist China but still existed in an illegal limbo created by unreasonable laws. Choy's demands echoed criticisms made by editor Dai-ming Lee through an early 1950s campaign waged in the *Chinese World* newspaper that publicized efforts by the PRC government to extort ransoms for relatives of Chinese Americans unable to immigrate to the United States. Lee called for the U.S. government to amend its laws that forced Chinese to enter illegally so that families could reunify and escape such vulnerability.[56] Choy also urged increasing the Chinese immigration quota, abolishing the Asian-Pacific Triangle, and extending refugee relief programs.[57]

Chinese Americans proposed reforms that placed Asian immigration on a basis closer to that of Europeans, changes that the State Department confidently projected would *not* produce significant increases in their numbers even if the Asian-Pacific Triangle was abolished. The State Department had issued a "confidential inquiry" to "all diplomatic missions and certain key consular posts" asking for estimates of Asians living within their jurisdiction and numbers "likely to apply for immigrant visas." This survey found that "the change would have a most favorable effect on our posture abroad," but some missions warned that if the proposed changes were made public but then not enacted, a "potentially adverse effect" would result. The countries of greatest concern were in the Western Hemisphere, for which there were no proposed immigration caps. Consular authorities estimated that Chinese visa applicants would be in the mere thousands—5,842 in total—with Ecuador claiming 3, El Salvador 28, and Haiti 6.[58] According to these projections, the laws could be amended to improve America's image abroad without fear of being overrun by Chinese.

That greater numbers of scientifically and technically trained individuals would immigrate was a key element attracting restrictionist support for proposed immigration reforms. The American Legion backed the measure because numerical ceilings would limit immigration while preferences for professionals and scientists "well may add significantly to the wealth and power of the United States." It correctly anticipated the influx of "scientific, technical, and professional migrants from less developed countries to the

United States," although it did not foresee the burgeoning of Asian immigration overall that would also result.[59]

Kennedy's assassination left Lyndon Johnson in charge of the fight for immigration reform, an issue in which he had previously expressed so little interest that he had voted for the now decried McCarran-Walter Act. His landslide victory in 1964 and the death of Francis Walter in 1963 made 1965 seem a year in which many previously unattainable changes might become possible. Representative Michael Feighan (D-OH), who had so alarmed the Hong Kong consulate during his inspection tour of 1955, replaced Walter as lead defender of the immigration status quo. Johnson's original proposal, drawing on Kennedy's priorities, featured a preference system that set aside 50 percent of visas for skilled immigrants, 30 percent for family reunification, and 20 percent for refugees. Feighan pressed for greater emphasis on family reunification in order to maintain America's racial and ethnic demographic mix and insisted on numeric caps for immigration within the Western Hemisphere, a concession that he won but with the unanticipated consequence of producing the intractable problem of immigration without permission that the United States still struggles with today.[60]

With these priorities established, the Hart-Celler Act dismantled the differential quota system and implemented instead a series of preferences that scaled back Kennedy's emphasis on economic considerations to allot 74 percent of visas for specified relatives of citizens and lawful permanent relatives and nonquota status for immediate relatives of citizens such as parents, spouses, and unmarried minor children. Occupational preferences dropped to third and sixth place from first with only 20 percent of quota slots, targeting professionals and other workers who filled jobs "for which qualified U.S. workers were not available" in fields such as accounting and auditing, aeronautical engineering, architecture, chemical engineering, chemistry, civil engineering, dietetics, electrical engineering, electronic engineering, industrial engineering, mathematics, mechanical engineering, metallurgy and metallurgical engineering, nuclear engineering, nursing, pharmacy, physical therapy, and physics.[61] Such applicants had to receive Department of Labor certification that they would not displace American workers. Investors and refugees received preferences as well.[62] These measures ensured that the Asian brain drain could become a steady flow after 1965 and evolve into a primary component of the growing numbers of Asians now able to immigrate to the United States. The act also accomplished the final exorcism of the paper son system of immigration fraud, for the twenty thousand annual allocation and nonquota immigration for immediate relatives rendered such illegality largely unnecessary for Chinese entry.[63] At the same time, the burden of illegal entry shifted to U.S. neighbors to the north and south who faced for the first time quantified limits on entry into the United States policed by heightened measures for border control and surveillance in a sundering of relations with those sharing land borders that has yet to find resolution. In contrast, Chinese and Asian immigration in general has not only increased but attained "model minority" standing largely through the preferences imbedded in the Hart-Celler Act of 1965.

Draining Asian Brains to America

As early as 1968 the British economist Brinley Thomas observed that changes in U.S. immigration laws dating to 1962 deliberately encouraged brain drain, particularly, although not intentionally, from Asia. He noted the rapid increase of professional immigrants from Asia, which stood at 24 percent of the total in 1963—a threefold increase over 1962 after the new law provided nonquota status for "alien scientists and engineers to achieve immigrant status within a relatively short period of time." In contrast, the influx of European scientists and engineers increased only 23 percent. Within one year Asian professionals had displayed "a remarkably high elasticity with respect to a moderate liberalizing of the restrictions" that made predictable the surge in their immigration after 1965.[64] Thomas's analysis summarized how the lack of economic opportunity and desire for higher education and professional opportunity in Asia, combined with fluent pathways to study and find employment in the United States now culminating in ready access to permanent residency and citizenship, produced high levels of brain drain. International consternation, including criticism from the United Nations, greeted this alarming pattern of the loss of the most value-added human resources from developing nations to the most advanced economy in the world. Rather than returning and helping their homelands gain ground economically and politically, educated elites from the Third World were staying in the United States. Over the long term, however, key elements of this brain drain have cycled back to their homeland in a circulation of knowledge, networks, capital, and strategies that has distributed economic development and integration more widely than as an endgame of absolute losses and gains.

The first outcries against this form of American theft came from Western European countries like England alarmed at high numbers of doctors and engineers pursuing higher salaries and better work conditions in the United States. In 1963 the British minister of science noted the annual departure of 7 percent of people with PhD degrees in science to work in the United States, which he charged with operating "parasitically on other people's brains." Unlike the Asian brain drain, which consisted primarily of students who changed status after gaining advanced degrees and finding jobs in America, Europe's was more costly because the knowledge workers had already received graduate training before relocating.[65] After U.S. laws dropped their racial restrictions, however, the number of educated Asians immigrating increased dramatically, turning developing nations into the main sources of brain drain.

Since World War II the number of Asian students has increased steadily (see fig. A.2). In 1970 Chinese students (from Hong Kong, Taiwan, and other areas) numbered 19,231, Indians 11,327, Japanese 4,156, and Koreans 3,991, accounting for 30 percent of the foreign student total.[66] Many Chinese chose scientific and technical careers as the most likely to bring fellowships and employment after graduation. In 1971 Charles Kao found that 82 percent of all Chinese receiving PhD degrees in the United States between 1955 and 1964 studied engineering and the sciences, commenting, "The preference for sciences and engineering among Chinese students come as no surprise. Greater demand and better rewards for such specialization at home and abroad provides the incentive and thereby accelerates the supply."[67] Students from Taiwan made strategic choices that facilitated their resettlement in America.

The U.S. government tracked the steadily increasing percentage of scientists, engineers, and physicians immigrating into the United States from developing countries, primarily from Asia. In 1956 Asian percentages hit 32.9, increasing to 42.6 percent in 1963, and by 1967 had risen to 51.8 percent.[68] Taiwan had the highest rates of brain drain if measured by student F visas converted to immigrant status at 86.1 percent, or 1,137 of 1,321. The average for all nations was 23.9 percent, or 3,648 of 15,272. India's rate was next highest at 75.4 percent, or 1,074 of 1,425, and then Korea at 71.7 percent, or 193 of 269.[69]

James A. Perkins, president of Cornell University, estimated that between 1949 and 1961, 43,000 scientists and engineers had immigrated to the United States, many from less developed countries. During the 1964–1965 fiscal year, some 11,000 out of 41,000 interns and residents in American hospitals had degrees from foreign medical schools, with 8,000 coming from developing nations. Perkins noted this serious situation in which "over 90 per cent of Asian students who arrive for training in the United States never return home."[70] Man Singh Das compiled statistics from 1967 that show the high numbers of Asian and particularly Taiwanese students converting to permanent status from F-1 visas. Of the 9,957 such conversions, 81.1 percent, or 8,073, were from Asia and 26.4 percent, or 2,629, were from Taiwan.

Shu Yuan Chang's survey of Chinese in the New York area in 1972 tracked the steady progression of Chinese immigrants into permanent residency. On arrival, 79 percent of survey participants entered with student visas, 8 percent came as immigrants, 6 percent as exchange scholars, 4 percent as visitors, and 3 percent as military or diplomatic personnel. By the time of the survey, however, only 47 percent were of solely Chinese nationality, 29 percent had gained U.S. permanent residency, 21 percent were naturalized U.S. citizens, and 3 percent were something else. In terms of occupation, 53

TABLE 8.2. Temporary Nonimmigrants (H-1, H-3, J-1, and F-1) Who Changed to Immigrant Status, by Country or Region of Previous Residence, Fiscal Year 1967

Country	Total	H-1 Visa	H-3 Visa	J-1 Visa	F-1 Visa
All countries	11,372	256	174	985	9,957
Total Europe	1,386	96	61	230	998
Total Asia	**8,904**	**85**	**87**	**659**	**8,073**
India	1,816	16	21	70	1,709
China (ROC)	**2,743**	**13**	**23**	**78**	**2,629**
Africa	254	7	2	23	222
North America	507	48	16	45	398
South America	171	5	4	17	145

Source: Man Singh Das, *Brain Drain Controversy and International Students* (Lucknow, India: Lucknow Publishing House, 1972), 64.

percent remained students, 45 percent were professionals, and 2 percent were other.[71]

These changes in the numbers and qualifications of Asian immigrants swiftly changed the demographic makeup of Asian communities in the United States. By 1969, immigrants entering under occupational preferences constituted 20.8 percent of those from Taiwan, 45 percent from India, 23.2 percent from South Korea, and 42.3 percent from the Philippines. By 1972, 86 percent of scientists and engineers and 80 percent of doctors immigrating came from less developed nations.[72] Asian immigrants had become significant assets for the American economy, even as their improved ability to resettle attracted vocal criticisms of U.S. immigration policy, albeit from the perspective of economic exploitation rather than racial discrimination.

Rationalizing Brain Drain: Neoliberalism and Global Labor Markets

International protests quickly identified these emerging migration patterns as deepening economic inequality around the world, a criticism that forced the United States to defend its new immigration policies. In 1966 the United Nations circulated a report calling for "drastic remedies . . . by individual governments and international agencies to curb the flow of talent from the underdeveloped areas."[73] In response, Congress convened hearings. After much testimony, scholarly analysis, and scrupulous consideration, the U.S. government exculpated itself, concluding that brain-drain migration flows operated according to rational market forces rather than deliberate policy choices and that state entities should protect individual free choices rather than intervening in rational economic processes. Such neoliberal principles have become naturalized and remain primary assumptions of contemporary U.S. immigration laws.

The Senate's Immigration and Naturalization subcommittee, under the leadership of Edward Kennedy (D-Massachusetts), met in 1967 to explore the contradiction between America's diplomatic outreach through educational and cultural exchanges and the impact of its recently changed immigration law. In opening the Senate hearings, Kennedy, the late president's brother and a key player in passage of the Hart-Celler Act, set out the key issues. Perceptions of a brain-drain crisis burdened America with "the brunt of growing criticism among countries of emigration" such as Europe and "the underdeveloped areas of the world," which labeled "this migration ... a major cause accentuating the gap between the rich and poor nations. It is viewed as a serious brake to progress in Asia and Africa and Latin America." In matters of foreign policy, Kennedy warned that "brain drain" "is threatening our relations with several governments, and the credibility of our national objective to assist the economic, social, and political development of other nations through foreign aid and other channels" while undermining "our efforts to assist the developing countries through foreign aid, the Peace Corps, and other programs." The loss of knowledge workers eroded American efforts to build stronger ties with poorer nations by helping them develop economically. These contradictory outcomes presented complex questions regarding whether and what kind of responsibility fell to the United States to redirect such migration flows, including whether there should be another change in U.S. immigration laws.

Alongside the damage to international relations, however, Kennedy also stressed core American ideals of freedom of choice to ask whether the United States should restrict "the freedom of movement and the right of an individual to choose his way of life in a manner which will develop his full potential for the benefit of all mankind."[74] In weighing the balance of a more equitable distribution of human resources around the world against advantaging the American economy, the Senate committee evoked the evenhanded rationality of free-market forces to mask the U.S. government's agency in privileging the entry and settlement of knowledge workers through the preferences legislated in 1965. The choice of legal "freedom of movement" was, and is, more available to those with certain levels of professional and educational credentials, and to those without, not at all.

Walter Adams, an economist at Michigan State University and adviser to Presidents Eisenhower, Kennedy, and Johnson, took a leading role in defending America's responsibility for stimulating brain drains by testifying as an expert witness and editing the pioneering anthology, *The Brain Drain*. As representative of the world's greatest collector of knowledge workers, Adams questioned the outcries of crisis by critiquing the so-called national model, which linked the possibility for economic progress to the retention of human capital. Adams summarized the accusations: "brain drains" impeded the development of poorer nations whose "top-grade professional manpower," often produced with "substantial doses of public investment," were relocating to wealthier countries, thereby becoming "a 'gift' from one country to another—typically from a poor country which cannot afford it to a rich country which does not need it." The growing numbers of Filipino doctors and nurses going to the United States during and after the 1950s illustrated this type of loss. According to Adams, perhaps most critically, "the 'nationalist' model points to the conclusion that unfettered migration of brainpower today favors the most advanced and affluent nations," producing calls to protect developing nations by ensuring the return of their educated workers.[75]

Adams minimized the agency of the United States in this imbalanced migration by invoking the logic of free markets and calling on developing nations to foster their own economic development rather than for industrialized countries to change their immigration laws. He identified the main problem as "the lack of absorptive capacity," which produced poor employment conditions in terms of salary, communities of comparably educated colleagues, and access to advanced research infrastructure, all of which deterred the most highly trained workers from returning. The problem was not selective immigration policies but that developing nations had not yet reached the stage of economic development in which they could usefully, and competitively, employ the highly skilled workers choosing to remain in the United States. What need did a primarily agricultural economy such as that of Taiwan in 1960 have for a world-class nuclear scientist? Adams proposed that advanced economies could "provide effective aid to the underdeveloped world" by providing "development assistance" and help less developed countries to "participate in world economic growth through international trade."[76] Through capitalist development, which would further entwine their economies with that of the United States, poorer nations could advance enough to compete eventually in international markets so that educated elites would choose to return.

In Adams's anthology, a single voice represented the "nationalist" perspective. V. M. Dandekar placed blame squarely on the immigration and economic policies of advanced economies and supported restrictions requiring students to return to India to work. Dandekar criticized educated fellow nationals who found employment abroad but also the complicity of democratic governments that facilitated their immigration through legal preferences. "It is the leading democracies which have the most stringent and discriminatory immigration laws." He described as "only specious" "the trade theory explanation of the Brain Drain [as] no more than a movement of factors in response to prices." Advanced nations such as the United States built into their immigration laws discriminations based on skills and educational credentials. If wealthy nations could choose primarily to admit and to grant permanent residency to educated and economically useful elites, poorer nations should also implement measures to prevent their departure or to ensure their return.

Dandekar pointed out that high salary differentials between advanced and developing nations existed not only for skilled and trained scientists and technicians but for housemaids as well. Despite such compelling market inequalities, there was no substantial outmigration of Indian housemaids because American laws gave manual workers few options for immigration. Dandekar called for greater defensive measures by developing nations: "In a contact between the rich and the poor, there is no more danger, if ever there was, of the rich being robbed. There is greater danger now of the poor being robbed. He must therefore protect himself."[77]

Offering perhaps the most balanced and far-reaching analysis in Adams's anthology, the British economist Brinley Thomas affirmed Dandekar's charge of government agency in the imbalanced flow of educated elites. Thomas described the mobility of educated knowledge workers as a migration flow new to the twentieth century, contrasting "the high proportion of international migrants who belong to the professional classes and the relative immobility of unskilled labor." He attributed the emergence of this pattern to deliberate intent. "Governments now regulate immigration according to strictly national interests, and there is a premium on highly qualified manpower." The modern world economy favored the most advanced nations already operating at the leading edge of scientific innovation, and "the international flow of these skills is heavily influenced by the rate of growth in the largest and richest sector, North America." In the emerging landscape of professional and technical migration, "Human capital is highly mobile internationally and is attracted to areas where real private productivity is highest. It constitutes a gift from the areas which incurred the costs of investment and a return flow of benefits to the investors is not inherent in the process." With such tight competition for educated manpower, "Immigration policy has come to resemble tariff policy as a flexible instrument for maximizing national advantage." Thomas pointed to the 1962 law as demonstrating these preferences and warned that through such immigration preferences, "United States growth policy . . . can inhibit the realization of other countries' growth policies."[78] Looking back from the twenty-first century, the entwining of fiscal and immigration policy identified by Thomas has become commonplace, particularly in other countries of high immigration such as Canada, Australia, and New Zealand. Such employment preferences, however, have not operated as detrimentally as initially feared for some developing economies because they have produced in the longer term not only the losses of brain drain but the more mutually beneficial phenomenon of knowledge exchange.

Adams concluded *The Brain Drain* anthology with "An Agenda for Action" that proposed eight solutions, seven of which required action by the governments *losing* knowledge workers, such as revising salary structures, increasing professional opportunities, and rationalizing manpower policies. Only his final recommendation suggested that "pull countries" remove monopolistic restrictions.[79] According to Adams's interpretation of brain drain, the United States should continue with its existing policies of foreign aid and immigration preferences rather than enacting controls to channel educated workers to return home.

The actual trajectories of Taiwan and India, which experienced the highest levels of brain drain during the 1960s, bear out Adams's projections that on reaching a certain stage of development, their economies would become competitive in the recruitment of knowledge workers. Even in 1972 Man Singh Das argued that most students actually did return to their homelands, particularly those with government scholarships who had the most useful skills and experiences. "The ones who decided to settle down permanently in the United States were those who were privately supported and those who specialized in subject matter areas of little functional consequences to their transitional societies," such as the humanities, social sciences, and highly specialized subjects such as nuclear physics. Das found that most brain-drain knowledge workers were from China, India, South Korea, Philippines, Iran, and Pakistan, where "most of the good government jobs are filled . . . and there are few places for the newer graduates. In some countries, indigenous universities already produce more highly qualified and technically trained people in some occupations than the national economies can absorb now or in the foreseeable future." In light of their inability to find appropriate employment at home, Das noted that most international students planned to obtain work experience and training abroad before returning, offering an additional bonus to their homelands after a delayed return.[80] Taking his analysis a step beyond that of Adams, Das viewed brain drain not so much as a crisis of loss and inequality as a stage in knowledge circulation.

Returns from Brain Drain

In the longer term, Taiwan has borne out Das's projection that knowledge circulation facilitates development by fostering capital investment and closer economic integration with the United States. More than other developing nations and despite Chiang Kai-shek's heavy military investments, Taiwan followed American guidelines for economic growth. In addition to sending a steady flow of college graduates for advanced studies, Taiwan received regular infusions of U.S. capital along with significant doses of economic and technological guidance in developing its economic infrastructure between 1950 and 1965. As projected by Adams, by the 1970s the Taiwanese economy had become sufficiently developed to woo back knowledge workers who, after years of working in the United States in some of the most technologically innovative research settings, had also gained sufficient experience and networks to function as highly effective global entrepreneurs. This return migration contributed significantly to Taiwan's emergence during the 1980s as a leading international manufacturer of computers and peripheral equipment in intimate cooperation with cutting-edge technologies developed in California's Silicon Valley.

This eventual success notwithstanding, Taiwan nonetheless experienced considerable anxiety for a couple of decades regarding its departed human resources. As early as 1955, even as the Bureau of Education implemented policies sending away the best and brightest of Taiwan's college graduates, the Executive Yuan established the Guidance Committee for Students Educated Abroad to facilitate the return and reintegration into Taiwan's society and economy of *liuxuesheng*, or students who studied abroad.[81] In 1969 the Guidance Committee issued *A Report on the Specialists Needed by Government Agencies and Academic Bodies* to be distributed overseas through Taiwan's embassies, consulates, cultural agencies, overseas Chinese organizations, and the overseas edition of the *Central Daily News* to publicize the need for 1,344 "specialists in all fields" with detailed statistics concerning what kinds of expertise were needed by each kind of prospective employer. In the early 1970s the Nationalists offered incentives such as free return transportation, job placement, and occasionally free housing and cash subsidies. Despite such efforts, Charles Kao found in 1971 that Taiwan had many jobs for doctoral degree holders, but that rates of return remained less than 10 percent, belying Adams's explanation that suitable jobs were lacking in economies suffering brain drain.[82]

Although in the early 1970s Taiwanese government officials and scholars could not yet know that knowledge circulation would turn toward Taiwan's advantage, Kao's study indicates that they nonetheless embraced the same neoliberal, market-driven analysis of their losses as did Adams in explaining American gains. He assessed motivations for knowledge workers to remain overseas as "gaining knowledge, gaining working ability, improving promotion opportunity, and improving social status."[83] All eight ethnic Chinese who have won Nobel Prizes in the sciences trained and worked in either the United States or England: Li Zhengdao, Yang Zhenning, Samuel C. C. Ting, Li Yuanze, Steven Chu, Daniel C. Tsui, Roger Y. Tsien, and Charles K. Kao.[84] Arguably they could not have attained such levels of success without access to major research facilities and communities of fellow scientists, a reality of scientific innovation that inspired thousands of less visible but ambitious Chinese scientists, engineers, and technicians who chose to work in the United States. Although not mentioned by Kao, concerns regarding political instability in both Chinas also shaped individual choices. Bearing in mind such factors, Kao's solution for brain drain affirmed those of Adams regarding salaries, work conditions, and special incentives. Kao did not ask for changes in immigration laws and seemed to trust that market forces would indeed eventually generate more equitable returns, optimistically noting a slight increase in those returning in the early 1970s that grew in the successive decades.[85]

Since the 1970s Taiwan's dramatic transformation into one of the four Asian "tigers," along with Hong Kong, Singapore, and South Korea, has produced a triumphalist narrative that rewrites "brain drain" as "knowledge circulation" into a key national asset. In 1982 the scholar Wu Yuan-li boasted of Taiwan's high returns from its "flow of human capital." "In the short run, human capital outflow represents a waste of investment in human capital; in the long run, however, it accumulates and grows abroad into an asset upon which interest can be drawn.... In Taiwan this principal has become rather large, and in recent years Taiwan has started to collect interest and probably a small proportion of the capital."[86] If brain drain facilitated the migration of value-added human capital, knowledge circulation further enriched the educated resource to the advantage of both sending and receiving economies.

In 1994 Sun Chen, a professor of economics, former president of National Taiwan University, and the then minister of national defense, described brain drain as a particular advantage that complemented the stages of Taiwan's economic development. As it assumed control of Taiwan, the Nationalist government invested few of its scant resources in higher education because there were so many highly educated immigrants from the mainland. The departure of college graduates for advanced studies abroad had limited impact because "of the availability of this highly educated group" during the 1950s.[87] Higher-education facilities developed in tandem with advances in industrial infrastructure and other forms of "technology of the economy." Eventually, capital- and technology-intensive industries become predominant. In 1965, however, only 3 percent of employed persons had any higher education, so that Taiwanese in fact appreciated America's generosity in providing educational opportunities that led to jobs and satisfactory homes for educated elites otherwise unemployable at home. By 1988, however, the proportion of educated workers had risen to 14.7 percent, of whom 55 percent had junior college degrees and 45 percent had university-or-higher-level education.[88]

The reversal of Taiwan's brain-drain flow occurred even as the numbers immigrating to the United States increased. After concerted lobbying efforts

TABLE 8.3. Number of Immigrants from Taiwan
Entering the United States, by Decade, 1950–2000

Decade	Taiwanese Immigrants to United States
1950–1960	7,373
1961–1970	26,873
1971–1980	86,109
1981–1990	147,511
1991–2000	123,173

Source: Lung Wen-pin and Huang Guo-nan. *Taiwan ji liang'an sandi huaren renkou tuigu fangfa—lilun goujian yu shizheng tantao (yi Meiguo wei lie)* [Methods for estimating the population of Chinese from Taiwan, PRC, and Hong Kong using the American example—discussion of theoretical structures and evidence] (Taipei: Overseas Chinese Affairs Commission, 2002), 25.

and the normalization of United States relations with the PRC, Taiwan received its own immigration quota of 20,000 in 1981. Taiwanese immigration rose from under 2,000 in 1965 to 14,895 in 1985, with surges in years of crisis.[89] Since 1987, political liberalization and economic growth have leveled off emigration from Taiwan.

During the 1980s more than 12,000 scholars and students returned from abroad with postgraduate degrees and considerable research and entrepreneurial experience. According to Chen, they enhance "the number of those at the highest levels of the work force and have contributed a great deal to Taiwan's rapid technological and economic development," particularly in high-tech industries. Benefits to Taiwan accrued even from those who remained abroad as they "contributed significantly to the development of the home country . . . by offering professional advice, by providing access to the most advanced sciences and technology in the world, and by short return visits." By the mid-1990s, Chen proclaimed brain drain as a critical asset in Taiwan's economic development: "The large number of students, scholars, and experts who have remained abroad form a potential supply of highly trained people that Taiwan can draw upon for its future development. They provide an advantage that few other developing countries possess."[90] Most visibly, Taiwan has benefited from the close ties to American high-tech industries developed through these transnational technical entrepreneurs.

Taiwan's brain exchange advantage has been most apparent in the information technology and manufacturing center based in the Hsinchu Science-Based Industrial Park, which in 1994 was home to 150 high-tech businesses that had generated nearly US$5 billion in sales in 1993. It produced half the world's supply in scanners, about 30 percent in network cards, and 10 percent of the personal computer market. Almost half of these companies had been started by Taiwanese engineers returned from the United States.[91] For example, David Lee (Sen Lin) was born in Beijing in 1937 but fled to Taiwan in 1949 with his family. The Lees migrated to Argentina in 1952 and eventually learned Spanish. The family opened a successful Chinese restaurant and then moved into the import-export business. Lee's father wanted him to study engineering in the United States, and in 1956 Lee enrolled in Montana State University in Bozeman. He worked his way through college and received his BS degree in mechanical engineering in 1960, then an MA degree from North Dakota State University. After working for established American firms, in 1969 Lee branched out to become one of the earliest successful Taiwanese Chinese entrepreneurs in Silicon Valley by developing computer peripherals such as the first daisywheel printer. Lee started a series of businesses and was bought out repeatedly by larger corporations such as Xerox, Qume, and ITT. Qume became the largest manufacturer of printers and floppy drives in the United States. Part of Lee's success stemmed from his use of cheaper Taiwanese manufacturers such as Acer and Mitac, which in turn helped Taiwan become a major exporter of PCs and computer peripherals.[92]

During the 1990s Taiwan extended its strategy of providing competitively priced manufacturing facilities and labor for global IT industry markets by expanding to the Chinese mainland, which had liberalized economically under Deng Xiaoping's leadership across the 1980s. In 2002 Taiwanese investors controlled two-thirds of China's IT output.[93] The growth in Taiwan's economy has been dramatic, with per capita income growing from US$200 per year in the 1950s to $12,465 in 2003.[94] In 2006 Taiwan's per capita GDP stood at $27,500, thirty-fifth in the world. In 2007 it gained further to reach $29,500, or thirty-third. In that year Taiwan's GDP was $375.6 billion, or twenty-third. Taiwan's economic development is notable for its close integration between cutting-edge research in the United States and lower-cost manufacturing facilities in Taiwan. The human resources once regarded as Taiwan's losses have turned into mobile knowledge workers and entrepreneurial bridges that have provided uncommon economic advantages in enabling Taiwan to build closer and mutually beneficial ties with the United States.

Exile in America

The students from Taiwan who became such instrumental knowledge workers and entrepreneurs experienced a relatively easier entry into American suburban, middle-class life compared to other minority groups and even American-born Chinese. By the 1960s statistical and anecdotal evidence celebrated the many Chinese entering professional and white-collar employment

Figure 8.2. I. M. Pei supervising construction of the John F. Kennedy Library during the 1970s. Pei had won the commission after charming Jaqueline Kennedy, who personally insisted on his hiring. Courtesy of John F. Kennedy Presidential Library and Museum.

and middle-class neighborhoods. The commissioning of I. M. Pei to design the Kennedy Library in 1964 was one such key landmark (see fig. 8.2). Many of the most visibly successful were immigrants who entered American society already bearing significant levels of education and skills. The repositioning of Chinese as model immigrants and their high levels of attainment gained them greater entry and acceptance in the United States; such attainments, however, did not assuage the sense of exile and dislocation on the part of those who were nonetheless refugees and whose repeated relocations as the consequence of over a decade of war and invasion tainted their settlement in America with uncertainty and nostalgic longings for their lost homeland.

In the late 1960s Chia-ling Kuo found that American-born and Taiwanese Chinese living on Long Island experienced discrimination in significantly different ways, with the latter claiming never to have encountered racism whereas the former appeared scarred by "the effect of discriminatory practices against their parents or themselves during their childhood."[95] The Cold

War had changed the parameters of acceptable discrimination against Chinese, who, for the purposes of cultivating American support abroad, had to be seen as enjoying equal opportunities in the United States. According to Christina Klein, "Questions of racism thus served to link the domestic American sphere with the sphere of foreign relations, proving their inseparability: how Americans dealt with the problem of race relations at home had a direct impact on their success in dealing with the decolonizing world abroad."[96] In a number of arenas, past practices of discrimination against Asians became untenable in light of how America might be viewed abroad in the 1950s.

The residential discrimination case of Sing Sheng reflects these changes. A former captain in the Nationalist Air Force, Sing Sheng married an American-born, ethnic Chinese woman, came to study in America, then decided to remain. In 1952 the couple attempted to buy a house in an all-white suburb in South San Francisco called Southwood. Their legal right to break the residential color barrier had been established with the Supreme Court case *Shelley v. Kraemer* in 1948, which invalidated racially restrictive housing covenants. Judicial proclamations did not, however, prevent their prospective new neighbors from bitterly protesting in the name of protecting their property values from racial "blockbusters" like the Shengs. To their surprise, these economic rationales became a national controversy, with Sing Sheng drawing parallels between his quest for a home and the international "fight with communism." According to Charlotte Brooks, "numerous observers commented on Southwood as if it were as much a foreign policy issue as a matter of civil rights. A *Life* magazine editorial argued that, after Southwood, 'in Asia they will . . . be asking whether American democracy is still worth betting on.' " In the end the Shengs decided to forgo the South San Francisco house and moved instead to Menlo Park, another unintegrated neighborhood but one that provided a warm welcome.[97] As friendly "foreigners" whose experiences of American democracy bore the weight of U.S. foreign relations aspirations in the western Pacific, Taiwanese Chinese encountered much more receptive conditions as they established new lives.

Despite such pressures to demonstrate egalitarian treatment of Chinese, the sociologist Peter Li observed that perceptions of growing numbers of professional Chinese were misleading and resulted instead from "the growth of a second generation of Chinese in recent years [and] the changing immigration policy which place a heavy emphasis on professional credentials as a qualification for immigration." Li stressed that the rising standard of Chinese Americans' socioeconomic standing was attributable more to immigration selection rather than the opportunities of American democracy. Li credited "selective recruitment by legislative control" for professionally credentialed Chinese immigrants, rather than upward mobility on the part of "the earlier immigrant cohorts of Chinese," for this change.[98] Rather than fostering opportunities for the multiple generations of Chinese American lodged in laundry and restaurant work, starting in the 1950s the United States had simply begun importing high-achieving scientists and engineers from overseas.

This patina of success masked the considerable personal difficulties experienced by many Taiwanese knowledge workers. Chinese students shouldered great responsibilities to their families to pay back the investment in their education by earning status and wealth as well as carving out a toehold to make possible the migrations of other family members, as described by the anthropologist Susan Greenhalgh. "They are expected to return the investment by such means as earning face-giving degrees; sending remittances to cover living expenses, younger brothers' schooling and so forth; making connections that can be exploited by other family members; and eventually perhaps helping younger siblings move to the city."[99] Such pressures increased the stakes of their presence in the United States, for if they did not succeed in school, work, marriage, and gaining legal status, they failed their families as well. With such pressures, most felt no choice but to complete graduate degree programs, enter white-collar or professional employment, marry and start families, and send their children to college.

Leslie Chang describes the personal and familial dysfunction of her mother and her three Beiyinu classmates. Although all attained the markers of socioeconomic success listed above, each experienced lives of discontent and discord, drawing on material but not spiritual groundings in America. Chang wrote her book in an attempt to understand her neglectful mother, whom she capsulizes as "the pragmatist, the assimilationist, able to move from world to world without ever belonging to any particular one." Delving into family history and exploring the consequences of her mother having lived in thirteen different cities and towns by the age of twenty-one, losing both parents, and becoming dependent on an abusive and manipulative uncle, Chang finds a way to forgive her mother and her generation's lack of introspection and preoccupation with material comforts by focusing on her disrupted life.

> Self-reflection was too painful. The women did not want to think. History was tragic. It had ended their childhood, killed their parents, driven them from their homes. Culture was useless. It had not given them rice when they were starving or found them a place to sleep when they were homeless. Success meant washing machines and air conditioning, college education for the children, and well-paying jobs. My mother and her friends had been too busy surviving life to ponder its mysteries.[100]

Such survivalist imperatives had produced varying degrees of quantifiable attainment in America: university degrees, suburban homes, educated children, and white-collar or professional jobs that nonetheless did not replace the losses and displacements they had sustained. Material prosperity and security could not dislodge the shadow of their irredeemable pasts. Despite the relative comfort of their American lives, the student immigrants had found their way to the Land of Opportunity through circumstances of compromised choices and considerable desperation.

Bai Xianyong's short story "Winter Night" depicts the psychic anguish of a successful Chinese professor teaching at UC Berkeley whose professional attainments and high status mask his existential turmoil. Wu Zhuguo has returned to Taiwan and pays a visit to his classmate and fellow former May Fourth protester, Professor Yu Qinlei, in his Taipei home. They reminisce about their history as youthful political activists, fervently demonstrating against Japanese aggression and calling for China's modernization. Memories of past idealism lead Yu, once half of "China's Romeo and Juliet of the day" couple, to admit the disappointments of his current life—his failure to publish, the limits of his teaching, the crass materialism of his mahjong-obsessed second wife, and his admiration for Wu's successes abroad, which have vindicated the blighted careers of Yu and other classmates trapped in Taiwan. Wu responds with intense regret that despite his international stature and speaking engagements, he regards himself as "a deserter abroad for so many years." Of late he has been particularly troubled. He attended a talk delivered by a young graduate student who criticized the May Fourth activists for having had little impact and as being "lost" in "spiritual exile . . . taking refuge in their isolation." Wu confesses he did not respond, for "On such an occasion how could my own pride permit me to stand up and speak for the May Fourth Movement?" and admitted his unwillingness to talk about the history of his own generation from a sense of complete failure. He also describes his many books as "empty talk," undertaken for no more reason than "to satisfy the requirements of the American universities. . . . If I didn't have to publish, I wouldn't have written a single one of them." Yu confesses in turn that for years he has longed to shed his Taiwanese poverty by gaining a fellowship to go to the United States. Although he knows that as a Chinese he will not be allowed to teach his specialization, Byron's poetry, he is willing to make the sacrifice and become a language teacher in order to afford better educational chances for his two sons. The two friends part, neither satisfied with his own existence and each longing for the purposeful life he thinks the other inhabits.[101] The irreconcilability of the men's aspirations, the impossibility for them to find both material and spiritual fulfillment while in exile from a China they could not save, in lives divided between Taiwan and the United States, leave them in tormented limbo.

Whether they came as refugees or students or immigrants, and regardless of their psychic discontent, these waves of post–World War II immigrants constituted a new class of Chinese Americans, "the uptown Chinese," in the coinage of Peter Kwong.[102] Associated with America's ally, the Nationalists on Taiwan, and originating from higher classes socio-economically and educationally, these immigrants outperformed the largely working-class Chinese who had borne the brunt of American discrimination during the exclusion era. Chia-ling Kuo observed:

> It seems that although the majority of the American-born Chinese are engineers by profession, the rest of the members hold less prestigious jobs, including post office clerks, small business proprietors, salesmen, elementary school teachers, etc. But most of the [Chinese immigrants] are engaged in prestigious professions other than engineering, such as university teaching, medical research or practice, or management in big corporations. Thus, the stranded-Chinese as a group are more successful in their professions than are the American-born. All of them have received the master's degree and many hold the Ph.D. degree. A small number of them occupy top-ranking teaching, executive, managerial, or research positions in American firms, corporations, banks, and universities.[103]

Both groups of Chinese had benefited from the diminishing of open discrimination and legislation regarding residence, employment, and educational access. The American-born Chinese, however, who reflect more clearly the ascent of racial minorities overcoming discrimination to leave behind the marginalized working classes to become middle class, did not succeed to the same striking degree as their Chinese immigrant counterparts. The latter not only attained middle-class status but showed up in increasing numbers in high-status occupations, such as teaching in elite universities and colleges, besides working as engineers, architects, and scientists.[104] Based on such examples, Chinese clearly had broken through to the inner circles of socioeconomic attainment in the United States. Much of their success, however, rested on the cultural and economic capital that they brought with them as immigrants screened by their educational capital and employment potential for entry.

The importation of educated elites also obscured the reworking of stereotypes of Asians, who became associated with middle-class attainments and integration into fields such as the sciences and engineering but were seen as lacking in leadership or creativity. The oddly invisible influence of Yi-fu Tuan reflects the simultaneous opening and obscuring of attainment available to Asian Americans. Tuan is highly celebrated within his discipline of geography, with the historian Simon Schama describing him as "one of the most remarkable and creative forces in the intellectual life of our time" but also as "the most influential scholar you've never heard of." Tuan attributes his lack of visibility to his ethnicity with the complaint that because he does not operate in "an accepted field, ethnic studies or physics," as a Chinese American he has not received greater public acclaim.[105] His capacity to transcend his racial attribution is striking, however, and reflects the opening of opportunities for ethnic Asians after World War II. Tuan's simultaneous accomplishment and disappearance seem to suggest the possibility for a postracial realm of ideas in which he could speak for human beings as a species in ways that rendered irrelevant race, gender, class, and a host of other modes of categorization. To be sure, while professionally active, Tuan emphasized his kaleidoscopic and eloquent ponderings of the general human condition while shrouding his marginality as a gay, Christian, ethnic Chinese.[106] Tuan attained great intellectual influence but at the cost of a kind of invisibility that reflects the new levels of attainment that became available to Asian Americans even as it suggests the necessity of certain kinds of conformity.

The broadening of Chinese access to previously restricted employments and neighborhoods also contributed to greater visibility through increasing numbers. The dismantling of Asian exclusion and the possibility of entering as nonquota students and refugees produced rising rates of population growth after World War II. In 1930 the Chinese American population had stood at 74,954, an increase of 21.6 percent over a decade earlier. The Great Depression sharply curtailed immigration over the next decade to increase by only 3.4 percent, with a population in 1940 of 77,504. Despite World War II, however, over the ensuing decade the Chinese American population grew by 51.8 percent to reach 117,629 in 1950. The very low national origins quota of the repeal in 1943 and the McCarran-Walter Act in 1952 did not prevent this population from doubling over the 1950s to reach 237,292, an increase of 101.7 percent by 1960. Most Chinese during this decade immigrated through nonquota statuses such as family reunification and as refugees.[107] Notably, the Chinese American population was already growing at geometric rates before passage of the Hart-Celler Act, the law most commonly credited with the dramatic increase in the number and proportion of skilled Asian immigrants. Decades before 1965, the United States had been working through principles of immigration selection that have become our common-sense priorities for border controls.

Although they chose different paths in the 1950s, with Yang Zhenning staying in the United States and Qian Xuesen returning to China, at the onset of the twenty-first century the two were both back in China. Yang was among the first Americans to visit the PRC in 1971 as relations began thawing. He actively facilitated student and scientific exchanges with the United States, as did Li Zhengdao, and moved back to China permanently in 1998 upon retiring from SUNY–Stony Brook to assume a position at Tsinghua University. Yang is perhaps the most visible example of a brain-drain intellectual recruited back to his ancestral homeland. Li Yuanze, Charles Kao, and Daniel C. Tsui are other Nobel Prize–winning scientists who also returned to work in Asia. Of the remaining four ethnic Chinese scientists to have attained this honor, three hold official affiliations with academic institutions in China, Taiwan, or Hong Kong.[108] In 1979 Li Zhengdao returned to China as a celebrated patriot, where he met again with Wu Ningkun after a twenty-eight-year separation.[109] I. M. Pei designed the Bank of China building that opened in Hong Kong in 1990. Yi-fu Tuan has also visited China, in 2005 after an absence of sixty-four years, as an academic star returned from abroad.[110] Notable examples of American-educated Chinese who returned to positions of great influence include two of the three democratically elected presidents of Taiwan and a majority of its cabinet ministers, along with thousands of well-connected, entrepreneurial engineers.

AnnaLe Saxenian has labeled such cosmopolitan operators "the new Argonauts" because they "are undermining the old pattern of one-way flows of technology and capital from the core to the periphery, creating far more complex and decentralized two-way flows of skill, capital, and technology." At the dawn of the twenty-first century, they operate at the cutting edge of international economic developments and collaborations because "they transfer first-hand knowledge of these financial [venture capital] institutions to the periphery" while disseminating and institutionalizing technological advances. Such individuals are often economic and technological vanguards in their homelands with transformative potential. "They form technical communities with the potential to jump-start local entrepreneurship, and the most successful returnees build alliances with technical professionals, businesses, and policymakers in their home countries." Taiwan during the 1970s and 1980s serves as an exemplary model for these transformations in the global economy. Taiwanese engineer-entrepreneurs started returning from Silicon Valley to pioneer "the model of early-stage high-risk investing" based on their capacities as "native-born investors [who] brought cultural and linguistic know-how as well as the capital needed to operate profitably in these markets. They also brought technical and operating experience, knowledge of new business models, and networks of contacts in the United States." Moreover, they function as "dynamic collaborators" who develop "incremental but cumulatively significant improvements in processes and products that now provide a distinctive competitive advantage" in niche markets that complement but do not compete directly with industry leaders in Silicon Valley.[111] New Argonauts not only integrate economic functions between core and peripheral economies by providing the near instantaneous linkages between cheaper manufacturing and labor costs in the latter to the most recent technological innovations in the former, they also enable research and development capacities in the periphery that propel two-way flows of technological innovation, which promotes diversification through the proliferation of small and medium-size businesses.

The economist Paul Collier notes additional benefits, such as the dissemination of "political and social attitudes that they have assimilated from their classmates." The capacity for political dissidents to organize while in America and then return significantly fueled Taiwan's political liberalization in the late 1980s. Generally, "their skills raise the productivity of the unskilled majority, and their attitudes accelerate democratization."[112] The success and global reach of Taiwan's bounding IT economic sector relied in no small part on the education and technical skills brought back by returned knowledge workers who imported as well business networks and experience, democratic values, and the financial expertise that jumpstarted this industry.

Despite the many criticisms of its first two decades, brain drain functioned as knowledge exchange, an early stage in the circulation of educated and influential leadership individuals whose migrations between China and America are privileged and facilitated. From the exemptions for Chinese students in the exclusion laws through the fostering of international education programs and the expansion of cultural exchanges during and after World War II, the perceived usefulness of educated Chinese leveraged greater access, resources, opportunities, and legal accommodations for continued rights of entry and, by the 1950s, permanent resettlement. The strategic value of this class of Chinese, particularly scientists and engineers during the throes of the Space Race, helped to press the cause of immigration reform and abolishing of the discriminatory national origins system. As will be discussed in the concluding chapter, the selective processes encouraging migration of educated elites also laid the foundations of the so-called model minority so celebrated in the first decades of the twenty-first century and now normative values for the privileging of knowledge workers that mask new forms of racial inequalities.

CHAPTER 9

Conclusion

THE AMERICAN MARKETPLACE OF BRAINS

MIGRATION FLOWS IN THE FIRST DECADE of the twenty-first century reflect the intensification and naturalization of immigration selection processes that favor the educated and technologically adept. Asians became the fastest-growing immigrant group in America for the first time in 2009, overtaking Latinos, who had held the lead since the 1950s. In 2010, 430,000 Asians—or 36 percent of all legal and illegal immigrants—became Americans compared to 370,000 Latinos at 31 percent.[1] This shift has provoked nary a flurry of protest or alarm, despite occurring amid a severe economic downturn. America's sense of immigration crisis now targets unsanctioned entries across its unruly southern border, a region that has experienced heightened surveillance, patrols, detentions, and deportations. In contrast, about 90 percent of Asians immigrate legally, in part because they must cross oceans to reach the United States. Screened through the preferences enshrined in the Hart-Celler Act of 1965, the Asian American population has nonetheless grown at geometric rates to reach 17.3 million, or 5.8 percent of the U.S. population in 2012, up from less than 1 percent when the legislation was first passed a half century earlier.[2] In stark contrast to the acrimonious reception of the few tens of thousands of Chinese who arrived during the mid-1800s, the immigration of hundreds of thousands of Asians now barely registers in America's public or legislative arenas as being a cause for alarm, much less restriction, reflecting general acceptance of a legal system that privileges immigrants understood to further America's economic interests.

As non-Europeans have come to dominate the ranks of immigrants to America, Asians have become "model minorities" perceived as exemplary immigrants with educational credentials, entrepreneurial ambitions, strong work ethics, valuable job skills, and exemplary family values. The outstanding career of I. M. Pei during the mid-twentieth century, celebrated so prominently in 1986, featured traits now normatively attributed to Asians who are imported for their education and useful skills to advance economic development while simultaneously undermining charges of racial inequality and discrimination in the United States by virtue of their successes as immigrants of color. As a model minority, Asian immigrants serve to rebuke less successful communities of color for their lack of attainment, which is attributed to obstructive cultural values rather than the successful "Asian" emphasis on family solidarity, hard work, and education. The Hart-Celler Act has enabled this reworking of the racialization and stigmatization of America's immigrant populations. Even as the law increased Asian admissions while imposing preferences for employment skills and education, it numerically capped for the first time immigration within the Americas, which magnified the illegal immigration problem in the United States. Geography and distance render U.S. limits and selection processes for Asian immigrants largely effective, an enactment of national sovereignty that is regularly undermined, however, by the proximity and long land borders shared with America's much poorer neighbors to its south. As this conclusion explores, the encoding of economic priorities and recoding of racial stigmas into immigration laws and employment preferences that began during the Cold War have transformed Chinese and other Asians into model immigrants even as they have been replaced by Latinos as the chief immigration threat, seen as incorrigible lawbreakers illicitly crossing into America with low educational and work attainment to become drains on public resources. Immigration debates and legislation of the late twentieth and early twenty-first centuries have underscored the overall movement toward enlarging the gateways that admit educated, technically and scientifically trained immigrants, now primarily Asians, while fortifying the gates lining America's southern border. The neoliberal logic configuring these transformations has become naturalized as a kind of common sense that governs and constrains America's ongoing discussions of immigration reform in ways that mask the deeply contentious racial choices and inequalities that the laws perpetuate.

A Pew Report titled "The Rise of Asian Americans" (2012) trumpeted this shift in immigration rates even as it proclaimed that "Asian Americans are the highest-income, best-educated and fastest-growing racial group in the United States. They are more satisfied than the general public with their lives, finances, and the direction of the country, and they place more value than other Americans do on marriage, parenthood, hard work and career success."[3] Immigration selection had fundamentally shaped this exemplary population, for 74 percent of Asian American adults were foreign-born, of whom 61 percent of those aged 25 to 64 arrived with at least a BA degree— double the percentage of non-Asian arrivals, "almost surely mak[ing] the recent Asian arrivals the most highly educated cohort of immigrants in U.S. history." Furthermore, Asians who are able to immigrate are more educated than those left behind. For example, nearly 70 percent of Japanese and South Korean immigrants hold BA degrees compared with roughly 25 to 27 percent in their homelands. According to 2010 census data, in this age range, 49 percent of Asian Americans held university degrees, compared to the national average of 28 percent, and earned higher average household incomes of $66,000, contrasted with $49,800. Whereas the national average for adults employed in management, professional, and related fields is 40 percent, the percentage for Asians is 50.[4]

Such comparatively high levels of attainment are shaped by the economic preferences of current immigration laws, for recent Asian immigrants were "about three times as likely as recent immigrants from other parts of the world" to receive their green cards through employer rather than family sponsorship, even though family reunification is still the most commonly used legal status to enter the United States for Asians, as with all other groups. "Recent arrivals from Asia are nearly twice as likely as those who came three decades ago to have a college degree, and many go into high-paying fields such as science, engineering, medicine and finance. This evolution has been spurred by changes in U.S. immigration policies and labor markets."[5] This book has explored the evolution of such processes of immigration selection for economically endowed immigrants enacted through the Hart-Celler Act, which had its roots in the exempt classes identified with the enactment of race-based immigration restriction against Chinese in 1882 and expanding programs for international education and cultural exchange through World War II and the Cold War. In the half-century since 1965, the growing clout of employers in immigration proceedings has institutionalized such economic preferences for those educated and trained to work in particular fields and has remade Asian Americans into model immigrants whose attributes dominate early twenty-first-century discussions of immigration reform and choices about who should be welcomed into the United States. Aihwa Ong describes these trends: "The most worthy citizen is a flexible *homo economicus*. In our age of globalization, the figure of entrepreneurial prowess is increasingly multiracial, multicultural, and transnational."[6] The rigors of conducting business internationally give bicultural, immigrant workers decisive advantages over monoculturally educated domestic ones. Immigration selection has positioned the United States to competitive advantage in the global economy.

As described in chapter 8, AnnaLe Saxenian's concept of "new Argonauts" evokes the globalization of scientific innovation, manufacturing advantage, and corporate competitiveness forged from the entrepreneurial energies of such transnational, technologically adept, economic performers from Asia, particularly ethnic Chinese and now Indians. "They have created dynamic collaborators in distant and differently specialized economic economies, while largely avoiding head-on competition with industry leaders" with Silicon Valley "at the core of this rapidly diversifying network" as "the largest and most sophisticated market as well as leading source of new technology." In the rapidly evolving, increasingly synchronized international economy, the "scarce competitive resource" that is at a premium "is the ability to locate foreign partners quickly and to manage complex business relationships and teamwork across cultural and linguistic barriers." Recent Asian immigrants "have a commanding professional advantage," for they "have the necessary language, cultural, and technical skills to function well in the United States as well as in their home markets."[7] Such considerations do much to explain the predominance of Asians in allocations of H-1B work visas and in American graduate science and engineering programs that feed directly into these corporate agendas.

This close integration of economic priorities with immigration controls draws on the much longer history of student migrations. Although students constituted but a small minority of the Chinese American population, their exempt status and relative welcome in the United States during the exclusion era help to explain the transition from the race- and national-origins-based systems that emerged with the Chinese Restriction Act of 1882 and remained in place until 1965. With the right filters in place, and with geography capping numbers at tolerable levels, immigration selection could serve national purposes, not only for matters of security but to propel economic development and advance America's standing abroad. The logic of favoring educated Chinese—many of whom were trained in STEM fields, first as visitors who would advance foreign and trade relations with China, then as wartime allies and useful skilled trainees, and then as critical resources in the Cold War competition against the communist world—advanced individual-based, economic criteria as compelling alternatives for the internationally offensive, race-based quota system. World War II had rendered racial nationalism unacceptable, and in the new world order that emerged, the United States needed to develop more egalitarian rationales for restricting its borders even as the emergence of postcolonial states in the developing world and hemispheric geopolitics transformed the number and origins of immigrants to America. As described by Aihwa Ong,

> The interweaving of ideologies of racial difference with liberal conditions of citizenship entered a new phase after World War II, when debates about who belonged came to be framed in business-economic terms of balancing the provision of security against the productivity of citizens . . . [giving] rise to the assessment of citizens as human capital, weighing those who could pull themselves up by the bootstraps against those who were economically dependent. . . . Ideological discourses contrasting the contributions to the nation of different races often conflated race and class, as . . . in the polarizing contrast between the "underclass" and the "model minority," two key categories for thinking about minoritization in postwar America.[8]

This bifurcation set Chinese onto the track toward becoming model minorities, even as Latino immigrants who committed unsanctioned entry in the greatest numbers since the 1920s became coded as an uncontrollable, invading force and burdens on public resources.

The trajectories of Chinese students reveal the range in American management of both racial differences and the international implications of race-based immigration restrictions. Even during the exclusion era, some Americans, particularly missionaries, educators, internationalists, and business interests, had distinguished among Chinese on the basis of their capacities to adapt to American culture and civilization. Such outreach sought to further U.S. influence abroad, priorities and strategies that gained ground with the liberalizations of immigration law that began with the 1943 repeal of exclusion. The employment categories that now admit so many Chinese and other Asian immigrants had antecedents in the 1940s "stranded students" who arrived and remained through the implementation of economic preferences with the Displaced Persons Act of 1948 and McCarran-Walter Act of 1952. Congressional and Department of State decisions enabled the stranded Chinese students and trainees to find gainful employment and regularize their status in the United States, accommodations made not only because of American benevolence but also because their educational and professional attributes made them valuable economic and technological contributors whose departures would benefit the communist enemy. The pragmatic possibilities of selecting immigrants on the basis of their economic value, in conjunction with the reality that distance sharply limited the number of Chinese who could enter the United States without gaining legal permission, repositioned Chinese as model immigrants. Through the tinkering with immigration laws during the 1950s and early 1960s, and with the dramatic shifts after 1965, the Chinese American population has nearly doubled every decade since 1950, immigrating in much greater numbers than anticipated but compensating for greater visibility and demographic impact through high educational and economic attainment, as table 9.1 illustrates.

Suggesting how effectively the 1965 law has worked, the percentages of recent Asian immigrants with college degrees have been steadily increasing since 1980, from 34.6 percent to 44.2 percent in 1990, then 59.3 percent in 2000 and 60.8 percent in 2010.[9]

Immigrants from Taiwan highlight the effects of the neoliberally framed Hart-Celler Act of 1965 in producing a class of immigrants with higher than average levels of education and employment in professional and white-collar fields. With few ties to pre–World War II Chinese American communities, greater percentages of Taiwanese Chinese immigrate through education or employment statuses, rather than family reunification, than those from Hong Kong or China. For example, 54 percent of China-born immigrants were admitted as immediate relatives of U.S. citizens, whereas only 15 percent of Hong Kong-born and 29 percent of Taiwan-born entered through the same status.[10] In 1990, 62 percent of Taiwanese had completed at least

TABLE 9.1. Educational Attainment, Employment, and Income Data
for Adults in the United States, 2010

	All Americans	Asians	Chinese	Asian Indians	Japanese	Filipinos	Koreans	Vietnamese
Foreign born (%)	16	74	76	87	46	69	78	84
BA degree (%)	28	49	51	70	32	47	53	26
Median family income (1999)	$49,800	$66,000	$65,050	$88,000	$65,390	$75,000	$50,000	$53,400
U.S. citizen (%)	91	70	69	56	79	77	67	80
Poverty rate (%)	13	12	14	9	8	6	15	15
In sciences and engineering (%)	5	14	18	28	9	7	8	10

Source: "The Rise of Asian Americans," 18. The data apply to adults ages twenty-five and
older.

four years of college, compared to 46 percent of Hong Kong Chinese, 31 percent of PRC Chinese, and 21 percent of non-Hispanic whites ages twenty-five to sixty-four. In contrast, almost 40 percent of immigrants from the PRC did not have high school diplomas, compared to 18 percent for Hong Kong, 8 percent for Taiwan, and 22 percent for Americans overall.[11] Commensurately higher percentages of Taiwanese Chinese were either in "managerial and professional specialty occupations" or in "technical, sales and administrative occupations" than Hong Kong or PRC Chinese, with comparable differences in average household incomes.[12] Modes of immigration clearly influence overall attainment levels, for Asian American groups that have immigrated in greater percentages through nonemployment statuses, such as Vietnamese and Cambodians, experience higher than national average rates of poverty.[13]

The model minority stereotype masks the sacrifices and downward mobility that many immigrants have made in order to succeed in America. The origins of this image is commonly traced to 1966, when the *New York Times Magazine* and *US News and World Report* printed laudatory accounts of the successes of Japanese and Chinese Americans attained through hard work, family values, and emphasis on education and white-collar and professional training. As critiqued by Ellen Wu, news reporting celebrating Asian American integration assiduously ignored community complaints regarding persistent issues of public health, unemployment, and juvenile delinquency.[14] During the Reagan era, the volume of reporting on the model minority phenomenon grew, with major newspapers and journals featuring covers that depicted clean-cut Asian American youth admitted in disproportionate rates to top universities such as Harvard, Berkeley, UCLA, and MIT. The Taiwanese American Kuo family of Flushing, New York, exhibited these essential characteristics when they came to national attention as their son, David, became their third child in as many years selected as a finalist for the Westinghouse Science Talent Search. The only family to accomplish this estimable feat, the Kuos had raised two elder sons who were both enrolled at Harvard, after having attended Bronx High School of Science as well. The parents, Mei-hui, a bank teller, and Hsien-Tsung, a respiratory hospital technician, spoke proudly of their efforts to provide a supportive environment for their sons' education and the better climate that had motivated them to move to the United States. Reaching these opportunities, however, had required sacrifices such as an extended period of separation and the loss of the parents' surgical and nursing careers in Taiwan owing to their inability to get reaccredited in the United States. Statistical data mask these significant losses even as they celebrate achievements.[15]

Even on the cusp of the early twenty-first century, the specter of Chinese exclusion lingers, for economic and educational attainment and the removal of discriminatory immigration barriers have not completely erased yellow peril fears that ethnic Chinese remain ineradicably loyal to their ancestral homeland. The rising economic and political clout of China, along with regular occurrences of corporate and military espionage and hacking, exacerbate entrenched, barely subcutaneous anxieties that Chinese remain perpetual foreigners in our midst ready to attack and betray America when beckoned by China. In 1996 Chinese American campaign donors were accused of participating in a PRC-oriented conspiracy to influence the Clinton White House through illegal campaign contributions in the so-called Bamboogate.[16] Although such cultivation of political networks is commonplace in American politics, only Chinese Americans were targeted as an ethnic group for federal investigation and a few instances of prosecution. Such racialized fears of Chinese as covert agents reemerged again in 1999 with the prosecution of the research scientist Wen Ho Lee (Li Wenhe, b. 1939), a Taiwanese American and naturalized U.S. citizen since 1974, on the suspicion that he had been spying for the PRC. The *New York Times* led the charge in attacking the Clinton administration for laxness in securing national secrets and fingering Lee as the leaker even though he was removed by several generations from China. The White House responded with a vigorous investigation that led to Lee's firing from his job of three decades at Los Alamos National Laboratory despite lie detector tests verifying his lack of wrongdoing. Charged with fifty-nine counts of mishandling classified information, rather than espionage, Lee was thrown into solitary confinement without bail by a judge who believed FBI testimony that he would otherwise give away the "crown jewels" of U.S. nuclear armaments secrets.[17] Once Lee hired attorneys, the government's case quickly unraveled, for there had been no security breach of nuclear top secrets, only the Clinton administration's need to show that it could be tough on China. Ultimately Lee pleaded guilty to one count of mishandling classified information, which he had downloaded onto a laptop computer. The readiness with which this low-key research scientist could be made a surrogate for America's fears of Chinese competition and military threat, however, inhibits U.S. companies from employing Chinese while making the latter less willing to seek work in the United States.[18]

In the twenty-first century Indians have become the highest achieving of all Asian American groups whose demographic trajectories underscore the ongoing shift toward neoliberal immigration priorities. About half of all Indian immigrants receiving green cards in 2011 did so through employer sponsorship, with the predictable outcome that Indian Americans lead *all* other Asian groups in income and education: 70 percent age twenty-five or older have completed a college degree.[19] The Indian community is perhaps the one most completely framed by the economic preferences built into immigration laws. The percentages of recent Indian immigrants holding college degrees hit 81.0 percent in 2010, up from 52.4 percent in 1980.[20] The effectiveness of U.S. immigration laws in screening for those with high levels of educational attainment is suggested by the mere 10 percent of the college-aged who are enrolled in tertiary education in India.[21] America's narrow gates now admit primarily those benefiting from the greatest investments of education and training, selective trends that are readily apparent among Indian Americans, whose demographics are chiefly framed by the Hart-Celler Act. Numbering but 12,296 as recently as 1960, the Indian community has since grown rapidly to become the third largest Asian American group at 3.2 million in 2012, following Chinese at 3.8 million and Filipinos at 3.4 million and surpassing the once-largest community, Japanese.[22]

Fast on the heels of the end of World War II, the United States became the destination of choice for Indian students studying abroad. Previously Britain had been the preferred metropole, receiving about 1,000–2,000 Indian students each year, with only at most 208 going to the United States.[23] This situation changed quickly starting in 1944 when the colonial government began funding Indian students to study in America in order to acquire greater scientific and technological capacity. The participation of Indians in American technical training programs in fall 1945 was part of this shift (see chapter 5). By 1946 Indians studying in America already outnumbered those going to Britain, and this preference has continued ever since. In 1949, for example, almost 1,700 Indians studied in the United States, more than double the 700 in the United Kingdom.[24] After India gained independence in 1947 and the United States emerged as the global leader in science and technology research and began courting nonaligned nations during the Cold War, Indian student numbers kept growing across the 1950s and 1960s, as shown in figure A.1. Graduates who had returned from the United States developed much of India's infrastructure for technical training and the computer industry. As in the case of China and Taiwan, their precedent laid the foundations for future generations to study in America, with the added advantage of native ability in the English language. By 2011 Chinese international students were the most numerous at nearly 160,000, followed by Indians at just over 100,000. South Koreans, Taiwanese, Japanese, and Vietnamese also claimed spots in the top ten most numerous national student groups.[25] In 2010 ethnic Asian students, both foreign- and U.S.-born, received a disproportionate percentage of graduate degrees, particularly in the STEM fields. Overall they collected 25 percent of the research doctorates granted in the United States—45 percent of all engineering PhDs, 38 percent of those in math and computer science, 33 percent of the physical sciences, and 25 percent of the life sciences.[26] As illustrated in chapter 8, the pathway to immigration through graduate study before 1965 has become a central road by which the neoliberal forces governing immigration now privilege the knowledge workers deemed most economically useful.

Like the large influxes of nurses from the Philippines that began arriving during the early 1960s through the Exchange Visitor Program described by Catherine Ceniza Choy, the Cold War reworking of immigration controls facilitated the immigration of educated and technically trained workers who had initially arrived with temporary visas for various forms of continuing education or training.[27] During the 1950s and 1960s, if Taiwan was the chief sufferer of brain drain, India came second, followed by South Korea (see table 8.2). In the past several decades, an estimated 80 percent of Chinese and Indian college graduates going abroad have not returned to their home countries.[28] Such patterns conjoin with the growing percentage of master's and doctoral students, particularly in fields such as engineering, who come from abroad. At present one-third of international students remain in the United States through temporary work visas, usually the H-1B. These high levels of educational attainment are a factor in the occupational profile of Asian Americans and particularly their concentration in the fields of science and engineering. As described in table 9.1, among adults, 14 percent of Asian Americans are employed in these fields, compared with 5 percent of the U.S. population overall. The percentage among Indians is even higher, at 28 percent.[29]

Immigration reforms within the past quarter century have widened the gates for such skilled workers. In 1990 Congress passed legislation doubling the number of work-based visas from 54,000 to 120,000, setting aside 80,000 for high-skills professionals, and enacted the H-1B program making available annually 65,000 temporary work visas for "specialty occupations." To qualify for the H-1B, applicants need to have at least a B.A. degree or its equivalent.[30] Until the mid-1990s the annual H-1B visa cap was never reached, but since then it has been exhausted with increasing speed, leading corporate interests to lobby for more such visas. Both Congress and successive presidents have been responsive in passing legislation for the sake of "American Competitiveness and Workforce Improvement" in 1998 and 2000 to temporarily almost double the ceiling to 115,000 in 1999 and 2000 and again up to 195,000 in 2001 through 2003.[31] Immigration law historian Bill Ong Hing observed, "After passage of the act, although the main thrust of immigration law continued to be family immigration, highly skilled immigrants would be deliberately encouraged to resettle in the United States more than ever before."[32]

Unlike other temporary worker visas, the H-1B provides means by which high-skilled workers can immigrate. Although it distributes nonimmigrant visas, the program permits dual intent so that recipients can simultaneously file for green cards. While these applications are being processed, the workers are permitted to remain in the United States on one- or three-year visa extensions that do not count against the annual cap. Through the late 1990s such conversions of status readily occurred, although more recently national limits on immigration from countries with large pools of applicants, such as India and China, have produced extended waits of a decade or longer. Meanwhile, such applicants are able to remain and work.

Statistics from 2011 offer a snapshot of the kinds of selective processes enacted through the H-1B visa program. That year the U.S. Citizenship and Immigration Service approved almost 270,000 petitions. Between 2008 and 2011 an average of 40 percent of petitions concerned first-time employment, with 18 percent aliens from outside the United States, 22 percent aliens already resident, probably as students, and 60 percent continuing employment. Indians now receive the most H-1B visas by far. In 2011 almost 60 percent of H-1B recipients were born in India and almost 10 percent in China, among a top ten that includes workers from the Philippines, South Korea, Japan, Taiwan, and Pakistan.[33] Almost 60 percent of H-1B recipients held post graduate degrees, and just over 50 percent worked in computer-related fields.[34] Since 2010 about 150,000 H-1B visa holders have filed for green cards, nearly a third of whom are from India, the largest block.[35] Those who depart have helped to develop India's IT sector in parallel to Taiwan's Hsinchu Science Park in locations such as Bangalore, Hyderabad, and Mumbai, which operate in close collaboration with Silicon Valley. The addition of the H-1B side door to immigration has most advantaged Asian, and particularly Indian, knowledge workers, for not all developing nations are positioned to produce knowledge workers employable in the United States. Only those that have already invested heavily in higher education systems, which prepare individuals for study or skilled employment, can engage in this kind of circulation of human resources.[36]

Immigration Reform for the Twenty-First Century

Senator Hiram Fong (R-HI), in 1959 the first Asian American elected to the Senate, participated actively in efforts to liberalize immigration laws and took seriously his responsibilities to gain greater access for Asians. In 1968 he acknowledged congressional agency in reforming immigration laws with "thorough consideration . . . of its impact on our complex technologically oriented economy." Congress had hoped that the "new law would enhance our economic growth, help stimulate our economy, and generate new employment opportunities because of provisions we wrote . . . giving high priority to the professionally skilled, technical, and other highly trained persons."[37] Despite criticisms of brain drain, the United States has stayed on the path of economic rationality, which has become naturalized as a "commonsense" logic governing immigration controls even as it reworks racial categories in the United States, with Asians becoming model citizens selected for their educational and employment attainment and work ethic.[38]

As suggested by the celebratory tone of the Pew Report, "The Rise of Asian Americans," Asian knowledge workers and entrepreneurs are welcome to become Americans, as proclaimed repeatedly by the economist and Pulitzer Prize–winning *New York Times* columnist Thomas Friedman. In the thick of the economic downturn in 2009, he proclaimed educated immigrants to be the solution. "When the best brains in the world are on sale, you don't shut them out. You open your doors wider. We need to attack this financial crisis with green cards not just greenbacks, and with start-ups not just bailouts."[39] In a related vein, Friedman wrote later that year: "Now is when we should be stapling a green card to the diploma of any foreign student who earns an advanced degree at any U.S. university, and we should be ending all H-1B visa restrictions on knowledge workers who want to come here. They would invent many more jobs than they would supplant. The world's best brains are on sale. Let's buy more!"[40] Such neoliberal logic calls for the intensification of immigration selection favoring knowledge workers, who are predominantly Asian.

While Americans can generally agree about the national advantages conferred by educated immigrants prescreened by employers and favor them with facilitated pathways to entry, jobs, and citizenship, far more discord attends the abiding problem of unscreened, only partially enforceable, migration across our southern border. About 80 percent of the estimated twelve million illegal immigrant population in the United States were born in Latin America.[41] Even though about 12 percent are unauthorized Asian immigrants, the same taint of illegality does not seem to apply.[42] Any meaningful immigration reform would have to address some normalization of status for this population as occurred with Chinese and the Confession Program. As during the exclusion era, many twenty-first-century unauthorized immigrants live and work in mixed-status families, find employment, pay taxes, and have committed no crime apart from their means of entry. Congress deadlocks on this issue despite the growing ranks of voters, many themselves immigrants or related to unsanctioned residents, pressing for reform.[43] Illegal aliens have become what Mae Ngai terms "impossible subjects," "a *new legal and political subject*, whose inclusion within the nation was simultaneously a social reality and a legal impossibility—a subject barred from citizenship and without rights."[44] Rather than developing strategies to normalize this population, states such as Arizona and South Carolina have sought to expel illegal aliens by encouraging "self-deportation" through measures intended to restrict those without legal identification and proof of residency from access to basic necessities. Even the Dream Act campaign, which seeks a pathway to citizenship on behalf of illegal migrants brought into the country as children, founders against entrenched opposition to any form of normalization for this kind of unscreened and unsanctioned entry even by those lacking culpability who have made their lives in the United States.

Representative Luis V. Gutierrez (D-IL) has protested the educational credentials favored in twenty-first-century calls for immigration reform by stating, "That is not America, there was no special line for Ph.D's and master's degree holders at Ellis Island."[45] However, this is precisely the agenda for current immigration reforms. In 1907, in the thick of the exclusion era, the Chinese student C.C.W. had questioned why Chinese laborers should face such tight restrictions when native-born and European Americans who worked for lower wages did not. "Why should they extend their courteous reception by locking up in the 'detention shed' even to those Chinese students and travelers, and say not a word to the Italians and Hungarians who come here by shiploads for the professed purpose of working?"[46] The United States has indeed implemented C.C.W's rationales for immigration control but in a way so that race continues to matter and immigrants of color gain the right to fuller inclusion by demonstrating their economic attributes.

By the time Ellis Island stopped functioning as America's chief immigration inspection station in 1954, Latin America had displaced Europe as the main source of immigrants, a trend that has only intensified with the transformation of the world after World War II—decolonization and the emergence of nation-states, improving communications, and growing awareness of global imbalances in economic opportunity—that has stimulated migration from poorer into wealthier parts of the world. Geography ensures that few from Asia can enter the United States except by fulfilling legal conditions requiring their employability through enhanced educational and economic attainments, whereas few physical barriers limit access from within the Americas.

What separates the welcome *homo economicus* from Asia and their decidedly unwelcome counterparts from Latin America is the degree to which their migrations are subject to the neoliberal agendas governing contemporary ideologies of border controls, which favor individuals who can find employers willing to sponsor their immigration for the educationally enhanced who bear the promise of conveying economic advantages to their workplace and the United States. Aihwa Ong has criticized the distinctions and hierarchies emerging from such preferences, which demarcate on the basis of perceived differences of class and race even as they successfully channel and manage immigrant ambitions. "Every day, celebrations of market freedom and progress, with their underlying assumptions about the relative moral worthiness of different categories of subjects, influence and shape social practices and the possibilities of citizenship. These social technologies can be conceptualized as a mode not of ruling through oppression, but of 'governing through the freedom and aspirations of subjects rather than in spite of them.'"[47] The opportunity to become American model minorities has enriched and liberated millions of Asian immigrants even as it has straitjacketed them with the requirement of educational and employment attainment and worked to discipline those who arrive without the economic skills required to gain legal entry, failings that now apparently condemn the less educated and economically adept to permanent second-class status, regardless of work ethic, moral values, creativity, or commitment. These are choices the United States has made regarding whom it allows to immigrate and to gain full standing as American citizens. These priorities have facilitated the movement away from the segregationist racial and national origins criteria prevailing before 1965 but have imposed new forms of orthodoxy and preferences that bear their own moral costs in enacting new systems of inequality. Without addressing how immigration reform has reworked hierarchies of race and class by importing knowledge workers from Asia, the American nation cannot reconcile the stark differences of racialization, privilege, attainment, and access to legal status that now mark and divide us.

Acknowledgments

As WITH MY FIRST, this book began when I failed to locate the strand of my family's history in customary narratives of America's past. In this case I was trying to work out how my father managed to stay in America despite having arrived as a graduate student in 1960, years before passage of the Hart-Celler Act of 1965, which is usually credited for the great influxes of engineers and scientists now so prominent among the ranks of Asian Americans. Before such immigration became commonplace, according to general understanding, my father somehow gained legal employment, got married and started a family, and became a citizen. He was one of an entire generation of educated Asians, chiefly Chinese, Indian, and South Korean, who arrived as students and intellectuals and managed to resettle in the United States before 1965, although often in a state of extended legal limbo owing to highly limiting quota restrictions. My father's regretful comment that only a few months after he married my mother in April 1962 a new law suddenly threw open the doors and ended the long waits for citizenship led me to recover passage of Public Law 87–885, "An Act: To facilitate the entry of alien skilled specialists and certain relatives of United States citizens, and for other purposes," a precursor to the 1965 act by several years. From this I traced back the much longer history of privileged migrations by students and knowledge workers whose mobility, in contrast to that of laborers, was endowed with strategic benefits for foreign relations, economic competition, imperial formations of power, and the advancement of world peace. As this account of educated Chinese migrations illustrates, the dramatic mid-twentieth-century transformation of Asians from "yellow peril" to "model minorities" draws on much older strands and practices of regarding educated Chinese as racially different but culturally adaptable and assimilable with Americans, patterns of interactions that have been obscured in our emphasis on Asian exclusion. My father participated in a transitional stage of migration in which the alliances and collaborations of World War II and the Cold War gained force in requiring emphasis on the compatibility of Asians leading to ideological shifts and legislative reforms that dismantled exclusion and have produced Asians as a class of supra-educated, employable, and entrepreneurial American subjects now upheld as the exemplary immigrants of the twenty-first century. I hope this book captures something of his story and that of his generation of fellow immigrants and their compromised choices.

This list of acknowledgments is long but will almost certainly fall short of thanking all who have contributed in some important way to the making of this book.

My research would not be possible without collections carefully ministered, organized, and made available by dedicated corps of archivists and librarians whose advice and guidance have been essential to this book. I particularly thank Paul Rascoe and Meng-fen Su of the Perry L. Castaneda Library at the University of Texas at Austin; Carol Leadenham and the staff of the Hoover Institution Archives; David Langbart and the staff of the National Archives II at College Park, Maryland; and Wei-chi Poon at the Ethnic Studies Library at the University of California, Berkeley. Other critical research collections that I consulted include the Kennedy Presidential Library; the National Archives in Washington, DC; the National Central Library and Academia Historica in Taiwan; the Burke Library Archives and C. V. Starr East Asian Library at Columbia University; the Widener, Schlesinger, and Harvard-Yenching Libraries at Harvard University; and the Library of Congress. Telling details have emerged from interviews with Connie Chan, Evelyn Hu-Dehart, Edward Huang, Burton and Lily Levin, Yi-fu Tuan, Dana Young, and Helen Zia.

Sometimes crafting a revisionist history such as this can be a daunting and isolating endeavor without encouragement and enthusiasm from likeminded others. I was fortunate to have the guidance and inspiration of Gordon Chang and Evelyn Hu-Dehart, two senior scholars who have generously directed me to key sources while sharing their intellectual and personal insights. The late Him Mark Lai informed and supported all my research agendas, even those far from the beaten path, and Lon Kurashige has always willingly provided a ready ear and open mind off which to bounce ideas.

This book simply would not have been possible without the collegial, institutional, and intellectual setting provided by the University of Texas at Austin. Alan Tully, the long-term chair of the History Department, has recruited an outstanding group of colleagues and found the resources to fund our research through the Scholarly Activity Grant funds. Under his leadership and that of founding director Julie Hardwick, the Institute for Historical Studies provides a stimulating and broad-ranging forum for the sharing and developing of first-rate scholarship. These resources have advanced my own work in immeasurable ways by enabling trips for research and travel, opportunities to collaborate with institute fellows such as Ellen Wu and Dominic Yang, and sponsorship of the conference "Transpacific China in the Cold War" in conjunction with Jeremi Suri's theme, "Rethinking Diplomacy," in 2013. In the capable hands of incoming chair Jackie Jones and new institute director Seth Garfield, these successes will certainly continue. Lok Siu stepped up at a key juncture to serve as interim director when I took a semester's leave that was critical to the formulation of this project. I also thank administrators in the College of Liberal Arts Randy Diehl, and Richard Flores for their leadership through phases of both institutional expansion and contraction. As do all UT faculty, I have also benefited from regular allocations of Faculty Travel Grants funding from the Graduate School and Special Research Grants from the Office of the Vice President for Research which also provided a subvention grant for this monograph.

A distinct advantage of the vibrant intellectual community at UT is that several friends and colleagues in Austin and elsewhere have provided references to sources and readings otherwise unfamiliar to me that have shaped this book in key ways. For these particularly critical insights, I thank Bob Abzug, Roger Daniels, Steve Hoelscher, Paul Kramer, Nhi Lieu, Mark Metzler, Franklin Ng, Edward Rhoades, Min Hyoung Song, Hugh Wilford, and Anand Yang.

Drafts of chapters and the book proposal have benefited from the close attention of many scrupulous readers. In particular I thank members of my writing groups: Julia Mickenberg, Robert Oppenheim, and Mary Neuburger; and within Asian American Studies: Julia Lee, Nhi Lieu, Naomi Paik, Snehal Shingavi, Lok Siu, Eric Tang, and Samuel Vong. Occasional readers include Eiichiro Azuma, Carl Bon Tempo, Donna Gabaccia, Sarah Griffiths, Christina Klein, Mae Ngai, Arissa Oh, and Meredith Oyen. I thank members of my Cold War Asia reading group as well: Mung-ting Chung, Peter Hamilton, and Michelle Hsiao.

This project has evolved over the course of many presentations that pushed me to process research, develop narratives, and articulate themes in forums with knowledgeable audiences that have offered invaluable and informed input and suggestions. I have appreciated generative opportunities to share my ideas and research at the following conferences: Association for Asian American Studies, American Historical Association, Organization of American Historians, Association for Asian Studies, and the Society for Historians of American Foreign Relations. I have particularly benefited from invitations to participate in specialized workshops, conferences, and speakers series. For these I thank Arthur Rosenbaum and the Atheneum at Claremont McKenna College; José Moya and the Forum on Migration at Barnard College; Roger Waldinger and Nancy Green for "A Century of Transnationalism: Immigrants and Their Homeland Connections" at UCLA; Glen Petersen, Laura Madokoro, and Elaine Ho for "Global Displacements and Emplacement: The Forced Exile and Resettlement Experiences of Ethnic Chinese Refugees" at the National University of Singapore; Nancy Abelman at the University of Illinois, Urbana-Champaign; Samuel Yamashita and Hong Thai of the Pacific Basin Institute at Pomona College; Min Hyoung Song at Boston University; Wing-kai To for "Chinese American Transnationalism in New England" at the University of Hong Kong; Ken Pomerantz for "Insiders and Outsiders in Chinese History" in honor of Jonathan Spence at Yale University; Bryan Roberts and Jonathan Brown for "China and Latin America in the Global Age" at Peking University, Beijing; and Henry Yu for "Migration and Taiwanese Identity" at the University of British Columbia.

Producing a book involves multiple moving parts, many of which involve nonintellectual but no less critical matters such as making travel arrangements, organizing events, manufacturing tables and graphs, and organizing information and files. The administrative side of my work, which informs, programmatically, the intellectual, benefited immeasurably from the professionalism and dedication of highly competent staff employed at UT. Barbara Jann, most especially, held together the Center for Asian American Studies (CAAS) as administrative associate. With the program coordinators Kenyatta Dawson and then Sona Shah, the CAAS staff made possible much more than I thought feasible despite highly constrained resources. Staff members from the History Department have been essential enablers for my research and conference travel and many programs. In particular, Courtney Meador and Nichole Powell have applied their calm and good humor to working out how to manage the often arcane UT budget systems to help me accomplish my ends. Gail Davis, Laura Flack, Art Flores, and Tony Araguz have also provided invaluable assistance, as has Jack Senakarn of the Liberal Arts IT Services team. Many student workers have devoted their ingenuity and diligence to this project, including Dana Nakano, Anju Reejsinghani, Cristina Salinas, Helen Pho, Lalini Pedris, Bridget Brewer, Jimena Perry, and Andrew Robichaud.

As this book took shape and I considered the most ideal venue for publication, I turned to the series that had produced the monographs most influential for this project. As my notes reveal, publications appearing in Princeton University Press's "Politics and Society in Twentieth-Century America" series have critically framed many of the issues addressed in *The Good Immigrants*. I thank Gary Gerstle, one of the series editors, for his receptiveness to my project and cogent feedback on both the book proposal and review manuscript. At both stages Gary read with understanding and critical engagement that greatly strengthened the final product. The balanced and nuanced comments of the second reader both affirmed this project and provided useful suggestions for reframing key points. At the Press, Eric Crahan, Jill Harris, and Eric Henney have been thoughtfully responsive and organized in guiding me through the stages and components of producing this book from its many pieces. I thank as well Anita O'Brien for her scrupulous attention and Richard Comfort for his meticulous indexing.

Parts of this book are revised and republished here, with permission, from the following: "Chinese and American Collaborations through Educational Exchange during the Era of Exclusion, 1872–1955," *Pacific Historical Review* 83, 2 (May 2014): 314–32; "The Disappearance of America's Cold War Chinese Refugees," *Journal of American Ethnic History* 31, 4 (Summer 2012): 12–33 (copyright © 2012 by the Board of Trustees of the University of Illinois); "Befriending the Yellow Peril: Chinese Students and Intellectuals and the Liberalization of U.S. Immigration Laws, 1950–65," *Journal of American East Asian Relations* 16, 3 (November 2009): 139–62; and "Domesticating the Yellow Peril: Students and Changing Perceptions of the Indigestibility of Chinese Immigrants, 1905–1950," in *Transpacific Interactions: The United States and China, 1880–1950*, ed. Vanessa Kuennemann and Ruth Mayer (New York: Palgrave Macmillan, 2009).

Any faults, shortcomings, and questionable interpretations that remain in this text are, of course, my own.

Over the course of the eventful decade that it has taken me to write this book, I have incurred many debts of friendship and affection without which such a difficult and often selfish project could not come to fruition. Relocation and divorce, both for myself and for my parents, as well as the passage of time, opportunities, and my own distractedness, have brought friends and loved ones in and out of my life, but the gifts of their companionship, understanding, and counsel are no less appreciated: Michael Adams, Ginny Burnett, Mia Carter, Jennifer Chan, Camilla Figueroa, Maria Cristina Garcia, Heather Hindman, Neville Hoad, Neil Kamil, Jenny Larson, Philippa Levine, Erika Lown, Maddalena Marinari, Tracie Matysik, Barbara Moran, Mary Neubuger, LeiLani Nishime, Maureen Nutting, Jamie Rhodes, Cathy Schlund-Vials, Nancy Stalker, Katie Stewart, Perri Strawn, and Melissa Vance Wilson. I particularly want to acknowledge friends who have generously shared their homes (in expensive cities) during my research trips: Kay Chu in Taichung, Taiwan; Mei Lin Kwan-Gett in New York; and most of all Isabelle Thuy Pelaud and Antoine St. Pierre in San Francisco. I thank my closest family members for their constancy: Arthur, Sally, Michael, and Mitchell Hsu; Tzu-Chinn Foo Lam; Chuen-chinn Hsuchen; Karen Lam; and Fay Ann Hsu.

Those who share my household have borne the brunt of my preoccupation with this project. I could not have managed as a working single parent without a sequence of several responsible and resourceful housemates who juggled full-time graduate studies to help me with childcare, dogsitting, and many other sundry household matters. Wu Bo, Tientien Tan, and Xiaoyin Li—thank you for spending with us the early stages of your American lives. I thank as well Sunny Vergara for his flexibility and generosity in coordinating parental visits with my sometimes hectic travel schedule.

My dependents are the most exposed to the very solitary and focused nature of an academic's life. It was with some ambivalence that I decided to dedicate this book to my daughter, Isabella Hsiangyi Hsu Vergara, who has been my most constant companion (apart from the dogs Shelby and Jack) for the past decade but also the chief obstacle to faster completion of this book. However, she tolerates with exceptional patience and good humor the precision and concentration of the unusual work that I do, and I have been privileged to share her journey into becoming a kind and thoughtful adult. Jack, whose greatest talent is to be exactly-in-the-way, has the misfortune to be the successor and near-twin to the incomparable Shelby. On their behalf, I undertake a seemingly unending stream of more and less mundane responsibilities—nutrition manager, scheduler, chauffeur, head buyer, fashion consultant, educational adviser and planner, bedtime reader, cheerleader-in-chief, moral compass, leash holder, and poop-scooper. This immersion into the quotidian provides constant reminders of the material and spiritual privileges of my everyday life. Being a parent has given me the incomparable opportunity to be a human being better, although it has slowed my progress as a professional. For this I thank Izzy, who embodies grace every day.

Appendix

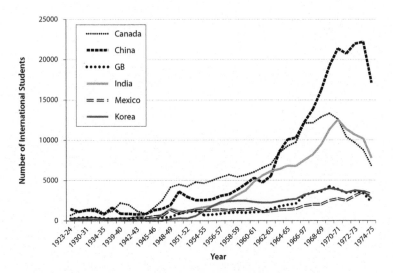

Figure A.1. International students from six major sending countries, 1923–1975. Statistics taken from Committee on Friendly Relations among Foreign Students, *Unofficial Ambassadors*, and Institute for International Education, *Open Doors*. After 1949 the category "Chinese" collapses students from Taiwan, Hong Kong, and China.

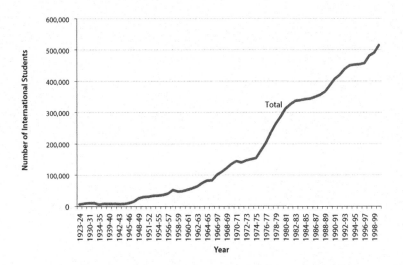

Figure A.2. Total international students in the United States, 1923–2000. Statistics taken from Committee on Friendly Relations among Foreign Students, *Unofficial Ambassadors*, and Institute for International Education, *Open Doors*.

Notes

Chapter 1. Gateways and Gates in American Immigration History

1. During this event, Reagan unveiled the Statue of Liberty for the first time since its restoration which had begun when he had asked Lee Iacocca in 1982 to chair the Statue of Liberty–Ellis Island Foundation. The foundation raised $500 million for both projects. Reagan's opening remarks praised not only the French and American friendship that the statue represented but also immigrants to America, "a special kind of people from every corner of the world, who had a special love for freedom and a special courage that enabled them to leave their own land, leave their friends and their countrymen, and come to this new and strange land to build a New World of peace and freedom and hope." ABC's Ted Koppel served as master of ceremonies for the programming.

2. Chang-Díaz is descended from an ethnically Chinese father and a Costa Rican mother and was the only Latino. Those of Jewish ancestry were well represented, including honorees such as Henry A. Kissinger, Itzhak Perlman, Irving Berlin, Albert B. Sabin, Elie Wiesel, and Hanna Holburn Gray. James B. Reston, Kenneth Clark, and Bob Hope rounded out the dozen.

3. "The Rise of Asian Americans," *Pew Research: Social & Demographic Trends*, http://pewsocialtrends.org/2012/06/19/the-rise-of-asian-americans/.

4. Rose Hum Lee, "The Stranded Chinese in the United States," *Phylon* 19, 2 (1958): 180, gives an estimate of 5,000 for the so-called stranded students, whom she set apart from Chinese American history as privileged and not sharing the struggles and discrimination faced by Chinese residing in Chinatown communities and confined largely to service businesses such as laundries and restaurants. She also asserts that the students deliberately set themselves apart from their Cantonese, working-class counterparts. Despite the great successes of some stranded students such as Pei, however, many educated Chinese refugees faced the same discriminations as their less educated co-ethnics and also had few options but to open a Chinese restaurant or some other small business. See Madeline Y. Hsu, "The Disappearance of America's Cold War Chinese Refugees," *Journal of American Ethnic History* 31, 4 (Summer 2012): 12–33.

5. Albert Einstein and many of the scientists working on the Manhattan Project provide additional examples of outstanding individuals for whom practical imperatives mandated the provision of new homes despite otherwise problematical group traits, such as Jewish ancestry.

6. The Chinese Restriction Act was not the first attempt to restrict the entry of poorer immigrants. In 1819 Congress passed legislation that both limited the number of passengers that ships could transport based on tonnage, in an effort to prevent overcrowding, and raised fares to limit the entry of Europeans with limited means or debts. Aristide R. Zolberg, *A Nation by Design: Immigration Policy in the Fashioning of America* (Cambridge, MA: Harvard University Press and

Russell Sage Foundation, 2006), 110–13. Concern for the potential economic costs of admitting incapable immigrants continued to animate restrictions. For example, the Immigration Act of 1882 banned the entry of "any person unable to take care of himself or herself without becoming a public charge," a status that in the Immigration Act of 1891 became the category of "persons likely to become a public charge." See Natalia Molina, *How Race Is Made in America: Immigration, Citizenship, and the Historical Power of Racial Scripts* (Berkeley: University of California Press, 2014), 92.

7. Naoko Shibusawa describes the Cold War's transformation of the gender and racial coding for Asians from male labor competition to feminine dependents. See *America's Geisha Ally: Reimagining the Japanese Enemy* (Cambridge, MA: Harvard University Press, 2006).

8. Cindy Cheng, *Citizens of Asian America: Democracy and Race during the Cold War* (New York: New York University Press, 2013); Charlotte Brooks, *Alien Neighbors, Foreign Friends: Asian Americans, Housing, and the Transformation of Urban California* (Chicago: University of Chicago Press, 2009), and *Between Mao and McCarthy: Chinese American Politics in the Cold War Years* (Chicago: University of Chicago Press, 2015), examine how civil rights activists cited America's image abroad to demand civil rights reforms. Other notable examples include Christina Klein, *Cold War Orientalism: Asia in the Middlebrow Imagination, 1945–1961* (Berkeley: University of California Press, 2003); Ellen Wu, *Color of Success: Asian Americans and the Origins of the Model Minority* (Princeton, NJ: Princeton University Press, 2014); Judy Wu, *Doctor Mom Chung of the Fair-haired Bastards: The Life of a Wartime Celebrity* (Berkeley: University of California Press, 2005); Chiou-ling Yeh, *Making an American Festival: Chinese New Year in San Francisco's Chinatown* (Berkeley: University of California Press, 2008); Xiaojian Zhao, *Remaking Chinese America: Immigration, Family, and Community, 1940–1965* (New Brunswick, NJ: Rutgers University Press, 2002); and Arissa Oh, "From War Waif to Ideal Immigrant: The Cold War Transformation of the Korean Orphan," *Journal of American Ethnic History* 31, 4 (Summer 2012): 34–55.

9. Zolberg, *A Nation by Design*, 22.

10. For example, Gordon Hirabayashi's (1918–2012) conviction for violating curfew was overturned in 1986 with the emergence of compelling evidence that information demonstrating that internment was not militarily necessary had been withheld from the Supreme Court.

11. For discussions of whiteness and U.S. citizenship, see Ian Haney López, *White by Law: The Legal Construction of Race* (New York: New York University Press, 1996); and Matthew Frye Jacobsen, *Whiteness of a Different Color: European Immigrants and the Alchemy of Race* (Cambridge, MA: Harvard University Press, 1998).

12. For an authoritative comparative account of the ideological, legal, and institutional lineage of the category "illegal alien," see Mae Ngai, *Impossible Subjects: Illegal Aliens and the Making of Modern America* (Princeton, NJ: Princeton University Press, 2004). Standard texts such as Zolberg, *A Nation by Design*; Sucheng Chan, *Asian Americans: An Interpretive History* (Boston: Twayne, 1991);

Ronald Takaki, *Strangers from a Different Shore: A History of Asian Americans* (Boston: Little, Brown, 1989); Roger Daniels, *Asian America: Chinese and Japanese in the United States since 1850* (Seattle: University of Washington Press, 1988); and Daniel Tichenor, *Dividing Lines: The Politics of Immigration Control in America* (Princeton, NJ: Princeton University Press, 2002), provide much greater detail on the expanding reach of Asian exclusion.

13. See Andrew Gyory, *Closing the Gate: Race Politics, and the Chinese Exclusion Act* (Chapel Hill: University of North Carolina Press, 1998), for more details on how California's anti-Chinese movement became legitimated through presidential politics.

14. On American beliefs about racial difference and the need to maintain separation from Chinese, see Stuart Creighton Miller, *The Unwelcome Immigrant: The American Image of the Chinese, 1785–1882* (Berkeley: University of California Press, 1969); Clarence Sandmeyer, *The Anti-Chinese Movement in California* (Urbana: University of Illinois Press, 1939); Alexander Saxton, *The Indispensable Enemy: Labor and the Anti-Chinese Movement in California* (Berkeley: University of California Press, 1971); Peggy Pascoe, *What Comes Naturally: Miscegenation Law and the Making of Race in the United States* (New York: Oxford University Press, 2009); and Phillip Choy, Lorraine Dong, and Marlon Hom, eds., *The Coming Man: 19th Century American Perceptions of the Chinese* (Seattle: University of Washington Press, 1995).

15. Erika G. Lee, *At America's Gates: Chinese Immigration during the Exclusion Era, 1882–1943* (Chapel Hill: University of North Carolina Press, 2002), 6–7, has most influentially argued this transformation.

16. See Shih-shan Henry Tsai, *China and the Overseas Chinese in the United States, 1868–1911* (Fayetteville: University of Arkansas Press, 1983), 58–61, for an account of these negotiations.

17. The very success of Chinese in defying U.S. immigration laws situated them in a no-man's-land of unsanctioned and fraudulent status liable for deportation with passage of the Geary Act in 1892. A shortlist of the extensive scholarship on this subject includes Lee, *At America's Gates*; Ngai, *Impossible Subjects*; Madeline Y. Hsu, *Dreaming of Gold, Dreaming of Home: Transnationalism and Migration between the United States and Southern China, 1882–1943* (Stanford, CA: Stanford University Press, 2000); Lucy Salyer, *Laws Harsh as Tigers: Chinese Immigrants and the Shaping of Modern Immigration Law* (Chapel Hill: University of North Carolina Press, 1995); Sucheng Chan, ed., *Entry Denied: Exclusion and the Chinese Community in America, 1882–1943* (Philadelphia: Temple University Press, 1991); and Mae M. Ngai, *The Lucky Ones: One Family and the Extraordinary Invention of Chinese America* (Boston: Houghton Mifflin Harcourt, 2010).

18. The racialized restrictions for entry and citizenship, contravening constitutional ideals of equality, capture the contestations between "racial nationalism" and "civic nationalism" explored in Gary Gerstle's *American Crucible: Race and Nation in the Twentieth Century* (Princeton, NJ: Princeton University Press, 2001).

19. Lee, *At America's Gates*, 9.

20. See Moon-ho Jung, *Coolies and Cane: Race, Labor, and Sugar in the Age of Emancipation* (Baltimore: Johns Hopkins University Press, 2006); Judy Yung, *Unbound Feet: A Social History of Chinese Women in San Francisco* (Berkeley: University of California Press, 1995); and George Anthony Peffer, *If They Don't Bring Their Women Here: Chinese Female Immigration before Exclusion* (Urbana: University of Illinois Press, 1999). According to Jung, the definition of "coolie" provided in the 1862 law was so vague as to be unenforceable in practice. The Page Act, however, led to serious declines in the number of Chinese women coming to the United States.

21. Adam McKeown, *Melancholy Order: Asian Migration and the Globalization of Borders* (New York: Columbia University Press, 2008), 7–8.

22. See Michael Hunt, *The Making of a Special Relationship: The United States and China to 1914* (New York: Columbia University Press, 1983), xi. I am using Akira Iriye's conceptualization of cultural internationalists. See *Pacific Estrangement: Japanese and American Expansion, 1897–1911* (Cambridge, MA: Harvard University Press, 1972), 122.

23. See table 2.2.

24. See Manuel Castells, *The Rise of the Network Society*, 2nd ed. (Oxford: Blackwell, 2000), 84–85.

25. For more general immigration history accounts, see Zolberg, *A Nation by Design*; Tichenor, *Dividing Lines*; and David Reimers, *Still the Golden Door: The Third World Comes to America* (New York: Columbia University Press, 1985).

26. Gordon Chang comments in "Asian Immigrants and American Foreign Relations," in *Pacific Passages: The Study of American–East Asian Relations on the Eve of the Twenty-First Century*, ed. Warren Cohen (New York: Columbia University Press, 1996), that diplomatic historians wrote extensively about immigration policy before World War II, but the topic disappears from studies of the Cold War era.

27. Jennifer C. Snow, *Protestant Missionaries, Asian Immigrants, and Ideologies of Race in America, 1850–1924* (New York: Routledge, 2007), 2–3. Also see Derek Chang, *Citizens of a Christian Nation: Evangelical Missions and the Problem of Race in the Nineteenth Century* (Philadelphia: University of Pennsylvania Press, 2012); Joshua Paddison, *American Heathens: Religion, Race, and Reconstruction in California* (Berkeley: University of California, 2012); William Speer, *The Oldest and the Newest Empire: China and the United States* (Hartford, CT: S. S. Scranton, 1870); and Otis Gibson, *The Chinese in America* (New York: Arno Press, 1978 reprint, 1877).

28. Snow, *Protestant Missionaries*, 16.

29. Paul A. Kramer, "Empire against Exclusion in Early 20th Century Trans-Pacific History," *Nanzan Review of American Studies* 33 (2011): 28n12. I thank Paul Kramer for sending me a copy of this article. Also see Beth Lew-Williams, "Before Restriction Became Exclusion: America's Experiment in Diplomatic Immigration Control," *Pacific Historical Review* 83, 1 (February 2014): 24–56; Gordon Chang, "China and the Pursuit of America's Destiny: Nineteenth-Century Imagining and Why Immigration Restriction Took So Long," *Journal of Asian American Studies* 15, 2 (June 2012): 145–69.

30. For these shifts in enforcement of immigration restrictions, see Michael Hunt, "The American Remission of the Boxer Indemnity: A Reappraisal," *Journal of Asian Studies* 31, 3 (May 1972): 539–59; Delber McKee, *Chinese Exclusion versus the Open Door Policy, 1900–1906: Clashes over China Policy in the Roosevelt Era* (Detroit: Wayne State University Press, 1977); and Stacey Bieler, *"Patriots" or "Traitors"? A History of American-Educated Chinese Students* (Armonk, NY: M. E. Sharpe, 2004).

31. Hunt, *The Making of a Special Relationship*, xi.

32. The varied and shifting understanding of what aspect of governance immigration most critically pertains to is illustrated by the migration of the Bureau of Immigration, founded in 1891, from its original home in the Department of the Treasury, as a matter of trade, to the Department of Commerce and Labor in 1903, completely into the Department of Labor in 1913, and into its present home in the Department of Justice in 1940, as a matter of national security. Donna Gabaccia, *Foreign Relations: American Immigration in Global Perspective* (Princeton, NJ: Princeton University Press, 2012), considers changing understandings of immigration restriction as a matter of trade, labor competition, national security, but also economic resource.

33. Akira Iriye, *Cultural Internationalism and World Order* (Baltimore: Johns Hopkins University Press, 1997), 3, 5–6.

34. See Liping Bu's excellent study of the emergence of international education programs, *Making the World Like Us: Education, Cultural Expansion, and the American Century* (Westport, CT: Praeger, 2003). I thank Paul Kramer for referring this work.

35. On "imperial openings," see Kramer, "Empire against Exclusion," 15. Kramer discusses imperial history more expansively in the review essay "Power and Connection: Imperial Histories of the United States in the World," *American Historical Review* (December 2011): 1348–91.

36. Y. C. Wang, *Chinese Intellectuals and the West, 1872–1949* (Chapel Hill: University of North Carolina Press, 1966), is a particularly strident critic of this problem.

37. See Weili Ye, *Seeking Modernity in China's Name: Chinese Students in the United States, 1900–1927* (Stanford, CA: Stanford University Press, 2001); Wang, *Chinese Intellectuals*; Bieler, *"Patriots" or "Traitors"*; R. David Arkush and Leo O. Lee, trans. and eds., *Land without Ghosts: Chinese Impressions of America from the Mid-Nineteenth Century to the Present* (Berkeley: University of California Press, 1989); and Liu Boji, *Meiguo huaqiao shi* (History of Chinese in America) (Taipei: Liming wenhua shiye gongsi, 1976).

38. Paul Kramer, "Is the World Our Campus? International Students and U.S. Global Power in the Long Twentieth Century," Bernath Lecture, *Diplomatic History* 33, 5 (November 2009): 783–88.

39. See Kramer, "Empire against Exclusion."

40. Klein, *Cold War Orientalism*; Henry Yu, *Thinking Orientals: Migration, Contact, and Exoticism in Modern America* (New York: Oxford University Press, 2001); Snow, *Protestant Missionaries*.

41. Klein, *Cold War Orientalism*, 224.

42. Ibid., 40. Klein attributes the intersection of foreign and domestic policy spheres to Arthur Schlesinger Jr. and Secretary of State Dean Acheson. Schlesinger "argued that the U.S. was losing the Cold War in Asia and Africa in part because the Soviet Union, untainted by colonialism, could claim the banner of racial equality and contrast itself to the Western democracies, whose domestic societies and colonies had been characterized by 'racial cruelties'" (43).

43. Ibid., 5.

44. Abba Schwartz, *The Open Society* (New York: Morrow, 1968), 140, 225–27. Schwartz's table does not include parolees. This table tallies a total of 778,660 refugee admissions, 695,773 of whom came from Europe and only 51,210 from Asia. Also see Hsu, "The Disappearance of America's Cold War Chinese Refugees."

45. See Carl Bon Tempo, *Americans at the Gate: The United States and Refugees during the Cold War* (Princeton, NJ: Princeton University Press, 2008). Oh, "From War Waif to Ideal Immigrant," describes the transformation by 1961 of Korean adoptees admitted through stopgap laws into relatives admissible under family reunification.

46. Klein, *Cold War Orientalism*, 23–24, 226.

47. Estimates for the numbers of Chinese refugees in Hong Kong ranged between 1 million and 1.5 million after the mid-1950s. In this book I use the estimate cited in the source immediately under discussion.

Chapter 2. *"The Anglo-Saxons of the Orient"*

1. I thank Dana Young, Yung Kuai's grandson, for his generosity in sharing his transcription from the original in the Yale Divinity School archives and checking this chapter for factual errors.

2. The PhB degree was a bachelor's in philosophy. Author's interview with Dana Young, Austin, Texas, November 15, 2012.

3. "Yung Kuai, 82, Dead: Chinese Ex-Diplomat: Former Embassy Counselor in Washington an Aide 50 Years," *New York Times*, March 21, 1943. Yung Kuai retained Chinese citizenship all his life and remained in the United States on a diplomat's visa. Although American-born, his children inherited his citizenship status as children of a diplomat. Dana Young interview.

4. Yung Kuai had roomed with Li Enfou, another convert to Christianity, who also managed to graduate from Yale and worked as a journalist in America under the name Yan Phou Lee. Li published the earliest memoir by a Chinese person written in English, *When I Was a Boy in China* (Lothrop, 1887), and penned the article "Why I Am Not a Heathen: A Rejoinder to Wong Chin Foo," *North American Review* (September 1887), responding to the journalist Wong Chin Foo's "Why Am I a Heathen?" *North American Review* (August 1887). Judy Yung, Gordon H. Chang, and Him Mark Lai, eds., *Chinese American Voices: From the Gold Rush to the Present* (Berkeley: University of California Press 2006), 70–85.

5. In 1882 Tan published an editorial described in *Harper's Weekly* (April 22, 1882, 243) as conceding that "the importation of coolies ought to be prohib-

ited, and [stating] that the Chinese government would most cordially co-operate in that good work," but he criticized the rationale that Chinese could not assimilate and would not become good citizens, blaming Americans instead for rejecting Chinese along with "Negroes" and Indians. For detailed information about the CEM and its participants, visit the website Mr. Young has compiled with two other descendants of CEM students: http://cemconnections.org/index.php?option =com_content&task=view&id=129&Itemid=55.

6. See Iriye, *Pacific Estrangement*, 122. In 1904 Secretary of State John Hay communicated with Secretary of War William Howard Taft regarding the need to modify immigration rules that caused so many "insurmountable" difficulties in U.S. relations with China.

7. Bu, *Making the World Like Us*, 25.

8. See Karen Sanchez-Eppler, "Copying and Conversion: An 1824 Friendship Album 'from a Chinese Youth,'" *American Quarterly* 59, 2 (June 2007): 309–10, about the mixed student population at the Foreign Mission School in Cornwall, which included not only Chinese and Native Americans but white students seeking to learn more about heathens and their cultures. I thank Julia Mickenberg for this reference.

9. Despite his English training, Morrison arrived under American auspices because the British feared Chinese reprisals against trade interests. During a quarter century of residence, and producing the first English-Chinese dictionary, Morrison baptized only ten Chinese. Ibid., 315–16.

10. In his memoir, *A Professor at Large* (New York: Macmillan, 1943), 18, Stephen Duggan, head of the Institute for International Education, claimed that the most cosmopolitan university campus he had visited was that of Utah because so many of its Mormon students had traveled abroad as missionaries and learned foreign languages.

11. See Walter La Feber, *The Clash: A History of U.S.–Japan Relations* (New York: Norton, 1997), 66; Jessie Gregory Lutz, *China and the Christian Colleges, 1850–1950* (Ithaca, NY: Cornell University Press, 1971), 6–7; Iriye, *Pacific Estrangement*, 123, who cites numbers of 3,107 out of 3,776 in 1905; and *China Christian Yearbook*, 1936–37 (Shanghai, 1937), 459, cited in Fred W. Riggs, *Pressures on Congress: A Study of the Repeal of Chinese Exclusion* (New York: King's Crown Press, 1950), 32.

12. Lutz, *China and the Christian Colleges*, 27.

13. Peter Tze Ming Ng, *Changing Paradigms of Christian Higher Education in China, 1888–1950* (Lewiston, NY: Edwin Mellen Press, 2002), 2.

14. Weili Ye notes that the first four Chinese women doctors were educated by missionaries. Jin Yunmei (1864–1934) was the first to receive a medical degree, in 1885, followed by Xu Jinhong (1865–1929), Shi Meiyu (Mary Stone, 1872–1954), and Kang Aide (Ida Kahn, 1873–1931). All four women grew up in Christian families, either through adoption by missionaries or by birth to Christian Chinese. Jin was the only one to remain in the United States; the rest returned to China. See Ye, *Seeking Modernity*, 112–29.

15. Unfortunately Zeng ran out of funds within two years and never graduated. Edward J. M. Rhoads, *Stepping Forth into the World: The Chinese Educational*

Mission to the United States, 1872–81 (Hong Kong: Hong Kong University Press, 2011), 3. See Sanchez-Eppler, "Copying and Conversion," for a nuanced analysis of the nineteen-page friendship album produced by "Henry Martyn A'lan" in 1824. Sanchez-Eppler observes that this is likely the first book produced by a Chinese on American soil, and it captures something of his perspectives regarding his missionary education. Alum returned to China but did not become a missionary, instead using his language skills to work in trade.

16. See K. Scott Wong, "The Transformation of Culture: Three Chinese Views of America," *American Quarterly* 48, 2 (June 1996): 201–32.

17. See Yung Wing's autobiography, *My Life in China and America* (New York: Henry Holt, 1909), 15. For more on the CEM, see Thomas La Fargue, *China's First One Hundred* (Pullman: State College of Washington, 1942); and Rhoads, *Stepping Forth*.

18. See Rhoads, *Stepping Forth*, chap. 2.

19. Wang, *Chinese Intellectuals and the West*, 74. Wang is translating a passage by Li Hongzhang. Also see Yung, *My Life in China and America*; and La Fargue, *China's First One Hundred*.

20. Wang, *Chinese Intellectuals and the West*, 75.

21. For the first 1872 cohort alone, the first request for host families received 122 responses. The hosts received payments to cover the costs of lodging, feeding, and teaching the students. In a parallel program, the Japanese diplomat Mori Arinori, one of the first Japanese to study abroad, had placed a teenage Japanese student with an American host family as a boarder in 1871. Rhoads, *Stepping Forth*, 50, 63–65.

22. CEM students were not the only Chinese teenagers to attain close, familial ties to Euro-Americans during this time. Lue Gim Gong (Lu Jingong, 1860–1925) came to North Adams, Massachusetts, in 1870 at the age of twelve to work in a shoe factory under a three-year contract. He was taken under the wing of Fanny Burlingame, his Sunday school teacher, who converted him to Christianity and remained a touchstone for the rest of his life in America. Although he lived a solitary life, Lue became famous by winning the Silver Wilder Medal from the American Pomological Society in 1911 for his innovations in hybridizing oranges in Florida.

23. "Yung Kuai, 82, Dead." Wang was highly critical of the CEM and in general complained of "denationalization" among Western-educated Chinese who became "uprooted from their own cultural tradition" See *Chinese Intellectuals*, xiii.

24. As Chung Mun Yew, or "Munny," Zhong led the Yale rowing team to victory twice over Harvard archrivals as coxswain in 1880 and 1881.

25. "Reminiscences of a Pioneer Student" in Yung, Chang, and Lai, *Chinese American Voices*, 37. Also see Qian Ning, *Chinese Students Encounter America*, trans. T. K. Chu (Seattle: University of Washington Press, 2002), 16–17, for a more extensive list of CEM student accomplishments.

26. See Gyory, *Closing the Gate*, regarding how the eccentricities of the electoral college and under-the-table negotiations contributed to national pressures for the restriction of Chinese immigration.

27. See Franklin Odo, ed., *The Columbia Documentary History of the Asian American Experience* (New York: Columbia University Press, 2002), 24–25.

28. Jung, *Coolies and Cane*, 26–38. During a lecture delivered in Boston in 1869, Frederick Douglass criticized the inegalitarian restriction of Chinese entry rights as violating principles of "eternal, universal, and indestructible" human rights. Douglass, "Our Composite Nationality," December 7, 1869, Boston, http:// teachingamericanhistory.org/library/document/our-composite-nationality/. I thank Kelly Lytle Hernandez for this reference.

29. Odo, *Columbia Documentary History*, 32. The American Anson Burlingame negotiated this treaty on behalf of the Qing government. It was a first for the Chinese government and considered a significant step toward securing Chinese rights overseas. Burlingame had been U.S. minister to China but had resigned to represent the Chinese government. Tsai, *China and the Overseas Chinese*, 24–27.

30. See Odo, *The Columbia Documentary History*, 38, for the text of "An Act Supplementary to the Acts in Relation to Immigration (a.k.a. The Page Law)."

31. T. Harry Williams, ed., *Hayes: The Diary of a President, 1875–1881* (New York: David McKay, 1964), 187–90, cited in Tsai, *China and the Overseas Chinese*, 46–47. For further discussions of the delayed passage and implementation of restrictions on Chinese immigration, see Chang, "China and the Pursuit of America's Destiny"; and Lew-Williams, "Before Restriction Became Exclusion."

32. Angell, *Reminiscences of James Burrill Angell* (New York: Longmans, Greens, 1912), 131; U.S. Commission to Evarts, 23 October 1880, Enclosure 2 in No. 8, USFR (China, 1881), 177–78. Cited in Tsai, *China and the Overseas Chinese*, 53–54, 57.

33. Tsai, *China and the Overseas Chinese*, 57.

34. Ibid., 66.

35. The difficulty of enforcing immigration restrictions quickly became clear after 1882 as Chinese continued to enter the United States by crossing land borders through Canada and Mexico or by claiming exempt status with elaborate verifications of identity as merchants, merchant sons and wives, tourists, and students. The Supreme Court case *Wong Kim Ark v. US* (1898) affirmed birthright citizenship for any person born in the United States regardless of race, which provided the basis for the "paper son" method of immigration fraud in which Chinese claimed citizenship by birth or derivation as the basis for legal entry. By the 1910s this had become the most common method of entry. The aggressive tactics developed by immigration authorities arose in part from frustration about the impossibility of securing U.S. land borders.

36. Minister Wu Tingfang made these protests in 1902 in pointing out that such enforcement of exclusionary laws violated the Angell Treaty of 1880. See George E. Paulsen's two articles about negotiation of the Gresham-Yang Treaty of 1894 and its abrogation in 1904, "The Gresham-Yang Treaty," *Pacific Historical Review* 37 (1968): 282–97, and "The Abrogation of the Gresham-Yang Treaty," *Pacific Historical Review* 40 (1971): 457–77. Failure of American authorities to enforce treaty stipulations securing the rights of exempt-class Chinese to enter the United States, and acceptable forms of documentation, led the Qing government to abrogate the treaty when it expired in 1903. Paulsen, "Abrogation," 467.

37. Ng, *Changing Paradigms*, 2. Of these institutions, 28 were colleges and 156 were teacher training schools.

38. The Chinese minister to the United States, Wu Tingfang, pressed for respect for the entry rights of exempt Chinese but accepted restriction for laborers. See Kramer, "Empire against Exclusion," 20; and McKee, *Chinese Exclusion*, 38–39.

39. McKeown, *Melancholy Order*, 8–10.

40. For example, on June 20, 1902, the International Missionary Union passed a resolution forwarded to the secretary of the treasury that immigration regulations be modified to remove "unnecessary obstacles . . . placed in the way of students . . . and of preachers of the gospel." McKee, *Chinese Exclusion*, 71.

41. See ibid., 69–71; and Luella Miner, ed., *Two Heroes of Cathay: An Autobiography and a Sketch* (New York: Fleming H. Revell, 1903).

42. Miner, *Two Heroes*, 3.

43. Ibid., 5–6.

44. Ibid., 6.

45. Hannah Pakula, *The Last Empress: Madame Chiang Kai-shek and the Birth of Modern China* (New York: Simon and Schuster, 2009), 7–9; and Elmer T. Clark, *The Chiangs of China* (Nashville, TN: Abingdon-Cokesbury Press, 1943).

46. McKee, *Chinese Exclusion*, 94.

47. Emily Hahn, *The Soong Sisters* (New York: Doubleday, Doran, 1941), 49.

48. Michael Hunt coined the term "Open Door constituency" as shorthand for the "set of interest groups . . . with a common commitment to penetrating China and propagating at home a paternalistic vision (conventionally associated with the open door) of defending and reforming China." Hunt, *The Making of a Special Relationship*, xi.

49. Hunt, "The American Remission," 542, 545–46.

50. Paulsen, "The Abrogation," 468; Guanhua Wang, *In Search of Justice: The 1905–1906 Chinese Anti-American Boycott* (Cambridge, MA: Harvard University Press, 2001), 8–11.

51. "The Awakening of China," *Chinese Students' Bulletin* 2, 6 (May 1907): 133–36.

52. Iriye, *Pacific Estrangement*, 114–20.

53. Roosevelt and his advisers first began planning for possible war against Japan in 1906. La Feber, *The Clash*, 89–92.

54. Iriye, *Pacific Estrangement*, 122–23.

55. Bieler, *"Patriots" or "Traitors,"* 44.

56. Bu, *Making the World Like Us*, 24.

57. Hunt, "The American Remission," 549, 556.

58. Bieler, *"Patriots" or "Traitors,"* 43. Some of the most prestigious of Chinese universities—Peking, Tsinghua, St. Johns, Nanjing, and Yenching—were founded under missionary auspices with all eventually coming under Chinese control.

59. Bieler, *"Patriots" or "Traitors,"* 41 (emphasis in original); Hunt, "The American Remission," 549–50. James came from a missionary background and arranged programs to recruit students directly from China to his institution. See Carol Huang, "The Soft Power of United States Education and the Formation of a Chinese American Intellectual Community in Urbana-Champaign, 1905–1954" (PhD dissertation, University of Illinois at Urbana-Champaign, 2001), 32. I thank Nancy Abelman for this reference.

60. Hunt, "The American Remission," 557–58, quoting Frank G. Carpenter in "The Awakening of China," *Daily Consular and Trade Reports*, no. 3636 (November 15, 1909), 8–9.

61. W. W. Yen "The Chinese Student's View," *Overland Monthly* (May 1911): 496–99, in Him Mark Lai Collection, UC Berkeley Ethnic Studies Library, AAS ARC 2000/80 44:3, 499. Yen graduated from Yale and would come to serve as a secretary with the Foreign Ministry.

62. Bieler, *"Patriots" or "Traitors,"* 41.

63. Hunt, "The American Remission," 550.

64. Ye, *Seeking Modernity*, 90.

65. See file on student visas from National Archives I, RG 85, 52082/81 Oct–Nov 1908, Washington, DC; Lee, *At America's Gates*, 131; Kramer, "Empire against Exclusion," 24; McKee, *Chinese Exclusion*, 207–9.

66. Lee, *At America's Gates*, 131.

67. Ye, *Seeking Modernity*, 90–91

68. Chen Wen-hsien, "Chinese under Both Exclusion and Immigration Laws" (PhD dissertation, University of Chicago, 1940), 378, 381. Chen cites the cases of *Moy Kong Chui v. U.S.* (246 Fed. 94 (1917)) and *Ex parte Lam Pui* (277 Fed. 456 (1914)).

69. Jiang Menglin, *Tides from the West: A Chinese Autobiography* (New Haven, CT: Yale University Press, 1947), 67–68. For the record of Jiang's relatively quick entry into the United States, see file on student visas from National Archives I, RG 85, 52082/81 Oct–Nov 1908. Unlike the thick files of Chinese attempting entry claiming citizenship, which contain extensive transcripts of interviews and other supporting evidence, the documents for student entry are largely procedural and consist only of notices of arrival and landing for each individual.

70. In Young, "China and the United States," *Chinese Students' Monthly* 4, 7 (May 1909): 444–48.

71. *Chinese Students' Monthly* 3, 5 (March 1908): 173–74.

72. "China, Japan and the United States in the Far East Drama," *Chinese Students' Monthly* 3, 6 (April 1908): 224, 227, 232–33.

73. "Editorial," *Chinese Students' Monthly* 4, 1 (November 1908): 5–6.

74. Wang, *Chinese Intellectuals*, 71.

75. Ye, *Seeking Modernity*, 51.

76. Ibid., 53–55.

77. Ibid., 58–60. Between 1909 and 1929, Boxer Fellows studied engineering (32.3%), science (11%), medicine (5.2%), agriculture (3.2%), military science (1.9%), humanities (5.5%), music (0.3%), and social sciences (23.8%), including law (2.8%), political science (9.2%), economics (10.4%), and sociology (1.5%), education (5%), and business (11.3%). Wang, *Chinese Intellectuals*, 111.

78. Ye, *Seeking Modernity*, 233n52. Ye relies on the estimate of *Jiaoyu zazhi* (Education magazine) to set the number at 1,600.

79. Bu, *Making the World Like Us*, 123–29. V. Everett Macy, a trustee of Teachers College, endowed the scholarships. Nominations came from the Ministries of Education of the foreign countries sending recipients of the grants.

80. Bieler, *"Patriots" or "Traitors,"* 40. Figures are somewhat speculative but according to Wang, an estimated 34,081 Chinese studied in Japan between 1900

and 1937, whereas only 20,906 did so in the United States between 1854 and 1953. Wang, *Chinese Intellectuals*, 119–20.

81. Ibid., 90.

82. Ibid., 89.

83. Tsung-kao Yieh, "The Adjustment Problems of Chinese Graduate Students in American Universities" (PhD dissertation, University of Chicago, 1934), 66–67.

84. Y. S. Tsao, "A Challenge to Western Learning: The Chinese Student Trained Abroad—What He Has Accomplished—His Problems," *News Bulletin (Institute of Pacific Relations)* (December 1927): 15.

85. Ye, *Seeking Modernity*, 61, 113.

86. Lee, *The Chinese in the United States of America*, 88–89, citing data about the National Tsinghua Research Fellowship Fund and the China Institute in America from *Chinese Students in American Universities and Colleges* (New York: China Institute in America, 1954), 6.

87. Wang, *Chinese Intellectuals*, 79.

88. Mei Hua-chuan, "The Returned Student in China," *Chinese Recorder* (March 1917): 158–59.

89. Wang *Chinese Intellectuals*, 79–80.

90. Ye, *Seeking Modernity*, 33.

91. Robert G. Cook, "China and the United States," *Chinese Students' Monthly* 16, 3 (June 1921): 193–95.

92. Duggan, *A Professor at Large*, 313.

93. U.S. Department of Labor, Bureau of Immigration, *Annual Report of the Commissioner General of Immigration to the Secretary of Labor, 1931* (Washington, DC: GPO, 1931), 52.

Chapter 3. The China Institute in America

1. Meng Zhi, *Chinese American Understanding: A Sixty-Year Quest* (New York: China Institute of America, 1981), 103. By the late 1940s, both of China's main philosophers and political thinkers had descendants living in America, with Confucius represented by his seventy-fifth-generation descendant, Kong Xiangxi.

2. Guo was a Presbyterian and Boxer Indemnity Fellow who studied at Wooster College before receiving his PhD degree in education from Columbia in 1914. He returned to found Nanjing's first modern Chinese university.

3. Meng, *Chinese American Understanding*, 104. Hu Shi, a Boxer Indemnity Fellow and 1917 graduate of Columbia, inspired many other Chinese to attend Teachers College through his example and by inviting John Dewey and Bertrand Russell for extensive speaking tours of China in 1919 and 1920. Hu was an influential literary scholar and diplomat who was one of the leaders of the May Fourth Movement and the New Culture Movement.

4. Meng claimed to be apolitical although he represented the Chinese government in distributing almost all fellowship funding for Chinese students during the 1930s and 1940s. The China Institute was legally "a private American corpo-

ration," but most likely Meng worked in the United States under a Chinese diplomatic passport as had Yung Kuai. Ibid., 187.

5. F. C. Yen, "The Alliance and the Students Coming to America," *Chinese Students' Monthly* (November 1907): 77–79.

6. Ye, *Seeking Modernity*, 94.

7. Ibid., 98. The *Chinese Students' Monthly* actually began publication in 1905, but the mimeographed issues are no longer extant.

8. Jiang, *Tides from the West*, 83–86.

9. Ye, *Seeking Modernity*, 99–104. This program petered out in 1912.

10. Marriages between international students and American-born Chinese were fairly common, even though between 1922 and 1932 women could lose their U.S. citizenship by marrying an "alien ineligible for citizenship." The sociologist Rose Hum Lee (1904–1964) and the journalist Flora Belle Jan (1906–1950) are prominent examples of Chinese American women who married Chinese students, whom they followed to China. See Yu, *Thinking Orientals*; Yung, *Unbound Feet*; and Jan, *Unbound Spirit*. After divorcing her husband, Lee returned to the United States and studied with the sociologist Robert Park, for whom Jan was an interview subject. Park celebrated Jan as a "Chinese American flapper" who illustrated the possibilities for Chinese assimilation.

11. Ye, *Seeking Modernity*, 91.

12. Ibid., 30–31.

13. This group also published the *Chinese Students' Annual* and the *Chinese Students' Quarterly*, but in the 1930s fiscal hardships disrupted the publications. The student clubs remained active but were not able to maintain the same level of national coherence. The earliest issues were mimeographs, which became print editions distributed nationally. *The Chinese Students' Monthly, 1906–1931: A Grand Table of Contents* (Washington, DC: Association of Research Libraries, Center for Chinese Studies Research Materials, 1974), vii–viii.

14. "Editorial," *Chinese Students' Monthly* 3, 1 (November 1907): 1–2; *Chinese Students' Monthly, 1906–1931*, viii.

15. Ye, *Seeking Modernity*, 26, 28; *Chinese Students' Monthly, 1906–1931*, vii–viii.

16. Yieh, "The Adjustment Problems of Chinese Graduate Students," 122.

17. See Iriye, *Pacific Estrangement*.

18. Bu, *Making the World Like Us*, 3, 51.

19. Ibid., 18.

20. Ibid., 20.

21. Ye, *Seeking Modernity*, 31–33.

22. CFRFS, *The Unofficial Ambassadors* (1945), 1. Meng Zhi describes a similar encounter but between Edmonds and a Hindu student who broke into tears when greeted with a "cheery 'Merry Christmas!'" See *Chinese American Understanding*, 106. Rockefeller also helped fund International Houses in New York, Chicago, and Berkeley with the motto "That Brotherhood May Prevail." See Mary Brown Bullock, *The Oil Prince's Legacy: Rockefeller Philanthropy in China* (Stanford, CA: Stanford University Press, 2011).

23. Bu, *Making the World Like Us*, 26.

24. Ibid.

25. See Anson Phelps Stokes, Jr., "Introductory Statement Made to the Conference," in *Unofficial Ambassadors* (1944), 3.

26. Bu, *Making the World Like Us*, 37.

27. Ibid., 25–26.

28. CFRFS, *The Unofficial Ambassadors* (1941), back inside page. A total of $2,070.68 went to the Japanese section. CFRFS began publishing *Unofficial Ambassadors* in 1928 and continued until its demise in 1953.

29. CFRFS, *The Unofficial Ambassadors: Report of the Consultative Conference, Bronxville 1944* (1944), 3.

30. Ibid., 4. This issue lists the Latin American section with a budget of $1,000 from the total of $18,261.06. The Chinese section received $2,475.

31. Stokes, "Introductory Statement Made to the Conference," in ibid., Bu, *Making the World Like Us*, 17.

32. Bu, *Making the World Like Us*, 17, 33.

33. Ibid., 19.

34. Duggan, *A Professor at Large*, 17–18.

35. See Bullock, *The Oil Prince's Legacy*.

36. Duggan, *A Professor at Large*, 52.

37. Bu, *Making the World Like Us*, 127.

38. Immigration Act of 1917, February 5, 1917. *Statutes at Large of the United States of America*, vol. 39, part 1 (Washington, DC: GPO, 1917).

39. Stephen Duggan, "The Foreign Student and the Immigration Law," *Fourth Annual Report of the Director* (New York: Institute of International Education, 1923), 1–3.

40. Bu, *Making the World Like Us*, 35–36, 62.

41. Liping Bu, email to author, June 24, 2012.

42. Act of May 26, 1924: The Immigration Act of 1924 ("Johnson-Reed Act") 43 Stat. 153; 8 U.S.C. 201.

43. Ruth Mitchell, *Foreign Students and the Immigration Law of the United States* (New York: Institute of International Education, 1930). I thank Paul Kramer for sharing this source with me.

44. Bu, *Making the World Like Us*, 78–80. While IIE programs focused primarily on European students, by the late 1930s the organization turned its attention to Asian and Latin American countries as well.

45. *The Handbook of Chinese Students in the U.S.A.* (New York: Chinese Students Handbook Co., 1935), Yuk Ow collection, UC Berkeley Ethnic Studies library, AAS ARC 2000/70 15:30.

46. Chih-ming Wang, *Transpacific Articulations: Student Migrations and the Remaking of Asian America* (Honolulu: University of Hawaii Press, 2013), 142.

47. Hongshan Li, *U.S.–China Educational Exchange: State, Society, and Intercultural Relations, 1905–1950* (New Brunswick, NJ: Rutgers University Press, 2008), 78–85.

48. Wang, *Chinese Intellectuals*, 99.

49. "Chinese Higher Education: A Brief Report," *China Institute in America Bulletin* 4, 1 (October 1939): 1.

50. Ng, *Changing Paradigms*, 5–6.

51. Lian Xi, *The Conversion of Missionaries: Liberalism in American Protestant Missions in China, 1907–1932* (University Park: Pennsylvania State University Press, 1997), 122, 192–93; Snow, *Protestant Missionaries*, 66–67, 117.

52. Bu, *Making the World*, 75; Duggan, *A Professor at Large*, 57–59.

53. By 1936 there were forty-one universities, thirty-eight colleges, and thirty-one professional schools in China. Twenty-eight were run by the national government, thirty-one by provincial and municipal authorities, and fifty-one by private organizations, including missionary societies. *China Institute in America Bulletin* (December 1936): 26.

54. Li, *U.S.–China Educational Exchange*, 80–81.

55. Bu, *Making the World Like Us*, 128.

56. "China Institute Founded with Second Boxer Fund," *New York Times*, December 19, 1926.

57. Li, *U.S.–China Educational Exchange*, 82–85.

58. Fan Yuan-lien, "Eastern Trends in the New Sciences: The China Foundation for the Promotion of Education and Culture," *New Bulletin (Institute of Pacific Relations)* (December 1927): 17–20.

59. Bieler, *"Patriots" or "Traitors,"* 79.

60. Li, *U.S.–China Educational Exchange*, 99–102, 110.

61. "China Institute Asks Charter in Jersey," *New York Times*, January 25, 1930.

62. "Paul Zhi Meng, 90, Headed China Institute," *New York Times*, February 7, 1990.

63. Meng, *Chinese American Understanding*, 102.

64. Ibid., 119–20.

65. Ibid., 118–39. Meng braved the uncertainties of travel through a country not yet fully controlled by the Nationalists to visit college and university campuses in Guangzhou, Fujian, Shanghai, Nanjing, Qingdao, Tianjin, Beijing, Manchuria, Moscow, Belgium, Germany, Holland, the United Kingdom, and France. At each of the Chinese institutions, he reported with pride the many American-educated administrators and faculty that he met. Meng comments evenhandedly about Sun Yatsen's consultation with Soviet representatives and the activities of leftist Chinese students in both Moscow and Paris. Although Meng worked well with the Nationalist government, he claims never to have been strongly partisan, unlike Zhao Yuanren. In the 1980s, after the rapprochement of the United States and the PRC, the China Institute readily incorporated staff, resources, and board members from the PRC.

66. Wang, *Chinese Intellectuals*, 113. The last two directors had been Mei Yiji and Zhao Yuanren, whose duties primarily concerned financial disbursements but not monitoring of students.

67. Meng, *Chinese American Understanding*, 169.

68. Ye, *Seeking Modernity*, 105–7.

69. Yieh, "The Adjustment Problems of Chinese Graduate Students," 3. Most of Yieh's survey subjects studied at four midwestern schools—University of Illinois, Purdue, Chicago, and Michigan—which may skew his results.

70. Ibid., 8.

71. Yieh cites U.S. Department of Labor, Bureau of Immigration, Second Amendment of General Order No. 195, Washington, DC, June 20, 1933.

72. Yieh actually judged the immigration clause to be "very flexible" with regard to temporary employment in the United States: "'In no case will a student be permitted to accept employment of a nature to interfere with his full course of studies.'"

73. Yieh cites "Foreign Students Barred from Jobs," *New York Times*, September 27, 1932.

74. Other students claimed the following religious affiliations: Buddhism (1), Confucianism (22), unclassified (39).

75. "China Institute Founded with Second Boxer Fund," *New York Times*, December 19, 1926.

76. Eugene Shen, "The China Institute in America," *China Institute in America Bulletin* (1927): 3.

77. Ibid., 5–6.

78. Ibid., 4.

79. The first issue, for example, publicized lectures on Chinese art and the situation in Manchuria, a listing of Chinese visitors to the United States and American visitors to China, selected books on China, and research fellowships and prizes for Chinese students. See *China Institute Bulletin* (January 1931).

80. Duggan, *A Professor at Large*, 42–43. By 1943 Hu had received fourteen honorary degrees, mostly from "our outstanding institutions."

81. Zhi Meng, "The American Returned Students of China," *Pacific Affairs* 4, 1 (January 1931): 1–16.

82. *China Institute in America Bulletin* (October 1936): 8–9.

83. *China Institute in America Bulletin* 4, 1 (October 1939): 9.

84. Y. S. Tsao, "A Challenge to Western Learning: The Chinese Student Trained Abroad—What He Has Accomplished—His Problems," *News Bulletin (Institute of Pacific Relations)* (December 1927): 13–16.

85. See, for example, "Chinese and Japanese Talk Here on Conflict: Zhi Meng's Assertion that Tokyo Would Annex Manchuria Is Denied by Bunji Omura," *New York Times*, October 17, 1931; Zhi Meng, "A Chinese Viewpoint," *New York Times*, November 7, 1931; and Zhi Meng, "Far East Leaders in Radio Broadcast," *New York Times*, February 29, 1932.

86. "Asks Our Aid in Far East Crisis," *New York Times*, March 10, 1933.

87. "In the Classroom and on the Campus: Chinese Leader Here Fears That Most Colleges in His Country Face Devastation," *New York Times*, September 5, 1937.

88. Yieh, "The Adjustment Problems of Chinese Graduate Students," 122.

Chapter 4. "A Pressing Problem of Interracial Justice"

1. Milton Caniff, *The Complete Terry and the Pirates, 1937–1938* (San Diego, CA: IDW, 2007), 227. During the height of the comic strip's popularity from 1934 until 1946, Caniff created, wrote, and drew panels based on contemporary events set in the South China Sea. He received the Cartoonist of the Year Award in 1946.

2. By 1942 Japan's Greater East Asia Co-Prosperity Sphere had displaced the colonial administrations of Indonesia, Burma, the Southeast Asian peninsula, the Philippines, and Hong Kong, advancing many of these areas closer to decolonization after World War II.

3. *The Good Earth* became a best seller again when selected for Oprah's Book Club in 2004. Buck left China in 1935 and never returned.

4. The China-born journalist John Hersey used the terms "symbols of understanding" and "permanent peace" to describe international students and their important global role at the Conference on Community Relations to Students from Abroad convened by the CFRFS in Bethlehem, Pennsylvania, in October 1946. CFRFS, *The Unofficial Ambassadors* (1947): 1–3.

5. Wilma Fairbank, *America's Cultural Experiment in China, 1942–1949* (Washington, DC: Bureau of Cultural and Educational Affairs, U.S. Department of State, 1976), 4–5. I thank Roger Daniels for referring me to this study.

6. Iriye, *Cultural Internationalism and World Order*, 114.

7. *China Institute in America Bulletin* 2, 3 (December 1937): 97–98.

8. Meng, *Chinese American Understanding*, 184–86. Meng discovered he had been placed on a Nationalist blacklist when he approached Song but was able to win him over through a combination of explaining his apolitical stance, noting his wide networks in the United States, and convening a selection committee combining both supporters and critics of the Nationalists. Also see Wang, *Chinese Intellectuals and the West*, 137–38.

9. *China Institute in America Bulletin* 6, 8 (July 1942): 1.

10. Meng, *Chinese American Understanding*, 189.

11. *China Institute in America Bulletin* 7, 1 (October 1942): 2–3. These included students in the fields of engineering (77), pure and applied sciences (114), social sciences (85), business (18), education (19), and others such as English, philosophy, and music (19). The State Department grants were awarded through a committee that comprised Duggan and Meng. A committee of Chinese like Song Ziwen and Yuanren Zhao, along with Meng, selected recipients for scholarships funded by the Chinese government. *China Institute in America Bulletin* 6, 8 (July 1942): 1.

12. Ching-Kun Yang, *Meet the USA: Handbook for Foreign Students in the United States* (New York: Institute of International Education, 1945), 37.

13. *China Institute in America Bulletin* 6, 6 and 7 (March–April 1942): 1–2. Nonquota students unable to support themselves by part-time work were to submit a sworn statement and documentation of resources and sponsors along with a letter from prospective employers. Two U.S. citizens had to vouch for the character of each applicant, who also had to document "his attitude towards the principles of democracy and to the government of the United States. The report should also include a statement by the alien that he has not in the past and will not in the future engage in any subversive activities." After receiving such clearance, each student had to keep the Immigration Service updated about any changes in address and employment.

14. Zhi Meng letter to Song, March 31, 1942, Box 3.2 China Institute in America, T.V. Soong Papers, Hoover Institution Archives.

15. Fairbank, *America's Cultural Experiment in China*, 114–15.

16. Ibid., 9–11, 20.

17. Ibid., vii. John King Fairbank was an outspoken critic of the Nationalists and U.S. policy toward the PRC after World War II, a stance underscored by Wilma Fairbank's acknowledgment of the influence of Joseph Stilwell and John Service in her account of the bureau. Her chief goal in writing the book was to counter China Lobby accusations that the United States "lost" China by inadequately supporting the Nationalists. Fairbank emphasizes that for the eight years the bureau existed, it enacted "a constructive program aimed directly at offering assistance to the Chinese people in education, public health, sanitation, agriculture, engineering, and the like" (vii).

18. Iriye, *Cultural Internationalism and World Order*, 112.

19. Fairbank, *America's Cultural Experiment in China*, 36–37.

20. Ibid., 36.

21. Her elder brother Song Ziwen faced the same difficulty and throughout his political career relied on Chinese secretaries. Yung Wing also had to relearn Chinese on his return in 1854.

22. Karen Leong, *The China Mystique: Pearl S. Buck, Anna May Wong, Mayling Soong, and the Transformation of American Orientalism* (Berkeley: University of California Press, 2005), 106.

23. Jonathan Fenby, *Chiang Kai-shek: China's Generalissimo and the Nation He Lost* (New York: Carroll and Graf, 2003), 246–47.

24. Meiling Song, *We Chinese Women: Speeches and Writings during the First United Nations Year by Mayling Soong Chiang (Madame Chiang Kai-shek)* (New York: Chinese News Service and John Day Company, 1943), 39–43.

25. Ibid., 43.

26. Pakula, *The Last Empress*, 418.

27. Ibid., 430.

28. Geraldine Fitch, Newsletter to "Friends," Huletts Landing, NY, July 1, 1943, Fitch Papers, Harvard-Yenching Library, Harvard University.

29. Madame Chiang was not the only Chinese politician to attain celebrity status in the United States. The visit of Viceroy Li Hongzhang to New York and Washington, DC, in 1896 also drew crowds of thousands of onlookers. His visit was so well received that some hearsay accounts attribute the popularity of chop suey to rumors that it was his favorite dish. However, the detailed records of his visit, including his daily meals, show no evidence that Li ever encountered the dish.

30. "Madame Chiang in Hollywood," *Life*, April 19, 1943.

31. Leong, *The China Mystique*, 141–42.

32. Committee on Immigration and Naturalization, House of Representatives, 78th Congress, Repeal of the Chinese Exclusion Acts: Hearings on HR 1882 and HR 2309: Bills to Repeal the Chinese Exclusion Acts, to Put the Chinese on a Quota Basis, and to Permit Their Naturalization," May 19, 20, 26, 27, and June 2 and 3, 1943. Representative Ed Lee Gossett (D-TX) questioned repeal's contribution to war efforts (24). The Reverend Albert O'Hara, considered an expert witness, who had lived in China from 1933 until 1941 and spoke Chinese, argued the necessity for "racial equality" and retaining China as an ally, arguing that without

China's help, many more American young men would die in battle. He also pointed out that anthropology had found "no evidence for any theory of superiority or inferiority among races" and argued that Chinese wanted a "practical" gesture of American friendship or might otherwise leave the war (42–45).

33. Many witnesses and letter writers testified to the recent retreat from extraterritoriality: Letter to Martin Kennedy from Frank Campbell, pastor of the Methodist Church in Neoga, Illinois, dated February 20, 1943 (6–7); Letter from Theodora Chan Wang, president of the Chinese Women's Association Inc. in New York, addressed to Eleanor Roosevelt, 12; Letter to Kennedy dated March 9, 1943, from George Kin Leung of New York: "Next to the abolition of extraterritoriality recently, your accomplishment will be hailed as a concrete step to bring the United States and China ever closer"; and Reverend John G. Magee, minister of St. John's Episcopal Church in DC (18). House Hearings on HR 1882 and HR 2309.

34. Riggs discussed repeal primarily as a study of legislative processes and how the "catalytic group" of the Citizens Committee managed at low cost to leverage public opinion, mitigate the criticisms of entrenched opponents, and forge the compromises necessary to gain enough votes in Congress for passage. Donald Dunham, a former U.S. consular official in Hong Kong, originated the idea of repeal after returning to the United States in the summer of 1941. He contacted Richard Walsh, and the two issued a letter recruiting other supporters of China to back the project. This group included influential backers who were nonetheless stymied by longstanding supporters of exclusion. Riggs, *Pressures on Congress*, 48–49, 51.

35. Wilkie had been the Republican challenger to Roosevelt in the 1940 presidential election. After winning the race, Roosevelt had sent Wilkie to China as his representative. According to some accounts, it was the beguiled Wilkie who urged Madame Chiang to come to the United States in late 1942 to charm the American public. Fenby, *Chiang Kai-shek*, 392; Pakula, *The Last Empress*, 412.

36. Riggs, *Pressures on Congress*, 116.

37. Duggan, *A Professor at Large*, 329.

38. House Hearings on HR 1882 and HR 2309. The bill under consideration was proposed by Martin J. Kennedy of New York. The Citizens Committee vetting and preparing of witnesses can be contrasted with the 1876 hearings held in California, which included few Chinese voices and largely favored Chinese exclusion.

39. Magnuson telegraphed William Green, president of the American Federation of Labor, to reassure him that quotas would severely limit the numbers of Chinese laborers. September 23, 1943, telegram to William Green, Accession Number 3181–002, Box 58, folder 21: "1943 HR 2309 Chinese Immigration 1 of 3," Warren Magnuson Papers, University of Washington Special Collections.

40. Although some witnesses would raise the issue of entry and citizenship rights for other Asians, such as Indians, Koreans, and Filipinos, these actually hindered the drive for repeal in raising the specter that America's gates might open too wide and admit too many Asians.

41. Das most likely was able to gain naturalized citizenship through his wife, Mary Keatings Morse, a cofounder of the NAACP. I thank Natalia Molina for scrutinizing this unusual case.

42. Allen systematically questioned supporters of repeal to see if they advocated "racial equality" along with "social equality" by which he meant "that all the various races should live together socially, eat, drink, and sleep together" (32–33, 37).

43. Allen was dismissive of witnesses who were women or of color. He questioned the right of Das to criticize the United States after he had "been so blessed by this country" with educational and teaching opportunities. Das in turn evoked constitutional principles in asserting his right to speak because he was "able to uphold the ideals of America by utilizing the opportunity that is given to every man who wishes to utilize it, and at the same time the democratic form of Government which gives us the privilege to express the convictions of a citizen without fear of anybody, so long as he knows that he is giving his conviction as the right of a citizen." After this exchange, Chairman Dickstein stated that he would protect Das's rights to free speech, although he was careful to distance himself from Das's criticisms of the United States. Allen remained intransigent and conveyed his hostility to nonwhite testimony: "I do not propose to let any man come here before my committee who is an oriental and born thousands of miles away, and criticize my country and my courts" (39–40).

44. Some witnesses supported greater racial equity in immigration legislation but by decreasing immigration for all for economic reasons rather than providing quotas for Asians. Royal C. Stephens of Philadelphia, a private citizen, opposed repeal but was concerned about immigration in general and requested deportation of immigrants already in the United States. He proposed that the Fourteenth Amendment be changed so that no children of alien immigrants could get citizenship (46–47).

45. Letter to Kennedy dated February 20, 1943.

46. In a letter dated March 30, 1943, the YWCA board of the University of California claimed that "the act, if passed immediately, would be an appropriate parting gift to our distinguished and beloved guest, Madame Chiang Kai-shek." House Hearings on HR 1882 and HR 2309, 8–9, 225–226.

47. Town Meeting, "Should We Repeal the Chinese Exclusion Laws Now?" moderated by Clifford Utley, September 18, 1943, broadcast September 2, featuring Walter Judd, John B. Bennett (Michigan), Monroe Sweetland of CIO, and E. B. Libonati, Chicago American Legion. In "1943 HR 3070 Chinese Immigration 2 of 3," Accession number 3181–002, Box 58, File 25, Warren Magnuson Papers, University of Washington Special Collections.

48. Li had corresponded extensively with Representative Magnuson throughout the summer and fall of 1943.

49. Thursday, October 7, 1943, Executive Session, HR 3073. A Bill to Repeal the Chinese Exclusion Acts, to establish quotas, and for other purposes. House of Representatives, Committee on Immigration and Naturalization, 13–15.

50. Riggs, *Pressures on Congress*, 173.

51. "President Urges Congress Repeal Chinese Exclusion Act as War Aid," *New York Times*, October 12, 1943.

52. Bill Ong Hing, *Making and Remaking Asian America through Immigration Policy, 1850–1990* (Stanford, CA: Stanford University Press, 1993), 48. This population increase included about 12,000 students and technical trainees stranded in

the United States by the Chinese Civil War and about 5,000 women arriving as war brides. Meng, *Chinese American Understanding*, 224.

Chapter 5. The Wartime Transformation of Student Visitors into Refugee Citizens, 1943–1955

1. *The Flower Drum Song*, with an introduction by David Henry Hwang (1957; Penguin reprint 2002), x. Also see "C. Y. Lee," in *Yellow Light: The Flowering of Asian American Arts*, ed. Amy Ling (Philadelphia: Temple University Press, 1999), 16–17; Andrew Shin, "'Forty Percent Is Luck': An Interview with C. Y. (Chin Yang) Lee," *MELUS* 29, 2 (Summer 2004): 77–104. I thank Min Hyoung Song for telling me about Lee's background.

2. S. W. Kung, *Chinese in American Life: Some Aspects of Their History, Status, Problems, and Contributions* (Seattle: University of Washington Press, 1962), 115. Under these terms, nonimmigrant residents either married to or parent of a U.S. citizen could petition to remain.

3. Officially titled *United States Relations with China with Special Reference to the Period 1944–1949*, the White Paper provided fuel for the China Lobby to criticize the United States for contributing to the Communist victory through its inadequate and wavering support. These charges led to the persecution of State Department officers and intellectuals considered complicit in this great loss, the earliest stage of the McCarthy witch hunts.

4. Christina Klein identifies the chief victims of "domestic containment" as "those who had left-liberal internationalist views on China" by the China Lobby, which consisted of "mostly right-internationalist politicians and private citizens who had supported Chiang Kai-shek's Kuomintang government" during and after the Chinese Civil War. The China Lobby "publicly attacked a number of American China experts who, having seen Mao's success in the civil war as all but inevitable, had recommended that Washington prepare to work with the new communist government." China experts who had their careers ruined included John Paton Davies, John Service, John Carter Vincent, O. Edmund Clubb, and Owen Lattimore. The Institute of Pacific Relations collapsed after being a leading sponsor of scholarship on China during the 1930s and 1940s. See Klein, *Cold War Orientalism*, 33–34; and Ross Koen, *The China Lobby in the United States* (New York: Harper and Row, 1974).

5. See William Kirby, "Engineers and the State in Modern China," in *Prospects for the Professions in China*, ed. William Alford and William Kirby (London: Taylor and Francis, 2010), 283–313, for the emphasis on "practical" knowledge in state initiatives for public education by both the Nationalists and Communists and the relatively high percentages of bureaucrats and politicians trained as engineers. Elliott S. Hanson, who ran the International Training Administration, coined the metaphor about "exporting know-how in human containers." CFRFS, *The Unofficial Ambassadors* (1946): 7.

6. Bu, *Making the World Like Us*, 71.

7. *China Institute in America Bulletin* (December 1927): 4.

8. *China Institute in America Bulletin* (October 1936): 8–9.

9. "Wanted: 5,000 Engineers," *China Institute in America Bulletin* 6, 4 (January 1941): 41.

10. Fairbank, *America's Cultural Experiment in China*, 27. Fairbank emphasized that with resources for education controlled by Minister of Education Chen Lifu, who would later head the Nationalist security apparatus in Taiwan, scholars "had no option but to obey" Nationalist government mandates regarding their conduct during the war (39).

11. *China Institute in America Bulletin* 5, 4 (January 1941): 47–48.

12. "Wartime Planning for Chinese Students in US: An Emergency—and an Opportunity," *China Institute in America Bulletin* 6, 4 (January 1942): 1–3.

13. *China Institute in America Bulletin* 6, 9 (September 1942) exhorted students to think about Chinese national welfare and their role in national economic development.

14. CFRFS, *Technical Trainees from Overseas* (New York: Committee on Friendly Relations among Foreign Students, 1945), 4. This pamphlet reported that most trainees came from China and Latin America and American motivations to sponsor such training included helping other countries develop, build ties for American machinery and methods, but also "being a good neighbor."

15. Fairbank, *America's Cultural Experiment in China*, 116.

16. Archives of the National Resources Commission (Guojia Ziyuan Weiyuanhui), Academia Historica, Xindian, Taiwan.

17. Educational reforms of the 1930s were apparently quite effective in developing China's infrastructure for scientific training. Nobel Prize–winning physicist Yang Zhenning praised the "excellent" education he received from Southwest Associated University in Kunming, Sichuan, up through the level of the master's degree in statistical mechanics that he received in 1944. See *Selected Papers 1945–1980 with Commentary* (San Francisco: W. H. Freeman, 1983), 3. Fairbank describes how "the pressing need for additional manpower at home to replace those absent on war service afforded openings for on-the-job technical training and for temporary assumption of roles in a wide variety of fields normally filled by Americans." Fairbank, *America's Cultural Experiment in China*, 83.

18. William Kirby, "Continuity and Change in Modern China: Economic Planning on the Mainland and on Taiwan, 1943–1958," *Australian Journal of Chinese Affairs* 24 (July 1990): 139–41. Kirby managed to interview several members of the "Society of 31," who remained in touch despite being dispersed in China, Taiwan, and the United States.

19. CFRFS, *The Unofficial Ambassadors* (1946): 7 and (1947): 6.

20. Ibid., (1945): 9–10. Almost as many trainees from Latin America arrived through this program.

21. *China Institute Bulletin* 27 (October 1945): 1.

22. CFRFS, *The Unofficial Ambassadors* (1946): 7.

23. Ibid.; *China Institute Bulletin* 27 (October 1945): 1–2.

24. With his brother Guofu, Chen Lifu headed the notorious C-C Clique and later became the much dreaded minister of security on Taiwan.

25. Fairbank, *America's Cultural Experiment in China*, 122–24. In China, Chen controlled university administrators by restricting their funds and had na-

tionalized certain universities to this end. "His manipulations reached well inside the institutions in an attempt to regiment the teaching by controlling the appointments of and allowances to faculty members." Chen also sought "to gain a measure of control over even the mission-supported colleges and universities." Wang, *Chinese Intellectuals and the West*, 131.

26. Fairbank, *America's Cultural Experiment in China*, 126, 130–33. Skeptical of Nationalist authoritarianism, the Bureau of Cultural Affairs attempted to work with entities apart from the Bureau of Education, such as the China Foundation, Academia Sinica, and the National Library of Peking (39).

27. CFRFS, *The Unofficial Ambassadors* (1945), 9–10. Sunduram was quoted in the *New York Times*, April 29, 1945.

28. See Kramer, "Is the World Our Campus?"

29. China Handbook Editorial Board, *China Handbook 1950* (New York: Rockport Press, 1950), 673–74.

30. Wang, *Chinese Intellectuals and the West*, 135–37. Confirming suspicions he had become anti-Nationalist, hence the efforts to remove him from China, Feng attempted to join the Chinese Communists by returning via Soviet Russia but died accidentally on the way back.

31. Excerpted from Institute of International Education, "Table Showing Comparison of the Number of Foreign Students in the Colleges and Universities of the United States during Recent Years," *Twenty-Eighth Annual Report of the Director* (New York: Institute for International Education, 1947), 97–99. Also see figure A.1.

32. Lee, *The Chinese in the United States of America*, 89. Lee is citing a survey conducted by CFRFS in 1947–48 published in *Wah Mei Yat Po* (New York Daily), January 9, 1954.

33. J. W. Fulbright, "Forward," in Walter Johnson and Francis J. Colligan, *The Fulbright Program: A History* (Chicago: University of Chicago Press, 1965), vii–viii.

34. Ibid., viii.

35. Institute of International Education, *Twenty-seventh Annual Report of the Director* (New York: Institute of International Education, 1946), 24.

36. Yang, *Meet the USA*.

37. On p. vi, Yang thanks Wilma Fairbank for helping with the guide.

38. Social interactions continued to be challenging. Yang acknowledged that Chinese men might encounter difficulties in dating "American girls," who "will talk to Chinese male students at social events but do not wish to have dates with them." However, in schools with fewer Chinese, some young women might "defy the conventions in this regard. This is specially true in a college having very few Chinese students and where character and academic records are outstanding" (126).

39. In his memoir, *A Professor at Large*, 290, Stephen Duggan considered justified Filipino resentments of American racism. "Because of the inferiority complex which has always existed in a colonial people of another race under white domination, the average intelligent Filipino felt that the Americans regarded themselves as a better folk, and the Filipinos resented it."

40. Buwei Yang Chao, *Autobiography of a Chinese Woman* (New York: John Day, 1947), 179–80. In "With This Lingo, I Thee Wed: Language and Marriage in

Autobiography of a Chinese Woman," Journal of American–East Asian Relations 18 (2011): 235–47, Jin Feng explores Buwei's rationalizations for relinquishing her professional aspirations for her marriage through her narrative strategies.

41. Ye, *Seeking Modernity*, 95, observes that none of the extensive biographical writings of either Zhao Yuanren or his good friend Hu Shi admit any personal encounters with working-class Chinese and their experiences of exclusionary enforcement.

42. Zhao, *Autobiography*, 181.

43. The Zhaos joined a growing list of Chinese Americans publishing English-language biographies and cookbooks. The bilingually published essayist Lin Yu-tang, author of *My Country and My People* (1935), *The Importance of Living* (1937), and the novel *Chinatown Family* (1948), wrote essays to accompany his wife and daughter's cookbooks, *Cooking with the Chinese Flavor* (1956) and *The Secrets of Chinese Cooking* (1960). American-born Pardee Lowe published *Father and Glorious Descendent* (Little, Brown) in 1943, and Jade Snow Wong *Fifth Chinese Daughter* (Harper) in 1945.

44. Ibid., 202.

45. Ibid., 205, 210.

46. Despite this claim, Zhao's translation of *Through the Looking Glass* had already been published in 1922.

47. "Immigration officials later grouped them all in a student classification because of their uncertain legal status." Shih-shan Henry Tsai, *The Chinese Experience in America* (Bloomington: Indiana University Press, 1986), 120–22. The China Institute of America tracked the total numbers of Chinese students in 1943–1944 (706); 1944–1945 (823); 1945–1946 (1,298); 1946–1947 (1,678); 1947–1948 (2,310); and 1948–1949 (3,914). Although 5,000 is the number cited in most Asian American and immigration history texts based on Rose Hum Lee's accounts, Meng Zhi estimates that by 1949, about 12,000 Chinese had "managed to escape to the United States." Meng, *Chinese American Understanding*, 224. With his close ties to students and the flows of Nationalist-affiliated visitors, Meng's estimate is probably more reliable.

48. Committee on Educational Interchange Policy, *Chinese Students in the United States, 1948–55: A Study in Government Policy* (New York: n.p., 1956), 7–8.

49. Ibid., 5–6.

50. Walter H. Judd Papers, Box 72, Folder 7 Sponsored Legislation/81st Congress Aid to Chinese Students (H.R. 5495), 1949–1955, Hoover Institution Archives.

51. *China Institute Bulletin* (November 1949): 5–6.

52. *China Institute Bulletin* (December 1950), 5.

53. *Chinese Students in the United States, 1948–55*, 8.

54. Kung, *Chinese in American Life*, 115.

55. See Lee, *The Chinese in the United States of America*, and Lee, "The Stranded Chinese in the United States," *Phylon* (1958): 256–69.

56. Lee, *Chinese in the United States*, 415. Lee cites a summary of reports of leading American newspapers and periodicals compiled by Chinese News Services and dated November 1–15, 1957.

57. Wu Ningkun with Li Yikai, *A Single Tear: A Family's Persecution, Love, and Endurance in Communist China* (New York: Atlantic Monthly Press, 1993), 5.

58. Wang An with Eugene Linden, *Lessons: An Autobiography* (Reading, MA: Addison-Wesley, 1986), 31.

59. Ibid., 83.

60. See Iris Chang, *Thread of the Silkworm* (New York: Basic Books, 1995) for a more extensive account.

61. Kung, *Chinese in American Life*, 112.

62. Ibid., 115; Ngai, *Impossible Subjects*, 343n40.

63. Kung, *Chinese in American Life*, 107.

64. Ibid., 110.

65. Ibid., 115–16.

66. See Reimers, *Still the Golden Door*, 37. Because they could be used to admit groups otherwise heavily restricted from entry, refugee laws also served to attract the lobbying efforts of ethnic and religious organizations to the cause of immigration reform.

67. Kung, *Chinese in American Life*, 108–9.

68. Lee, *Chinese in the United States*, 381.

69. This percentage had decreased significantly from the 30.4 percent of 1940. See Betty Lee Sung, *A Survey of Chinese-American Manpower and Employment* (New York: Praeger, 1976), 75.

70. Yang, *Selected Papers*, 56–57.

71. Cited in *Chinese Students in the United States, 1948–55*, 13–14.

Chapter 6. "The Best Type of Chinese"

1. William Brinkley, "The Agonizing Odyssey of Two People in Love," *Life* 40, 10 (March 5, 1956): 100–102, 165–74.

2. Mrs. Grace Li Case, Subject Files Related to the Refugee Relief Act, 1953–1958; Box 9, accession E#5496, Office of Refugee and Migration Affairs, Bureau of Security and Consular Affairs, Department of State, RG 59, National Archives II, College Park, MD.

3. "US Admits Chinese after 8-Year Fight," *New York Times*, June 19, 1956.

4. Mary Dudziak, *Cold War Civil Rights* (Princeton, NJ: Princeton University Press, 2000), describes how concern for America's image abroad contributed to advances in domestic civil rights.

5. See Bon Tempo, *Americans at the Gate*.

6. Klein, *Cold War Orientalism*, 240–41.

7. Kung, *Chinese in American Life*, 114, table 21.

8. Tai K. Oh, *The Asian Brain Drain: A Factual and Casual Analysis* (San Francisco: R&E Research Associates, 1977), 4.

9. Ngai, *Impossible Subjects*, 236; Kung, *Chinese in American Life*, 115.

10. The McCarran Report, issued April 20, 1950, downplayed racial theories but justified retention of the national origins quotas in order to restrict immigration "to best preserve the sociological and cultural balance of the United States"

by giving preference to immigrants "more readily assimilable, because of the simi-larity of their cultural background to those of the principle components of our population." Quoted in Zolberg, *A Nation by Design*, 311.

11. Schwartz, *The Open Society*, 138, 170, 225.

12. Richard Ferree Smith, "Refugees," *Annals of the American Academy of Po-litical and Social Science* 367, "The New Immigration" (September 1966): 43. Ac-cording to Bon Tempo's account, neither the Hungarians nor Cubans experienced as much scrutiny for their educational or employment qualifications as did Chinese.

13. Kung, *Chinese in American Life*, 107.

14. Ibid., chap. 6; Zolberg, *A Nation by Design*, 324.

15. ORM officials debated whether someone so wealthy could be considered a refugee. They found in Song's favor and approved his plan to apply for an RRP visa from the American consulate in Havana. Aide to Chinese government offi-cials to land, "Chinese facilitation of landing" file, 1947; Refugee Relief Act of 1953, file 56351/4.13, Box 3381, accession 85–58A734, RG 85; National Ar-chives, Washington, DC.

16. See Reimers, *Still the Golden Door*, 37. Because they could be used to admit groups otherwise heavily restricted from entry, refugee laws also attracted the lobbying efforts of ethnic and religious organizations to the cause of immigra-tion reform. Also see Papers of Abba Schwartz, Box 10, Schwartz files, John F. Kennedy Library.

17. See Chi-Kwan Mark, *Hong Kong and the Cold War* (Oxford: Oxford Uni-versity Press, 2004).

18. "Refugee Problem in Hong Kong and Macao," Hearings before the Sub-committee to Investigate Problems Connected with Refugees and Escapees of the Committee of the Judiciary, United States Senate, 87th Congress, 2nd session. (Washington, DC: GPO, 1962), 17.

19. Memorandum for the Board Assistants, Report on Assistance Programs in Behalf of Refugees and Escapees of Interest under NSC 86/1, November 17, 1955, 2; Operations Coordinating Board, OCB Activities, Subject Files RRP 1953–1958, Office of Refugee and Migration Affairs, Bureau of Security and Consular Affairs, Department of State, RG 59; National Archives II, College Park, MD. See Edvard Hambro, "Chinese Refugees in Hong Kong," *Phylon Quarterly* 18, 1 (1957): 69–81. Hambro (81) reports that Hong Kong had a population of 2.225 million in 1954. Conveying the preference that solutions for Chinese refugee problems should be found within Asia, Hambro expressed his dissatisfaction with the limited actions taken by the Nationalist government and noted the reluctance of most refugees to settle in Taiwan, commenting unpersuasively, "None of these suffice to justify any complacency or passivity in regard to these unhappy people."

20. See Mark, *Hong Kong and the Cold War*; Chi-kwan Mark, "The 'Problem of People': British Colonials, Cold War Powers, and the Chinese Refugees in Hong Kong 1949–62," *Modern Asian Studies* 41, 6 (2007): 1145–81; and Glen Petersen, "To Be or Not to Be a Refugee" *Journal of Imperial and Commonwealth History* 36 (2008): 171–95.

21. Both Harold Oram and Marvin Liebman were campaigners for the China Lobby. Oram mentored Liebman, whose first project was fundraising for ARCI.

Dissatisfied with its limited focus on refugee resettlement and relief, Liebman later became instrumental in the more overtly political Committee of One Million campaign.

22. Liebman's memoir credits Moy for conceiving ARCI and describes Moy as "a slight man who certainly did not look like a general . . . full of vim and vigor, a real operator." For reasons unknown to Liebman and which do not show up in available documents, Moy was "quietly dropped from the organization." Marvin Liebman, *Coming Out Conservative: An Autobiography* (San Francisco: Chronicle Books, 1992), 89. As late as April 1957, Moy was still in touch with B. A. Garside but committed suicide on January 31, 1958. ARCI Records, "Letters from Hong-kong and Taiwan." January 1–June 30, 1958, February 1, 1958; Hong Kong–Taiwan Office Correspondence 1958, Hoover Institution Archives.

23. Flora Belle Jan, *Unbound Spirit: Letters of Flora Belle Jan* (Urbana: University of Illinois Press, 2009), 224.

24. Fitch Collection, Box 22, ARCI and Christopher Emmet, Moy for China Institute, July 21, 1951, Harvard-Yenching Library, Harvard University; "Extracts from *Chinese Weekly* 'Shih Pao Tsa Chi,' " vol. 17, no. 2, dated February 23, 1957; 1957 briefing for James Pilcher, deputy chief of mission, from Orville Bennett FERP/T, 050—Ernest Moy, March 26, 1957, Foreign Service Posts, Taiwan, U.S. Embassy and Consulate, General Records 1941–1963, Box 11, RG 84, National Archives II, Washington, DC.

25. Fitch Collection, Box 22, Fitch Papers, Moy to Geraldine Fitch, March 13, 1951, Harvard-Yenching Library, Harvard University.

26. Fitch Collection, Box 22, ARCI and Christopher Emmet, Moy to Geraldine Fitch, March 27, 1951; Geraldine Fitch to Moy, April 2, 1951; Moy to B. A. Garside, April 30, 1951; Moy letter to H. H. Jung, August 25, 1951, and three-page memo by Moy for China Institute, Harvard-Yenching Library, Harvard University. Also see letters dated March 12 and August 14, 1951, to prospective leaders. Despite frequent contacts with Moy and vague promises, Meng Zhi provided little concrete support for ARCI. See November 5, 1951, memo Moy to Meng, Fitch papers. In contrast, Han Liwu served as chairman of the ARCI Taiwan board and was also head of the China Institute in America branch in Taiwan.

27. Fitch Collection, Box 22, Moy to Geraldine Fitch, November 17, 1951, Harvard-Yenching Library, Harvard University.

28. Emmet was a devoted anticommunist activist who soon left ARCI to focus on events in Europe.

29. Liebman, *Coming Out Conservative.* Cf. George Fitch, *My Eighty Years in China* (Taipei: Mei Ya Publications, 1974); B. A. Garside, *Within the Four Seas* (New York: Fredrick C. Beil, 1985); and Lee Edwards, *Missionary to Freedom: The Life and Times of Walter Judd* (New York: Paragon House, 1990), and the Judd papers at the Hoover Institution. Despite the significant levels of involvement with ARCI, none provides much detail except to note that about 97 percent of the ARCI registrants who came to the United States repaid their travel loans.

30. Anon., "Background of Committee to Aid Chinese Refugees," n.d., Box 1, folder Background Material, Aid Refugee Chinese Intellectuals, Inc., Papers, Hoover Institution Archives; Anon., "The Purpose and Program of Aid Refugee

Chinese Intellectuals, Inc.," n.d., Box 1, folder Purpose and Program of ARCI, ARCI papers; Liebman, *Coming Out Conservative*, 92–93; Hugh Wilford, *The Mighty Wurlitzer: How the CIA Played America* (Cambridge, MA: Harvard University Press, 2008), 91, 295–96n36. My thanks to Hugh Wilford for explaining patterns of how the CIA's goal of supporting anticommunist efforts led it to work with and fund a variety of anticommunist organizations across the political spectrum, such as the *Paris Review* and the National Student Association. The object, in most instances, was to enable such work rather than control operations to the extent that seems to have occurred with ARCI. Email to the author, May 8, 2014. Besides funding and anticommunism, other aspects of ARCI's operations reflect standard CIA procedures, including placing agents as salaried staff and the illusion of widespread support through a letterhead masthead featuring prominent names. See Wilford, *The Mighty Wurlitzer*, 8–12.

31. Rose served as director of "Special Projects" within the Office of Refugee and Migration Affairs before becoming associate director of ARCI's Hong Kong office in the late 1950s. Fletcher joined ARCI as a staff member implementing the Refugee Relief Program in 1954. Both men became active in the American Emergency Committee for Tibetan Refugees, another CIA front presenting itself as a nongovernmental, humanitarian relief organization.

32. ARCI Records, Box 19, LeClerq letters to Hong Kong, March 8, 1954, November 6, 1954, and November 15, 1954, Hoover Institution Archives.

33. "Summary of Agreement" dated April 1, 1953, in letter from Garside to George Fitch, May 8, 1953; ARCI Records, Box 26, Letters to Formosa 1953, Agreement with U.S. Government, April 1, 1953, and B. A. Garside to George Fitch, March 30, 1953. Support for ARCI's goals extended to the Office of the President. In a memo to President Eisenhower, the Office of the Director for Mutual Security concurred with the Department of State in determining that "it is important to the security interests of the United States and to our over-all objectives in the Far East that this Government assist in the movement of Chinese refugees out of Hong Kong to Formosa and other suitable areas where they can be productively employed." Executive Office of the President, Office of the Director for Mutual Security, Memorandum for the President dated March 20, 1953. Subject: Special Assistance for Chinese Refugees. Declassified Documents. Dwight D. Eisenhower Library, Abilene, Kansas. I thank Gordon Chang for sharing these documents.

34. Nancy Bernkopf Tucker, *Taiwan, Hong Kong, and the United States, 1945–1992: Uncertain Friendships* (New York: Twayne, 1994), 21–22. On the China Lobby, see Koen, *The China Lobby in the United States*.

35. Tucker, *Taiwan, Hong Kong, and the United States*, 58. Jonathan Fenby's biography, *Chiang Kai-shek*, argues that Chiang manipulated more support from the United States by exaggerating his determination to attack the PRC.

36. Liebman, *Coming Out Conservative*, 92. Liebman states the first meeting occurred on January 30, 1952. However, ARCI records contain meeting minutes dated February 14, 1952. ARCI Records, Box 2, "Minutes of Executive Committee Meetings 1st 2/14/52 to 30th 12/8/55," Hoover Institution Archives. Taylor was head of the Russian and Far Eastern studies department at the University of

Washington from 1939 to 1969 and was one of the Pacific Northwest's leading Asian studies specialists.

37. Liebman, *Coming Out Conservative*, 92–93.

38. ARCI Records, Box 8, Dinner 4/28/52, Harold Oram, memo reopening Dinner Initiating Campaign for Public Support, February 14, 1952, Hoover Institution Archives.

39. ARCI Records, Box 1, Purpose and Program of ARCI, Message on Refugee Chinese Intellectuals, n.d., Hoover Institution Archives.

40. ARCI Records, Box 8, Dinner 4/28/52, Marvin Liebman, April 28, 1952, Hoover Institution Archives.

41. ARCI Records, Box 8, Dinner 4/28/52, Harold Oram, memo reopening Dinner Initiating Campaign for Public Support, February 14, 1952. Rusk's speech urged generosity and concern for intellectual Chinese on the basis of past relationships: "We are not talking about abstractions but personal friends. Old acquaintances, classmates in Chinese, American or European schools and colleges, students of ours, teachers of ours, business associates, fellow workers in any one of the learned professions or in laboratories where we jointly attacked ignorance or disease, comrades in arms at a moment of great peril, diplomatic colleagues as Chinese and Americans have labored together for decades to build a tolerable life among nations." ARCI Records, Box 8, Dinner 4/28/52, Extract from Remarks by Mr. Dean Rusk at Dinner Meeting of ARCI.

42. "A Good Place for Help," *New York Times*, December 28, 1952; *New York Times* advertisement cited in Petersen, "To Be or Not to Be a Refugee," 178. The ads that Petersen refers to appeared on October 14 and 15, 1953.

43. Between September and December 1952, Arthur M. Cox of the Psychological Strategy Board, which often acted as a clearinghouse for CIA front organizations, corresponded with Christopher Emmett and Harold Oram regarding ARCI's limited success in fundraising from private donors and the imminent exhaustion of its accounts. Cox communicated with colleagues with memoranda describing ARCI's programs, goals, and financial situation, recommending that stopgap funds be allocated through pressure on the Rockefeller Foundation until U.S. government funds could be appropriated in the spring. I thank Hugh Wilford for sharing these records. Memorandum from Cox to Sherman, September 1, 1952, and Memorandum from Cox to Taylor, December 2, 1952, folder 4 080, ARCI, Box 4, Records of the Psychological Strategy Board Files, Harry S. Truman Library, Independence, Missouri.

According to State Department records, Judd first approached Allen Dulles of the CIA to support ARCI in December 1952 but was refused unless funds could be funneled through the Title III military program, if approved by the director of mutual security, as the Escapee Program in Europe had done. Secret Memorandum to Norman S. Paul, Office of the Director for Mutual Security, March 9, 1943; Louis H. Frichtling, Office of the Special Assistant to the Secretary for Mutual Security Affairs, Funds for Support of Aid Refugee Chinese Intellectuals, Inc.; "General-Escapee Program, (ARCI)," Bureau of Far Eastern Affairs, 1953 Records Related to Economic Aid, 1948–1958, RG 59, National Archives II, College Park, MD.

Until its demise in 1970, ARCI relied almost entirely on State Department funding channeled through a revolving door of agencies such as the Foreign Operations Administration (FOA), the International Cooperation Association (ICA) under the Mutual Security Bureau, and the US Escapee Program (USEP). See "Summary of Agreement," April 1, 1953, in letter from Garside to George Fitch, May 8, 1953; ARCI Records, Box 26, Letters to Formosa 1953, Agreement with U.S. government, April 1, 1953, and B. A. Garside to George Fitch, March 30, 1953.

44. ARCI Records, Box 26, Letters to Formosa, B. A. Garside to George Fitch, February 19, 1953, Hoover Institution Archives.

45. During Father McGuire and James Ivey's inspection of Hong Kong's refugee crisis, one Mr. Aldington, a political officer with the colonial government, "urged upon us the necessity of avoiding any notoriety, any publicity in our operation." ARCI Records, Box 5, ARCI Agenda, 1952, Report on Survey Mission to Hong Kong, Frederick C. McGuire, Executive Committee Meeting Agenda, March 19, 1952, Hoover Institution Archives.

46. ARCI Records, Box 26, Letters from Taiwan, George Fitch to Karl Compton, December 2, 1953, Hoover Institution Archives.

47. ARCI Records, Box 28, Letters from Taiwan, George Fitch to B. A. Garside, July–December 1956, Hoover Institution Archives.

48. ARCI Records, Box 26, Letters to Formosa, B. A. Garside to George Fitch, January–July 1956, April 20, 1956, Hoover Institution Archives.

49. Ibid., Jan. 8, 1953.

50. The Fitches attended chapel with the Chiangs and spent some Christmases at their home. As late as 1955, George Fitch expressed his belief that Chiang Kai-shek could still retake the mainland: "Personally I feel convinced that after perhaps 3 or 4 attempts at achieving a bridgehead one could ultimately be held and that there would be uprisings among the peasants and defections from the army that would result in a gradual but successful penetration." ARCI Records, Box 28, Letters from Taiwan, George Fitch to B. A. Garside, January–June 1955, Hoover Institution Archives.

51. ARCI Records, Box 8, Compton–Dr. Karl Correspondence, Walter Judd to Dr. Karl T. Compton November 9, 1953, Hoover Institution Archives.

52. ARCI Records, Box 4, ARCI Minutes 1953, Taiwan Advisory Board Minutes of the Eighth Meeting, June 9, 1953, Hoover Institution Archives.

53. ARCI Records, Box 26, Letters to Formosa, Chang to Marvin Liebman, reporting arrival of first settlement case in Taiwan, September–December 1952, Hoover Institution Archives.

54. ARCI Records, Box 2, Minutes of Executive Committee meetings 1st 2/14/52 to 30th 12/8/55, George Taylor to Christopher Emmet, May 20, 1952, Hoover Institution Archives.

55. ARCI Records, Box 19, Letters from Hong Kong, William Howard to George Fitch, May–September 1954, Hoover Institution Archives.

56. ARCI Records, Box 27, Letters from Taiwan, 1/1/54 to 6/30/54, George Fitch to B. A. Garside, May 8, 1954, Hoover Institution Archives.

57. ARCI Records, Box 26, Letters to Formosa, Budget, November 6, 1953; ARCI Records, Box 27, Letters from Taiwan, 7/1/54 to 12/31/54, Advisory Board Meeting, October 23, 1954, Hoover Institution Archives.

58. Nash's practical proposal that ARCI provide much needed rice to distribute to refugees on Hong Kong's coronation celebration had been refused as inconsequential to ARCI's real objectives. ARCI Records, Box 18, Letters from Hong Kong, Ernest Nash telegram to B. A. Garside, May 19, 1953, Hoover Institution Archives.

59. Ibid., Ernest Nash to B. A. Garside, January–May 1953.

60. ARCI Records, Box 26, Letters to Formosa, B. A. Garside to George Fitch, January 8, 1953, Hoover Institution Archives. For a more extended discussion of ARCI's Taiwan programs, see "Refugees as Resources in Aid Refugee Chinese Intellectuals, Inc. (ARCI) Programs to Support Nationalist Taiwan, 1952–1956," in "Global Displacements and Emplacement: The Forced Exile and Resettlement Experiences of Ethnic Chinese Refugees," special issue of *Journal of Chinese Overseas*, 10, 2 (2014).

61. U.S. Statutes at Large, PL 203, chap. 336, pp. 400–407. Palestinian refugees also received an allocation of two thousand refugee visas.

62. Kung, *Chinese in American Life*, 108–9; Hing, *Making and Remaking Asian America*, 252n28.

63. Arthur Hummel, PAO in Hong Kong, authored "Overseas Chinese," Secret, February 5, 1954, Records of the Foreign Service Posts, Hong Kong, U.S. Consulate General, Classified General Records of the USIS, 1951–1963, "Chinese Students," RG 84, National Archives II, College Park, MD. Hummel testified in Support of repeal in 1943.

64. Pierce J. Gerety, Office Memorandum-Conversation with Congressman Judd, March 27, 1956, Subject Files Related to the RRP, 1953–1958 Far East, Bureau of Security and Consular Affairs, Office of Refugee and Migration Affairs, RG 59, National Archives II, College Park, MD. Some Japanese claimed refugee status as victims of earthquakes while others were sponsored as agricultural workers.

65. Despite the cessation of active warfare after 1945, propaganda remained a significant tool wielded by the State Department within the United States and in many parts of the world. See Kenneth Osgood, *Total Cold War: Eisenhower's Secret Propaganda Battle at Home and Abroad* (Lawrence: University Press of Kansas, 2006); and Nicholas Cull, *The Cold War and the United States Information Agency* (Cambridge: Cambridge University Press, 2008). I thank Chi-kwan Mark for referring me to Cull's work.

66. The State Department kept a tight rein on ARCI activities by distributing funds only by reimbursement so that any expenditures of which the International Cooperation Agency disapproved would not be compensated. This financial arrangement reflects State Department support for the direct channeling of refugees into Nationalist employment but also its pressure on ARCI to send registrants to the United States. See "Summary of Agreement" dated April 1, 1953, in letter from Garside to George Fitch, May 8, 1953; ARCI Records, Box 26, Letters to

Formosa 1953, Agreement with U.S. Government, April 1, 1953, and B. A. Garside to George Fitch, March 30, 1953.

67. ARCI Records, Box 28, Letters to Taiwan, 1/1/55 to 12/31/55, B. A. Garside to George Fitch, February 3, 1955, Hoover Institution Archives.

68. Carole McGranahan has written about Fletcher's CIA activities working with Tibetan refugees after completing his Hong Kong assignment. See "Love and Empire: The CIA, Tibet, and Covert Humanitarianism," paper presented at Intimacies of War conference, Yale University, New Haven, CT, April 25, 2014. Cited with permission of the author.

69. In 1956 George Fitch corresponded privately with Fletcher to describe a potential recruit he had identified in Taiwan, one C. George Hoh, for "one of those Laos assignments." Fitch Collection, Box 22, Harvard-Yenching Fitch Papers, George Fitch to Travis Fletcher, May 13, 1957, Harvard-Yenching Library, Harvard University.

The PRC may have fielded their own agent in the ARCI office. In October 1954, T. C. Tseng, one of the Chinese staff in the Hong Kong branch who had been employed from its beginning, abruptly disappeared. A March 1955 *Shanghai Daily News* article located him studying in Beijing. See ARCI Records, Box 27, "Letters from Taiwan," 7/1/54 to 12/31/54, October. 5, 1954, letter from Fitch to Garside, Hoover Institution Archives; ARCI Records, Box 28, Letters to and from Taiwan, 1955–1956, March 30, 1955, letter from Fitch to Garside, Hoover Institution Archives.

70. LeClerq joined ARCI at the same time as Fletcher, with many complementary responsibilities, but available records do not reveal his later activities. I am unable to determine if he was also working on behalf of the CIA or State Department. Many of his statements and actions, however, suggest that he was fully attuned to Fletcher's activities.

71. "M'leod Still Holds Refugee Plan Role," *New York Times*, June 11, 1955. A previous director of the program, Edward J. Corsi, had been ousted for criticizing his supervisor, McLeod, for "sabotaging" the program. "Entry of Refugees Said to Be on Rise," *New York Times*, August 30, 1955. McLeod, in contrast, was criticized for overzealously enforcing details of the program with the priority of keeping out possible communists. See "Visa Aides Speed Refugee Plans," *New York Times*, July 3, 1955.

72. "Refugee Program Facing a Paradox: Applications May Be Closed in Some Areas while Visas Go Begging in Others," *New York Times*, May 14, 1956.

73. ARCI Records, Box 19, Letters to Hong Kong, 1/1/54—12/31/54, B. A. Garside to William Howard, April 3, 1954, Hoover Institution Archives.

74. ARCI Records, Box 19, Letters from Hong Kong, William Howard to B. A. Garside, May–Sept. 1954, Hoover Institution Archives. See *Oakland Tribune*, January 5, 1955.

75. ARCI Records, Box 20, Letters to Hong Kong, B. A. Garside to George Fitch and William Howard, January–December 1955, January 3, 1955, Hoover Institution Archives.

76. ARCI Records, Box 19, "LeClercq letters to Hong Kong" November 15, 1954–November 6, 1956, LeClercq to Travis Fletcher, March 23, 1956, November 15, 1954, and November 6, 1954, Hoover Institution Archives.

77. ARCI Records, Box 26, Letters to Formosa, LeClercq to George Fitch, February 28, 1956, and January–July 1956, Hoover Institution Archives.

78. Pierce J. Gerety, Office Memorandum-Conversation with Congressman Judd, March 27, 1956; Subject Files Related to the RRP, 1953–1958 Far East; Bureau of Security and Consular Affairs, Office of Refugee and Migration Affairs, RG59, National Archives II, College Park, MD.

79. Many of the compromised reforms of the McCarran-Walter Act first appeared in bills proposed by Judd, such as HR 5004 (1948) and HR 199 (1949). Walter H. Judd Papers, Box 36, Folder 9, Asian Immigration 1947–1953, Hoover Institution Archives.

80. ARCI Records, Box 19, LeClercq letters to Hong Kong, LeClercq to William Howard and Travis Fletcher, and March 8, 1954, November 15, 1954, and November 6, 1956, Hoover Institution Archives.

81. Ibid.

82. ARCI Records, Box 20, LeClercq Letters to Hong Kong, LeClercq to Travis Fletcher, January–December 1955, May 18, 1955, Hoover Institution Archives.

83. ARCI Records, Box 19, LeClercq letters to Hong Kong, LeClercq to Travis Fletcher, November 15, 1954, November 23, 1955, and November 6, 1956, Hoover Institution Archives.

84. ARCI Records, Box 28, Letters to Taiwan, 1/1/55 to 12/31/55, LeClercq to George Fitch, February 10, 1955, Hoover Institution Archives.

85. ARCI Records, Box 19, LeClercq letters to Hong Kong, LeClercq to Travis Fletcher, November 15, 1954, October 18, 1955, and November 6, 1956.

86. Author's interview with Evelyn Hu-Dehart, June 29, 2010, and February 9, 2013.

87. Mae M. Ngai, "Legacies of Exclusion: Illegal Chinese Immigration during the Cold War Years," *Journal of American Ethnic History* 18, 1 (Fall 1998): 3–35. After his Hong Kong posting, Drumright became ambassador to China stationed in Taiwan 1958 to 1962.

88. Peter Kwong and Dusanka Miscevic, *Chinese Americans: The Immigrant Experience* (Southport, CT: Hugh Lauter Levin Associates, 2000), 224.

89. For these reasons, and because of Hong Kong's major role as an intelligence gathering post, the consulate was unusually large for a small city. For political reasons the U.S. Embassy in China had to be stationed in Taiwan. Cheng, *Citizens of Asian America*, 178–80, describes the alarmist tone of Drumright's report, which associated the paper son system with both communist infiltration and unchecked, transnational criminal networks.

90. Louis Goetz, interview by Charles Stuart Kennedy, July 23, 1992, 9, Association for Diplomatic Studies and Training, Foreign Affairs Oral History Project, Abba Schwartz Award Program, John F. Kennedy Library, Boston.

91. Halleck Rose to Pierce Gerety, Refugee Relief Program/Far East, January 31, 1956; Subject Files Related to the RRP, 1953–1958 Far East; Bureau of Security and Consular Affairs; Office of Refugee and Migration Affairs, RG 59, National Archives II, 3, Washington, DC.

92. Advisory Opinions on Refugee Relief Program from Coordinator, RRP/FE to All Consular Offices, Far East, August 3, 1955; "RRP/FE Advisory Opinion

21002; " Office of Refugee and Migration Affairs; Subject Files, Refugee Relief Program 1953–1958; Bureau of A&CA, RG 59, National Archives II, Washington, DC.

93. Michael Feighan, n.d., Summary of "Report of Inspection of the Administration of the Refugee Relief Act of 1953, as Amended, and Related Problems in the Countries of South East Asia and North Asia"; Program Files 1953–1957; Bureau of Security and Consular Affairs, Office of Refugee and Migration Affairs, RG 59, National Archives II, Washington, DC.

94. Michael Feighan, "Report of Inspection of the Administration of the Refugee Relief Act of 1953, as Amended, and Related Problems in the Countries of South East Asia and North Asia," file "Congressional Letters," Box 14, accession A1 E5495, Office of Refugee and Migration Affairs, Bureau of Security and Consular Affairs, Department of State, RG 59, National Archives II, College Park, MD.

95. Hing, *Making and Remaking*, 44–53.

96. Ngai, *Impossible Subjects*, 240–48.

97. Zolberg, *A Nation by Design*, 320–21.

98. Ngai, *Impossible Subjects*, 218. Ngai underscores that the confession program did not offer amnesty. Some confessions were used to incriminate Chinese Americans suspected of leftist sympathies and activities who lost their status, with some being deported to Taiwan or to China.

99. Cheng, *Citizens of Asian America*, 187.

100. Ngai, *Impossible Subjects*, 222–23.

101. Records Pertaining to the Refugee Relief Program at Foreign Service Posts, 1953–1958; "Hong Kong from December 1, 1955, to June 30, 1956 [Folder 1/2]"; General Records, BSCA, ORM, RG 59, National Archives II, College Park, MD.

102. Ibid.

103. Eric G. Lindahl, vice consul, Hong Kong to F. J. Noble, immigration officer, Hong Kong, Office Memorandum, December 21, 1955, about "Opinion for preliminary determination of eligibility under PL 203 in the case of LI Li Hwa"; "LI Li Hwa," Bureau of Security and Consular Affairs, Office of Refugee and Migration Affairs; Subject Files 1953–1958; Refugee Relief Program, RG 59, National Archives II, College Park, MD.

104. American Consulate General, Hong Kong, to Department of State, Operations Memorandum, January 11, 1956; "LI Li Hwa," Bureau of Security and Consular Affairs, Office of Refugee and Migration Affairs; Subject Files 1953–1958; Refugee Relief Program, RG 59, National Archives II, College Park, MD.

105. Lindahl, vice consul, Hong Kong, to F. J. Noble, immigration officer, Hong Kong, Office Memorandum, December 21, 1955; Proposed Refugee Visa for Li Li-Hwa, to FE/P John Henderson from RRP-Pierce J. Gerety, January 24, 1956; Eric G.; "LI Li Hwa," Bureau of Security and Consular Affairs, Office of Refugee and Migration Affairs, Subject Files 1953–1958; Refugee Relief Program, RG 59, National Archives II, College Park, MD; Frank C. Tribbe of USIA to Halleck Rose, RRP, Secret Office Memorandum concerning "Immigration of Li Li-Hua; Hong Kong," to coordinate publicity, March 19, 1956: Treat connection to USIA as a "classified matter." Don't want USIA's involvement being used for communist propaganda; Bureau of Security and Consular Affairs, Office of Refugee and Mi-

gration Affairs, Subject Files 1953–1958, Refugee Relief Program, Department of State, RG 59, National Archives II, College Park, MD.

106. *International Screen* 13 (November 1956). Also see "Hollywood Bound," *Port Angeles Evening News*, July 9, 1956.

107. "Refugee Program Facing a Paradox."

108. Kung, *Chinese in American Life*, 120; and Zolberg, *A Nation by Design*, 325. Subcommittee on Immigration and Naturalization, Report of the Committee on the Judiciary, United States Senate, 85th Congress, 2d Session, March 5, 1959 (Washington, DC: GPO, 1959); 86th Congress, 1st Session, Report No. 78, 4–5.

109. Kung, *Chinese in American Life*, 120–21.

110. *Statutes at Large* 72:546, Hing, *Making and Remaking*, 282n28.

111. ARCI Records, Box 20, Letters to Hong Kong, B. A. Garside to William Howard, January–December 1955, August 11, 1955, and October 8, 1956, Hoover Institution Archives. "Dimensions of Unfinished Task." Another 12,639 were dismissed as having "no qualifications which could fit them for any employment within the present scope of the ARCI program."

112. ARCI Records, Box 15, State Department-USEP, McCollum to Walter Judd, December 31, 1956, July 1, 1956, August 14, 1956, December 10, 1958, December 31, 1958, January 1, 1958. ARCI Records, Box 19, LeClercq letters to Hong Kong, LeClercq to Travis Fletcher, November 15, 1954, August 17, 1956, November 6, 1956, Hoover Institution Archives. Showing another close connection between ARCI and the State Department, LeClerq proceeded to work for ICA after completing his assignment with ARCI.

113. ARCI Records, Box 25, Letters from Hong Kong, Halleck Rose to B. A. Garside, January 1, 1961, August 16, 1962, and December 31, 1968, Hoover Institution Archives.

114. Edwards, *Missionary to Freedom*, 190.

115. ARCI Records, Box 15, State Department-ORM, 1/1/1961–1970, B. A. Garside to Elmer M. Falk, July 2, 1965, Hoover Institution Archives.

116. In his biography, *Within the Four Seas*, 118, Garside claimed that registrants' debts were all "repaid entirely voluntarily." According to correspondence files, however, Garside worked hard to keep track of registrants with outstanding loans, sometimes going to great lengths to locate those who had "disappeared," and sent regular reminders of funds owed.

117. Louis Goetz, interview by Charles Stuart Kennedy, July 23, 1992, 10–11. The Association for Diplomatic Studies and Training, Foreign Affairs Oral History Project, Abba Schwartz Award Program, John F. Kennedy Library, Boston.

118. Hu would depart the United States in 1958 to head the Academia Sinica in Taipei.

119. See Madeline Hsu, "From Chop Suey to Mandarin Cuisine: Fine Dining and the Refashioning of Chinese Ethnicity during the Cold War Era," in *Chinese Americans and the Politics of Race and Culture*, ed. Sucheng Chan and Madeline Hsu (Philadelphia: Temple University Press, 2008), 184–89.

120. Betty Lee Sung, *Mountain of Gold: The Story of the Chinese in America* (New York: Macmillan, 1967), 208–9.

121. Ibid., 159.

122. Robert McG. Thomas Jr., "Eileen Chang, 74, Chinese Writer Revered Outside the Mainland," *New York Times*, September 13, 1995; David Der-Wei Wang, foreword to *The Rice Sprout Song* (Berkeley: University of California Press, 1998 reprint, 1955). In 1961 C. T. Hsia's authoritative *A History of Modern Chinese Fiction* (New Haven, CT: Yale University Press) named Zhang as one of the great writers of the 1940s alongside Eudora Welty and Flannery O'Connor. After she died her estate included a bundle of unpublished fiction and other writings, which have since been published through the auspices of her literary agent's family. Joyce Hor-chung Lau, "Chinese Writer Cements a Legacy," *New York Times*, October 1, 2010.

Chapter 7. *"Economic and Humanitarian"*

1. "Refugee Problem in Hong Kong and Macao," Hearings before the Subcommittee to Investigate Problems Connected with Refugees and Escapees of the Committee of the Judiciary, United States Senate, 87th Congress, 2nd session (Washington, DC: GPO, 1962), 123.

2. Donald Janson, "First Chinese Refugees Welcomed in Chicago," *New York Times*, June 6, 1962. One son could not come because he had tuberculosis. After they arrived, the Engs found out that he had been cleared by immigration officials to come as well and would arrive a couple of days later. See "Chinese Refugee Family Quitting Hong Kong for US," *New York Times*, June 4, 1962.

3. Janson, "First Chinese Refugees Welcomed in Chicago."

4. "Father of Chinese Refugee Admitted by Kennedy Dies," *New York Times*, June 11, 1962.

5. Ellen Wu, *Color of Success*, 2–5.

6. "Robert Kennedy Welcomes First of Hong Kong Refugees," June 5, 1962, and "How Hong Kong Provides for Refugees," June 1, 1962; file "570.1 Refugees: Hong Kong," Box 25, accession EUD3257, Foreign Service Posts, Taiwan, U.S. Department of State, RG 84, National Archives II, College Park, MD.

7. Lee, *Flower Drum Song*, 133.

8. A nightclub singer and recording artist who performed in both Japanese and English, Umeki immigrated to the United States in 1955. She was the first Asian American actor to receive an Academy Award and also received a Tony nomination for her Broadway performance as Mei Li.

9. The largest proportion of ethnic Chinese refugees arrived from Hong Kong, but they also came from Taiwan, Southeast Asia, and some Latin American countries as well.

10. In chapter 6 of *Color of Success*, "Chinatown Offers Us a Lesson," Ellen Wu describes insistent media depictions of Chinatowns as havens of family and community stability stemming from Chinese cultural values despite efforts by community activists to attract attention and resources to problems of juvenile delinquency, high school dropout rates, and poor sanitation and health during the 1950s and 1960s.

11. See, for example, Grace Chou, *Confucianism, Colonialism, and the Cold War: Chinese Cultural Education at Hong Kong's New Asia College, 1949–63* (Leiden: Brill, 2011), for details of U.S. foundation funding for Chinese-language higher education in Hong Kong.

12. Osgood, *Total Cold War*, 5, 33.

13. Speakers' Bureau, Circular Airgram 1816, November 20, 1952; file "Exchange of Persons," Box 2, accession EUD 2689, Records of the Foreign Service Posts of the Department of State, Hong Kong, U.S. Consulate-General, Classified General Records of the USIS, 1951–1963; RG 84, National Archives II, College Park, MD. Declassified NND842810.

14. Report on the Public Affairs Officers Meeting on Overseas Chinese, May, 12, 1954, 33, 35; file "Overseas Chinese," in ibid.

15. Washington to USIS, Taipei, April 8, 1954 regarding "Proposed Re-Statement of Mission, USIS/Formosa," 1, 3; file "Cultural Affairs July–Dec," Box 1, in ibid.

16. John Foster Dulles, "US Escapee Program Activities in the Far East," Department of State Instruction CA-5243, February 10, 1955, 3; file "Taipei Jan. 31, 1955 to May 31, 1955" [Folder 2/2], Box 3, accession EUD 2689; Office of Refugee and Migration Affairs, Bureau of Security and Consular Affairs, U.S. Department of State, RG 59, National Archives II, College Park, MD. Declassified NND979038. The instruction was actually drafted by China Affairs officer Richard Cashin. Taiwan figured prominently in this campaign "to strengthen Free China as a symbol of haven and refuge for freedom-loving Chinese, and as the custodian of traditional Chinese culture." The settlement of "prominent intellectuals" on Taiwan where they "are being assisted there to reestablish their lives in occupations and professions for which they are technically trained and qualified" provided hope that different homes awaited and "to enhance the prestige and influence of Free China among the overseas Chinese communities throughout Southeast Asia."

17. Timothy J. Larkin, ORM/USEP to Douglas N. Forman, CA, Office Memorandum, July 16, 1957, concerning Data on Hong Kong Requested in Telephone Conversation of July 12, 1957; "3P Hong Kong," Bureau of Far Eastern Affairs, Office of Chinese Affairs, Decimal Files 1954–1956; RG 59, National Archives II, College Park, MD.

18. Joint State-USIA-FOA Secret memorandum to Hong Kong, Manila, Saigon, Seoul, Taipei, Feb. 10, 1955, 3–4; file "Refugee Program Escapee Acts," Box 6, accession EUD 2689, Records for the Foreign Service Posts, U.S. Consulate General; Classified General Records USIS, 1951–1963; U.S. Department of State, RG 84, National Archives II, College Park, MD. Declassified NND 842810.

19. Under "Cautions," Dulles warned that U.S. aid to Taiwan had provoked negative perceptions that "Taiwan is 'an American colony' and the Nationalist Government 'American puppets'" (6).

20. ARCI Records, Box 15, Lawrence Dawson letter to B. A. Garside, July 16, 1958; file "State Department-USEP," January 1, 1958–December 31, 1958; Hoover Institution Archives.

21. Letter from Chen Foh-yu, Operations Memorandum: Case of Lau Wen-ngau, U.S. Information Service, Hong Kong, to U.S. Information Agency, Washington, DC,

June 22, 1955; file "Refugee Program Escapee Acts," Box 5, accession EUD 2689, Records of the Foreign Service Posts, U.S. Consulate General, Hong Kong, Classified General Records of the USIS, 1951–1963, U.S. Department of State, RG 84, National Archives II, College Park, MD.

22. Secret Memorandum from Laurence Dawson to D. N. Forman, September 13, 1957, file "570.1 Racial Disturbances, DP's, Refugees," Box 28, accession E#P255, U.S. Department of State, RG 59, National Archives II, College Park, MD. Declassified NND877213.

23. "5 Chinese Refugees on Way to New Connecticut Home," *New York Times*, September 16, 1955.

24. Peggy Durdin, "The Chinese Scroll Called Hong Kong," *New York Times*, December 7, 1958.

25. "Chinese Refugees Crowd Hong Kong," *New York Times*, January 15, 1960.

26. Restricted: General Precautions Concerning Your Testimony, n.d., file "Congress-Committee-Subcommittee on Immigration & Naturalization"; Box 27, accession A1 E5498; U.S. Department of State, RG 59, National Archives II, College Park, MD. Declassified NND 979039.

27. See Tichenor, *Dividing Lines*, chap. 7.

28. John F. Kennedy, *A Nation of Immigrants* (New York: Anti-Defamation League of B'nai B'rith, 1959), 37. Aristide Zolberg points out that this bill represented a significant concession by reformers who adopted restrictionists' insistence on capping overall immigration. See *A Nation by Design*, 319.

29. Press release from Office of John F. Kennedy, United States Senate, August 2, 1953, Legislation Files '53-'60: '53-'55; Box 647, Senate Files, John F. Kennedy Library and Archives.

30. John F. Kennedy to Arthur Watkins, July 15, 1954, ibid.

31. John F. Kennedy to Francis Walter, June 27, 1955, ibid.

32. Walter P. McConaughey, "Memorandum of Conversation, January 25, 1957, regarding Chinese Refugees and US Immigration Laws," file "570.1 Racial Disturbances, DP's, Refugees"; Box 28, accession E#P225, U.S. Department of State, RG 59, National Archives II, College Park, MD.

33. Aide-Memoire, February 21, 1957, file "570.1 Racial Disturbances, DP's, Refugees"; ibid. Declassified NND877213.

34. Press release from Office of John F. Kennedy, United States Senate, June 27, 1957, Legislation Files '53-'60: '56-'57: Immigration Legislation 6/19/57–7/8/57, Box 670, Senate Files, John F. Kennedy Library and Archives.

35. Shing-Tai Liang letter to Senator John F. Kennedy, August 27, 1957, "Immigration Legislation 8/23/57–9/15/—," Box 670, Senate Files, John F. Kennedy Library and Archives.

36. Mark Damon letter to Senator John F. Kennedy, January 5, 1958, "Legislation Files, 1958: Immigration 11/20–2/6/58," Box 695, Senate Files, John F. Kennedy Library and Archives.

37. Jack Lotto, Exclusive-Refugees, October 18, 1956, file "210.4 Chinese Communist Pressures on Chinese Aliens in the U.S.," Box 23, accession E#P225; Bureau of Far Eastern Affairs, Office of Chinese Affairs; Decimal Files 1954–1957; U.S. Department of State, RG 59, National Archives II, College Park, MD.

38. John F. Kennedy to Mark Damon, January 10, 1958, "Legislation Files, 1958: Immigration 11/20–2/6/58," Box 695, Senate Files, John F. Kennedy Library and Archives.

39. John F. Kennedy letter to Peter Y. F. Shih, June 25, 1959, "Immigration Files 53–60, 1959," Box 719, Senate Files, John F. Kennedy Library and Archives.

40. Anthony Lewis, "Walter Pushes Bill to Admit Refugees Outside of Quotas," *New York Times*, March 25, 1960.

41. Report on Hong Kong and Macao, 17.

42. Louis Goetz, interview by Charles Stuart Kennedy, July 23, 1992, 8; Association for Diplomatic Studies and Training, Foreign Affairs Oral History Project, Abba Schwartz Award Program, John F. Kennedy Library, Boston. 8. Goetz was stationed in Hong Kong from 1961 to 1966. He also noted that "the fortunate or unfortunate part of . . . the problem was that most of our local employees qualified and went to the States."

43. Max Frankel, "Hong Kong Crisis on Refugees Puts US in a Dilemma," *New York Times*, May 23, 1962.

44. "Chinese Refugees Trouble Macau," *New York Times*, March 4, 1962. Kennedy and his wife had visited Hong Kong and American charitable projects, including a resettlement estate, a community center run by the Maryknoll sisters, a Church World Service milk station, and the Bishop Ford Center. Publicity also described the $27 million in American agricultural surplus distributed since 1954. "Robert Kennedys Visit Refugees and Swim in Bay in Hong Kong," *New York Times*, February 12, 1962.

45. "Return of Refugees from Red China." Congressional Record—Senate. 1089 Cong. Rec. 8112, 1962. May 10, 1962—Senator Bush requested entering into record the *Greenwich Times* article "Hungry Refugees from China Sent Back Home."

46. "The Refugee Problem in Hong Kong." Congressional Record—Senate. 1089 Cong. Rec. 8145, 1962. May 10. The *Life* editorial also advocated passage of the Hart bill. Fong entered it into the Congressional Record along with several other relevant articles including *Life*, May 4, 1962, "China's Refugees: Something Can Be Done Now"; *Washington Star*, May 9, 1962, "Refugees in Hong Kong Seek Free World Aid."

47. "Hong Kong Refugees." Congressional Record—Senate. 1089 Cong. Rec. 8824, 1962. May 21.

48. "Nationalist Chinese to Accept Refugees from Red China." Congressional Record—Senate. 1089 Cong. Rec. 8913–14, 1962. May 22.

49. Frankel, "Hong Kong Crisis on Refugees Puts US in a Dilemma." Taiwan was not a viable solution also because many refugees, who were mostly Cantonese, preferred not to go there. See "Most Refugees Shun Taiwan," *New York Times*, June 12, 1962. According to the Free China Relief Association, 17,616 refugees from Hong Kong resettled in Taiwan from January 1952 to March 1962. Taiwan's total resettlement over that period was 71,297. "Aid for Refugees from China Asked," *New York Times*, June 3, 1962.

50. Max Frankel, "U.S. to Ease Chinese Quota for Hong Kong Refugees," *New York Times*, May 24, 1962.

51. Ibid. Walter thought 7,800 had already been cleared by consular authorities although State Department figures were closer to 5,000. Also see Davis, "Impetus for Immigration Reform," 140.

52. "The Hong Kong Refugee Situation," May 24, 1962; S569-S570, Congressional Record; file "570.1 Refugees: Hong Kong"; Box 25, accession EUD3257, Foreign Service Posts, Taiwan, U.S. Embassy and Consulate, Taipei, General Records, 1941–1963, U.S. Department of State, RG 84, National Archives II, College Park, MD.

53. "The Hong Kong Refugee Situation." Congressional Record—Senate. 1089 Cong. Rec. 9245–46, 1962. May 24.

54. Ibid.

55. "Walter Presents Bill," *New York Times*, May 25, 1962. Considerable publicity also attended the arrival of forty-eight adopted children from Hong Kong later that June. See Choy, *Global Families*, 56–57.

56. "Refugee Problem in Hong Kong and Macao," 1.

57. Ibid., 3.

58. Ibid., 10–11.

59. Ibid., 16.

60. *Communism Failed Her . . . Will We?* (Chinese Refugee Relief fundraising brochure), n.d., Papers of Anna Chennault, Schlesinger Library; Walter H. Judd Papers, Box 185, folder 3, Hoover Institution Archives..

61. AR7277-A. President John F. Kennedy with Anna Chennault, Chairwoman of Chinese Refugee Relief, Meeting with Anna Chennault, Chairwoman of Chinese Refugee Relief, 10:17AM, White House Photographs, John F. Kennedy Presidential Library and Museum, Boston.

62. "Aid for Refugees from China Asked," *New York Times*, June 3, 1962.

63. Officially, Chennault remained head until 1970. Press reports of the time identify Chennault as the founder of Chinese Refugee Relief, although she credits President Kennedy in her memoir. Both versions are challenged by David Lee, who asserts that actually it was he and Jack Anderson, a journalist neighbor with long-standing interests in China, who came up with the idea after Lee's trip to Hong Kong where he personally witnessed the plight of Chinese refugees. Anderson knew Kennedy and gained his backing. Lee claimed that he and Anderson recruited Chennault to the organization after failing to convince the Chinese ambassador Jiang Tingfu (T. F. Tsiang) to take the lead. Li Dawei (David Lee), "Zhongguo nanmin jiujihui shiliao gengzheng" (Historical correction for Chinese Refugee Relief), *Hua fu youbao* (Washington Post) April 10, 1998, 7.

64. According to Wilford, IRC was not an actual front organization. See *The Mighty Wurlitzer*, 176. The IRC handled about two thousand of the first group of parolees in 1962. Wallace Turner, "5,000th Refugee of China Arrives," *New York Times*, February 20, 1963.

65. ARCI Records, Box 2, "Aid Refugee Chinese Intellectual Executive Committee II," February 20, 1958, report to 41st meeting of the executive committee, 2, Hoover Institution Archives.

66. "13-Year Wait Ends in Joy for Chinese Girl," *New York Times*, June 7, 1962. Another sister was a student at UC Berkeley and saw Deanna on a stopover in San Francisco.

67. Wallace Turner, "5,000th Refugee of China Arrives," *New York Times*, February 20, 1963.

68. "Admission of Chinese Refugees by Special Act of Attorney General Robert F. Kennedy," September 29, 1964, 2–3, Abba Schwartz papers, [folder title illegible], Box 8, John F. Kennedy Presidential Library and Archives. In September 1964 Abba Schwartz, Kennedy's and then Lyndon Johnson's administrator of the Bureau of Security and Consular Affairs, reported that from May 1962 until September 1, 1964, 12,024 Chinese nationals had been authorized for admission and 11,348 had arrived. Schwartz projected that an additional 4,000 to 5,000 would be admitted by the end of February or March 1965, for a total of 15,000 to 17,000.

69. Richard Ferree Smith, "Refugees," in *Annals of the American Academy of Political and Social Science*, vol. 367, *The New Immigration* (September 1966): 43; Davis, "Impetus for Immigration Reform," 141.

70. Yueh Hu, "The Problem of the Hong Kong Refugees," *Asian Survey* 2, 1 (March 1962): 33.

71. Frankel, "US to Ease Chinese Quota for Hong Kong Refugees."

72. "Hong Kong Firm on Refugee Policy: Says US Plan Does Not End Population Pressure," *New York Times*, May 25, 1962. The article included a photograph of a man jumping from a truck rather than be returned to China.

73. "Hong Kong Wary on Refugee Issue," *New York Times*, June 17, 1962.

74. "Aggression by Refugee?" *New York Times*, May 26, 1962.

75. "Opinion of the Week: At Home and Abroad," *New York Times*, May 27, 1962.

76. Russell Baker, "Refugees Called a Bane to Peiping," *New York Times*, May 30, 1962.

77. "Refugee Problem in Hong Kong and Macao," 26; Davis, "Impetus for Immigration Reform," 139. Hart had the backing of religious leaders such as Rabbi Maurice Eisendrath, president of the Union of American Hebrew Congregations. "We cannot successfully compete with the communists for the loyalties of the people of the world, until the United States stands before the world as we always did, as a free nation of immigrants, a haven for the oppressed, an open society, generous and compassionate which judges all human beings within and beyond our borders only on the basis of character and individual worth."

78. "Heart-warming Response to Chinese Refugee Plight," Congressional Record—Senate. 108 Cong. Rec. 9593, 1962. June 1.

79. "Refugee Problem in Hong Kong and Macao," 30.

80. He also made a pitch for the lifting of the trade embargo, which burdened the Hong Kong economy and trade.

81. "Extension of Remarks of Hon. John W. McCormack," "Plight of the Chinese Refugees," Congressional Record-Appendix A4319, June 13, 1962; House of Representatives, June 12, 1962. Chennault was born in Beijing, although her mother and grandmother had been born in the United States.

82. Christopher's welcome included the historically inaccurate qualifier, "with our traditional friendship for the Chinese people."

83. "Hong Kong Refugee Situation." Congressional Record—Senate. 1089 Cong. Rec. 10747–48, June 18, 1962. Hart also noted that the last immigration

reform took place in 1961, in which transnational adoptees could enter through family reunification statuses rather than as refugees.

Chapter 8. Symbiotic Brain Drains

1. Tuan's professional career flourished in several institutions far from centers of Chinese American life: Indiana University at Bloomington, University of New Mexico, University of Toronto, and University of Minnesota.

2. Tuan, *Who Am I? An Autobiography of Emotion, Mind, and Spirit* (Madison: University of Wisconsin Press, 1999), 92.

3. Peter Monaghan, "Lost in Place," *Chronicle of Higher Education*, March 16, 2001, http://chronicle.com/article/Lost-in-Place/11412. Tuan has criticized the Civil Rights Movement, observing that although he has become sensitive to racial slurs and slights, "whether this constitutes an improvement in the direction of greater social harmony and personal happiness, I do not know. I rather doubt it." *Who Am I?*, 92; author's interview with Yi-fu Tuan, 25 June 2010. Since his retirement Tuan has written more extensively about his personal experiences of being Chinese in America in memoirs such as *Who Am I?* and *Coming Home to China* (Minneapolis: University of Minnesota Press, 2007). I thank Steve Hoelscher for introducing me to his graduate mentor, reading a draft of this chapter, and guiding me to key readings in the field of geography.

4. Yi-fu Tuan, *Topophilia: A Study of Environmental Perception, Attitudes, and Values* (New York: Prentice-Hall, 1974, reissued in 1990 by Columbia University Press); Tuan, *Space and Place: The Perspective of Experience* (Minneapolis: University of Minnesota Press, 1977); Tuan, *Landscapes of Fear* (Oxford: Blackwell, 1979); Tuan, *Cosmos and Hearth: A Cosmopolite's Viewpoint* (Minneapolis: University of Minnesota Press, 1999).

5. "Yi-Fu Tuan," in *Key Thinkers on Space and Place*, ed. Phil Hubbard, Rob Kitchin, and Gill Valentine (London: Sage, 2004), 307; Paul C. Adams, Steven Hoelscher, and Karen E. Till, eds., "Place in Context: Rethinking Humanist Geographies," in *Textures of Place: Exploring Humanist Geographies* (Minneapolis: University of Minnesota Press, 2001), xiv.

6. See the overview by J. Nicholas Entrikin, "Geographer as Humanist," in Adams et al., *Textures of Place*, 427.

7. Monaghan, "Lost in Place."

8. Tuan, *Who Am I?*, 10.

9. Zolberg, *A Nation by Design*, 22, contrasts the political and ideological contestations over "front-gate" and "back-door" immigration to which this book adds "side-door."

10. Lee, *The Chinese in the United States of America*, 91. These numbers dropped to 2,918 in 1952 owing to cuts in financial support from the Nationalist government, which started urging students to finish their courses and return as soon as possible, or find financial support from sources available in the United States. See Archives of the National Resources Commission, Academia Historica, Xindian, Taiwan. These records span 1939–1952 and are available in digitized form.

11. See Gordon Chang, *Friends and Enemies: The United States, China, and the Soviet Union, 1948–1972* (Stanford, CA: Stanford University Press, 1990). Chang argues that well into the 1950s American leadership believed that the PRC would simply collapse and the Chinese people would rise up and turn to America for help.

12. Tucker, *Taiwan, Hong Kong, and the United States*, 69.

13. "Act for International Development," Title IV, Sec. 402 (c), Public Law 535, passed June 5, 1950.

14. Walter Johnson and Francis J. Colligan, *The Fulbright Program: A History* (Chicago: University of Chicago Press, 1965), viii.

15. Among the copious accounts and analysis of the February 28 Incident, the following reflect key perspectives: George Kerr, *Formosa Betrayed* (Boston: Houghton Mifflin, 1965); Lai Tse-han, Ramon H. Myers, and Wei Wou, *A Tragic Beginning: The Taiwan Uprising of February 28, 1947* (Stanford, CA: Stanford University Press, 1991); Stephane Corcuff, ed., *Memories of the Future: National Identity Issues and the Search for a New Taiwan* (Armonk, NY: M. E. Sharpe, 2002). The terms of Taiwan's transfer from Japanese to Nationalist control are still disputed today by China, which regards the island as a renegade province. The Taiwanese Chinese had initially welcomed Nationalist rule but quickly resumed their campaign for independence or even protectorate status with the United States.

16. Author's interview with Lily and Burton Levin, January 8, 2011. Levin served in the American Embassy in Taiwan evaluating visa applications during the mid-1950s.

17. May-Lee and Winberg Chai, *The Girl from Purple Mountain: Love, Honor, War, and One Family's Journey from China to America* (New York: Thomas Dunne Books, 2002), 255.

18. Chung-ping Chang, "The United Board for Christian Higher Education in Asia in the Development of Tunghai University in Taiwan, 1955–1980" (PhD dissertation, Southern Illinois University, 1982), 14.

19. Expressions of Taiwanese identity, along with political organization, remained suppressed through the late 1980s when Chiang Kai-shek's son and successor, Chiang Ching-kuo, ended martial law and allowed the island to democratize. The February 28 Incident remains the foundational event for the Taiwan independence movement. Many political dissidents fled abroad to Japan, the United States, and Hong Kong but returned after the lifting of martial law.

20. Dominic Meng-hsuan Yang and Mau-kuei Chang, "Understanding the Nuances of *Waishengren*: History and Agency," *China Perspectives* 3 (2010): 119.

21. Ibid.; also see Dominic Meng-hsuan Yang, "Wuling niandai waisheng zhongxia jieceng junmin zai Taiwan de shehui shi chutan—dangguo, jieji, shenfun liudong, shehui mailuo, jianlun waisheng da qianxi zai lisan yanjiu zhong de dingwei" (A preliminary study of the mid- and lower-class mainlanders in Taiwan in the 1950s—party-state, social mobility, social network, and discussion of the great mainland exodus in diaspora studies), in *Zhonghua minguo liuwang Taiwan liushinian ji zhanhou Taiwan guoji chujing* (The sixtieth anniversary of the Republic of China's exile in Taiwan and the international status of postwar Taiwan), ed. Chen Yi-shen et al. (Taipei: Qianwei, 2010), 560–74.

22. Yang and Chang, "Understanding the Nuances," 120.

23. Tucker, *Taiwan, Hong Kong, and the United States*, 69.

24. Yang and Chang, "Understanding the Nuances," 121. Yang and Chang cite evidence from *Free China* (*Ziyou Zhongguo*) and publications from various mainlander native place associations indicating a transition from "sojourning" (*luju*) mentalities in the 1950s to "cultural nostalgia" (*wenhua huaixiang*) during the early 1960s. These shifting expectations contributed to the founding of *Free China* magazine by liberal intellectuals who sought democratic reforms as an alternative to authoritarian rule on Taiwan.

25. Perry Anderson, "Stand-Off in Taiwan," *London Review of Books* 26, 11 (June 3, 2004).

26. Shu Yuan Chang, "China or Taiwan: The Political Crisis of the Chinese Intellectual," *Amerasia Journal* (Fall 1973): 47–81.

27. Charles H. C. Kao (Gao Xijun), *Brain Drain: A Case Study of China* (Taipei: Mei Ya Publications, 1971), 19. Also see Chang, "China or Taiwan," 77.

28. Iris Chang, *The Chinese in America: A Narrative History* (New York: Penguin, 2003), 302.

29. Dori Jones Yang, ed., *Voices of the Second Wave: Chinese Americans in Seattle* (Seattle: East-West Insights, 2011), 246.

30. Leslie Chang, *Beyond the Narrow Gate: The Journey of Four Chinese Women from the Middle Kingdom to Middle America* (New York: Dutton, 1999), 76.

31. Chang does not mention whether Suzanne received a scholarship arranged by Archbishop Yu Bin.

32. Author's interview with Burton and Lily Levin, January 8, 2011.

33. Father Chan organized social events that helped the students meet and find eligible marriage partners. Many of the male students became engineers and academics and supported middle-class families. Chan oriented students to work in the Catskills through "lectures in the ballroom . . . introducing them to the Jewish culture they would encounter. . . . He demystified lox, gefilte fish, and matzoh ball soup, and . . . he visited them throughout the summer to make sure they were all right."

34. "Information on U.S. Efforts to Influence Youth on Taiwan," Paul Popple to Leonard L. Bacon, March 11, 1964, "Educ. & Cul. Exch. R.C.: EDX 10 Foreign Student Program 1964," RG 59, Department of State, Bureau of Far Eastern Affairs (FE), Office of East Asian Affairs (FE/EA) Central Files, 1947–1964, Box 1, E5315, Secret Declassified NND842810, 2. The United States also trained an estimated 12,000 members of the Chinese armed forces. See p. 5.

35. Ibid., 3.

36. Walter H. Judd papers, Box 99, folder 2, "State Department; Educ. & info. Programs/Chinese and Korean Students, 1947–1955," Hoover Institution Archives.

37. In 1952 most students were in New York (563), California (353), Illinois (206), Massachusetts (140), Michigan (137), Pennsylvania (124), Ohio (106), Indiana (101), or Washington (100). Lee, *Chinese in the United States*, 90.

38. Susan Greenhalgh, "Networks and Their Nodes: Urban Society on Taiwan," *China Quarterly* 99 (September 1984): 531–32. Greenhalgh observed the prevalence of emigration: "Just how many of Taiwan's families have gained foot-

holds abroad is unclear. What is clear is that the internationalization of Taiwan's society is not limited to the upper class . . . [where it] is most advanced. . . . Mainlanders are believed to have even more members overseas than Taiwanese" (550).

39. Chang, "China or Taiwan," 54.

40. Ibid., 53.

41. Kung, *Chinese in American Life*, 118, 120–21.

42. *Statutes at Large* 72:546; Hing, *Making and Remaking Asian America*, 282n28.

43. Zolberg, *A Nation by Design*, 324. Chapter 6 of Kung, *Chinese in American Life*, is dedicated to "Relief through Private Legislation." Appealing for immigration relief through congressional representatives seems to have been a generally known strategy although with low chances of success. See Yang, *Voices of the Second Wave*, 321, for an example.

44. For a more extended discussion of these legal shifts, see my article, "The Disappearance of America's Cold War Chinese Refugees," *Journal of American Ethnic History* 31, 4 (Summer 2012): 12–33.

45. Author's interview with Edward Huang, May 22, 2005.

46. Yang, *Voices of the Second Wave*, 310.

47. Ibid., 247.

48. Zolberg, *A Nation by Design*, 304.

49. Cited in ibid., 314. This coalition stressed individual qualifications as fundamentally more democratic and asserted that that "integration" had been happening among southern and eastern Europeans, thereby invalidating the need for quotas based on national origins.

50. Myer Feldman letter to Philip Hart, January 4, 1963, and Philip Hart letter to Theodore Sorensen, December 14, 1962, Subject Files, LE/IM1, Box 483, John F. Kennedy Library and Archives.

51. "A New Immigration Proposal: A Fact Sheet on S. 747 Introduced in the United States Senate on February 7, 1963," White House Files, Subject Files, LE/IM, Box 482, John F. Kennedy Library and Archives 260.

52. "Principal Provisions of State Department's Tentative Proposal for Immigration Legislation," May 27, 1963, from Bureau of Security and Consular Affairs, ibid.

53. Lyndon Johnson letter to Kennedy, July 23, 1963, ibid., 5.

54. In 1966 Lim P. Lee became the first Chinese American postmaster-general of San Francisco through his close connections to local power brokers John and Phil Burton.

55. "The Law That Stinks," *Chinese World*, June 8, 1963, LE/IM1, Subject Files, Box 483, John F. Kennedy Library and Archives. During a trip to Washington, DC, Hatcher arranged for Lee to tour the White House and meet Kennedy's aid, Myer Feldman. Lim P. Lee letter to Andrew Hatcher, May 18, 1963, and Hatcher to Lee, May 22, 1963, ibid.

56. Cheng, *Citizens of Asian America*, 160–66.

57. J. K. Choy, "The Discriminatory Chinese Immigration Laws," December 1, 1961, Subject Files, LE/IM1, Box 483, John F. Kennedy Library and Archives, 4–5.

58. "Summary Report on the Anticipated Effect of the Proposed Elimination of the Asia-Pacific Triangle Provisions from Our Immigration Laws," 1963, Bureau

of Security and Consular Affairs, White House Files, Subject Files, LE/IM, Box 482, John F. Kennedy Library and Archives.

59. Ngai, *Impossible Subjects*, 260.

60. See Michael Davis, "Impetus for Immigration Reform: Asian Refugees in the Cold War," *Journal of American-East Asian Relations* 7, 3–4 (1998): 147, 149–51. Also see Reimers, *Still the Golden Door*. The earlier champion of Asian immigration, Walter Judd, lost his congressional seat in 1962.

61. Oh, *The Asian Brain Drain*, 6.

62. Bill Ong Hing, *Defining America through Immigration Policy* (Philadelphia: Temple University Press, 2004), 95–96.

B.A. Garside, the long-term ARCI executive director, kept track of the 1965 reforms noting the drop in priorities of professional and skilled workers from 1 to 3 and 6. He received an invitation to attend the Oct. 3 signing ceremony on Liberty Island from the White House. See ARCI Records, Box 1, "Information re: 1965 Immigration Law;" Box 15, "State Department—ORM" 1/1/1961 through, Oct. 2, 1965 telegram from Lawrence F. O'Brien to Garside, Hoover Institution Archives.

63. Willard B. Devlin, oral history interview, Georgetown University, October 15, 1986, 11.

64. Brinley Thomas, "'Modern' Migration," in *The Brain Drain*, ed. Walter Adams (New York: Macmillan, 1968), 37.

65. "Britain: The Brain Drain," *Time*, March 15, 1963.

66. Oh, *The Asian Brain Drain*, 1.

67. Kao, *Brain Drain*, 10.

68. Research and Technical Programs Subcommittee of the Committee on Government Operations, House of Representatives, *The Brain Drain of Scientists, Engineers, and Physicians from the Developing Countries into the United States* (Washington, DC: GPO, 1968), 2. Absolute numbers of international students increased as well: 5,373 (1956), 5,956 (1962), 7,896 (1963), 7,810 (1964), 7,198 (1965), 9,534 (1966), 15,272 (1967).

69. "Proportion of Scientific Immigrants Who Entered United States Originally as Students with F Visa, Fiscal 1967," in ibid., 3.

70. Cited in Walter Adams, "Introduction" in Adams, *The Brain Drain*, 1.

71. Chang, "China or Taiwan," 48–49, 51.

72. Ngai, *Impossible Subjects*, 260, 262.

73. Subcommittee on Immigration and Naturalization of the Committee on the Judiciary, U.S. Senate. *International Migration of Talent and Skills* (Washington, DC: n.p., 1968), 1.

74. Ibid., 1–2.

75. Adams, *The Brain Drain*, 4–5.

76. Ibid., 248–62. Former U.S. senator Paul Douglas affirmed Adams's defense of the United States in his introduction to *The Brain Drain*, baldly claiming: "The American Government has not sought to stimulate this migration." Ibid., xii.

77. V. M. Dandekar, "India," in Adams, *The Brain Drain*, 227–29. Brain drain had critics in advanced economies. The Reverend William J. Gibbons, director of the Scientific Manpower Survey at Fordham University, testified before a House

committee that refugee resettlement programs had privileged applicants with special skills, contributing to the brain drain even in humanitarian relief efforts. Gibbons cited Brinley Thomas in finding the United States responsible "to take major action to counter 'brain drain' " although he acknowledged the complexity of the situation. "A very delicate balance exists between proper concern for human freedom and initiative, and the meeting of needs for specialized manpower in developing countries." Research and Technical Programs Subcommittee, *The Brain Drain of Scientists*, 6, 11, 13.

78. Thomas, "'Modern' Migration," 29, 40, 37, 47–48.

79. Adams, *The Brain Drain*, 248–62.

80. Das, *Brain Drain*, 88, 91.

81. Executive Yuan, Guidance Committee for Students Educated Abroad, *Fudao liuxuesheng huiguo fuwu shouce* (Service guidebook to guide returned overseas Chinese students) (1963), 24.

82. Das, *Brain Drain Controversy*, 97. See *The Asian Student*, February 22, 1969, 3; November 21, 1970, 7; *China Post* "How To Stop Brain Drain," November 4, 1970; Kao, *Brain Drain*. During the 1960s Taiwan had limited need for graduates in the humanities, social sciences, and even agriculture but strong demand for "engineering, science and medical students." Of 315,000 people with college education, only 2,000 were unemployed in 1971.

83. Kao, *Brain Drain*, 122. Taiwan's Fifth Economic Development Plan for 1968 through 1972 projected shortfalls of 18,000 college graduates and postgraduates. In the early 1970s Taiwan experienced shortages of experts in education, engineering, sciences, medicine, and other fields, with surpluses only in the humanities.

84. Of these eight, only Chu and Tsien were born in the United States and the other six are immigrants. Tsien is related through his father to Qian Xuesen and several other successful scientists.

85. Ibid., xx.

86. Sun Chen, "Investment in Education and Human Resource Development in Postwar Taiwan," in *Cultural Change in Postwar Taiwan*, ed. Stevan Harrell and Chun-chieh Huang (Boulder, CO: Westview Press, 1994), 102. See also Yuan-li Wu, "Capital Flow between the United States and China: Conceptual Reorientation," in *ROC and USA 1911–81*, ed. Tung-hsin Sun and Morris Wei-hsin Tien (Monograph Series No. 2. American Studies Association of the Republic of China, 1982).

87. Chen, "Investment in Education," 98–99.

88. Ibid., 95–96, 100.

89. According to the Overseas Chinese Affairs Commission (OCAC), about 391,000 Taiwan residents immigrated to the United States from 1949 to 2000. Pei-te Lien, "Ethnic Homeland and Chinese Americans: Conceiving a Transnational Political Network," in *Chinese Transnational Networks*, ed. Tan Chee-beng (London: Routledge, 2007), 111.

90. Chen, "Investment in Education," 103–4.

91. Edward Gargan, "High-Tech Taiwanese Come Home," *New York Times*, July 19, 1994. The geographer Shengling Chang has compared the homes, neighborhood settings, and community resources of Taiwanese "astronauts," so called

because they spend so much time shuttling over the Pacific between Hsinchu and Silicon Valley. See *The Global Silicon Valley Home: Lives and Landscapes within Taiwanese American Transpacific Culture* (Stanford, CA: Stanford University Press, 2006).

92. Chang, *The Chinese in America*, 304–5.

93. Suzanne Berger and Richard K. Lester, "Globalization and the Future of the Taiwan Miracle," in *Global Taiwan: Building Competitive Strengths in a New International Economy*, ed. Berger and Lester (Armonk, NY: M. E. Sharpe, 2005), 3.

94. Ibid., 4.

95. Chia-ling Kuo, "The Chinese on Long Island—A Pilot Study," *Phylon* 31, 3 (1970): 285, 283.

96. Klein, *Cold War Orientalism*, 40.

97. Charlotte Brooks, "Sing Sheng vs. Southwood: Residential Integration in Cold War California," *Pacific Historical Review* 73, 3 (2004): 463–64, 467–70, 474, 492. Brooks argues that "numerous white Californians still saw Asian Americans as foreigners, but with Japan, South Korea, the Philippines, and Taiwan now allies, and the rest of Asia seemingly up for grabs, the significance of being 'foreign' had changed since the early twentieth century. 'Foreignness' set Asian Americans apart from African Americans, Mexican Americans, and other non-white Californians" thereby strengthening their cases against residential discrimination" (489).

98. Peter S. Li, *Occupational Mobility and Kinship Assistance: A Study of Chinese Immigrants in Chicago* (San Francisco: R&E Research Associates, 1978), 52.

99. Greenhalgh, "Networks and Their Nodes," 546–47.

100. Chang, *Beyond the Narrow Gate*, 279, 270.

101. Bai Xianyong, "Winter Night," in *Wandering in the Garden, Waking from a Dream*, edited by George Kao and translated by Bai Xianyong and Patia Yasin (Bloomington: Indiana University Press, 1982), 172–88.

102. Peter Kwong, *The New Chinatown* (New York: Hill and Wang, 1987).

103. Kuo, "The Chinese on Long Island," 286.

104. In 1961 a Chinese Embassy survey found that more than 1,300 ethnic Chinese were faculty at 88 U.S. institutions of higher learning, including 30 department heads, 130 full professors, and more than 300 associate professors. Harvard, Princeton, and Yale employed a total of 98 Chinese professors. Sung, *Mountain of Gold*, 252.

105. Monaghan, "Lost in Place." Tuan's two brothers are both physics professors.

106. Tuan did not reveal these aspects of his personal life until retirement and publication of several memoirs and personal writings. See *Who Am I?* (1999). He credits his impartiality as an interpreter of "the big picture" to the multiple layers of his marginal positionality, observing: "each of us, in fact, is a minority person—a minority of one. It is when we don't think of ourselves as bound to a particular ethnicity or culture, it is when we see ourselves in all our irreplaceable individuality, that, paradoxically, we regain a sense of the centrality of our being and our duty as such a being to our kin, neighbor, and humankind." In Tuan's view, his outsider status *is* the source of his deepest humanity. See *The Last Launch: Messages in the Bottle* (Staunton, VA: George F. Thompson, 2014), 146–

47. I thank Yi-fu Tuan and Steve Hoelscher for sharing this manuscript with me in advance of publication.

107. Hing, *Making and Remaking Asian America*, 48; Kung, *Chinese in American Life*, 114, table 21.

108. American-born Chu holds affiliations with both the Academia Sinica in Taiwan and the Chinese Academy of Sciences in China. Tsien has not accepted these Chinese honors.

109. Wu and Li, *A Single Tear*, 341, 359. On the occasion of their reunion, Wu compared the hero's welcome extended to Li, who had chosen to pursue his career away from China, and his own marginal status and decades of persecution as a Western-educated intellectual living under communist rule.

110. Yi-fu Tuan, *Coming Home to China* (Minneapolis: University of Minnesota Press, 2007).

111. AnnaLe Saxenian, *The New Argonauts: Regional Advantage in a Global Economy* (Cambridge, MA: Harvard University Press, 2006), 6, 7–8.

112. Collier, "Migration Hurts the Homeland."

Chapter 9. Conclusion

1. Kirk Semple, "In a Shift, Biggest Wave of Migrants Is Now Asian," *New York Times*, June 18, 2012; "The Rise of Asian Americans," Pew Research: Social & Demographic Trends. http://pewsocialtrends.org/2012/06/19/the-rise-of-asian-americans/. The Pew Report draws on 2010 census data and a survey of 3,511 households conducted in English and seven Asian languages.

2. Sudip Bhattacharya, "Caught in the Middle: Asian Immigrants Struggle to Stay in America," April 8, 2013, http://www.cnn.com/2013/04/08/politics/asian-american-immigration. Bhattacharya lists the total Asian American population at 17.3 million, of which 1.3 million are resident illegally, which tallies to about 10 percent of Asian immigrants.

3. "The Rise of Asian Americans," 1. The report did acknowledge that there are higher than average poverty rates among Koreans, Vietnamese, Chinese, and "Other Asians," while Indians, Japanese, and Filipinos have lower rates.

4. Ibid., 1, 18.

5. Ibid., 1.

6. Aihwa Ong, *Buddha Is Hiding: Refugees, Citizenship, the New America* (Berkeley: University of California Press, 2003), 9.

7. Saxenian, *The New Argonauts*, 6, 5.

8. Ong, *Buddha Is Hiding*, 12.

9. "The Rise of Asian Americans," 63. The percentages of non-Asian recent immigrants with college degrees steadily increased as well, although not by as much as Asians, growing from 19.6 percent to 1980 to 29.7 percent in 2010.

10. According to a 2002 report issued by the Taiwanese Overseas Chinese Affairs Committee, in 1990, 41 percent of Taiwanese Americans emigrated to study, 30 percent for jobs, and 20 percent for family-related reasons. Of those age twenty-five and above, 35 percent had college degrees and 43 percent had advanced

degrees. Lung Wen-pin and Huang Guo-nan, *Taiwan ji liang'an sandi huaren renkou tuigu fangfa—lilun goujian yu shizheng tantao (yi Meiguo wei lie)* (Methods for estimating the population of Chinese from Taiwan, PRC, and Hong Kong using the American example—discussion of theoretical structures and evidence) (Taipei: Overseas Chinese Affairs Commission, 2002), 25.

11. Min Zhou, "Chinese: Once Excluded, Now Ascendant," in *The New Face of Asian Pacific America: Numbers, Diversity, and Change in the 21st Century*, ed. Eric Lai and Dennis Arguelles (San Francisco: AsianWeek, 2003), 41.

12. Eric Lai, "A People of Their Own: Taiwanese Americans," in ibid., 43.

13. "The Rise of Asian Americans."

14. William Petersen, "Success Story, Japanese-American Style," *New York Times Magazine* (January 9, 1966); "Success Story of One Minority Group in U.S.," *U.S. News & World Report* (December 26, 1966); and Wu, *The Color of Success*.

15. Anna Quindlen, "The Drive to Excel," *New York Times Magazine*, February 22, 1987.

16. The March 1997 issue of the *National Review* featured stereotypical caricatures of the Clintons and Al Gore, complete with queue and buck teeth, under the title "The Manchurian Candidate," evoking the paranoid conspiracy film from 1962 about brainwashing and planned presidential assassination by North Korean communists.

17. Lars-Erik Nelson, "Washington: The Yellow Peril," *New York Review of Books*, July 15, 1999.

18. See Wen Ho Lee and Helen Zia, *My Country versus Me: The First-hand Account by the Los Alamos Scientist Who Was Falsely Accused of Being a Spy* (New York: Hyperion, 2001). Lee lost his retirement accounts when fired but in June 2006 won a $1.6 million settlement from the U.S. government and various press outlets for violations of privacy. See also Sam Dillon, "US Slips in Attracting the World's Best Students," *New York Times*, December 21, 2004. Dillon describes a decline of 28 percent in international student visas in 2004 due to greater difficulty with additional immigration screening after September 11, 2001. In particular, apart from students from the Middle East, Chinese students faced more delays in their visa processing. The explanation was that many specialize in the sciences, which triggers a screening process "intended to prevent the transfer of sensitive technology." One congressional study found that more than half of visa investigations in one three-month period in 2003 concerned Chinese students. Chinese student applications fell 45 percent. Meanwhile, more international students went to Britain, Germany, and Singapore.

19. "The Rise of Asian Americans."

20. Ibid., 63. The next highest rates of college-educated are Koreans at 69.5, Japanese at 67.6, Filipinos at 57.8, then Chinese at 56.1.

21. Philip G. Altbach, "The Giants Awake: Higher Education Systems in China and India," *Economic and Political Weekly* 44, 23 (June 5–12, 2009): 39, 47; Pawan Agarwal, "Epilogue: Higher Education in India—the Twelfth Plan and Beyond," in *A Half-Century of Indian Higher Education: Essays by Philip G. Altbach*, ed. Pawan Agarwal (New Delhi: Sage India, 2012), 596, cites a figure of

15.2 percent for 2006–2007 and an estimated 20.2 percent for 2011–2012. I thank Anand Yang for these references.

22. "Indian Americans Third Largest Asian Community in US," *Times of India*, March 22, 2012. Vietnamese are now the fourth largest Asian American group, but many have entered through refugee status.

23. This pre-World War II peak occurred in 1928–1929; numbers then dropped during the 1930s. *Unofficial Ambassadors* (1929), 11.

24. Ross Bassett, "Aligning India in the Cold War Era: Indian Technical Elites, the Indian Institute of Technology at Kanpur, and Computing in India and the United States," *Technology and Culture* 50, 4 (October 2009): 788–89. Bassett describes the leading role of American-educated scientists and educators in developing Indian research institutions and the computing industry and their collaborations with American companies such as IBM.

25. "The Rise of Asian Americans," 62. The total number of international students was 723,277. International student numbers have increased steadily since World War II, rising from just over 10,000 in 1946.

26. Ibid., 26.

27. See Catherine Ceniza Choy, *Empire of Care: Nursing and Migration in Filipino American History* (Durham, NC: Duke University Press, 2003).

28. Altbach, "The Giants Awake," 50.

29. "The Rise of Asian Americans," 27. Some 28 percent of college graduates in India specialized in science or engineering in 2009. Pawan Agarwal, *Indian Higher Education: Envisioning the Future* (New York: Sage, 2009), 204.

30. Characteristics of H-1B Specialty Occupation Workers: Fiscal Year 2011 Annual Report to Congress, October 1, 2010–September 30, 2011 (March 12, 2012), U.S. Department of Homeland Security, U.S. Citizenship and Immigration Services, 2–3. An emendation in 2004 exempted from the annual cap up to 20,000 H-1B petitions for aliens with U.S.-earned M.A. or higher degrees. Certain entities are also exempt from the cap, such as higher education institutions and affiliated nonprofits, and nonprofit research or governmental research institutions. I thank Richard Jung for this reference. The program does include protections for domestic workers. Each prospective employer must submit to the Department of Labor a Labor Condition Application "attesting that the foreign worker's employment does not adversely impact similarly employed U.S. workers" who must be paid the prevailing wage and labor under comparable working conditions. See Deborah Woo, "Labor, Workplace, and the Glass Ceiling," in *The New Face of Asian America: Numbers, Diversity, and Change in the 21st Century*, ed. Eric Lai and Dennis Arguelles (San Francisco: Asianweek, 2003), 228; and Hing. *Defining America through Immigration Policy*, 110.

31. Characteristics of H-1B Specialty Occupation Workers, 3–4.

32. Hing, *Defining America through Immigration Policy*, 108.

33. Characteristics of H-1B Specialty Occupation Workers, 4–6.

34. Ibid., 10, 13.

35. Somini Sengupta, "Engineers See a Path Out of a Green Card Limbo," *New York Times*, May 22, 2013, citing a Brookings Institution report. In 2014

the White House proposed measures to allow spouses of H-1B visa holders to work as well, to ameliorate long-standing complaints.

36. Saxenian, *The New Argonauts*, 6–7. The economist Paul Collier points out that the emigration of knowledge workers affects large and small countries differently. "Many poor countries have too much emigration. . . . The big winners from the emigration of the educated have been China and India. Because each has over a billion people, proportionately few people leave." In comparison, Ghana's "rate of skilled emigration [is] 12 times that of China," while Haiti "loses around 85 percent of its educated youth, a rate that is debilitating." "Migration Hurts the Homeland," *New York Times*, November 29, 2013.

37. Subcommittee on Immigration and Naturalization of the Committee on the Judiciary, U.S. Senate. *International Migration of Talent and Skills* (Washington, DC: GPO, 1968), 3.

38. John McCain uses this description for immigration reforms proposed in 2013 that included expanding the H-1B visa program and reducing family reunification percentages but also enacting Dream Act terms. A 1912 proposed measure met with significant resistance. Bill Keller, "Liberals vs. Immigration Reform," *New York Times*, July 7, 2013.

39. Thomas L. Friedman, "The Open-Door Bailout," *New York Times*, February 11, 2009. Friedman is citing research by Vivek Wadhwa, a Harvard Law School Labor and Worklife Program research associate, showing that more than half of Silicon Valley's start-ups were founded by immigrants in the past decade, employing 450,000 workers. I thank Maddalena Marinari for directing me to Friedman's editorials.

40. Thomas L. Friedman, "Invent, Invent, Invent," *New York Times*, June 28, 2009.

41. Haeyoun Park, "Recession's Toll on Hispanic Immigrants," *New York Times*, March 24, 2009. Pew Hispanic Center estimated there were 11.9 million illegal immigrants in the United States in 2008; 59 percent were born in Mexico and 22 percent in other Latin American countries, with 12 percent originating from Asia.

42. Karthick Ramakrishnan and Farah Z. Ahmad, *Immigration: Part of the 'State of Asian Americans and Pacific Islanders' Series* (Riverside, CA: Center for American Progress, 2014), 9.

43. The Latino vote reached 10 percent in 2012, up from 6 percent in 2000, and constituted a critical difference in battleground states such as New Mexico, Nevada, Colorado, and Florida. Julia Preston and Fernanda Santos, "A Record Latino Turnout, Solidly Backing Obama," *New York Times*, November 7, 2012. Some 73 percent of Asian Americans voted for Obama in 2012 and constituted 3 percent of the vote, with more than 60 percent of those surveyed supporting comprehensive immigration reform. See Asian American Legal Defense and Education Fund, "New Findings: Asian American Vote in 2012 Varied by Ethnic Group and Geographic Location," January 17, 2013, http://aaldef.org/press-releases/press-release/new-findings-asian-american-vote-in-2012-varied-widely-by-ethnic-group-and-geographic-location.html.

44. Ngai, *Impossible Subjects*, 4–5. The emphasis is Ngai's.

45. Jeremy W. Peters, "House Votes to Ease Visa Limits for Some Foreign Workers," *New York Times*, November 30, 2012.

46. C.C.W., "When the Chinese Exclusion Act Will Be Repealed," *Chinese Students' Bulletin* 2, 4 (March 1907): 83–86.

47. Ong, *Buddha Is Hiding*, 9.

Bibliography

Archival and Other Primary Sources
Manuscript Collections

Academia Historica, Xindian, Taiwan
Archives of the National Resources Commission (Guojia ziyuan weiyuanhui)
Columbia University, New York
Burke Library Archives
C. V. Starr East Asian Library
Harvard University, Cambridge, MA
Fitch Collection, Harvard-Yenching Library
Papers of Anna Chennault, Schlesinger Library
Hoover Institution Archives, Palo Alto, CA
Aid Refugee Chinese Intellectuals Inc. (ARCI) Collection
T. V. Soong Papers
Walter Judd Papers
United States National Archives and Records Administration
John F. Kennedy Library, Boston
U.S. Department of State, Record Group 59, College Park, MD
U.S. Department of State, Records of Foreign Service Posts, Record Group 84, College Park, MD
U.S. Immigration and Naturalization Service, Record Group 85, Washington DC
University of California, Berkeley, Ethnic Studies Library
Him Mark Lai Collection
University of Washington, Seattle, Special Collections
Warren Magnuson Papers

Published Government Documents

Characteristics of H-1B Specialty Occupation Workers: Fiscal Year 2011 Annual Report to Congress, October 1, 2010–September 30, 2011 (March 12, 2012). U.S. Department of Homeland Security, U.S. Citizenship and Immigration Services.
Committee on Educational Interchange Policy. *Chinese Students in the United States, 1948–55: A Study in Government Policy.* New York: n.p., 1956.
Committee on Immigration and Naturalization, House of Representatives, 78th Congress. Repeal of the Chinese Exclusion Acts: Hearings on HR 1882 and HR 2309: Bills to Repeal the Chinese Exclusion Acts, to Put the Chinese on a Quota Basis, and to Permit Their Naturalization," May 19, 20, 26, 27 and June 2 and 3, 1943.
Research and Technical Programs Subcommittee of the Committee on Government Operations, House of Representatives. *The Brain Drain of Scientists,*

Engineers, and Physicians from the Developing Countries into the United States. Washington DC: GPO, 1968.

Subcommittee on Immigration and Naturalization. Report of the Committee on the Judiciary, United States Senate, 85th Congress, 2d Session, March 5, 1959. Washington, DC: GPO, 1959. 86th Congress, 1st Session, Report No. 78.

Subcommittee on Immigration and Naturalization of the Committee on the Judiciary, U.S. Senate. *International Migration of Talent and Skills.* Washington, DC: GPO, 1968.

U.S. Department of Labor, Bureau of Immigration. Annual Report of the Commissioner General of Immigration to the Secretary of Labor, 1931. Washington, DC: GPO 1931.

U.S. Senate. "Refugee Problem in Hong Kong and Macao." Hearings before the Subcommittee to Investigate Problems Connected with Refugees and Escapees of the Committee of the Judiciary, United States Senate, 87th Congress, 2d Session. Washington DC: GPO, 1962.

Newspapers, Periodicals, and Serials

Annual Report of the Director (Institute for International Education)
Bulletin (China Institute in America)
China Handbook
Chinese Recorder
The Chinese Students' Bulletin
Chinese Students' Monthly
Congressional Record
Life
News Bulletin (Institute of Pacific Relations)
New York Times
Open Doors
Pacific Studies
Time
The Unofficial Ambassadors (Committee on Friendly Relations among Foreign Students)

Published Primary Sources

Brinkley, William. "The Agonizing Odyssey of Two People in Love." *Life* 40, 10 (March 5, 1956): 100–102, 165–74.

Chao, Buwei Yang. *How to Cook and Eat in Chinese.* New York: John Day, 1945.

Committee on Friendly Relations among Foreign Students. "Technical Trainees from Overseas." New York: Committee on Friendly Relations among Foreign Students, 1945.

Executive Yuan, Guidance Committee for Students Educated Abroad. *Fudao liuxuesheng huiguo fuwu shouce* (Service guidebook to guide returned overseas Chinese students). 1963.

Fitch, Geraldine. *Formosa Beachhead.* Chicago: H. Regnery, 1953.

Flower Drum Song. Directed by Henry Koster. Universal Studios, 1961.

Gibson, Otis. *The Chinese in America.* New York: Arno Press, 1978 reprint (1877).

Hambro, Edvard. "Chinese Refugees in Hong Kong." *Phylon Quarterly* 18, 1 (1957): 69–81.

Kennedy, John F. *A Nation of Immigrants.* New York: Anti-Defamation League of B'nai B'rith, 1959.

Lee, C. Y. *The Flower Drum Song with an introduction by David Henry Hwang.* New York: Penguin, 2000 reprint (1957).

Lin, Qingfen, ed. "Taiwan zhanhou chuqi liuxue jiaoyu shiliao huibian," Vols. 1–5 (Documentary collection on students overseas of postwar Taiwan). Xindian, Taiwan: Academia Historica, 2007.

Mitchell, Ruth. *Foreign Students and the Immigration Law of the United States.* New York: Institute of International Education, 1930.

Open Doors: Report on International Educational Exchange, 1948–2004. CD-ROM. New York: Institute for International Education, 2005.

Song, Meiling. *We Chinese Women: Speeches and Writings during the First United Nations Year by Mayling Soong Chiang (Madame Chiang Kai-shek).* New York: Chinese News Service and John Day, 1943.

Speer, William. *The Oldest and the Newest Empire: China and the United States.* Hartford, CT: S. S. Scranton, 1870.

Yang, Ching-Kun. *Meet the USA: Handbook for Foreign Students in the United States.* New York: Institute of International Education, 1945.

Yieh, Tsung-kao "The Adjustment Problems of Chinese Graduate Students in American Universities." PhD dissertation, University of Chicago, 1934.

Interviews, Oral Histories, and Memoirs

Burton, Lily, and Levin Burton. Interview by Madeline Hsu. Wellesley, MA, January 8, 2011.

Chai, May-lee and Winberg. *The Girl from Purple Mountain: Love, Honor, War, and One Family's Journey from China to America.* New York: Thomas Dunne Books, 2002.

Chao, Buwei Yang. *Autobiography of a Chinese Woman.* New York: John Day, 1947.

Devlin, Willard B. Oral history interview. Georgetown University, October 15, 1986.

Duggan, Stephen. *A Professor at Large.* New York: Macmillan, 1943.

Fitch, George Ashmore. *My Eighty Years in China.* Taipei, Taiwan: Mei Ya Publications, 1974.

Garside, B. A. *Within the Four Seas.* New York: Fredrick C. Beil, 1985.

Goetz, Louis. Interview by Charles Stuart Kennedy. July 23, 1992. Association for Diplomatic Studies and Training, Foreign Affairs Oral History Project, Abba Schwartz Award Program, John F. Kennedy Library, Boston.

Huang, Edward. Interview by Madeline Hsu. Lafayette, CA, May 22, 2005.

Hu-Dehart, Evelyn. Interview by Madeline Hsu. Austin, TX, June 29, 2010, February 9, 2013.

Jan, Flora Belle. *Unbound Spirit: Letters of Flora Belle Jan*. Urbana: University of Illinois Press, 2009.

Jiang, Menglin. *Tides from the West: A Chinese Autobiography*. New Haven, CT: Yale University Press, 1947.

Liebman, Marvin. *Coming Out Conservative: An Autobiography*. San Francisco: Chronicle Books, 1992.

Meng, Zhi. *Chinese American Understanding: A Sixty-Year Quest*. New York: China Institute of America, 1981.

Miner, Luella, ed. *Two Heroes of Cathay: An Autobiography and a Sketch*. New York: Fleming H. Revell, 1903.

Tuan, Yi-fu. *Coming Home to China*. Minneapolis: University of Minnesota Press, 1999.

———. Interview by Madeline Hsu. Madison, WI, June 25, 2010.

———. *The Last Launch: Messages in the Bottle*. Staunton, VA: George F. Thompson, 2014.

———. *Who Am I? An Autobiography of Emotion, Mind, and Spirit*. Madison: University of Wisconsin Press, 1999.

Wang An with Eugene Linden. *Lessons: An Autobiography*. Reading, MA: Addison-Wesley, 1986.

Wu, Ningkun, and Yikai Li. *A Single Tear: A Family's Persecution, Love, and Endurance in Communist China*. New York: Back Bay Books, 1994.

Yang, Dori Jones, ed. *Voices of the Second Wave: Chinese Americans in Seattle*. Seattle: East-West Insights, 2011.

Yang, Zhenning (Chen-ning Yang). *Selected Papers 1945–1980 with Commentary*. San Francisco: W. H. Freeman, 1983.

Young, Dana. Interview by Madeline Hsu. Austin, TX, November 15, 2012.

Yung, Kuai. "Recollections of the Chinese Educational Mission." N.p., n.d. Courtesy of Dana Young.

Yung, Wing. *My Life in China and America*. New York: Henry Holt, 1909.

Selected Secondary Sources

Adams, Walter, ed. *The Brain Drain*. New York: Macmillan, 1968.

Agarwal, Pawan. "Epilogue: Higher Education in India—the Twelfth Plan and Beyond." In *A Half-Century of Indian Higher Education: Essays by Philip G. Altbach*. Edited by Pawan Agarwal, 595–611. New Delhi: Sage India, 2012.

Altbach, Philip G. "The Giants Awake: Higher Education Systems in China and India." *Economic and Political Weekly* 44, 23 (June 5–12, 2009).

Anderson, Perry. "Stand-Off in Taiwan." *London Review of Books* 26, 11 (June 3, 2004).

Arkush, R. David, and Leo O. Lee, trans. and eds. *Land without Ghosts: Chinese Impressions of America from the Mid-Nineteenth Century to the Present*. Berkeley: University of California Press, 1989.

Asian American Legal Defense and Education Fund. "New Findings: Asian American Vote in 2012 Varied by Ethnic Group and Geographic Location," January

17, 2013. http://aaldef.org/press-releases/press-release/new-findings-asian-amer ican-vote-in-2012-varied-widely-by-ethnic-group-and-geographic-location. html.

Bai, Xianyong. "Winter Night." In *Wandering in the Garden, Waking from a Dream.* Edited by George Kao and translated by Xianyong Bai and Patia Yasin, 172– 88. Bloomington: Indiana University Press, 1982.

Basset, Ross. "Aligning India in the Cold War Era: Indian Technical Elites, the Indian Institute of Technology at Kanpur, and Computing in India and the United States." *Technology and Culture* 50, 4 (October 2009): 783–810.

Bieler, Stacey. *"Patriots" or "Traitors"? A History of American-Educated Chinese Students.* Armonk, NY: M. E. Sharpe, 2004.

Bon Tempo, Carl. *Americans at the Gate: The United States and Refugees during the Cold War.* Princeton, NJ: Princeton University Press, 2008.

Brooks, Charlotte. *Alien Neighbors, Foreign Friends: Asian Americans, Housing, and the Transformation of Urban California.* Chicago: University of Chicago Press, 2009.

———. *Between Mao and McCarthy: Chinese American Politics in the Cold War Years.* Chicago: University of Chicago Press, 2015.

———. "Sing Shen vs. Southwood: Residential Integration in Cold War California." *Pacific Historical Review* 73, 3 (2004): 463–94.

Bu, Liping. *Making the World Like Us: Education, Cultural Expansion, and the American Century.* Westport, CT: Praeger, 2003.

Bullock, Mary Brown. *The Oil Prince's Legacy: Rockefeller Philanthropy in China.* Stanford, CA: Stanford University Press, 2011.

Caniff, Milton. *The Complete Terry and the Pirates, Vol. 2, 1937–1938.* San Diego, CA: IDW, 2007.

Castells, Manuel. *The Rise of the Network Society.* 2nd ed. Oxford: Blackwell, 2000.

Chan, Sucheng. *Asian Americans: An Interpretive History.* Boston: Twayne, 1991.

———, ed. *Entry Denied: Exclusion and the Chinese Community in America, 1882–1943.* Philadelphia: Temple University Press, 1991.

Chang, Chung-ping. "The United Board for Christian Higher Education in Asia in the Development of Tunghai University in Taiwan, 1955–1980." PhD dissertation, Southern Illinois University, 1982.

Chang, Derek. *Citizens of a Christian Nation: Evangelical Missions and the Problem of Race in the Nineteenth Century.* Philadelphia: University of Pennsylvania Press, 2012.

Chang, Gordon. "Asian Immigrants and American Foreign Relations." In *Pacific Passages: The Study of American-East Asian Relations on the Eve of the Twenty-First Century.* Edited by Warren Cohen, 103–118. New York: Columbia University Press, 1996.

———. "China and the Pursuit of America's Destiny: Nineteenth-Century Imagining and Why Immigration Restriction Took So Long." *Journal of Asian American Studies* 15, 2 (June 2012): 145–69.

———. *Friends and Enemies: The United States, China, and the Soviet Union, 1948–1972.* Stanford, CA: Stanford University Press, 1990.

Chang, Leslie. *Beyond the Narrow Gate: The Journey of Four Chinese Women from the Middle Kingdom to Middle America*. New York: Dutton, 1999.

Chang, Shenglin. *The Global Silicon Valley Home: Lives and Landscapes within Taiwanese American Transpacific Culture*. Stanford, CA: Stanford University Press, 2006.

Chang, Shu Yuan. "China or Taiwan: The Political Crisis of the Chinese Intellectual." *Amerasia Journal* (Fall 1973): 47–81.

Chen, Sun. "Investment in Education and Human Resource Development in Postwar Taiwan." In *Cultural Change in Postwar Taiwan*. Edited by Stevan Harrell and Chun-chieh Huang, 91–110. Boulder, CO: Westview Press, 1994.

Chen, Wen-hsien. "Chinese under Both Exclusion and Immigration Laws." PhD dissertation, University of Chicago, 1940.

Cheng, Cindy. *Citizens of Asian America: Democracy and Race during the Cold War*. New York: New York University Press, 2013.

The Chinese Students' Monthly, 1906–1931: A Grand Table of Contents. Washington, DC: Association of Research Libraries, Center for Chinese Studies Research Materials, 1974.

Choy, Catherine Ceniza. *Empire of Care: Nursing and Migration in Filipino American History*. Durham, NC: Duke University Press, 2003.

———. *Global Families: A History of Asian International Adoption in America*. New York: New York University Press, 2013.

Choy, Phillip, Lorraine Dong, and Marlon Hom, eds. *The Coming Man: 19th Century American Perceptions of the Chinese*. Seattle: University of Washington Press, 1995.

Cull, Nicholas. *The Cold War and the United States Information Agency*. Cambridge: Cambridge University Press, 2008.

Daniels, Roger. *Asian America: Chinese and Japanese in the United States since 1850*. Seattle: University of Washington Press, 1988.

Das, Man Singh. *Brain Drain Controversy and International Students*. Lucknow, India: Lucknow Publishing House, 1972.

Davis, Michael. "Impetus for Immigration Reform: Asian Refugees in the Cold War." *Journal of American–East Asian Relations* 7, 3–4 (1998): 127–56.

Dudziak, Mary. *Cold War Civil Rights*. Princeton, NJ: Princeton University Press, 2000.

Edwards, Lee. *Missionary to Freedom: The Life and Times of Walter Judd*. New York: Paragon House, 1990.

Entrikin, J. Nicholas. "Geographer as Humanist." In *Textures of Place*. Edited by Paul C. Adams, Steven Hoelscher, and Karen E. Till, 426–40. Minneapolis: University of Minnesota Press, 2001.

Fairbank, Wilma. *America's Cultural Experiment in China, 1942–1949*. Washington, DC: Bureau of Cultural and Educational Affairs, U.S. Department of State, 1976.

Fenby, Jonathan. *Chiang Kai-shek: China's Generalissimo and the Nation He Lost*. New York: Carroll and Graf, 2003.

Ferree Smith, Richard. "Refugees." *Annals of the American Academy of Political and Social Science*, vol. 367, *The New Immigration* (September 1966): 43–52.

Gabaccia, Donna. *Foreign Relations: American Immigration in Global Perspective*. Princeton, NJ: Princeton University Press, 2012.

Gerstle, Gary. *American Crucible: Race and Nation in the Twentieth Century*. Princeton, NJ: Princeton University Press, 2001.

Greenhalgh, Susan. "Networks and Their Nodes: Urban Society on Taiwan." *China Quarterly* 99 (September 1984): 529–52.

Gyory, Andrew. *Closing the Gate: Race, Politics, and the Chinese Exclusion Act*. Chapel Hill: University of North Carolina Press, 1998.

Hing, Bill Ong. *Defining America through Immigration Policy*. Philadelphia: Temple University Press, 2004.

———. *Making and Remaking Asian America through Immigration Policy, 1850–1990*. Stanford, CA: Stanford University Press, 1993.

Hsu, Madeline Y. "The Disappearance of America's Cold War Chinese Refugees." *Journal of American Ethnic History* 31, 4 (Summer 2012): 12–33.

———. *Dreaming of Gold, Dreaming of Home: Transnationalism and Migration between the United States and Southern China, 1882–1943*. Stanford, CA: Stanford University Press, 2000.

———. "From Chop Suey to Mandarin Cuisine: Fine Dining and the Refashioning of Chinese Ethnicity during the Cold War Era." In *Chinese Americans and the Politics of Race and Culture*. Edited by Sucheng Chan and Madeline Hsu, 173–93. Philadelphia: Temple University Press, 2008.

———. "Refugees as Resources in Aid Refugee Chinese Intellectuals, Inc. (ARCI) Programs to Support Nationalist Taiwan, 1952–1956," for "Global Displacements and Emplacement: The Forced Exile and Resettlement Experiences of Ethnic Chinese Refugees." Special Issue. *Journal of Chinese Overseas* 10, 2 (2014): 137–64.

Hu, Yueh. "The Problem of the Hong Kong Refugees." *Asian Survey* 2, 1 (March 1962): 23–37.

Hubbard, Phil, Rob Kitchin, and Gill Valentine, eds. *Key Thinkers on Space and Place*. London: Sage, 2004.

Hunt, Michael H. "The American Remission of the Boxer Indemnity: A Reappraisal." *Journal of Asian Studies* 31, 3 (May 1972): 539–59.

———. *The Making of a Special Relationship: The United States and China to 1914*. New York: Columbia University Press, 1983.

Hunter, Jane. *The Gospel of Gentility: American Women Missionaries in Turn-of-the-Century China*. New Haven, CT: Yale University Press, 1984.

"Indian Americans Third Largest Asian Community in US." *Times of India*, March 22, 2012. http://articles.timesofindia.indiatimes.com/2012-03-22/other-news/31224360_1_asian-american-population-census-bureau.

Iriye, Akira. *Cultural Internationalism and World Order*. Baltimore: Johns Hopkins University Press, 1997.

———. *Pacific Estrangement: Japanese and American Expansion, 1897–1911*. Cambridge MA: Harvard University Press, 1972.

Jacobsen, Matthew Frye. *Whiteness of a Different Color: European Immigrants and the Alchemy of Race*. Cambridge, MA: Harvard University Press, 1998.

Johnson, Walter, and Francis J. Colligan. *The Fulbright Program: A History*. Chicago: University of Chicago Press, 1965.

Jung, Moon-ho. *Coolies and Cane: Race, Labor, and Sugar in the Age of Emancipation*. Baltimore: Johns Hopkins University Press, 2006.

Kao, Charles H. C. (Gao Xijun). *Brain Drain: A Case Study of China*. Taipei: Mei Ya Publications, 1971.

Kerr, George. *Formosa Betrayed*. Boston: Houghton Mifflin, 1965.

Kirby, William. "Continuity and Change in Modern China: Economic Planning on the Mainland and on Taiwan, 1943–1958." *Australian Journal of Chinese Affairs* 24 (July 1990): 121–41.

———. "Engineers and the State in Modern China." In *Prospects for the Professions in China*. Edited by William Alford and William Kirby, 283–313. London: Taylor and Francis, 2010.

Klein, Christina. *Cold War Orientalism: Asia in the Middlebrow Imagination, 1945–1961*. Berkeley: University of California Press, 2003.

Koen, Ross. *The China Lobby in the United States*. New York: Harper and Row, 1974.

Kramer, Paul. "Empire against Exclusion in Early 20th Century Trans-Pacific History." *Nanzan Review of American Studies* 33 (2011): 13–32.

———. "Is the World Our Campus? International Students and U.S. Global Power in the Long Twentieth Century." Bernath Lecture. *Diplomatic History* 33, 5 (November 2009): 783–88.

———. "Power and Connection: Imperial Histories of the United States in the World." *American Historical Review* (December 2011): 1348–91.

Kung, S. W. *Chinese in American Life: Some Aspects of Their History, Status, Problems, and Contributions*. Seattle: University of Washington Press, 1962.

Kuo, Chia-ling. "The Chinese on Long Island—A Pilot Study." *Phylon* 31, 3 (1970): 280–89.

Kwong, Peter. *The New Chinatown*. New York: Hill and Wang, 1987.

Kwong, Peter, and Dusanka Miscevic. *Chinese Americans: The Immigrant Experience*. Southport, CT: Hugh Lauter Levin Associates, 2000.

La Fargue, Thomas. *China's First One Hundred*. Pullman: State College of Washington, 1942.

La Feber, Walter. *The Clash: A History of U.S.–Japan Relations*. New York: Norton, 1997.

Lai, Eric, and Dennis Arguelles, eds. *The New Face of Asian Pacific America: Numbers, Diversity, and Change in the 21st Century*. San Francisco: AsianWeek, 2003.

Lee, Erika G. *At America's Gates: Chinese Immigration during the Exclusion Era, 1882–1943*. Chapel Hill: University of North Carolina Press, 2003.

Lee, Rose Hum. *The Chinese in the United States of America*. Hong Kong: Oxford University Press, 1960.

———. "The Stranded Chinese in the United States." *Phylon* 19, 2 (1958): 180–94.

Leong, Karen. *The China Mystique: Pearl S. Buck, Anna May Wong, Mayling Soong, and the Transformation of American Orientalism*. Berkeley: University of California Press, 2005.

Lew-Williams, Beth. "Before Restriction Became Exclusion: America's Experiment in Diplomatic Immigration Control." *Pacific Historical Review* 83, 1 (February 2014): 24–56.

Li, Hongshan. *U.S.–China Educational Exchange: State, Society, and Intercultural Relations, 1905–1950.* New Brunswick, NJ: Rutgers University Press, 2008.

Li, Peter S. *Occupational Mobility and Kinship Assistance: A Study of Chinese Immigrants in Chicago.* San Francisco: R&E Research Associates, 1978.

Lien, Pei-te. "Ethnic Homeland and Political Participation: The Case of Chinese Immigrants from Taiwan," paper presented at Annual Meeting of the American Political Science Association, Chicago, September 2–5, 2004.

Ling, Amy, ed. "C. Y. Lee." In *Yellow Light: The Flowering of Asian American Arts*, 11–16. Philadelphia: Temple University Press, 1999.

Liu Boji, *Meiguo huaqiao shi* (History of Chinese in America). Taipei: Liming wenhua shiye gongsi, 1976.

López, Ian Haney. *White by Law: The Legal Construction of Race.* New York: New York University Press, 1996.

Lung Wen-pin and Huang Guo-nan. *Taiwan ji liang'an sandi huaren renkou tuigu fangfa—lilun goujian yu shizheng tantao (yi Meiguo wei lie)* (Methods for estimating the population of Chinese from Taiwan, PRC, and Hong Kong using the American example—discussion of theoretical structures and evidence). Taipei: Overseas Chinese Affairs Commission, 2002.

Lutz, Jessie Gregory. *China and the Christian Colleges, 1850–1950.* Ithaca, NY: Cornell University Press, 1971.

Mark, Chi-Kwan. *Hong Kong and the Cold War.* Oxford: Oxford University Press, 2004.

———. "The 'Problem of People': British Colonials, Cold War Powers, and the Chinese Refugees in Hong Kong 1949–62." *Modern Asian Studies* 41, 6 (2007): 1145–81.

McKee, Delber. *Chinese Exclusion versus the Open Door Policy, 1900–1906: Clashes over China Policy in the Roosevelt Era.* Detroit: Wayne State University Press, 1977.

McKeown, Adam. *Melancholy Order: Asian Migration and the Globalization of Borders.* New York: Columbia University Press, 2008.

Miller, Stuart Creighton. *The Unwelcome Immigrant: The American Image of the Chinese, 1785–1882.* Berkeley: University of California Press, 1969.

Molina, Natalia. *How Race Is Made in America: Immigration, Citizenship, and the Historical Power of Racial Scripts.* Berkeley: University of California Press, 2014.

Monaghan, Peter. "Lost in Place." *Chronicle of Higher Education*, March 16, 2001. http://chronicle.com/article/Lost-in-Place/11412.

Ng, Peter Tze-Ming. *Changing Paradigms of Christian Higher Education in China, 1888–1950.* Lewiston, NY: Edwin Mellen Press, 2002.

Ngai, Mae M. *Impossible Subjects: Illegal Aliens and the Making of Modern America.* Princeton, NJ: Princeton University Press, 2004.

———. "Legacies of Exclusion: Illegal Chinese Immigration during the Cold War Years." *Journal of American Ethnic History* 18, 1 (Fall 1998): 3–35.

Ngai, Mae M. *The Lucky Ones: One Family and the Extraordinary Invention of Chinese America*. Boston: Houghton Mifflin Harcourt, 2010.

Oh, Arissa. "From War Waif to Ideal Immigrant: The Cold War Transformation of the Korean Orphan." *Journal of American Ethnic History* 31, 4 (Summer 2012): 34–55.

Oh, Tai K. *The Asian Brain Drain: A Factual and Casual Analysis*. San Francisco: R&E Research Associates, 1977.

Ong, Aihwa. *Buddha Is Hiding: Refugees, Citizenship, the New America*. Berkeley: University of California Press, 2003.

Osgood, Kenneth. *Total Cold War: Eisenhower's Secret Propaganda Battle at Home and Abroad*. Lawrence: University Press of Kansas, 2006.

Paddison, Joshua. *American Heathens: Religion, Race, and Reconstruction in California*. Berkeley: University of California, 2012.

Pakula, Hannah. *The Last Empress: Madame Chiang Kai-Shek and the Birth of Modern China*. New York: Simon and Schuster, 2009.

Pascoe, Peggy. *What Comes Naturally: Miscegenation Law and the Making of Race in the United States*. New York: Oxford University Press, 2009.

Paulsen, George E. "The Abrogation of the Gresham-Yang Treaty." *Pacific Historical Review* 40 (1971): 457–77.

———. "The Gresham-Yang Treaty." *Pacific Historical Review* 37 (1968): 282–97.

Peffer, George Anthony. *If They Don't Bring Their Women Here: Chinese Female Immigration Before Exclusion*. Urbana: University of Illinois Press, 1999.

Petersen, Glen. "To Be or Not to Be a Refugee." *Journal of Imperial and Commonwealth History* 36 (2008): 171–95.

Ramakrishnan, Karthick, and Farah Z. Ahmad. *State of Asian Americans and Pacific Islanders Series*. Riverside, CA: Center for American Progress, 2014.

Reimers, David M. *Still the Golden Door: The Third World Comes to America*. New York: Columbia University Press, 1985.

Rhoads, Edward J. M. *Stepping Forth into the World: The Chinese Educational Mission to the United States, 1872–81*. Hong Kong: Hong Kong University Press, 2011.

Riggs, Fred W. *Pressures on Congress: A Study of the Repeal of Chinese Exclusion*. New York: King's Crown Press, 1950.

"The Rise of Asian Americans." *Pew Research: Social & Demographic Trends*. http://pewsocialtrends.org/2012/06/19/the-rise-of-asian-americans/.

Salyer, Lucy. *Laws Harsh as Tigers: Chinese Immigrants and the Shaping of Modern Immigration Law*. Chapel Hill: University of North Carolina Press, 1995.

Sanchez-Eppler, Karen. "Copying and Conversion: An 1824 Friendship Album 'from a Chinese Youth.'" *American Quarterly* 59, 2 (June 2007): 301–39.

Sandmeyer, Clarence. *The Anti-Chinese Movement in California*. Urbana: University of Illinois Press, 1939.

Saxenian, AnnaLee. *The New Argonauts: Regional Advantage in a Global Economy*. Cambridge, MA: Harvard University Press, 2006.

Saxton, Alexander. *The Indispensable Enemy: Labor and the Anti-Chinese Movement in California*. Berkeley: University of California Press, 1971.

Schwartz, Abba. *The Open Society.* New York: Morrow, 1968.

Shibusawa, Naoko. *America's Geisha Ally: Reimagining the Japanese Enemy.* Cambridge, MA: Harvard University Press, 2006.

Shin, Andrew. "'Forty Percent Is Luck': An Interview with C. Y. (Chin Yang) Lee." *MELUS* 29, 2 (Summer 2004): 77–104.

Snow, Jennifer C. *Protestant Missionaries, Asian Immigrants, and Ideologies of Race in America, 1850–1924.* New York: Routledge, 2007.

Sung, Betty Lee. *Mountain of Gold: The Story of the Chinese in America.* New York: Macmillan, 1967.

———. *A Survey of Chinese-American Manpower and Employment.* New York: Praeger, 1976.

Takaki, Ronald. *Strangers from a Different Shore: A History of Asian Americans.* Boston: Little, Brown, 1989.

Thomas, Brinley. "'Modern' Migration." In *The Brain Drain.* Edited by Walter Adams, 29–49. New York: Macmillan, 1968.

Tichenor, Daniel. *Dividing Lines: The Politics of Immigration Control in America.* Princeton, NJ: Princeton University Press, 2002.

Tsai, Shih-shan Henry. *China and the Overseas Chinese in the United States, 1868–1911.* Fayetteville: University of Arkansas Press, 1983.

———. *The Chinese Experience in America.* Bloomington: Indiana University Press, 1986.

Tuan, Yi-fu. *Cosmos and Hearth: A Cosmopolite's Viewpoint.* Minneapolis: University of Minnesota Press, 1996.

Tucker, Nancy Bernkopf. *Taiwan, Hong Kong, and the United States, 1945–1992: Uncertain Friendships.* New York: Twayne, 1994.

Wang, Chih-ming. *Transpacific Articulations: Student Migrations and the Remaking of Asian America.* Honolulu: University of Hawaii Press, 2013.

Wang, Guanhua. *In Search of Justice: The 1905–1906 Chinese Anti-American Boycott.* Cambridge, MA: Harvard University Press, 2001.

Wang, Y. C. *Chinese Intellectuals and the West, 1872–1949.* Chapel Hill: University of North Carolina Press, 1966.

Wilford, Hugh. *The Mighty Wurlitzer: How the CIA Played America.* Cambridge, MA: Harvard University Press, 2008.

Wu, Ellen. *Color of Success: Asian Americans and the Origins of the Model Minority.* Princeton, NJ: Princeton University Press, 2014.

Wu, Judy. *Doctor Mom Chung of the Fair-haired Bastards: The Life of a Wartime Celebrity.* Berkeley: University of California Press, 2005.

Wu, Yuan-li. "Capital Flow between the United States and China: Conceptual Reorientation." In *ROC and USA 1911–81.* Edited by Tung-hsin Sun and Morris Wei-hsin Tien. Monograph Series No. 2. American Studies Association of the Republic of China, 1982.

Xi, Lian. *The Conversion of Missionaries: Liberalism in American Protestant Missions in China, 1907–1932.* University Park: Pennsylvania State University Press, 1997.

Yang, Dominic Meng-hsuan, and Mau-kuei Chang. "Understanding the Nuances of *Waishengren*: History and Agency." *China Perspectives* 3 (2010): 108–22.

Ye, Weili. *Seeking Modernity in China's Name: Chinese Students in the United States, 1900–1927*. Stanford, CA: Stanford University Press, 2001.

Yeh, Chiou-ling. *Making an American Festival: Chinese New Year in San Francisco's Chinatown*. Berkeley: University of California Press, 2008.

Yu, Henry. *Thinking Orientals: Migration, Contact, and Exoticism in Modern America*. New York: Oxford University Press, 2001.

Yung, Judy. *Unbound Feet: A Social History of Chinese Women in San Francisco*. Berkeley: University of California Press, 1995.

Yung, Judy, Gordon H. Chang, and Him Mark Lai, eds. *Chinese American Voices: From the Gold Rush to the Present*. Berkeley: University of California Press, 2006.

Zhang, Ailing. *The Rice Sprout Song*. Introduction by David Der-wei Wang. Berkeley: University of California Press, 1998 reprint (1955).

Zhao, Xiaojian. *Remaking Chinese America: Immigration, Family, and Community, 1940–1965*. New Brunswick, NJ: Rutgers University Press, 2002.

Zolberg, Aristide R. *A Nation by Design: Immigration Policy in the Fashioning of America*. Cambridge, MA: Harvard University Press and Russell Sage Foundation, 2006.

Index

The page numbers for charts, tables, and illustrations are in italics. The names of national leaders may refer to the individual or the administration or both.

Abbot, Lawrence, 41–42
Abbot, Lyman, 41
academia, U.S., ethnic Chinese and, 305n104
Adams, Walter, 220–21; *Brain Drain, The,* 220–21
adult educational attainment, employment, and income, U.S., *241*
Aid Refugee Chinese Intellectuals, Inc. (ARCI), 19, 133–43, 161, 285n22, 286n36, 287n43; children of registrants and, 152; China Lobby and, 140–41; CIA and, 139–40; financial responsibility of registrants and, 162; functions and goals of, 141–42; Hong Kong and, 135–36, 143; identifying "future leaders" and, 144–45; incorporation of, 139; key mission of, 139–40; latter stages of, 161; Nationalists and, 135–36, 145; promotional dinner of, 142, 287n41; Refugee Relief Program and, 148–49; resettlement programs of, 146; State Department and, 143, 147, 149, 289n66; visa applications and, 149
Allen, A. Leonard, 93, 101, 102, 278nn42–43; on immigration reform, 94
American Asiatic Association, 13
American Immigration Policy (Bernard), 213
Anderson, Jack, 298n63
Angell, James B., 33
Angell Treaty of 1880, 12–13
Arthur, Chester A., 34
Asian exclusion. *See* exclusion, Asian
Asian-Pacific Triangle, 102, 194, 214–15

Asian Survey (Hu), 188
Autobiography of a Chinese Woman (Zhao), 116–18

Bailie, Joseph, 107
Bai Xianyong [Pai Hsien-yung], 206; *Taibeiren,* 206–7; "Winter Night," 231
Barred Zone Act of 1917, 7–8, 65
Bernard, William S., 213; *American Immigration Policy,* 213
Bernkopf Tucker, Nancy, 141
Beyond the Narrow Gate (Chang), 209
Bon Tempo, Carl, 17
Boxer Indemnity Fellowships, 13, 18, 45, 46–47, 269n77; Zhao Yuanren and, 116
Boxer Uprisings, 38, 39–40; indemnity and, 40–41, 42, 56, 71. *See also* Righteous Harmony Society
Boym, Michael, 28
brain drain, 3, 15–16, 20–21, 22, 235; European countries and, 217–18; human capital and, 225; international relations and, 220; as knowledge circulation, 225; neoliberal principles and, 220; Taiwan and, 305n83
Brain Drain, The (Adams), 220–21
Brooks, Charlotte, 306n97
Bu, Liping, 60
Buck, John Lossing, 87
Buck, Pearl, 27, 84, 91, 117; Congressional testimony of, 96–97; *Good Earth, The,* 84
Bureau of Cultural Affairs, U.S., 281n26
Burlingame-Seward Treaty, 30, 32
Burnham, Mary, 23, 24
Butler, Nicholas M., 63, 76

Caniff, Milton, 82, 274n1
Carnegie, Andrew, 84–85
Carnegie Endowment for International Peace, 64
Carusi, Ugo, 213
Central Daily News, 224
Chai, Winberg, 205
"Challenge to Western Learning, A" (Tsao), 79–80
Chan, Father, 210, 301n19
Chang, Leslie, 230; *Beyond the Narrow Gate*, 209
Chang, Shengling, 305n91
Chang, Shu Yuan, 218
Chang-Díaz, Franklin, 1, 259n2
Chen Da, 59
Chen Hengzhe, 58
Chen Lifu, 109–10
Chennault, Anna, 169, 186, 191–92, 298n63; JFK and, 170, 186
Chennault, Claire, 167
Chen Sun, 225
Chen Wen-hsien, 44
Chen Yinke, 52, 281n25
Cherrington, Ben, 87
Cheung, Dominic, 165
Chiang, Cecilia, 164
Chiang, Meiling Song (Madame Chiang), 18, 56–57, 83–84, 88–91; Americans and, 89; *China Shall Rise Again*, 89; immigration reform and, 94, 97; publications in English and, 89–90; *This Is Our China*, 89; U.S. speaking tour of, 90–91
Chiang Kai-shek, 18, 56–57, 88–89, 122, 138, 204, 206; education, international study and, 70–71; Nationalists and, 89
Chicago Daily News, 189
Chien, Linsan, 164
Chin, Irving Sheu Kee, 193–95
China Area Aid Act of 1950, 19, 124
China Foundation: directors of, 70–71; founding of, 70
China House, 72–73; opening of, 73
China Institute in America, 18, 56–57, 77, 111; agendas of, 77–78; *Bulletin*, 274n79; Bureau of Cultural Affairs and, 88; *China Institute Bulletin* and, 78–80, 85; *China Institute Monthly* and, 78; Hu Shi and, 78; IIE and, 78; incorporation of, 71; Meng Zhi and, 71, 72–74; Sesqui-Centennial Exposition (Philadelphia) and, 78; World War II and, 86
China Lobby, 38, 302n21; ARCI and, 135, 137, 139–40; Nationalists and, 105, 140–41; U.S. interests and, 204, 276n17, 279n3, 279n4
China Shall Rise Again (Chiang), 89
China Speaks (Meng), 80
Chinese Americans: achievements of, 22, 162; Cold War and, 171; as community members, 192; confession program and, 157–58; illegal status and, 157; immigration reform and, 178, 215; immigration selection and, 229; integration of, 185; loyalty of, 243, 292n98; middle-class standing and, 200; as model minority stereotype, 242; population growth of, 233; PRC and, 215; publications in English and, 282n43; public relations, U.S., and, 158; refugee relief programs and, 132; testimonies of, 98; as "uptown Chinese," 231–32; visibility of, 180. *See also* Chinese Exclusion Act of 1882
Chinese American Understanding (Meng), 71
Chinese Civil War, 104, 105
Chinese Consolidated Benevolent Association (CCBA), 158
Chinese Educational Mission (CEM), 15, 23, 28, 29–31, 266n15, 266nn21–22; Chinese careers and, 31; generations of students and, 52; New England and, 30; reestablishment of, 47–48
Chinese Exclusion Act of 1882, 6–7, 12–13, 16, 23, 34, 58, 259n6; Citizens Committee to Repeal Chinese Exclusion and, 91–92; repeal of, 91–103, 277n40, 278n44; testimony

concerning, 94–101, 276n32, 277n33;
World War II and, 103
Chinese Refugee Relief, 169, 185
Chinese Restriction Act of 1882. *See*
Chinese Exclusion Act of 1882
"Chinese Scroll Called Hong Kong,
The" (Durdin), 174–75
Chinese students. *See* students, Chinese
Chinese Students' Alliance, 59–60,
61–62, 63
Chinese Students' Monthly, 46–47, 58,
59–60
Chinese World, 215
Ching, Thomas Lee, 187, 188
Choy, Wayson, 215
Chu, Deanna, 187, 191
Chu, J. P., 51; "Training Received by the
750 Leading Men in China," 51
Chu Shee, U.S. v., 44
Collier, Paul, 234–35, 309n30
Columbia University Teachers College,
48–49
Committee on Friendly Relations
among Foreign Students (CFRFS),
57, 60–61, 63–64, 110, 272n28, 280n14;
Chinese Christian Student Monthly
and, 62, 72; CSCA and, 63; founding
of, 14; port of entry services and, 66
Cosmopolitan Clubs, 60–61, 74–76
Cressey, George, 87
cultural internationalism. *See*
internationalism
Currie, Lauchlin, 86

Dandekar, V. M., 221–22
Das, Man Singh, 223, 277n41
Das, Taraknath, 95
Dawson, Lawrence, 161, 174
DeMille, Cecil B., 159
Dickstein, Samuel, 93, 102
Displaced Persons Act of 1948, 19, 104,
123, 126, 134, 211, 240
Dodd, Thomas, 184, 186
Douglas, Paul, 184, 186
Dragon Lady, 81
Drumright, Everett, 149, 154, 186

Duggan, Lawrence, 64
Duggan, Stephen, 18, 57, 63–64, 65, 66, 71,
74, 78, 84, 265n10; on American
racism, 281n39; immigration reform
and, 93; *Meet the USA* and, 112–13
Dulles, John Foster, 158, 171–72; on Far
East Refugee Program, 173
Durdin, Peggy, 174; "Chinese Scroll
Called Hong Kong, The," 174–75

Eastland, James, 214
Eby, Kermit, 96
Edelstein, Jules, 156–57
education, international, 273n53,
280n17; Boxer Indemnity Fellowships
and, 47; Chinese modernization and,
51; Chinese nationalism and, 67;
Chinese social classes and, 52; Qing
dynasty and, 47–48; technical fields
and, 48; U.S. and, 48, 49. *See also*
under Nationalists; Qing dynasty
Einstein, Albert, 259n5
Eisendrath, Maurice, 299n77
Eisenhower, Dwight D., 176; on the
McCarran-Walter Act, 177
Emmet, Christopher, 139
Eng, Frank J., 166
Engle, Clair, 184
Eng Se-suey, 166–67; family of, 184, 192
entry of skilled specialists, relatives
(PL 87–885 of 1962): effects of, 196–97,
211; passage of, 196; pressure for
general immigration reform and,
184–85, 189; refugee relief advocates
and, 190–91
Evans, Theodore, Mrs., 174
Exchange Visitor Program, 245
exclusion, Asian, 91; barred zone and,
7–8; California and, 31–32; Chinese
workers and, 58–59; educational
exchange and, 45–47; Japanese
"enemy aliens" and, 5; legacies of,
5–11; missionary establishment and,
36; political exigencies and, 102–3;
student counternarratives to, 47–51;
students and, 35, 57–58. *See also*

exclusion, Asian (*continued*)
  Chinese Exclusion Act of 1882;
  restriction

Fairbank, John King, 87, 109, 276n17,
  280n10
Fairbank, Wilma, 87
Farquharson, Mary, 96
Federated Educational Association of
  China, 68
Fei Chihao, 36
Feighan, Michael, 156, 216
Feng Yuxiang, 111, 281n30
Fifteen Passenger Act of 1879, 33
Fitch, George, 137, 140, 145, 288n50,
  290n69
Fitch, Geraldine, 90, 137; *Formosa
  Beachhead*, 139
Fletcher, Travis, 140, 149, 186
Flower Drum Song (Lee), 19, 104; film of,
  168; musical and film of, 167
Flying magazine, 110
Fong, Hiram, 180, 181, 246, 297n46
Formosa Beachhead (Fitch), 139
Frankel, Max, 181
Freeman, Mansfield, 141
Frelinghuysen, Frederick T., 34
Fulbright, J. W., 111
Fulbright Act of 1946, 105, 110, 111–12, 171

Garside, B. A., 139, 140, 141, 143, 161–62,
  293n116, 304n62
Geary Act of 1892, 34, 261n17
Gerety, Pierce J., 131, 150
Gibbons, William J., 305n77
Gibson, Otis, 12
Goelz, Louis, 154, 162–63, 180
Good Earth, The (Buck), 84
Gossett, Ed, 92
Greene, Roger, 85, 87
Greenhalgh, Susan, 230
Guo Bingwen, 55, 71–72, 270n2
Gutierrez, Luis V., 247

H-1B program, 5, 21–22, 245–47, 309n30,
  309n35

Hambro, Edvard, 284n19
*Handbook of Chinese Students in the
  U.S.A., The*, 66–67
Handlin, Oscar, 178
Han Liwu, 145
Hanson, Elliott S., 279n5
Harriman, Averill, 185
Harrison, Earl, 213
Hart, Philip A., 20, 183, 184–85, 189; on
  contributions of Chinese immi-
  grants, 192–93; on Hong Kong
  refugees, 190; on the parolee
  program, 195–96
Hart-Celler Act of 1965, 3, 4, 10–11, 18, 20,
  93, 201, 216–17, 240; model minority
  standing and, 217; paper son system
  and, 216; preferences and, 216; Taiwan
  and, 240, 242
Hatcher, Andrew, 214
Hausske, Al, 158
Hay, John, 13
Hayes, Rutherford, 33
Hines, Lewis G., 95
Hirabayashi, Gordon, 260n10
Hirabayashi v. United States, 5
Hocking, William Ernest, 69, 116
Hong Kong: ARCI and, 141–43, 148;
  China Lobby and, 137; Chinese
  refugees and, 135–36, 143–44, 264n47,
  286n33, 295n49; CIA and, 149;
  conditions in, 141–42; focus on,
  181–82; Hart-Celler Act of 1965 and,
  240–41; immigration effects and, 154,
  188–89; immigration fraud and, 154;
  immigration policies, U.S., and,
  19–20; immigration quotas, U.S., and,
  100, 102; population of, 135–36, 175, 181;
  PRC and, 136; press and, 174; refugee
  reception and, 181–82; refugee relief
  advocates and, 156, 172, 185; Taiwan
  and, 137, 144; U.S. consulate in,
  291n89
Hoover, Herbert, 185
Hoover, J. Edgar, 154
How to Cook and Eat in Chinese (Zhao),
  117–18

Hu, Yueh, 188; *Asian Survey*, 188
Huang, Edward, 211
Hu-Dehart, Evelyn (Hu family), 152–53
Hull, Cordell, 86
Hume, Edward, 71, 85
Hummel, Arthur, 97, 147–48
Humphrey, Hubert, 183, 184
Hunt, Michael, 9, 13, 268n48
Hu Shi, 48, 52, 55, 71, 141, 163, 270n3;
    China Institute and, 78

illegal immigrants, U.S., 1, 236, 310n41.
    See also paper son system
Immigration Bureau, U.S., 43–44, 45, 65,
    263n32; on Chinese students, 53;
    treatment of Chinese and, 35. *See also*
    immigration policies, U.S.
immigration exemptions, enforcement
    of, 35–37
immigration policies, U.S., 102; 1943
    reform of, 91–103; 1950s and, 133–34;
    1960s brain drain and, 200–202; Aid
    Refugee Chinese Intellectuals, Inc.
    (ARCI), and, 19, 133–35; authority and,
    32–33; Boxer Indemnity Fellowships
    and, 13; boycott of 1905 and, 40–41;
    brain drain and, 3–4, 15–16, 20–21, 22;
    China White Paper and, 105, 279n3;
    Chinese Confession Program and,
    157–58; citizenship and, 5–6, 124; Cold
    War and, 17, 20; coolie trade and, 8,
    32; cultural internationalism and, 60;
    detention and, 125; Division/Bureau
    of Cultural Relations/Affairs and, 87;
    Division/Bureau of Cultural
    Relations and, 85, 86; Economic
    Cooperation Administration (ECA)
    and, 122–23; economic preferences
    and, 238; educational and cultural
    exchanges and, 2, 196; educational
    levels and, 290; enforcement of,
    24–25, 39, 43–44 (*see also* Immigration
    Bureau, U.S.); Escapee Program and,
    172–73; Exchange Visitor Program
    and, 244–45; exclusion and, 5, 25, 34;
    from exclusion to selection and, 4;

FBI, INS, and, 156–57; Food for Peace
    program and, 183; "front gate," "side
    door," and, 5; gatekeeping and, 10;
    H-1B program and, 5, 21–22, 245–47,
    309n30, 309n35; illegal immigration
    and, 154; imperialism and, 14–15;
    individual attainment, merit, and, 11;
    Information and Educational
    Exchange Act of 1948 and, 171;
    international relations and, 2, 11–12,
    16; Lehman Bill and, 176; Magnuson
    bill and, 93; McCarthyism and, 105;
    missionary establishment and, 12;
    national interests and, 2, 4, 8, 222;
    neoliberal principles and, 22; paper
    son system and, 20, 132, 154, 156–57;
    parole of refugees in Hong Kong
    and, 167, 188; parole program and,
    187–89; policy goals, economic
    criteria and, 134–35; PRC and, 122;
    presidents and, 10; Protestant
    missionaries and, 12; quota system
    and, 133–34; race, culture, and, 16;
    racial and civic nationalism and,
    261n18; refugee programs and, 135;
    refugees and, 17, 19, 20; restriction
    and, 8; side door into America and, 5,
    200–201, 208–11, 213, 246, 300n9;
    skilled and experienced Chinese and,
    125; STEM fields and, 21–22, 239, 244;
    "stranded students" and, 127, 201;
    Technical Assistance Program and, 87,
    101, 203; World War II, Cold War,
    quotas, and, 128–29; World War II
    and, 10, 95. *See also* exclusion, Asian;
    Immigration Bureau, U.S.; restric-
    tion; *specific legislation*
imperial history, 14–15
India/Indians, 243–44
In Young, 45–46
Institute for International Education
    (IIE), 14, 15, 18, 60, 63–64, 66, 272n44;
    Meet the USA and, 112
internationalism, 39–41, 87–88, 109–12,
    136–37, 171–73; China/Chinese and,
    24–25, 47–48, 59–60, 87–91, 112–20;

internationalism (*continued*)
  Chinese Exclusion Act of 1882 and,
    98; culture and, 14, 60, 85; definitions
    of, 13–17; international education and,
    14–15, 36–37, 60–67, 75–77, 84–86,
    111–15. *See also* China Institute in
    America; education, international;
    Iriye, Akira; Meng Zhi [Paul Chih
    Meng]
International Missionary Union,
    268n40
International Training Administration
    (ITA), 109
Iriye, Akira, 14, 60, 85
Ivy, James, 141

James, Edmund J., 42–43
Jan, Flora Belle, 138
Japan/Japanese, 275n2; Gentlemen's
    Agreement and, 7, 34; militarization
    of, 81–84; students and, 50; Treaty of
    Shimonoseki and, 34; U.S. and, 13, 18,
    39–41, 43; World War II and, 5
Jiang Menglin [Chiang Monlin], 44–45,
    52, 55, 58, 70, 110, 269n69
Jiang Tingfu, 185
Johnson, Lyndon, 214, 216
Johnson-Reed Immigration Act of 1924,
    6, 66, 92–93, 132
Judd, Walter, 19, 91, 93, 97, 99–101, 123,
    141, 186; ARCI and, 137, 151; student
    scholarships and, 210

Kao, Charles, 208, 218, 224–25, 233
Keating, Kenneth, 185, 186; on employ-
    ment issues, 190
Kellogg, Mary, 30
Kennedy, Edward, 220
Kennedy, John F., 20, 22; Anna Chen-
    nault and, *170*; ARCI and, 161;
    immigration reform and, 177–78, 214;
    internationalism, civil rights and, 176;
    Nation of Immigrants, A, 178; parole of
    Chinese refugees and, 134–35, 166
Kennedy, Martin J., 92, 277n38
Kennedy, Robert F., 181, 183, 297n44

Kingman, Dong, 167
Kirby, William, 108–9
Klein, Christina, 16, 17, 264n42, 279n4
Knowland, William, 123
Kong Xiangxi [H. H. Kung], 36, 38, 52,
    53, 139, 140, 270n1
Koo, V. K. Wellington, 52, 59, 70, 141
Korean War, 122
Korematsu v. United States, 5
Kraemer, Shelley v., 229
Kramer, Paul, 14–15, 110
Kung, S. W., 160
Kuo, Chia-ling, 228, 232
Kuomintang [KMT]. *See* Nationalists
Kwong, Peter, 231

Latino versus Asian immigration, 236,
    239–40; legality and, 247, 310n41;
    neoliberal principles and, 248–49.
    See also paper son system
Latino votes, U.S., 310n43
"Laundry Song, The" (Wen), 74
Lau Wen-ngau, 173–74
LeClerq, Frederick, 149–50, 151, 290n70
Lee, C. Y., 19, 104, 211; *Flower Drum Song*,
    104, 167
Lee, Dai-ming, 215
Lee, David [Li Dawei], 166, 186, 227,
    298n63
Lee, Erika, 44
Lee, Lim P., 214
Lee, Rose Hum, 124, 127, 259n4
Lee, Wen Ho, 22, 243, 308n18
Lee Ying, 181, *182*
Lehman, Herbert, 131
Leong, Karen, 89
Levin, Lilly, 209
Li, Grace, 130–32
Li, Min Hin, 98
Li, P. C., 130–32, 147
Li, Peter, 229
Liang Dunyan, 31, 36, 42
Liang Shing-Tai, 178
Liebman, Marvin, 139, 285n21
Li Enfou [Yan Phou Lee], 264n4
Lieu, Patrick, 150

Life, 181
Li Hongzhang, 52, 276n29
Li Li-hwa, 159–60
Lin Yutang, 186
Li Yuanze, 233
Li Zhengdao [T.D. Lee], 3, 105, *106*, 124, 179, 234
Low Chia, Doris, 155–56
Luce, Henry B., 27, 73, 84, 140
Lu Hancheng, 163
Lyford, Harry, 173

MacCracken, John H., 76; on immigration reform, 190
MacGuire, Frederick A., 141
Magee, John G., 94
Magnuson, Warren, 92, 277n39
Manhattan Project, 259n5
Mao Zedong, 105
Marco Polo Incident, 27, 83, 85
Marshall, George C., 105
McCain, John, 310n38
McCarran Report, 300n10
McCarran-Walter Act of 1952, 126–27, 132, 133, 134, 175–77, 240, 291n79; quotas for Chinese refugees and, 177
McCarthy, Eugene, 186
McCarthy, Richard, 173
McCormack, John W., 186
McGranahan, Carole, 290n68
McKeown, Adam, 35
McLeod, Scott, 150
Meet the USA (Yang), 112–16; educational and cultural exchanges and, 115–16; racism, U.S., and, 114–15
Mei Guangdi, 52
Mei Yiji, 72, 110
Meng Zhi [Paul Chih Meng], 18, 71–74, 77, 141, 270nn3–4, 271n22, 273n65, 274n72; China Institute and, 72–73, 79–80; *China Speaks*, 80; China-U.S. relations and, 78–79; *Chinese American Understanding*, 71; *Chinese Christian Students Monthly* and, 62, 72; as Chinese internationalist, 74; on

Chinese-Japanese conflicts, 80; on discrimination, 72; education, development of, 55–57; Japanese invasion and, 83; Nationalist blacklist and, 275n8; professional influence of, 72; Sino-Japanese War and, 85; "stranded students" and, 123; student employment and, 108; World War II and, 86–87
Metcalf, Victor, 43
Mexico. *See* Latino versus Asian immigration
Miner, Luella, 36–37
missionaries in China: accomplishments of, 25–26; exclusion movement and, 26; increasing numbers of, 27; May Fourth Movement and, 70; Qing dynasty and, 28, 30; schools and, 27, 35
"model minorities," 1, 4, 21–22, 186, 217, 236–37, 239–40, 242, 248–49
Molina, Natalia, 259n6
Monroe, Paul, 70, 71, 74
Moore, Elizabeth Luce, 141
Morrison, Robert, 27, 265n9
Mott, John R., 26, 72
Moy, Ernest, 71, 137–39, *138*
Mundt, Karl, 183, 184

Naked Earth, The (Zhang), 163
Nash, Ernest, 146, 289n58
Nationalists, 56–57, 88–89, 103, 206, 275n8; Cold War and, 105–11, 122–24, 136, 140–41, 148, 165, 198, 204–7, 276n17; immigration reform and, 91–92, 177; international education and, 18–19, 70–71, 77, 86, 203–5, 207–8, 224–25, 273n65, 279n5; refugee relief and, 136–37, 141–46, 148, 158, 166, 177, 189, 284n19; World War II and, 80, 83
Nationality Act of 1790, 1, 5–6, 196
Nation of Immigrants, A (Kennedy), 178
New York Herald Tribune, 181
New York Times, 23, 76, 77; on Hong Kong refugees, 174, 175
Ngai, Mae M., 134, 158, 248
Northern Expedition, 70

O'Farrell, John J., 97, 98
Ong, Aihwa, 238, 239
"Open Door constituency," 39, 43
Opium Wars, 27, 28, 29
Oram, Harold, 139, 141, 285n21
Osgood, Kenneth, 171
Overbach, John, 166

Page Act of 1875, 8, 32, 262n20
paper son system, 20, 132, 148, 154, 156,
    162, 178, 215–16, 291n89
Pei, I. M., 1, 3, 9, 21, 106, 124, 196, 234;
    John F. Kennedy Library and, 228
Peng, Jack, 209, 213
Perkins, James A., 218
Pew Research, 237; "Rise of Asian
    Americans, The," 237–38
Philippines, 40–41, 110, 244–45, 246;
    brain drain and, 223
Pierson, Arthur Tappan, 27
PL 85–316 of 1957, 160
PL 87–885 of 1962, 20
Powderly, Terence, 35
Pressures on Congress (Riggs), 92
propaganda, U.S., 289n65; parole
    program and, 167, 187–89

Qian Xuesen, 105, 124, 125, 233
Qing dynasty, 28, 31, 35, 36; Boxer
    Uprisings and, 39–40; CEM and,
    47–48; missionaries in China and,
    28–30; Tsinghua College and, 47
Quota Act of 1921, 65

Rankin, Karl, 149
Reader's Digest, 104
Reagan, Nancy, 2
Reagan, Ronald, 1, 2, 259n1
"Recollections of the Chinese Educa-
    tional Mission" (Yung), 23
Refugee Relief Act of 1953, 19, 127, 133,
    147, 150, 151, 164; expiration of, 160. See
    also PL 85–316 of 1957; see also under
    immigration policies, U.S.
refugees: admission to the U.S. and, 17;
    crisis of 1962 and, 20, 136–37, 143, 147,

180–85; relief programs and, 171,
    283n66, 284n16
restriction, 8, 33–34; Chinese students
    and, 9–11, 14, 25, 35, 37, 48; "corporate
    internationalist" migrations and,
    15–16; internationalism and, 14; Open
    Door constituency and, 9, 13, 36, 39,
    43; Page Act and, 8; race and class
    and, 32; world wars and, 18. See also
    exclusion, Asian; see also under
    immigration policies, U.S.
Ricci, Matteo, 26
Rice Sprout Song, The (Zhang), 163
Richmond Times-Despatch, 187, 189
Rieger, John F., 158
Riggs, Fred W., 91, 92, 102, 277n34;
    Pressures on Congress, 92
Righteous Harmony Society, 39, 206
"Rise of Asian Americans, The" (Pew),
    237–38
Rockefeller Foundation, 64
Rogers, Will, 97
Roosevelt, Eleanor, 86, 185
Roosevelt, Franklin D., 102
Roosevelt, Theodore, 13, 18, 36; Chinese
    students and, 43
Root, Elihu, 36, 63–64, 84
Rose, Halleck, 140, 151, 155, 286n31
Rusk, Dean, 142

San Francisco Chronicle, 13
Sargent, Frank P., 35
Saxenian, AnnaLe, 234; "new Argo-
    nauts" and, 234, 238–39
Sayonara (film), 168–69
Schama, Simon, 232
Scott Act of 1888, 13, 34
Selznick, David O., 91
Severinghaus, Emmavail Luce, 141
Shelley v. Kraemer, 229
Sheng Sing, 228
Shi, Alfred Zhaoji, 52
Shibusawa, Naoko, 260n7
Shih, Peter, 179
Sia, Frank Tze-tun, 166
Smith, Arthur, 41, 42

Smith, Judson, 36
Song, Charlie Jones, 38
Song Ailing, 38–39; Theodore Roosevelt and, 39
Song Meiling, 38, 44. *See also* Chiang, Meiling Song (Madame Chiang)
Song Qingling [Soong Chingling], 38, 44
Song Ziwen [T. V. Soong], 38, 48, 86, 105, 135, 140, 302n15
Soon, E. Ling, 40
Speer, Robert, 122
Speer, William, 12
Sputnik, 124, 179, 211, 213
Stothart, William, 91
"stranded students," 3, 5, 19, 239–40, 259n4; brain drain and, 205; China Area Aid Act of 1950 and, 124; Chinese Civil War and, 103; discrimination and, 127; ECA funds and, 123; hardship and, 120; professional success and, 232, 240; World War II, Cold War, and, 201
Stuart, John Leighton, 27
students, Chinese, 9–10, 223, 239; adverse conditions and, 76–77; in America, 1903–1945, 48; brain drain and, 200; Chinese Students' Alliance and, 59, 271n13; Christianity and, 76; classification of, 282n47; discrimination and, 74, 75; Displaced Persons Act of 1948 and, 211; Eastern Alliance of Chinese and, 58–59; educational and cultural exchanges and, 14, 111, 203; employment and, 66, 76, 86, 201, 275n13; employment options and, 25; fellow countrymen and, 58; government exchange programs and, 210; Hart-Celler Act of 1965 and, 201, 211; Immigration Bureau, U.S., and, 53; immigration hassles and, 72; Institute grants and, 275n11; marriages to American-born Chinese and, 271n10; May Fourth movement and, 68–69; McCarran-Walter Act and, 211; missionaries in China and, 25–28; Nobel prizes and, 224; as nonquota

entries, 210; permanent residency and, 201, 218–19, *219*; after World War II, 201; PRC and, 105–6; as refugees, 123–24, 126; remaining in the U.S. and, 211; side door into America and, 5, 200–201, 208–11, 213, 246, 300n9; successes of, 203; technical fields and, 107–8, 218; in U.S., by year, *48*; usefulness of, 24–25; World War II and, 86, 104–5, 109
students, international. *See* education, international
students, international, by country of origin, *49*
Student Volunteer Movement (SVM), 27
Sung, Betty Lee, 164
Sun Jia'nai, 52
Sun Yatsen, 38, 95, 137
Swanstrom, Edward E., 180, 190–91
Swift, John F., 33
Swing, Joseph, 156–57

Taft, William Howard, 41
Taibeiren (Bai), 206–7
Taiwan: brain drain and, 203, 305n83; brain drain reversal and, 225–26; Chinese students and, 205; college graduates studying abroad and, *212*; economic development and, 207; economic growth model of, 223; emigrants from, 307n10; employment options and, 206; February 28th Incident and, 205, 301n19; foreign study and, 207–8; Fulbright Act of 1946 and, 204; Hsinchu Science Park and, 226–27; immigrants to the U.S. and, 225, 305n89; industry expansion to Chinese mainland and, 227; Nationalist rule and, 207; White Terror and, 206
Tan, S. H., 177, 265n5
Tang Shaoyi, 31, 42
Tan Yaoxun, 24
Taylor, George, 141; on Hong Kong intellectuals, 145

technology start-ups, U.S., 310n39
Terry and the Pirates, 81–82
This Is Our China (Chiang), 89
Thomas, Brinley, 21, 216–17, 222
Tien, C. C., 211, 213
Tien, Chang-lin, 208
Toynbee, Arnold, 95
"Training Received by the 750 Leading Men in China" (Chu), 51
Treaty of Guadalupe Hidalgo, 6
Trescot, William H., 33
Tribbe, Frank, 159
Truman, Harry, 185
Tsao, Y. S., 79–80; "Challenge to Western Learning, A," 79–80
Tsinghua College, 47, 71
Tsui, Daniel C., 233
Tuan, Yi-Fu, 196–200, *199*, 202, 232–33, 234, 300n1, 307n106; on Civil Rights Movement, 300n3; *Who Am I*, 200

Umeki Miyoshi, *168*, 294n8
United States, Hirabayashi v., 5
United States, Korematsu v., 5
United States Information Agency, 171–73
US, Wong Kim Ark v., 267n35
U.S. v. Chu Shee, 44

Vanden Heuvel, William J., 187, 191
Versailles, Treaty of, 68
"Vocational Opportunities and Problems" (Yieh Tsung-kao), 51, 74–75, 76–77

Wadhwa, Vivek, 310n19
Walsh, Richard, 84, 91, 277n34
Walter, Francis, 176, 179, 186, 216; on Chinese refugee crisis, 183–84; immigration policies, U.S., and, 183
Wang, An, 105, 108, 269n80
Wang, Theodora Chan, 98
Wang, Y. C., 30, 48, 52, 111; on salary structures in China, 50–51, 109, 124
Wang Bingnan, 3, 125, 179
Ward, Bishop, 151–52

Waters, Agnes, 95–96
Wei Daoming, 73
Wen Bingzhong, 31
Wen Yiduo, 74; "Laundry Song, The," 74
Who Am I (Tuan), 200
Who's Who, 51
Wilford, Hugh, 285n30
Wilkie, Wendell, 92, 277n35
Williams, S. Wells, 33
"Winter Night" (Bai), 231
Wittfogel, Karl, 79
Wong, C. C., 162
Wong, K. Scott, 29
Wong Kim Ark v. US, 267n35
Worley, Lloyd, 97
Wu, Ellen, 167, 242, 294n10
Wu Mi, 52
Wu Ningkun, 124, 234
Wu Tingfang, 40, 267n36, 268n38
Wu Yuan-li, 224

Xi'an Incident, 84

Yang, Ching-kun, 112; on American girls, 281n38; *Meet the USA*, 112–16
Yang, Dominic, 206
Yang Zhenning [C. N. Yang], 3, 105, *106*, 124, 127–28, 179, 233
Yan Huiqing, 70
Ye, Weili, 48, 58, 266n14
Yee, Paul, 98, 108
Yee, Samuel E., 195
Yeh, George, 141
"yellow peril," 4, 22, 25, 81, 82, 132, 195, 243
Yen, W. W., 43
Yieh, Tsung-kao, 51, 80; "Adjustment Problems of Chinese Graduate Students in American Universities, The," 51, 74–77; on Chinese students in America, 80; "Vocational Opportunities and Problems" (Yieh Tsung-kao), 51, 74–75, 76–77
Young, Dana, 23
Young Men's Christian Association (YMCA), 14, 63, 66, 72

Yu, Bin [Paul], 186, 209, 210
Yuan Shikai, 59
Yung Kuai, 17, 23–25, 24, 264n3; "Recollections of the Chinese Educational Mission" and, 23
Yung Wing, 24, 28, 29–30

Zeng Laishun, 29, 52, 266n15
Zhang Ailing, 163–64, 165; Naked Earth, The, 163; Rice Sprout Song, The, 163
Zhang Boling, 70, 72
Zhan Tianyou [Tien Yow Jeme], 31
Zhao family, 121, 282n43

Zhao Yang Buwei [Buwei Yang Chao], 116–21; Autobiography of a Chinese Woman, 116–19; How to Cook and Eat in Chinese, 117–18
Zhao Yuanren [Yuen Ren Chao], 47, 52, 116–21; Boxer Indemnity Fellowships and, 116; education of, 116; skills of, 120
Zheng, Andreas, 28
Zheng, C. C., 145
Zheng, T. H., 145
Zheng Caoru, 34
Zhong Wenyao, 31, 266n24
Zolberg, Aristide, 5

Lightning Source UK Ltd.
Milton Keynes UK
UKOW04f0956190917
309458UK00003B/94/P